The Making
of a Socialist

T.C. Douglas, Premier of Saskatchewan, 1944.

The Making of a Socialist

The Recollections of T.C. Douglas

Edited by Lewis H. Thomas

1726 37588

 The University of Alberta Press

First published by
The University of Alberta Press
Edmonton, Alberta, Canada

ISBN 0-88864-070-6

Copyright © The University of Alberta Press 1982

Canadian Cataloguing in Publication Data

Douglas, T.C. (Thomas Clement), 1904–
    The making of a socialist

    Includes index.
    ISBN 0-88864-070-6

    1. Douglas, T.C. (Thomas Clement), 1904–
2. Statesmen — Canada — Biography. 3.
Saskatchewan — Politics and government.
I. Thomas, Lewis H., 1917–   II. Title.
FC3525.1.D68A3   971.24'009'94   c81-091230-9
F1072.D68A3

Typesetting by The Typeworks
Mayne Island, British Columbia

Printed by John Deyell Company
Willowdale, Ontario

To
Gertrude S. Telford
1887–1978

Contents

Foreword

Thou of an independent mind,
With soul resolv'd, with soul resign'd;
Prepar'd Power's proudest frown to brave,
Who wilt not be, nor have a slave;
Virtue alone who dost revere,
Thy own reproach alone dost fear.

Robert Burns, "For an Altar of Independence"[1]

In the following pages, the recollections of Thomas Clement Douglas are reproduced from a series of taped interviews recorded between 21 September and 21 December 1958. The interviewer was C.H. (Chris) Higginbotham, a well-known journalist and radio commentator.

T.C. Douglas was a Member of Parliament from 1935 to 1944, and again from 1962 to 1979, for a total of twenty-six years. In the intervening seventeen years, a period of office so far unequalled in the history of the province, he was Premier of Saskatchewan. The setting and circumstances of the interviews were described by Mr. Higginbotham in a statement from their last recording session:

In 1958 Saskatchewan was in the throes of great activity and change. Premier Douglas was right in the midst of it. He therefore couldn't possibly find the time to sit down and write his experiences in the usual way. It was felt, however, that an effort should be made to get these recorded before time dimmed his memory and the memory of people living at this date. It was therefore decided to press into service the burgeoning science of electronics. For two hours at a time, mostly on Sundays and afternoons in the fall and winter of 1958, the premier casually and completely without notes told his story to a tape recorder. The recording sessions were held in the Executive Council Chamber of the Legislative Building. The chamber, by the way, is a replica of a room in the Vatican. It was believed to be the most perfectly appointed room of its kind in the Dominion. The walls are covered with red silk tapestry, woven to represent Roman tapestry seven hundred years old. This is the room in which the Saskatchewan cabinet met on Tuesdays and Fridays. One of the features of the room is a large beautifully polished oval table, around which the cabinet ministers sit. It is at this table, too, where Premier Douglas told his story. He'd stride into the room armed with three large pipes. It was evident, however, that he was no tobacco addict. He would take a few puffs from one pipe, put it down, and then repeat the process with another pipe. It could be said he was almost a dead loss to the tobacco industry.

He has just now entered his office on this last Sunday before Christmas, 21 December 1958. His office is just a few steps from this Council Chamber. It's a beautiful room, bright with flowers despite the bitter weather without. The portraits looking down on the premier while he works include those of Abraham Lincoln, J.S. Woodsworth, founder of the C.C.F. party, Prime Minister Mackenzie King, and some family pictures, and M.J. Coldwell, who at this date has

C.H. (Chris) Higginbotham, interviewer, 1962.

retired as leader of the C.C.F. Party. There's also a portable television set in the office, a symbol of the times in which we're in at this moment.

It would have been impossible to find a better interviewer than Chris Higginbotham, who had known at first hand every political leader of Saskatchewan from the late 1920s through to 1958. Born in Altricham, near Manchester, England, in 1901, he served with the Royal Flying Corps and the R.A.F. in the First World War. He emigrated to Canada shortly after the armistice. He worked for a time on cannery boats in Vancouver, and then obtained a position with a west coast weekly. Later he moved to Saskatchewan, joining the Regina *Leader-Post* in 1927, and served its Moose Jaw bureau until 1931. In 1933 he became city editor of *The Leader-Post*, and stayed on as city editor and acting editor until 1944. The next two years were spent as *The Leader-Post*'s Ottawa correspondent. He served on the *Vancouver Sun* for a year and then returned to Regina, where he worked as a radio and television broadcaster, and as a free-lance correspondent for *Time* and other magazines and newspapers. In 1968, Higginbotham published a book on Saskatchewan political history entitled *Off the Record*.[2] The work is replete with interesting anecdotes and shrewd characterizations covering the years from the turn of the century to 1966.

The interviews were really conversations between the two men. They were both articulate, with a twinkle in their eyes. Higginbotham was noted as an ebullient conversationalist. Both men were about the same height (the premier was 5 feet, 5 inches), but here the resemblance ceased. Douglas was slight of figure while Higginbotham tended to rotundity.

These transcribed interviews are a significant contribution to the history of Canadian politics. Douglas's recollections are notable for their incisiveness and candour. And they display a generosity of spirit in a man who was subjected, during the early years of his premiership, to more vilification than any other politician of his day. Yet despite it all, T.C. Douglas never lost his magnanimity. The perceptive reader will recognize that the premier and the party he led were articulating principles and policies that aroused extreme hostility in conservative circles at the time, but which are now regarded as conventional political wisdom.

A number of additional prefatory comments are in order. The preparation of these interviews was a project of the Archives of Saskatchewan, then headed by Dr. John H. Archer, provincial archivist from 1957 to 1962. The tapes comprise about twenty-six hours of conversation. On the whole, the sound reproduction is good, except in a few instances when Mr. Douglas was not facing the microphone. The sequence of topics to be covered was arranged in advance by Mr. A.R. Turner, assistant archivist and later Archer's successor, and Mr. Higginbotham, in consultation with the premier. The typed transcription of the interviews was prepared shortly after the last interview, and number 524 foolscap double-spaced typed pages. More than one stenographer was involved in the transcription, and some proper names were spelled phonetically. It is from this transcript that the following work has been assembled. The last chapter is a summary of the chief events of the last three years of Douglas's term of office (1959–61), written by the editor.

To prepare a manuscript of publishable length and form involved some omissions. The criteria applied included the avoidance of repetition, unnecessary detail, and some references of purely family interest. Correction of some errors in syntax have been made. In a few instances, sections were rearranged so that a strict chronological account was consistently maintained. Interpolations and explanations by the editor appear in square brackets.

A number of friends have been most helpful in assisting the preparation of this work. I would like to thank Mr. T.C. Douglas for granting access to this record; Mr. Ian Wilson, provincial archivist of Saskatchewan, and his staff, for innumerable favours; Mr. Leslie Gutteridge, director of the University of Alberta Press from 1971 to 1979, for enthusiastic support; his successor, Mrs. Norma Gutteridge, and Mrs. Katherine Wensel for excellent editorial assistance. I am grateful to Mrs. Olive Baird of the staff of the Department of History for expert typing, and to my wife for careful proof-reading and excellent suggestions. The University of Alberta provided assistance from the general research fund for consultations in Regina.

Photographs are courtesy of the Archives of Saskatchewan.

Edmonton, Alberta   Lewis H. Thomas
August 1979

1

Scottish immigrant

I was born on 20 October 1904 in the town of Falkirk, Scotland.[1] This is a well-known town in Scottish history, lying half-way between Glasgow and Edinburgh, the scene of many battles between the English and the Scotch and later the scene of a very famous battle when Bonnie Prince Charlie was trying to seize the throne of the United Kingdom.

> What's it like in appearance? You have been back, have you?

Many times. It's a little town in the centre of a large industrial area. The main industries there are the great ironworks. Close to that area are coal-mining districts, and so the ironworks have grown up close to the coal deposits. The bulk of the people in the town of Falkirk and the surrounding towns and villages are men engaged in the great blast furnaces, the steel mills, and the ironworks. Most of my relatives worked in the ironworks and the steel mills. My father was an iron-moulder as were most of his brothers.

I don't know a great deal about my family for any great distance back. My grandfather, whom I remember quite well, was an iron-moulder and also a painter. In his younger days he had done a good deal of oil-painting, and as a matter of fact, he had painted William Ewart Gladstone. He was also an amateur orator and politician. He was the Burns speaker for a number of Burns banquets in the surrounding countryside. My earliest recollection of him is hearing him quote Burns as he sat by the fireside. I can dimly remember him picking me up, putting me on his knee, and saying to me the lines from "Tam o'Shanter": "Ah, Tam! ah, Tam! thou'll get thy fairin! / In hell they'll roast thee like a herrin!" I think one of the outstanding things of his life was the fact that he was the chairman at the meeting in the town hall when William Ewart Gladstone opened his famous Midlothian campaign [in 1880]. My grandfather on my father's side was a very strong Liberal and a tremendous admirer of William Ewart Gladstone.

And on the maternal side?

My mother's people were all highlanders. Both my grandfather and grandmother on my mother's side came from two places in the Highlands, Auchterarder and Crieff. They came to the city of Glasgow when they were twenty-two and twenty-one years old respectively. They spoke Gaelic and only started to learn English after they came down to Glasgow. My grandfather on my mother's side worked for the Scottish Co-operative Wholesale, and was a great co-operator all his life. I remember visiting him at his work and going with him to his work sometimes when I was on holidays. He was a strong Conservative and belonged to the famous Plymouth Brethren, a very devout sect. But he later became a Baptist and lay preacher and often I went to hear him conduct services. He wasn't an orator in the tradition of my paternal grandfather, but he was a very kindly and very fine Christian gentleman.

Do you have any clear and sharp recollections of your own childhood?

I have very distinct recollections of starting kindergarten in Scotland. I remember visiting my grandparents in Glasgow and in Falkirk. I distinctly recollect leaving—I remember first of all my father coming to Canada [in 1911]. My father came ahead of us, and I remember us going to the boat to say goodbye to him. I remember later saying goodbye to our friends at the docks in Glasgow, and coming to Canada [in 1912]. My mother, my two sisters, and myself came in the company of my father's brother, Mr. William Douglas.

Do you remember what the house was like?

Yes. My grandfather owned two small houses at the foot of a Scottish brae called Sunnybrae, and my grandfather and grandmother lived in one of them with the members of their family; I think they had eight sons and one daughter. They had another house on the adjoining lot where my father and mother lived, where I was born.

What were you grandfathers' names?

My paternal grandfather was Thomas Douglas, and my father had the same name. We had a tradition in our family that the eldest son was called Thomas Douglas, and this went back quite a distance. I believe my great-grandfather was a city councillor of Dunfermline. On the maternal side, my grandfather's name was Andrew Clement or Cle(e)ment we call it generally, but in the Highlands they called it Clement. [Douglas's mother's maiden name was Annie Clement.]

In your own family, how many children were there?

I am the only son and eldest in the family. I have two sisters, one Annie or Nan, who is now Mrs. Talney, the wife of Dr. M.A. Talney of Portland, and Isabel, now Mrs. A.E. Bergstrom in the city of Saskatoon.

Who is left of the family in Scotland now?

My father's eldest brother, William Douglas, lives in the family house, one of the houses owned by my grandfather. His son, also William Douglas, lives in the other house. Also, my father's only sister, the only other surviving member of his family, Mrs. Duncan Stewart, lives in Falkirk.

> In Scotland many houses were in greystone with a slate roof. Do you remember any like this? Did you have a small fireplace for heating?

Ours was a stone house, and earlier had had the thatched roof, but my first recollection of it was with a slate roof. The heating was by fireplaces. Later on my family moved, and I remember being in a place called Sunnyside, which is fairly close to Sunnybrae, where we lived in a house in a terrace. The last time I was in Falkirk I visited this house, and a cousin of mine, Mr. Willie Deans, is now living there.

> Were the early days in the Scottish tradition? Just what kind of a discipline was there, what kind of an atmosphere?

There was a good religious atmosphere in the home. My mother was a Baptist, and my father had been raised as a Presbyterian. My father and my mother sang in the choir. My father wasn't an organist, but he played the little organ we had in the parlour, and one of my earliest recollections is the neighbours and us sitting around singing hymns and some of the old songs of Bobbie Burns. We always said Grace at the table, and when we went to my grandparents' place, quite often there would be readings from the Scriptures — something of the old tradition of the cotter's Saturday night that Bobbie Burns portrayed.

But it certainly wasn't a strict religious home. My grandparents on my mother's side, who were Plymouth Brethren originally and later Baptists, were more strict in the sense of their own personal observance. But they never tried to impose upon a boy a lot of religious scruples. There was no harsh discipline. I think my father thought that my grandfather had mellowed a great deal. He said that when he and his brothers were young, they were compelled to shine their shoes on a Saturday night and prepare the fire for Sunday morning. But by the time that I came along those very stern Scottish Sabbaths were beginning to disappear.

> What were the main enjoyments? Meeting and conver-
> sation and music?

Yes, there was music. The Scottish people would visit in the
homes. There was a good deal of singing and rolling up the carpet
and dancing the Scottish *schottische* and the reels. Then there
were always the pubs in Scotland, to which everybody went. I can
look back and remember a wedding held in my grandfather's
house. Before anybody took a drink of the whisky that was being
passed around, the minister got the first glass. That happened on
the Presbyterian side of my ancestry. On my maternal side, this
would have been a most shocking incident.

> The family must have been quite broadminded on a lot
> of issues. You don't call drinking Scotch whisky a sin in
> any language.

That's right. Both my father and my mother said that when they
were young, there had been a good deal of objection to them
going dancing, but this had disappeared by the time I came along,
and dances in the homes were quite common.

> The family had moulders on one side and soldiers on the
> other.

Yes. Falkirk is in Stirlingshire where Stirling Castle is located, and
Stirling is the home of the Argyll and Sutherland Highlanders.
For a good many generations, some member of the family had
served with Argyll and Sutherland Highlanders. My father served
with them in the South African War. Some of our forefathers had
been with the Argyll Sutherlands in the Middle East and at
Waterloo. Two of my father's brothers were killed in the First
World War. The long connection between our family and the
Argyll Sutherlands is characteristic of most of the families around
Stirling. In the last war when the Fifty-first Division was almost
wiped out because they were used in the rearguard at Dunkirk,
there was hardly a family in Stirling that didn't lose someone in
that retreat.

> There is one other question about your home. Would you
> call yours, in material terms, poor or rich or middle?

Poor and rich are relative terms. First of all, it was a working-class family who lived on their weekly wages, and by working-class standards it was a comfortable home. My father, his brothers, and his father were all good tradesmen. They had served their time as iron-moulders and as blast-furnace men, and so they received good wages for working people. But by middle-class or upper-class standards, of course, it was a poor home. Also, if work got scarce, even the best artisan would have quite difficult times.

When we came to Canada and went through the depression of 1913–14, my father, who carried on his trade in Winnipeg as an iron-moulder, was reduced to three days of work a week; we knew then what it was to be worried about where the next dollar was coming from.

By the standards in Scotland of the other people in the community who worked, our family was comfortably fixed, because the men were good workers, and if there was employment they managed to get it. Compared with the unskilled workers or people who had had some misfortune, we were comparatively well off.

> Was there any any particular personal or general tragedy that happened during the days you spent in Scotland?

No, there was no great tragedy. Just before coming to Canada, and while living in Falkirk, I injured my knee by a fall, with the result that osteomyelitis set in. It has been with me ever since. My father had already left for Canada and I had my leg operated on a number of times by doctors in Scotland.

> I have heard that your early associations with this first serious illness created your interest in public health. Did those thoughts nag at you?

Yes. Although I was very young to recollect much from the Scottish period, I do remember the operations. The typical old country doctor came to the house with his top hat, frock coat, and his bag of instruments, and the operation was performed on the kitchen table with my grandmother and my mother assisting, along with a neighbour woman who was a practical nurse. They performed an operation in which the femur was scraped—an operation that today would be considered quite serious. It was done with just a gauze mask and some chloroform.

After three of these operations, it was hoped that I had been cured. Later on in Winnipeg, the osteomyelitis recurred, and I went through a long period of hospitalization. The doctors attending me told my parents that the leg would have to be amputated and they were given some time to decide whether or not to agree to the amputation. During that period in Children's Hospital in Winnipeg, about 1913 or 1914, Dr. R.J. Smith, a very famous orthopaedic surgeon, was going through the wards with a group of students and became interested in my case. He interviewed my parents and told them that he was prepared to take over, providing they would allow the students to observe. As a result of several operations, he saved my leg.

I always felt a great debt of gratitude to him; but it left me with this feeling that if I hadn't been so fortunate as to have this doctor offer me his services gratis, I would probably have lost my leg. My parents were having quite a difficult time during the depression, money was very scarce, and they couldn't possibly have hired a man of Dr. Smith's standing. I felt that no boy should have to depend either for his leg or his life upon the ability of his parents to raise enough money to bring a first-class surgeon to his bedside. And I think it was out of this experience, not at the moment consciously, but through the years, I came to believe that health services ought not to have a price-tag on them, and that people should be able to get whatever health services they required irrespective of their individual capacity to pay.

> You have taken various trips back to your birthplace and met the people. I wonder, were the people impressed? What was their feeling when they found that one of their sons became a Premier of Saskatchewan? Can you recall anything about your impact on the people of Falkirk? Were there any other famous men out of Falkirk?

In 1945 I went overseas for about three months to visit Saskatchewan units who were serving in the United Kingdom and on the Continent.[2] When I got back to the United Kingdom, I visited Glasgow, and happened to be having lunch with the directors of the Scottish Co-operative Wholesale at 110 Morrison Street, only a few blocks from where my maternal grandparents had lived, and where my mother, my sisters, and I had lived during the First World War. The directors, when they found I had been born in Falkirk, thought I should go back and visit my relatives. I expressed the opinion that they probably wouldn't remember me. I hadn't very much time; I was flying back to Canada on a Lancaster Bomber the following day, and so I saw very little value in my going and trying to look up relatives. But they insisted that I should. So one of the co-operative directors put a car at my disposal and I set out from Glasgow to visit Falkirk.

I found the address of my father's brother, Mr. William Douglas, who lived in the house where my grandfather had lived, and next door to the house where I was born. I recognized the brae, although it had been some years since I had been there. When I knocked, my aunt came to the door and I was wondering how I would explain who I was, but she said "Hello, Tommy, come on in." And I said, "How did you know who I was?" and she said, "We heard about you on the wireless." In a few minutes the message went over the grape vine, and all the relatives from far and near were pouring in. I had a wonderful family reunion in the spring of 1945.

I also went back in 1948. This time was on a more formal basis. I was attending the Commonwealth Parliamentary Conference in London with the Liberal senator [Arthur Roebuck] from Toronto. He was also a member of the Canadian delegation to the parliamentary conference, and I told him I was going to Falkirk, where my parents came from, and he said, "That is interesting, I want to go to Falkirk, too. My great-grandfather started the Carron Ironworks during the Napoleonic wars. My father and his father and his father before him had all worked in the Carron Ironworks."[3] So we set out together to go to Falkirk via Glasgow. When we got there, the city fathers, the Lord Mayor, and the city council, had arranged a big dinner for us and we were both given an official welcome and the key to the city, myself as a former Falkirk bairn returning home, and the senator as a grandson of the founder of the Carron Ironworks. We both spoke on that occasion.

Can you remember anything that you said?

It was fairly formal. I don't recall anything particular that I said at that time, except the usual thanks for their kindness and my pleasure at visiting Falkirk again. I think, however, I had a little fun with the gathering, because a by-election was going on for the constituency of Stirling, and my grandfather, of course, had been known all throughout Falkirk as a great Liberal. However when my father came back from the South African War, he decided to throw in his lot with the Labour party, which caused quite a rift in the family. For about a year my father and my grandfather didn't speak to each other. That was when we moved our home from Sunnybrae to Sunnyside. But when I was born, there was a reconciliation, because I was the first grandchild and my grandfather finally broke down and decided that even if his son was an awful Socialist, he had a grandson now and so the family peace was restored.

It was rather amusing to address this banquet in Falkirk during a by-election campaign. The man who sat on my right, a squire, was the coalition candidate running for both the Liberals and the Conservatives. The mayor, of course, was a very prominent Labour man. Most of the people there knew of my family's old traditional Liberal background, and the fact that practically all of the sons had broken with the father and were supporting the Labour party.

I had spent the morning travelling around the town of Falkirk, and had seen this great poster everywhere telling people to vote for the squire, for he was the richest man in the community, owned most of the land, and was running on the Liberal-Conservative ticket. I was rather appalled at the fact that there were no Labour posters and no trucks going around with loud-speakers telling people to support the Labour candidate, while on almost every street corner the trucks were telling people to support the Liberal-Conservative candidate. So I said to the Lord Mayor at the dinner, "Is there a Labour candidate in the field?" And he said, "Oh, aye." I said, "I don't see any posters up or any loudspeakers out. They all seem to be supporting my friend on my other side." "Well," he said, "Dinna fret yourself about that, lad," he said, "You'll see where we are when the vote comes in." And he was right. The Labour candidate won the seat by a resounding majority. You have to remember that Stirling was the home of Keir Hardy, the first Labour M.P. to be elected to the House of Commons. He went from Stirlingshire with his muffler and his cloth cap down to the House of Commons to sit with the gentry with their top hats and frock coats. Stirling and Falkirk had a great tradition of support of the Labour Party.

> Would the Liberal party be regarded by townspeople there as radicals in the sense that we know the term down through the last half of the century?

Oh, yes. In the days when my grandfather was a supporter of Gladstone, he was part of the rebel party, as opposed to the landed gentry. The workers in those days were mostly Liberals. This is one of the strange things you find about Canadian politics. The Scotchmen who came to this country thirty or forty years ago were Liberal when they left Scotland and are still Liberal here, but the relatives they left behind, who were Liberal because liberalism meant radicalism, have switched over to the Labour party. The Scotchmen in this country can hardly reconcile the fact that the Liberal party in the old country is no longer a radical party; the Labour party has taken its place.

> Were there some good speakers in your family?

My grandfather on my mother's side was a quiet speaker. He was a lay preacher, as I said, and would give quiet little talks that simply shone with the man's own sincerity and his kindly personality. I never heard him use a cross word to anyone. He was gentleness personified, a fine Christian gentleman. But he was not an orator.

But my father's father was one of the finest speakers I ever heard. He had a tremendous capacity for extemporaneous speaking, and a very gifted memory. He could quote lengthy poems like "The Cotter's Saturday Night" or "Tam o'Shanter" completely from memory, and when he was celebrating Hogmanay, which is the Scotchman's New Year's Eve, and partaking of Scotland's national beverage, he could do even better.

> You were really, then, brought up in an atmosphere of words. Words were important in your youth.

Yes. Remember that we came to Canada in 1912. We returned to the United Kingdom when the First World War broke out. My father went overseas. He was a British reservist, and was called back and later got transferred to the Canadian army, but since he had gone overseas and was in France, there wasn't much point in my mother and my sisters and myself, with no relatives in this country, continuing to live in Canada, so we went back to the old country and lived in Glasgow, close to my mother's people, throughout the entire First World War. So my impressions of Scotland are not only of the period before I was eight years of age, but from when I was ten until I was fourteen. We came back to Canada in 1919.

You say I was in an atmosphere of words. First of all, nobody could be in my grandfather's house on my father's side without being in a welter of words. Unfortunately, my grandfather had eight sons, all of whom seemed to like to argue even more than he did, and so there was a constant bedlam of discussion: politics, religion, and philosophy, any one of which could finally be solved by a quotation from Bobbie Burns.

> They extended beyond the patron saint of Scotland in their reading, did they not? Were they great readers?

Yes. There was a great deal of reading done. Not systematic reading, but nevertheless a great deal of reading on fairly serious subjects. You have to realize that this was the great period of change in Britain, from the beginning of the century until the First World War. There were tremendous changes under Lloyd George. You had the upsurge of the Labour party. You had the great battles with the trade union movement. At the beginning of the First Great War, the ten- and twelve-hour day were still common. There was revolutionary social change in the air, about which there was constant discussion and reading.

 Now, some of your impressions of your arrival in Winnipeg [in 1911]. Was it a cold bitter day, or can you think of anything on your voyage across, or anything that would bring us to Winnipeg?

I can remember the voyage across. There was a good deal of fog. We were about seventeen days coming out. We were delayed because of fog, and I recollect that there were some ships in difficulty. We were practically motionless for several days with ice. We arrived in Winnipeg in April. My father was already here, and his brother, with whom we came, had been here before.

You'll tell us why you came, will you?

We came for the same reason that most people came from the old country. We felt there was better opportunity. Britain was badly crowded and there were limited opportunities, limited housing. There were always people in every family who felt that they should get away to the colonies to improve their lot. And my father's brother had already spent some years in Canada, and had come back to Scotland. He was largely instrumental in persuading my father to come to Canada. He escorted my mother and my sisters and myself, and subsequently went back to Scotland.

How did you travel from the seaboard?

By train, in the old colonist cars, and we cooked our meals in a little kitchen at the end. They were pretty dilapidated. We slept on the hard boards. It took us about five days. I can remember my father meeting us. I can remember coming out of the C.P.R. station and seeing the old Countess of Dufferin, the old locomotive. I can remember a few days after arriving, the big Decoration Day parade. They had a parade to decorate the graves of the men who fought in the Riel Rebellion. My father, as a South African veteran, was in the parade. I can still remember seeing him in the parade, and after it was over, he came and joined us, and we all went out to Kildonan Park.

Winnipeg in those days was a fascinating place.[4] People were pouring in between 1910 and 1912 from all over central Europe and the United Kingdom. Housing was hard to get. Most of the houses that people like ourselves lived in were out in the suburbs, in Elmwood, houses that were not modern, where you had to carry the water.

Did you have a house to go to when you first arrived?

Yes. My father had rented a house. We lived in rented houses right up until my father joined the army and we went back to Scotland.

You started school in Winnipeg?

Yes, at a little Norquay Street school.

Do you recall very much of that period? What kind of a teacher did you have? Who was she? Do you remember?

No. I don't remember a great deal. I remember the school and I remember playing some football. But that period was broken up quite a lot because of this osteomyelitis. I must have had at least three of four operations and spent from eighteen months to three years in and out of hospital in broken periods.

That would have been an unhappy time.

It was probably the most unhappy period of my life. However, I had one fortunate bright spot in what was a fairly difficult period. I say difficult, first of all, because of the economic depression at that time. There were a tremendous number of people in Winnipeg who had come from all over and hadn't been absorbed yet. Unemployment was high. Even the men who were working, like my father, were working on short time, three days a week. A man would go down and stand around maybe even half a day, to find out if he was going to get any work, and finally at noon be told there was nothing, and come back home not having earned a five-cent piece. Those were pretty grim times for us. We didn't suffer, but there was a feeling of uncertainty and we didn't have very much other than just the bare necessities.

But I was very fortunate in starting to go to All People's Mission. The mission was started by the Reverend J.S. Woodsworth, whom I remember very well. I also remember the director of boys' activities and sports, a Reverend Harry Atkins, who worked with Mr. Woodsworth. It was my first contact with Mr. Woodsworth and when I was reading his biography by his daughter, *A Man To Remember*,[5] it brought back a whole host of memories of the work he did amongst these new Canadians. We played basketball and there was a swimming pool, we had games of all sorts and club work, boxing and other sports, and a small library from which I used to get books regularly.

I think that period did two things for me. First, I realized how much (what I would call) underprivileged boys need help, and how little the organized church and society was supplying at that time. It's much better now, but certainly there wasn't much then. If there hadn't been an All People's Mission, I don't know what we'd have done in what were almost the slums of Winnipeg. They weren't slums in the sense that they were pestilence-ridden spots, but they were poor homes: frame buildings, outdoor toilets, restricted conditions. And the fact that somebody was interested enough to come and live amongst these people, and provide some type of social centre for the boys and girls of our community, meant a great deal to us.

The other lasting impression from that period is the fact that I was tossed into the middle of what was a Tower of Babel. There were people from the Ukraine (Galicia as they called it in those days), Austria, the Scandinavian countries, and all over the world. You lost all sense of national or racial pride, and began to realize the value and worth of people of other races. They were wrestling the same problems we were. They were trying to get established. They were trying to get jobs. They were trying to get decent houses to live in. They were trying to speak the language properly and adapt themselves to the country. The fact that they had sheepskin coats and the women wore babushkas was secondary. You found that basically you were the same.

I always remember when I came out of the hospital once and could only walk with crutches. I could get to school in good weather; and of course no one thought of having a car. There was one family in the whole district who had a Ford car; it was the wonder of the world, and we were just allowed to look at it and touch it. I got along fairly well with crutches but when the wintertime came it was very difficult, and a Polish boy and a Ukrainian boy came knocking at the house with a sleigh, and told my mother that they would pull me to school and bring me back each day. This would be about 1914. These boys speaking broken English, the kind of people that some folks referred to as dagos and foreigners and bohunks, these were the people who came and took an interest in another immigrant boy. Otherwise I just wouldn't have got to school. I think this has had an impression on me all through my life, and is part of the reason why I have always had such a strong sense of disapproval against any kind of racial or religious intolerance.

◻ For a moment, sir, we're going back to Scotland for a little while—to talk about your father.

I suppose my father would fit the description of a great many other Scottish working men. He had a very limited education. He went to school until he was thirteen. When he was thirteen it was the custom of his day to go on what they called half time. He went to school in the morning and worked in the foundry in the afternoon. By the time he was fourteen he was working full time in the foundry. He worked in the foundry until he was a young man and became a soldier in the Sutherland Highlanders, and fought in the South African War. He served some time in India and then caught enteric fever and was invalided back, and for quite a time had to take a job as head gardener at the hospital because he wasn't fit to go back to his trade. I remember him just indistinctly during that period. Then he was well enough finally to go back and work in the foundry.

Then he fought again in the First World War. He died in 1936 before the Second World War.

I sometimes wish, you know, that it were possible to put into words what a man like him could mean. It's now twenty-two years since he died, and yet in many ways he's more alive than when I was a boy. I recall things he said, advice he gave me, and I realize as I get older how much basic wisdom he really had. As I said, he didn't have a lot of formal education. He had a tremendous memory. I mentioned the family's capacity for argument; he and I were able to argue.

What was your father's take-home pay?

I'm depending entirely on the memory of a very early period in my life, but it seems to me that it was two pounds ten, the wages of a fairly good artisan in those days. A pound was considered fairly good wages for unskilled labour. Skilled labour earned wages anywhere from thirty shillings to two pounds ten.

> Where did the family live in Winnipeg during the first period?

I don't recall the exact numbers. The first house was on Jarvis Street. We were only there for a short time. Then we moved onto Gladstone Street which was just off Sutherland Avenue. My father worked in the Vulcan Ironworks on Sutherland Avenue. The All People's Mission was at the corner of Sutherland and Norquay, I think.

> Can we go to where you lived in Glasgow on the return trip? Do you remember the district, address, and so on?

Oh, yes, very well. When we returned to Glasgow during the years of the First World War when my father was overseas, we lived at 63 Clarence Street, as it was called in those times. I noticed when I was back in Glasgow that the name has changed to Dalentopid Street. We lived only about a hundred yards from the head office of the Scottish Co-operative Wholesale, which is at the corner of Dalentopid Street and Morrison Street.

> Did you see that when you went to school each day?

Oh, yes. My grandfather on my mother's side worked in the Co-operative Wholesale.

> Now, where in Winnipeg did you live during the second period?

When we returned to Canada in 1919, we came back before my father was discharged from the army, so my mother and my sisters and myself returned on our own and we lived at 44 Gordon Avenue. We lived there until after my father's return and then in 1920 we bought a house at 132 McPhail Street, and lived there until the time of my father's death.

> We might go into such things as your father's philoso-
> phy, his social, moral, and general attitude. What were
> his hobbies, what did he read? Tell us everything you
> think we should know to give a background.

It's very difficult to sum up a man's personality and his philosophy in minutes, and the passage of years makes you tend to idolize a person, I suppose. I have always felt that I owed a great deal to my father. He had the Douglas failing of a quick temper, which he usually regretted about five minutes after exposing it. He would never sulk. If he was angry, he told you, and he told you in fairly profuse and descriptive language of his displeasure and then it was all over with. There was no bad feeling. Like myself, when he lost his temper he was usually so penitent about it, and he would try to do something for you to make up for the fact that he'd been cross with you.

To me, he had very great assets, and the longer I live the more I appreciate them. He had a scrupulous sense of honesty. He was the kind of man that would owe no one, with the exception of buying our house, of course, which we had to buy by paying so much a month. That was foreign to him. But he never in his life bought anything on credit. This was his pride, that he owed no one any money. He was careful to a penny about paying his debts and was quite honest in returning anything he borrowed. He was also generous to a fault about helping other people, and we always used to think that he was a bit of a soft mark for anybody who was in trouble and would come around to play on his sympathy. This sense of integrity he had is something I appreciate more as the years go by.

But he also had a certain intellectual and moral integrity. He hated hypocrisy. Sometimes he would lean over backwards to make sure nobody would think he was trying to pretend to be something he wasn't. I can still recollect one of the things he used to do when he would come home from working in the foundry. He still had the black sand on him, and although he had had a bit of a wash at the works, he would never be quite cleaned up. When he came into the house, the first thing he did was sit down with a bottle of beer. He worked over a 200-degree furnace all day and perspired heavily, and so he'd have a bottle of beer and go and have a bath and then he'd come down and have his supper. He came in one day and the minster was in visiting our home. My mother and the rest of us were all on our best behaviour. So the minister wouldn't be under any misapprehensions, my father said to him, "I'm going to have a bottle of beer. Would you like one?" This embarrassed my mother and sisters and myself considerably, and undoubtedly the minister, who was a strict Baptist teetotaller. But my father felt that he wasn't going to do without his beer, not because he minded doing without the beer, but because he didn't want anyone to get the impression that he was trying to keep the minister from knowing that he had a glass of beer when he came in. This is the sort of thing he did all his life.

He hated sham and pretence and I liked that about him. The other characteristic he had was something he inherited from Burns, a great feeling of independence. I think one of the things that made him want to leave Scotland, one of the things that made me, even as a boy, glad to be leaving Scotland, was his hatred of class distinction. The idea of taking off your cap to a squire and touching your cap to the doctor and preacher was foreign to him. He felt that he was as good as any man, and that a man's a man: "The rank is but the guinea's stamp, / The man's the gowd for a' that."[6] If he were honest and upright with God and man, he had as much right to walk the earth with dignity as any lord or knight or king.

On the other hand, although he thought he was as good as any man, he took the position that any man was as good as him. He had a marvelous tolerance about people of other nationalities. When we came to Winnipeg in the days when people were pouring in there, my father could be seen coming home from work with some poor chap from central Europe who was trying to learn the language and who had been having a tough time at work, and my father would help him so that he wouldn't lose his job and would be able to understand the foreman. They used to come to our house, people of all sorts. I remember one of my father's best friends was a Chinese laundryman he had helped out. I never realized how much that was true until the funeral. He died quite suddenly. It was in January, a cold winter day, but people we had never even seen before came to the funeral. People of different languages and different ethnic groups came to my mother and myself to mention little kindnesses that my father had done for them.

He had this feeling of independence and pride. One of his favourite sayings was an old Scottish one: "I hear guid conceit of yourself," which means respect yourself, don't let people trample on you, you're as good as the next man. And at the same time he never looked down on any man of any race or colour. The only people he despised were those who lied, cheated, or pretended to be something they weren't.

What did he do at nights after work? What were his diversions or hobbies?

When he was younger, he gardened. He was very fond of gardening, which is something I've never inherited. He had a green thumb and could grow almost anything. We used to joke and tell him that he could put a broomstick in the ground and make it grow.

He played croquet, he used to play soccer football, or soccer as we called it. He played on one of the teams in Winnipeg, mostly made up of old country fellows like himself. He liked to go down to the Legion clubrooms and sit around with the boys and talk over the First World War and the South African War. But mostly he stayed at home, and throughout the latter years of his life he stayed home a good deal. He worked in the foundry from 7 A.M. till 6 P.M. Later on the hours were shorter. He was very punctual. He walked to work, even when we lived in Elmwood and the foundry was way over on Sutherland Avenue. He was always at work twenty minutes before the whistle went, which gave him time to change his clothes and lay out his tools and smoke a cigarette. The moment the whistle went, he started to work. After he'd finished work he put away his clothes and tools and washed up on his own time. This was part of his old Scottish training to give the boss a good day's work for a good day's pay. So this meant that he was up at 5:30 or six o'clock in the morning.

What was he like in appearance? Was he a big man?

He was a tall man. I have taken my short stature from my mother's side. My father was close to six feet, very muscular but lean. He didn't go to flesh at all, but weighed I suppose 180–85 pounds. He was quite strong and very well built.

What did he read?

His reading was scattered. He had no organized system of reading. He read a good deal of old country papers, some of the books put out by the Labour party and the Fabian Society, and current magazines, trying to keep in touch with political events and international affairs in a sort of general way.

Was he active in politics?

No, he was never active in politics. He was a member of the Labour party and supported the Labour party and voted for the Labour party when he was in Britain. And when he came to Canada, we were living in North Winnipeg and Winnipeg Centre, and he voted for Mr. Woodsworth when he ran, Mr. Heaps on other occasions. But he took no active part either as a canvasser or chairman for any meetings. He wasn't as active as his father had been in politics except that he was a strong supporter and cast his ballot.

So you would hear quite a bit about politics?

Oh, yes. My father and I argued about politics at every meal. At the drop of a hat my father would have a discussion about politics, national and international and British politics.

I wonder if you would care to talk about your mother for a time. There's one particular question I wanted to ask you. Apart from her influence and attitude, did she think that her son should be this or that? Did she have certain ambitions for you? Would it be the church, or law, or medicine?

If she had, she certainly didn't express them. She was very good about taking the position that her children would decide for themselves. However, when I decided to go into the ministry, she told me that this was what she had always hoped I would do. Certainly she was the religious influence in our home, and in terms of public speaking and elocution, she was the most influential. Whenever any of us had to say a piece at the Christmas Tree, we would say it before my mother twice a day for a week before, and she would drill us on it. She used to do reading or recitation at different little public functions, and had a native ability for histrionics. She had the Highland strain in her, the imagination. I can remember our main family treat when we were small was Sunday evening, when we would all sit around and she would read to us Dickens or Scott or some book, and she would read a given number of chapters. Then it was put away and continued the next Sunday evening.

She read beautifully and with imagination. The characters became alive. She was largely responsible for my great interest in English literature and dramatics.

> Were the days in Glasgow happier than they were in Winnipeg?

By that time I was over the worst of the osteomyelitis. Yes, they were very happy days in Glasgow.

> Your health was good. Could you engage in any sports at all? How old were you then?

Mostly soccer. A little cricket but mostly soccer, and just general rough-and-tumble games that boys played.

We were in Glasgow when the armistice was signed on 11 November 1918. I became fourteen on 20 October 1918. So I was fourteen when the First World War ended and we left to come back to Canada on New Year's Eve, 1918. We were at sea on New Year's Day, 1919.

> How were you academically in those days? Were you getting good marks as they called them in England?

I was never considered a bookworm or had any great ambition to be a good student. I had a fairly good memory, with the result that I used to be one of the top six in the class. But I was never striving and certainly got no encouragement at home to strive to be at the top of the class. Having a good memory, it was comparatively easy to write exams, and with a reasonably good facility of expression, it was easy to put down what you knew. But I really never was the type of student who tried very hard for academic distinction.

> In that respect, what did you think of the Scottish public school compared with what we have today? We're now speaking in 1958, when there's a great turmoil about education. Have you any thoughts on that?

It's not fair to compare the British school system of 1918 with the Canadian school system of 1958, but remember that I had gone to school in Winnipeg, and then we had gone back to Glasgow, and I certainly knew a great deal of difference in the two school systems. I didn't like the Scottish school system. Looking back now I can see some advantages in it. But the discipline was very strict, to the point sometimes of what seemed to be almost brutality. It's one thing to discipline children for misbehaving, but we were disciplined for more than three mistakes in spelling. The teacher went down the row and gave you a cut across the fingers with a cane or with a strap. I've never been convinced that this will improve your spelling ability. It is better to take you back over your mistakes and show you what was wrong. This idea of caning you and strapping you for mistakes, for being late, and that sort of thing was, I thought, overdone. I'm not saying that is still done in the old country, but it certainly was then.

On the other hand I have to admit that we could do with some of their discipline. They had excellent discipline. The children were disciplined not only in terms of doing what they were told and saying "Yes, sir," and "No, ma'am," to the teachers, being polite and conducting themselves properly, not slouching in their seats, and being punctual, but they also had a certain intellectual discipline. In grammar, we parsed every word in a sentence. You not only had to know that it is more correct to say, "It is I," rather than "It's me," but why it was more correct. Now I know these intellectual disciplines of memorizing a lot of grammar rules are considered out of date by some, but the fact remains that even now in universities our English students write with better facility, better command of English, and better grammar than we do.

> Does any particular teacher stand out in your mind?

Yes, the principal of Scotland Street School, Mr. David Strachan. He had graduated from Edinburgh and Oxford, and yet he had buried himself, some people would say, down in the working-class district of Glasgow as principal of a public school. He spent practically all of his adult life as principal of that school. When I was there he had already been principal for thirty years or more, and he stayed for many years afterward.

He wasn't sadistic at all. When I spoke of people sometimes getting cut across their hand for mistakes in spelling, this didn't extend to Strachan, although he was a very strict disciplinarian, and would cane a boy for disobedience, particularly for being boisterous or hurting a girl. He would never cane a girl. This was one of the rules of the school, although in other schools it was done. There was no caning of girls in his school. But he did a great deal for us. He used to have the classes read selected portions of the Bible for half an hour in the morning, and sometimes sing Scottish psalms. He used to give us little talks, little homely things about honesty and dependability and loyalty, punctuality, the difference between being a gentleman and being just a boor, personal cleanliness, and the fact that when you went to look for a job how important it was that you look neat, that your shoes were shining, your fingernails clean. When you were given responsibility by your boss, every penny must be accounted for; this was a great trust and you must never betray it. These things sunk in.

Interestingly, every Wednesday afternoon at high school was a half-day off, and we'd play football till about 3:30 and then we'd all go over to our old school and visit Dumpy Davey as we called him. He was short and stout. We didn't call him Dumpy Davey to his face. He was always glad to see us.

I remember once by some accident I'd come up at the top of the class on something and somebody had told him about it, and I remember how pleased he was. He always kept these contacts with us. I think this will be an interesting little sidelight: In 1945 I was in Glasgow during the war after I'd come back from visiting Canadian troops in Holland and Belgium and Germany, and walked up to the Scotland Street School. The black-out was still on, and I stood there in the school grounds looking around and thinking again of all the youngsters I had known and with whom

I'd played football. I was thinking of Dumpy Davey and wondering where they all were.

While I was standing there, someone came up. I could see the lighted end of a cigarette, and it turned out to be the school caretaker. And he asked me if there was anything I was looking for, and I said, "No, I was just living again over old memories," and he said, "Did you go to school here?" I said "Yes" and mentioned Mr. Strachan. And he said, "You know, there's hardly a week goes by that some boy doesn't come here in his kilt or with Canada on his shoulder or New Zealand or Australia, and come and stand here for a minute like you're doing." He said, "I suppose Davey has boys all over the world." I think that was a fine tribute to a Scottish schoolmaster.

> As I recall my own school days in England, we were quite different from Canadian boys, and I've often wondered why. I mean, I used to have a fight every day.

I think maybe we've become more civilized. I think the mores of the group have gone down to children, because what you say about the old country schools is certainly true, there was a fight every day. But that was equally true in Canada. In the Canadian schools you had a fight with somebody almost every day, and it was quite the common thing to have a circle of boys and a couple of fellows in the centre squaring off. And I can remember, even when I was sixteen or seventeen years of age in Winnipeg, having a fight behind the police station on Selkirk Avenue — a great place to have one. But in those days fighting was just sort of accepted as a way of settling who was the best man.

That seems to have died out. I've had a number of boys' Sunday school classes, boys' groups over the last twenty or thirty years, and the boys don't fight much now. I think they've probably become more sensible, they've come to recognize that sheer ability to knock another fellow down is no indication of your superiority.

> I want to ask you about the books you read. Not just the books you read in school — you said you weren't a bookworm — but you obviously did a lot of reading in those

days, did you not? For instance, I suppose you'd read such things as *Boys' Own Paper* and *Chums?*

Oh, yes, I read. There was a library very close to us in Glasgow, right on Paisley Road, and I read all of the Henty adventure books for boys one by one, and all of the Ballantyne books, *The Last of the Mohicans*, Fenimore Cooper's book, all the typical regular type of boys' books.

Detective stories, too, I suppose.

Not so much in those days. More of the adventure stories — pirates, trappers, explorers, and above all, soldiers. In Glasgow, living three blocks from the Broomielaw, you could go down any evening and see ships from all the seven seas tied up at the docks, and the sailors from every country in the world. Of course, every boy was going to be a sailor. As a matter of fact I would think that two-thirds of the boys with whom I went to school ended up by going to sea.

Did you have any early ambition yourself in any direction, through your reading or your environment?

Oh, yes. Like every other boy I said I wanted to go to sea as soon as I was old enough.

Did you ever do anything toward that ambition?

No, not at all, because we came back to Canada when I was still fourteen, which knocked that on the head.

We'll go from there to the high school. How long did you go to that high school? You started at twelve years of age.

I only went to that high school for a couple of years. My father was still in France and my mother did not have too much influence over a boy of fourteen. My mother was working. Since my father was now transferred to the Canadian army, we didn't get the full amount of money a Canadian soldier would get due to the fact that we were not living in Canada, and so my mother was working, and it was hard paying high school fees and keeping a family. And so in the fall of 1918 when school started up again, I didn't go back. I didn't tell my mother anything about it. I got myself a job in a cork factory.

Can you remember the name of the cork factory?

No, I don't remember the name of it, but the man who owned it was a man called Hunter. The factory was right beside the suspension bridge across the River Clyde. I worked there all summer and instead of going back to school, I stayed on that fall.

What were you doing precisely?

I was really working in the office as Hunter's assistant. He was very kind to me, and as a matter of fact wanted me to stay and go to night-school and learn Spanish and Portugese, and then go with him on buying trips and gradually take over the buying of cork. He went to Spain and Portugal to buy cork two or three times a year. This was a factory that made corks of all sorts, from corks for barrels down to corks for little medicine bottles, and for the whole whisky trade. Then they printed the bottles or branded the corks. But my main work was in the office. I wasn't tending any of the machines.

Were you keeping figures?

No, I answered the telephone and took orders, saw that orders were shipped out, that they went to the warehouse, and that sort of work.

Did you have any particular liking for a life of commerce?

I liked the idea of travelling to Spain and Portugal and learning foreign languages. I always had a great liking for languages, and this I would have enjoyed very much.

In other words, you were not interested in the commercial aspect?

No. It was the adventure that appealed to me, not the making of money.

My father came home on leave just after the armistice. He had said when he came over to the old country that he thought he'd take his discharge and we'd stay there. It had been pretty tough in Canada during the economic depression, with my father only working part time and the trouble with my leg. And all our people were in the old country. So my father thought he would take his discharge and continue to live in Scotland. But when he came home on leave he'd had time to look around a bit, and saw the old class distinctions in Scotland, which were more marked then than they are now, although they certainly have by no means disappeared.

But this idea that you were in classes, and that the working-class boy didn't get up into the professional class and the professional class into the ranks of the gentry, and that the gentry would never expect to get into the ranks of the nobility, this irked my father. He said, "Oh, you people, as soon as you can, get a boat, go back to Canada, and I'll come back when we are shipped back. I'll take my discharge in Winnipeg so we'll start again in Canada."

> In those days, I mean in Scotland generally, the father's decision held, did it not?

Oh, yes. And, of course, we all wanted to go back, too. My sisters weren't very old, but my mother and I certainly wanted to go back.

> What were your own personal reasons?

Even as a boy I felt very strongly about class distinction. One of the things that bothered me, for instance, was that I had been raised in Winnipeg where you could go wherever you liked. In Scotland we would go for our holidays to a place like Largs or Dinoon or Roxy, which are resorts down at the mouth of the River Clyde. There were little public beaches where hundreds of thousands of people crowded to the square foot, and all the rest of the country was marked off. These were the shooting grounds of the Duke of Argyle, or some other landed gentry, who had six or eight thousand acres of land for grouse shooting or deer shooting, and signs were up all over: "Trespassers will be prosecuted."

Where was there to go except on the public beach, and walk up and down the rows? Tramping over the hills and doing the kind of things that a boy wants to do, these you couldn't do in a large part of Scotland. This class distinction and this social framework had been fastened on so tightly.

> It would affect you in another way, wouldn't it? If the father had been a postman, I mean the whole community would say the son's got to be a postman too—that kind of attitude we find in the north of England. The boy should have no ambition beyond following the trade of his father despite how poor it might be and how restricted.

Yes. However, I find that when I go back to Scotland, this attitude is broken down now. But certainly when I was a youngster, people said to my father, "Now, Tom, I suppose you're going to make the young fellow a moulder," and my father would say, "Like hell I'll make him a moulder. I'll break his neck if he ever goes near a moulding shop."

> Surely there's a family ambition.

All his life my father said, "You're going to get out of this and break this tie, this staying a slave to a foundry."

When you got back to Winnipeg you had been in high school for two years. The family now lived at Gordon Avenue.

Just my mother and sisters and I. My father didn't come till later, so in a sense this matured me. I was the man of the family and had to look after things: see that the storm windows were put up, and that my sisters would start school—I went with them and got them placed—and this sort of thing. And this isn't bad for a boy. We got settled down, and then the question came, of course, of what was I going to do. Because my father was still overseas there seemed to be only one thing for me to do, and that was to get a job. So I bought a bicycle and began as an errand boy. One of my first jobs was for a drugstore at the corner of Higgins and Main, the one that used to have those fancy lights, across from the Royal Alex Hotel. I worked as a messenger boy for quite a while. But each job I took, I stayed just for a few weeks, until I could find another one that paid a little more money.

> What were you paid when you were working in the office of the cork factory? Do you remember?

I did very well. I started at thirty shillings, and I was up to about three pounds in a few weeks. During the war, men were scarcer than hens' teeth, and any boy who could show any aptitude at all at answering the phone and taking some of the work off the boss's shoulders was paid very good money.

When I came back to Canada I was looking for something more permanent than being a messenger boy, and finally I went into the printing business. I worked for the *Grain Trade News*, which was operated by Dawson Richardson, a brother of James Richardson. I remember going into the print-shop and telling the foreman I was looking for a job. They had been advertising for a boy to learn the printing trade. He looked me over and tried me out on two or three things, and then said, "I'll teach you all I know, and you still won't know anything."

> You formally apprenticed?

Yes, and I was recognized by the Typographical Union as an apprentice.

> How long did it normally take to become a journeyman, or was there a set term?

Five years.

> So you were formally apprenticed for five years to that company?

Oh, not exclusively for that company. You could move around. When you got to having three years, you were what they called a two-thirder. This entitled you to a different salary schedule. And you moved around, but the union kept tab of your time for five years. Then the union gave you some tests and gave you a journeyman's certificate. I used to go to night-school and study printing.

What were your first jobs in the print-shop?

I started out as a printer's devil, breaking up forms, stripping the type, putting away the slugs and the furniture on a ledge, scrubbing the forms as they came off the press, scrubbing off the ink with gasoline. I did that for a few months, and then began setting type.

What were your working hours as an apprentice at twelve dollars a week?

In those days we worked from 8 A.M. to 6 P.M. and till 12 noon on Saturday.

Is the firm still in existence?

Oh, yes. I sometimes go back and visit the fellows there.

Your father returned in 1919. These were days of tremendous unrest in Winnipeg. Tell us what impressed you about this turbulent atmosphere in Winnipeg. What had happened?

We arrived in Winnipeg in January 1919. Throughout the balance of the year soldiers were being brought back and being discharged almost every few days. They were looking for work. Quite a lot of people were walking the streets. There was no unemployment insurance and no orderly transition of the economy from war to peace. The union in Winnipeg was called the One Big Union, which was really ten or twenty years before its time. It was an attempt to duplicate the C.I.O. [Congress of Industrial Organizations], to bring their craft or their occupation into one big union and act as a single unit.

They finally called a strike in Winnipeg when they couldn't get any definite answer to their demands. The strike tied up everything: streetcars, policemen, firemen, milk deliveries. At the same time, more veterans were coming home, and there was quite an attempt to play off the veterans against the men who were on strike. [The Winnipeg General Strike began on 15 May 1919. It was not organized by the One Big Union, which was formed after the strike began. It was the craft unions of the Trade and Labour Congress (T.L.C.) that resorted to this weapon to challenge employers on the issues of higher wages, the eight-hour day, union recognition, and the closed shop. The unions were also embittered by the recent refusal of the Manitoba government to outlaw court injunctions in labour disputes. The employers and their political allies pictured the strike as a conspiracy of the radical One Big Union.][7]

I remember going to some of the outdoor meetings. I can still see Mr. Woodsworth speaking from the steps of the Norquay School in Elmwood, and Mr. S.J. Farmer and John Queen. One of the most outstanding men was Fred Dixon, who would have been a powerful political figure had he lived. He died sometime later, but for a while he was a member of the Manitoba Legislative Assembly. Heaps and Bob Russell and many others were leaders among the strikers.

Most people know the story. The committee of one thousand was formed and Eaton's turned their fine horses over to them. Some of the veterans were told that the strikers were just slackers who lived in Canada during the war, made a lot of money, and now wanted to get even more. The I.W.W. [Industrial Workers of the World] were characterized as "I Won't Work." A lot of these veterans were fooled into joining the committee of one thousand, trained to ride the horses, and supplied with sawed-off baseball bats and hoe handles. We had a very bad situation.

I was coming home from work one day, and several other young fellows and I climbed up on the roof of a building to see the mounted police charge the workers in Market Square in front of City Hall. The police opened fire and killed a man who stood on the corner of Main Street and Williams Avenue, not very far from where we were. We saw the mounted police and the men who had been taken in as sort of vigilantes riding from North Main straight down toward the corner of Portage and Main, then reforming on Portage Avenue and coming back down again, riding the strikers down and breaking up the meetings, breaking up their parade.

You actually saw the shooting?

Yes. There was quite a good deal of shooting. Most of the
mounted policemen were shooting into the air, but some of them
shot into the crowd. One particular man was killed and several
others were wounded. [This was Bloody Saturday, 23 June 1919 at
about five or six o'clock, which ended the strike, the workers
having failed to achieve any of their objectives.]

Mr. Woodsworth was thrown into jail. Do you remember any impressions of that incident?

We have to remember that Mr. Woodsworth was our minister. He
had been head of the All People's Mission for years. We'd gone
there to church and I'd gone to the boys' clubs, and although we'd
been away, when we came back we still had recollections. We'd
gone to hear him speak on behalf of the strikers. He was editing a
paper [the *Western Labour News*], which was trying to tell the
strikers' story, and we read it. Our sympathies naturally were all
with him and with the Labour people. So it was with a good deal
of dismay that we learned that he was thrown into jail. Certainly,
as the years went by, the Winnipeg General Strike left a very
lasting impression on me. Not until the Estevan riot and later the
Regina riot did I realize that this was all part of a pattern. Whenever the powers that be can't get what they want, they're always
prepared to resort to violence or any kind of hooliganism to break
the back of organized opposition.

[The Estevan riot took place in this south-eastern Saskatchewan coal-mining town, fifty-four miles south of Weyburn.
The miners had been on strike since 7 September 1931 in an effort
to secure increased wages and better working conditions. A
parade organized by the strikers on 29 September ended in a
bloody clash between the police and several hundred strikers and
their families. Three strikers were killed, and a number were injured. Many strikers were arrested.

The Regina riot was an episode in the "On-to-Ottawa" trek of
single unemployed men who resented conditions in the Dominion government relief camps of British Columbia. The leader of
the trek, which began in Vancouver, was a Communist, although

most of the thirteen hundred men who travelled east on boxcars were not. Their objective was to press Prime Minister Bennett to adopt a "work with wages" programme. The C.P.R. co-operated by allowing the men to "ride the rods," but on 14 June the Dominion government ordered a stop in Regina. There was widespread sympathy in the city for the "strikers," as they were now called, exhibited in donations of food and money. Ottawa's reaction was to plan the arrest of the strike leaders by charging that they were members of an "unlawful organization" forbidden by the criminal code of Canada.

On 1 July a peaceful fund-raising meeting was held at Market Square attended by fifteen hundred men, women, and children, and including only about three hundred trekkers and their leaders. The R.C.M.P. seized this occasion to make the arrests by charging into the crowd swinging their batons. The citizens reacted violently, and police on horseback rode into the crowd firing their revolvers. When, after three and a half hours, peace was finally restored, one city policeman was dead, a number injured, and forty citizens and trekkers were in hospital, seventeen with bullet wounds. It was the most violent riot in Canadian history. Fortunately, the Government of Saskatchewan, which had not been involved in either the trek or the riot, intervened to feed the trekkers and supervise their return to their homes.][8]

> I remember that I first met you at the Estevan riot. You'd come to look into it all the way from Weyburn. What were you doing in the days following the Winnipeg General Strike?

I was working in the print-shop all day. One or two nights a week I was at night-school to polish up my printing. You didn't have to go to night-school, but if you did you had a chance to be a better printer. When I was sixteen I was already operating a linotype machine, and I was the youngest linotype operator in Canada. I was getting the full journeymen's wages before my five years were up. I was drawing forty-four dollars a week, which was the union wage, before I'd even completed my time because I was running a linotype and was able to complete four thousand ems an hour, which was the regular amount, and the union insisted that I be paid union wages. So that's why I went to night-school to try to improve my techniques.

The other nights in the week I belonged to church groups. I first became a Scout and later a troop leader, patrol leader, Cub-master, and Scoutmaster.

My father being a Mason, I also joined the order of DeMolay, which provided me with good training in public speaking and meeting people. By this time I was also beginning to copy some of my mother's tricks, and gave little readings and recitations at various concerts and after-dinner affairs.

> You went in for monologues, which were very popular at the time.

Oh, yes. I did Alfred Noyes's "The Highway Man," Pauline Johnson's "Legend of Qu'Appelle Valley," and Kipling's "If." I took lessons for one evening a week from Jean Campbell, the famous elocutionist, a pupil of Jean Alexander, whose books are very well known. Jean Alexander and Jean Campbell had toured all over Canada doing monologues. I used to go to Bobbie Burns dinners to give the Scottish monologues and sometimes to Masonic events to do an item on the programme. In those days there were a lot of concerts. The Scouts used to charge twenty-five cents for tickets, and we'd make up a programme. Usually I'd get stuck doing a monologue and probably get stuck for a quarter, too.

> It was rather good training though, wasn't it? You lost any fear of audiences you might have had.

That's right. It was excellent training.

> Were there any other people who helped you in those days?

Two men helped me a great deal. One was Dr. Howden, who owned the Winnipeg Theatre, one of the dads of the DeMolay. The Masons select certain men as dads or an advisory committee to the DeMolay order, and they help you and advise you. Dad Howden was a very good friend to some of us including myself, and used to take us to the Winnipeg Theatre. We met a number of people there and occasionally got a small part, sometimes as a butler. I got a couple of little Scotch parts with my Scottish accent, which was very good for me. Dr. Howden also had a share in the Walker Theatre, which at that time was the place for impressarios to bring their stars. I saw John Martin Harvey playing in *Hamlet*.[9] We made first-class contacts through Dr. Howden. At one time he tried to persuade me to go onto the stage, and offered to send me away for dramatic training if I would quit my job to join his repertory theatre.

I didn't do it, but I did agree to something else. He used me as the understudy for the part of Jacques DeMolay in one of the DeMolay plays. Having a fairly good memory, I knew the lines cold when the leading man had to drop out, so I got the chance of playing the part of Jacques DeMolay in the old Board of Trade Building at a Masonic convention in front of five thousand Masons.

How old were you then?

I was about seventeen or eighteen. My father, who was sparing of praise as he was of most things, was somewhat pleased when we got out of the Board of Trade Building. He said, "Let's walk." I knew from that he'd been deeply moved by the performance. We never exchanged a word all the way home, but as we were going up the front step, he tapped me on the shoulder and said, "You did no bad." That was as close as he ever came to giving me a word of praise. He might tell my mother that he was pleased, but he found it very difficult to tell me.

And the other person who helped you?

The other person I wanted to mention was W.J. Major, who was also one of our dads and later became Attorney-General of the Province of Manitoba. Eventually he was a judge of the Queen's Bench Court. W.J. Major was one of the men who was largely responsible for persuading me to quit printing and go to school again. He told me that he thought I had some ability that would be of some use, but having quit school when I was only fourteen years of age and not completing high school, there were very decided limitations on how far I could go.

He thought I should go to university. At that time I was chaplain for the DeMolay organization and, being chaplain, I suppose he thought in terms of the ministry. I was certainly thinking in terms of the ministry.

> Were there any other influences? You've almost finished your apprenticeship by this time.

I finished my apprenticeship before I went to college, but I hadn't by this time. I was eighteen, in my last year. As a printer setting up type all day long, books and articles, it was easy to do quite a bit of reading. There was a foreman in one print-shop I worked in, the Kingdom Press, whose name was Tom Campbell. He was like so many printers who had started work just as I did at fourteen years of age. He had moved all around, all over the North American continent, because a printer can go anywhere in the English-speaking world. A print-shop is the same whether it's in Nome, Alaska, or Louisville, Kentucky, or Winnipeg, Manitoba. Campbell finally settled down in Winnipeg, was married and raising a family. He was an omnivorous reader, and particularly became interested in archaeology and Old Testament documents, largely as a result of having set up a book by an archaeologist. He got me reading quite a bit along those lines, particularly the Old Testament, the old story of the early scrolls and the early documents that produced the various sacred scriptures. He also influenced me to think in terms of scholastics.

> At this time of your life you were interested in sports, too, weren't you?

Oh, yes. I was very interested in sports. I had a troop of Scouts. At this time I think I was assistant Scoutmaster and also a Cub-master, and had a group of small boys under my care from the Baptist church in Elmwood. I was interested in various kinds of sports, but I wasn't too good at some of them. I did a bit of sprinting, but I don't think I ever got a hundred-yard dash much below twelve seconds. I was always too clumsy on my feet to be much good at the high jump. But I went into it with the other young fellows who worked around there. The Scout troop we had was a cycle troop of all working boys. All the boys in Elmwood worked for a living, so we all owned our own bicycles. We painted them red with grey trimmings, and on the week-ends, we'd put packs on our backs and go out on the open road by east St. Paul and camp out. We'd go out on Saturday afternoon, and come back Sunday night or early Monday morning.

We'd play baseball and various sports. I became quite interested in boxing at the O.B.U. [One Big Union] gym. I used to box with people like Lloyd Peppen, who later became the Canadian lightweight champion, and spar with people like Charley Balongey, who later became the heavyweight champion. I was on a number of preliminaries with Jack Taylor, the Canadian heavyweight wrestling champion. He was the man famous for his great toe hold, a very fine wrestler. It was a very interesting period, because some of the preliminaries I was in were on nights when some of the American champions like Ed "Strangler" Lewis, Zabisco, Husam Turk, and Swedenburg from Chicago were wrestling. "Strangler" Lewis was probably the most colourful.

At what age did you have your first bout?

I began boxing when I was around fifteen. I boxed at 135 pounds in the lightweight class.

How long did you continue boxing?

Until I left to go to university, and then I started boxing again at university.

Did you win any championships?

I had the Manitoba Lightweight Championship for a couple of years.

Who did you beat for that one?

Cecil Matthews. He had the championship and then I took it in 1922. We fought in the old arena that used to be across from Union Station by the Fort Garry Hotel. Cecil Matthews got a return match in 1923 and I held the championship for the second year.

How long or how many rounds did it go? Was it on points or was it a knock-out?

It was on points. It was a six-round bout. They had an elimination contest all through the year, and in the final week we'd be narrowed down to about ten, and then we would have bouts every night and the final fight on the Saturday night. The next year I had it much easier because contestants had to eliminate each other and when they came to me, I was still comparatively fresh.

What did your mother think about this?

My mother wasn't happy about it. My father was quite disgusted. For a man who had been a soldier and who had been in the odd fight himself, he didn't look on it kindly. My father and my mother wouldn't come to the bouts at all. They thought I was very silly. The first time I fought in the championship, I already had a broken nose, a couple of teeth out, a strained right hand, and a sprained thumb by the time we came to the finals. My father looked me over before I went the last night and said, "It serves you right. If you're fool enough to get into this sort of thing, don't ask for any sympathy." I didn't get any.

It was rather an achievement for you, winning any kind of a boxing match, considering the time when you didn't think you'd even be able to walk again.

Not really. After the last operation on my leg just before we had gone back to Britain, about 1914, I had no trouble until I got my leg banged up in Germany in 1945.

I don't want you to get the impression that I was a great athlete. I was fairly average, and I wasn't a particularly outstanding boxer. I was too short in the arm to be a good boxer, but I was fast on my feet and could hit fairly hard, and as far as matches were concerned, I got a very lucky break. My opponent tried to come in fast and go under my guard, dropped his, and left himself wide open.

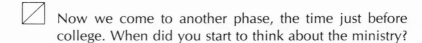 Now we come to another phase, the time just before college. When did you start to think about the ministry?

In about 1922 or 1923. I had always been active in church work, particularly with boys. Then when I became chaplain of the order of DeMolay, that made me think of it some more. I had joined the Baptist church when I was fourteen. My mother, of course, was greatly interested in the church. The general feeling was that if I had any useful contribution to make at all it was probably in the Christian church.

> It was this whole accumulation of your family back-ground and your early activities in church work. But there must have been some other factor there, such as your experiences with poverty.

Yes, although I don't think that was so much of a factor then. I think it came to me later. At that time I think my main feeling was that I liked church work, I liked working with young people, I liked working particularly with boys. I found making little talks to boys and at young people's meetings comparatively easy. The minister we had in the Baptist church would periodically ask the young people to take charge of the Sunday evening church ser-vice for some variety, and I would be roped in to give the talk. With the reading I was doing as a printer, it wasn't too difficult to sit down and prepare a little ten- or fifteen-minute talk. And so I found myself gradually working into it. I was becoming a part-time worker in the church doing the odd bit of preaching.

> At that time you couldn't have been interested in a career that would make money for you. You must have known of the strictness of clerical life.

When I left the printing business to go to college for six or eight years of training, I knew that when I finished I wouldn't be earning as much money as I was as a printer.

2

Baptist minister

◩ How did you prepare yourself to go to college?

First of all, I had to start saving some money. My father was
working, but he was making less than I was. I had been putting
every dollar I earned into the family coffer so we could pay off the
house and kept just a few dollars for my own pocket money. I
wanted my parents to own the house and have some economic
security. Although my father had a marvellous constitution, we
never knew when he might have serious complications from
having been gassed overseas. I had no money when I decided to
go to college, so I spent a year saving and reading as much as I
could. I got books from the church minister and Mr. Major. I did a
good deal of reading and studying at nights, although not in an
organized way but in a reasonably haphazard way. Dr. W.C.
Smalley, who later became general secretary of the Baptist Union

of Western Canada, was at that time Manitoba Superintendent of Missions, and he helped me out a good deal. He knew that I wanted to go to college. He knew that the only hope I had of getting through college was working while I was studying and the only work I could get would be preaching on Sundays and during the summer holidays. And to do that I had to get some experience.

So he got me a little week-end supply around Winnipeg in country churches. One of the first he sent me to was Stonewall, which is just outside of Winnipeg. At that time I was either eighteen or nineteen. I looked quite boyish. When I see the pictures now, I think I looked about fourteen. Away I went on the morning train, and when I got off there was a great crowd of people looking around for someone, and I got off completely unobserved. Since no one had paid any attention to me, I went up to a boy who was leaning against his bicycle and said, "Can you tell me how I get to the Baptist church?" He said, "What do you want at the Baptist church?" I said, "I'm supposed to be taking the service this morning." And then in a voice as though he were an auctioneer, he yelled down the whole length of the platform, "Mom, this kid says he's the new preacher!" whereupon the eyes of the entire congregation who had come down to meet the supply for the week-end were focused on me. The apparent disappointment in their faces was very noticeable.

But when I got through the service, they invited me back. So in the last year while still in the printing business I went out as many week-ends as I could to get preaching experience.

> How did your pals in the printing trade regard this business of your going to become a minister?

They didn't mind. It really wasn't too much of a shock. I was a bit of an oddity in the print-shop; I was always good friends with everyone, but I didn't join the lads in the evenings. I didn't go to the drinking parties and didn't play poker, as most printers do. And at noon hour, whenever there was a poker game, I was usually memorizing a recitation for the evening or getting a talk ready.

Did they kid you about it at all?

I was provincial lightweight champion, and so they didn't kid too much. Tom Campbell, of whom I spoke previously, was tremendously pleased. He said, "You're going to get out of this blankety-blank printing business and it's a good thing; you should be out of it." My employers were very accommodating if I needed time off to go somewhere.

And you met many of them later in life.

Oh, yes. I always went back and saw the boys. I have always gone back; they are among my best friends and my greatest boosters.

When you were going into the church, did you consider any phase of church work that might interest you more than any other, for example, missions or home missions?

No, I was mainly thinking in terms of religious education. I think if I'd had a choice of that kind, it would have been in boys' work. I recognized that I needed basic training.

Every boy that went into the Baptist ministry thought he was going to be another Charles Hadden Spurgeon,[1] certainly the greatest Baptist preacher ever produced, and maybe one of the greatest preachers of the English-speaking world. I was saturated with Spurgeon's lectures, sermons, and the stories of his life.

Why did you decide to go to Brandon College?

I had quit school near my fourteenth birthday, and so I had really no academic standing in Canada at all. I only had a couple of years of Scottish high school. In connection with its university, Brandon College ran an academy, which offered grades 9, 10, and 11. After this you went straight into arts. So I went to the academy to complete my high school prerequisites.

When I went to Brandon, I had in mind that I would take the English theology course, in which there was no Greek or Latin or Hebrew. You also didn't need your grade 11. I'd thought of doing that; it would have only taken me three years. Dr. Sweet, the president, a very capable man who died a short time after that, took me into his office and chatted to me about the course, and said, "How old are you?" and I said, "I'm nineteen, I'll be twenty in a few days." And he said, "Mr. Douglas, if you had only ten years to live, you'd be better to take six years to do four years of good work than to take three years to do seven years of mediocre work. Don't try any short cuts. Take your academy, take your high school, take your arts, take your theology, take a full course. Certainly it will take you six or eight years, but we need trained men, and partly trained men are never happy themselves, and never do effective work." That was the best advice I ever got, and I passed it on to many young boys I met who were trying to take short cuts.

> In the fall of 1924 you started your course at the academy to get your qualifications. How long did it take you?

I was six years at Brandon.

> How did you support yourself? You only had this small supply during the summer.

The supply during the summer was while I was still a printer, and I wasn't paid for it. They paid me my train fare, but they were only putting up with me. I was practicing on them.

I started at Brandon College with ninety dollars in my pocket. That's all I had managed to save. Of course my parents wouldn't have seen me starve, but they were not in a position to help me very much. I had a promise from Mr. Smalley to try to get me a preaching appointment every third week, or maybe once a month. This was the best he could hope for. Usually during your first year you didn't get any money. But he knew my financial position and he offered to try to help me in this regard.

I was very fortunate. On my way to Brandon they told me that I was to stop and take a service at a little place called Austin, which is about half-way between Portage la Prairie and Brandon. The purpose of going there was to close the church up. The church had been going to pieces; they'd had a row and half the congregation had become British Israelites. (This is why I became an authority on British Israelite literature.) And so I was to go and have this service, close them off formally, and bury the dead. At twenty years of age, you're brash and ready to hand out advice to people three times your age with complete equanimity. So I proceeded to preach a sermon saying it was disgraceful that they were closing this church. The young people in the community needed religious education, and because of differences about biblical interpretations, these people were depriving the young of religious education. When I finished and they were singing the last hymn, the head deacon sent me a note asking me to tell the congregation to stay. They had a bit of an argument, admitted they had been a little foolish, and said that if I would agree to come every Sunday, they'd try it for another year.

When I went to the college and told them, they said, "You can't go every Sunday, not with your two years of high school and year of theology all crammed into one. But we will let you go every other Sunday."

My future brother-in-law had decided to come to Brandon College in the meantime.

What was his name?

Mark Talney. Mark and I had decided to go to college together, although he decided some six months after I did. It was agreed that he and I would alternate in carrying this charge at Austin. And so we got through the first winter.

Did Mr. Talney stay with the church?

Oh, yes. He is a Doctor of Divinity in Portland, Oregon, where he is the secretary for social services and evangelism for the Presbyterian church of Oregon.

Mark and I did any odd jobs, waiting tables or tending night-bells for the students who came in late and got fined two-bits. They came in late and you collected the two-bits. You kept the twenty-five cents for getting up and opening the door. Any fellow who wakes you up at one o'clock in the morning deserves to pay two-bits. I wouldn't do it for two-bits now.

I had another little racket on the side during my college days. I used to go around to all the fowl suppers, for five dollars an evening and my expenses, doing monologues.

What was the strong item on your programme?

Oh, mostly the humorous monologues.

Do you remember any of them?

Oh, yes: "Is He at the Weddding?" and "Shopping in Eaton's," and one or two others I wrote myself, which were really a combination of corny jokes I still inflict on political audiences.

I had quite a repertoire. I went to one place where they actually paid me twenty dollars, and I put on the entire programme of monologues, with the local choir interspersing musical numbers in between. I made up a whole programme for the evening. This was when I was getting into the semi-professional class.

And you still recall quite a number of those, don't you? Did you keep them on file?

I've never kept a file. I should, but I depended on pure memory. People meet me now and tell me about a story they remember me telling fifteen years ago, and I've forgotten the story.

And you could adapt the stories to modern conditions.

Yes, you can always bring them up to date.

You always seem to come up with some that are completely new. I don't think I've ever heard them before. Where do you get them?

I make them up. A humorous incident happens, and then you dress it up. Over the years I've collected some of the amusing little things that have happened to chairmen introducing me, and then I put them all together and it makes a little monologue. Or I take humorous incidents that have happened in debates with Mr. Tucker and Mr. Rupert Ramsay, or interruptions I've had from the audience. Sometimes someone in the audience has the better of me on an interruption. The best jokes are always those in which somebody gets the better of you.

Apart from these activities, were there any other college diversions?

Not much with the heavy programme I had, and going out every second Sunday, and after the first year, every Sunday all through college. Even after I was married I didn't skip any of the Sundays.

We got married on a Saturday and I preached on Sunday. When you need the income, you don't miss it.

I met my wife at Carberry, Manitoba.

She didn't go to Brandon, did she?

She went to Brandon later, but I met her at Carberry. One Saturday when I was going down on the train from Brandon to Austin, I ran into the superintendent of the Presbyterian church who saw me reading the *Sunday School Times* and he came over and sat down and started chatting. He found out I was going down to take the service at Austin, and he said, "We're in a terrible predicament." At that time the Presbyterian church had stayed out of the union, and was having an awful job getting ministers. He said, "We need a man for Carberry for the summer. Would you be interested?" I said, "I don't think I could very well, I'm a Baptist." He said, "If we cleared it with your people, would it be alright?" He took it up with Mr. Smalley, who agreed to my going. He had quite a number of students around and it was a chance to place one of them near Brandon.

And so I went to Carberry to preach for the Presbyterians for two years. I went every Sunday and then took the services all summer. It was considered alright in those days. My future wife was a Methodist, but she started coming to the Presbyterian church. We got acquainted, and later she came to Brandon to study music. She was a music teacher.

I finished at Brandon in the spring. After two years at Carberry, the Baptists said they wanted me back because they were running short of men, and so my leave of absence was cancelled. They sent me up to Shoal Lake and Strathclare, which is close to Dauphin. So I went there for two years every Sunday and each summer. The first two years of college I went to Austin, the second two years to Carberry, the third two years to Shoal Lake–Strathclare, which was one of Mr. Smalley's former ministries for many years, so he was anxious I should go there. I had two very happy years at Shoal Lake–Strathclare.

Before graduation in 1930, we were all wondering where we were going to go, and different churches were offering us calls, asking us to come and be looked over. One of my best friends at

Brandon College was a fellow called Stanley Knowles, who had come to Brandon about half-way through my course. Knowles and I were both asked to go to Weyburn, Saskatchewan, in the fall of 1929, and preach for a call that we wouldn't take until after we had graduated in the spring of 1930.

So Knowles and I went alternate Sundays to Weyburn all through the winter of 1929–30, and then in the spring of 1930 they looked us both over and finally decided to call me. Later, when I became a C.C.F. politician, some of the deacons were thinking that probably they'd made a mistake, and that they should have taken Knowles. But eventually Knowles became a C.C.F. politician, too, and they'd have been stuck either way.

Did Stanley hold it against you at all?

Oh, no. As a matter of fact, Stanley did much better. He went as assistant minister to First Baptist Church in Winnipeg. He was really better off, although I'd much rather have been at Weyburn than at First Baptist Church.

[Stanley Howard Knowles was born in Los Angeles in 1908. His parents were Canadians who returned to Canada in 1924. Knowles studied at Brandon College, United College (Winnipeg), and the University of Manitoba. He received his B.A. degree in 1930 and the B.D. in 1934. He became a printer and minister. Knowles was elected as a Winnipeg alderman (1941–42) and was an unsuccessful candidate in the federal elections of 1935 and 1940 and the provincial election of 1941. He became an active member and office holder in the C.C.F. in Manitoba beginning in 1934. He was first elected to the House of Commons in a by-election in 1942, occasioned by the death of J.S. Woodsworth. Subsequently he won every successive federal election except in 1958, but was again returned in 1962, and in subsequent general elections, including the one in 1979. During his long parliamentary career he has been involved with numerous international Labour and United Nations organizations. His unrivalled knowledge of parliamentary procedure is recognized by all political parties in the Commons. He was honoured by appointment to the Queen's Privy Council of Canada in 1979.]

So my formal education, as far as going to college was

concerned, finished in the spring of 1930. Weyburn people were very good to me, and each summer they gave me a leave of absence so I could work on my Ph.D. in Chicago. During the winter I was studying my master's degree courses by correspondence with McMaster University. I wrote my thesis on Christian Sociology, particularly the problem of the subnormal and underprivileged family, in 1933. The work I was doing in Chicago each summer toward my Ph.D. was in the same field.

I didn't get back to Chicago to finish my doctor's degree, which I had hoped to do. My ordination was in June 1930.

Where were you ordained?

In the Baptist church in Weyburn. When a church ordains you all the other churches in the association meet and the ministers and their deacons come. They examine you on your faith and beliefs and theology, and above all, on your academic training. They had to be satisfied as to your personal views and so on, and your acceptance of certain church beliefs. The Baptist church has no fixed set of doctrines. Rather, the New Testament sets forth the beliefs, and there is no dogma, as in the Presbyterian or Anglican church.

You'd be precisely what age on your ordination day?

I was a few months away from being twenty-six.

Did you debate at university? Were any of your opponents men who later gained renown in public life? What about Stanley Knowles, didn't you beat him in a debate at one time?

Most of ours were inter-departmental debates. There would be a team from each of the years in the arts faculty and the science faculty and the theological faculty, and the gold medal was given for the debating team that eventually, after a process of elimination, won the college championship. I was on the winning debating team about four years in succession. We also debated against a number of other universities, notably the universities in Manitoba, Ontario, and Alberta. One year, in 1928 I think, we had the satisfaction of debating the Imperial Team from Great Britain. We had the good fortune to be the only group in Canada to beat the Imperial Team. They'd made a very successful tour up until that time.

Stanley Knowles was, if I recollect properly, on one of the teams against which I debated in an intercollegiate debate. Stanley was a top-grade student, but he didn't take much part in either athletics or student activities.

One of the men against whom I debated was B.T. Richardson, who later became editor of the Saskatoon *Star-Phoenix*, and is currently editor of the *Toronto Telegram*. He was on the Manitoba team, in about 1926 or 1927. He's the only one I recall who has since become at all prominent.

> Did you have any memorable experiences as senior stick?

As senior stick in my last year, director of the debating executive in previous years, and in other positions on the student executive, I developed some techniques in administration and some ideas of leadership in group activities. Our student body was organized so that you had a number of departments: athletics, debating, drama, treasurer, secretary for the student body, and senior stick, who was really the chairman of the executive. The person who was elected to head each of these branches became a member of the executive, and the senior stick was the presiding officer. In effect it was a student cabinet. For my last four years at Brandon, I served on the executive in one capacity or another: one year in charge of drama, a couple of years in charge of debating, one year heading up the literary group that got out the college paper, and in my last year as senior stick.

Presiding over these student activities was very good training. I often thought afterward that I might have spent more time on my studies and less time on extracurricular activities. Looking back on it, these extracurricular activities were equally important, maybe more important, than academic studies. I learned a great deal about working with people and helping organize activities.

> You were married on 30 August 1930. How did a Baptist going to preach at a Presbyterian church come to know and attract a Methodist?

I'm not much of an authority on the attraction of the sexes. But when I was in the Presbyterian church at Carberry, I was the only young minister there. The minister at the United church was a very distinguished gentleman who had had a long record in the United church, and before that, in the Methodist church, but he was seventy-five years old. So a good deal of community work among young people became my responsibility, irrespective of churches: Girl Guides, Boy Scouts, Wolf Cubs, Brownies, and basketball teams for both boys and girls. And in this way I met my wife.

> Did any of the professors at Brandon have any special influence on you? Do you remember some of their teachings that were very impressive, and were some guide to your future life?

I always thought I owed a great deal to Dr. J.R.C. Evans, who at that time was the head of the Science Department and the Dean of Men. He is now president of Brandon College. He was not only very kind to me personally, but he was an excellent teacher with a very logical type of mind. He was also the coach for our debating team. I still follow his system of laying out a speech. He had a scientific approach. He didn't just get into a subject and wallow around. He set out in the introduction what he was trying to say, and then he elaborated on the different points, and then he summed up all his material in the conclusion. This was a tremendous help to all of us who worked under him.

The other was Dr. H.L. MacNeill, who was the professor of Greek and the New Testament. He had a profound influence on me. He was a radical for his day, not in political and economic terms, but certainly in religious terms. That was the period of the great controversy between the modernists and the fundamentalists, and this man was under constant attack by the fundamentalists. It didn't take me very long to realize that he had much more of the spirit of Christ than the people who were attacking him for not being a Christian. Although he was reviled, he reviled not again; despite the attacks made upon him he never indulged in personalities. When he was called before boards of inquiry, as he sometimes was, he answered questions truthfully, refusing to take refuge in long, wordy, evasive replies. He had certain convictions as a result of his studies, and he stated them honestly and fearlessly.

What were those convictions?

He had come to the conclusion, which is not uncommon now, but certainly was thirty years ago, that refused to accept literal interpretation of the Scriptures. He took the position that the Bible was a library made up of poems like the Psalms, drama like the Book of Job and the Book of Esther, historical books, letters such as the Epistles of St. Paul, and prophecies and actual biographical accounts like the Gospels. He thought that each of these should be interpreted in the light of the purpose for which they were written.

He took the view that divine inspiration meant that God was speaking to man, but that the same literal application shouldn't be applied both to a verse of the Psalms and a statement from the Acts. I think he set an excellent example. We had many fundamentalists among the students who were prepared to argue this question. Dr. MacNeill believed that Jesus was essentially a child of his time. He thought in the framework of his time, and therefore thought of the Kingdom of God as Jewish prophets have thought of it for centuries. But he projected this and gave it a new meaning; rather than an earthly kingdom based on power and might and on the sword, it was to be a Kingdom of the spirit in men's hearts, made up of righteousness and justice. This was considered fairly radical thirty or thirty-five years ago.

That would have considerable influence on you, would it not? In the aggregate.

That's right. In the aggregate. It liberalized my views.

The other man who had much the same influence was Professor Cyrus Richards, who taught philosophy and psychology. He had graduated in medicine and when he was finished had decided that things of the mind, ideas, were going to be much more important in the long run than things of the body. So he had turned to philosophy and psychology. He was a very stimulating individual, and I think he did a good deal to break down any of our misconceptions and to open our minds to broader concepts.

◻ What is the name of the Baptist church in Weyburn?

The Calvary Baptist Church. Compared to most churches it was well off financially. Not that it had a lot of wealthy people, but it had developed over the years a reputation for regular contributions by its people, with a genuine sense of sacrifice. Most of the congregation were working people, with one or two professionals and a few business people. But I can recollect men who worked on railroads, who made a pledge to contribute four or five dollars regularly every week. In the thirties that was a lot of money. I was later staggered when I went to Ontario to find congregations in which wealthy industrialists made contributions of two dollars a week.

Because of the people we had in Weyburn, particularly the kind of leadership we'd had under Mr. Norman McKinnon, the deacon and the moving spirit, finances weren't a big problem.

What would be the number of the congregation?

The actual members would run in the neighbourhood of between 100 to 150; with adherents, people who attended the church but weren't actual members, it would run between 250 and 300.

Did you find the people responsive to a young minister?

I found them exceedingly responsive. Mr. Norman McKinnon really had a genius for religious education. He had done a great deal of work among young people and children and built up a particularly different kind of Sunday school or church school as they called it than any I've ever seen. Lots of older people attended

Calvary Baptist Church, Weyburn, Saskatchewan (Courtesy Soo Line Historical Museum, Weyburn).

there, but it was a young people's church. This fitted in exactly with my whole background. From the time I'd been sixteen or seventeen years of age, I'd done Scout work and athletics and drama among young people and young people's organizations of various sorts. So this was a very natural habitat for me and I suited their specific demands for a pastor. They wanted a young people's man. And I was at the age when I was interested in the whole question of religious education.

But how did the older people receive you?

They were wonderful. Again, I think it was due to the influence of the type of people in that church. The older people felt that the primary purpose of churches was to get young people to carry on a programme of religious education. The church wasn't just for old people and sermons every Sunday. They were interested in young people. They were remarkable. I have very happy memories of the Deacon's Board, and the men and women who made up the backbone of that congregation. I think they were probably the finest congregation I have ever known.

> Speaking objectively, did the congregation increase or did it decline in your days? There was a return to spiritual things underway at that time, am I correct?

That's right, there was quite an increase. The men who had preceded me hadn't been particularly interested in young people's work, but once we started activities among the young people, a good many new things got going. Once a month we put on a religious drama instead of a church service on Sunday evening. It was one of the things I had been studying in Chicago when I went to university — religious drama under Dr. Eastman. I wrote a couple of the plays myself. And once a month we'd have the young people conduct the service.

> Where were you married?

We were married in Brandon. Some of my wife's people were living in Brandon at the time. And then we went on to Winnipeg where my people were, and spent a week or two with them.

> Who was the best man at your wedding?

Stanley Knowles was my best man and my brother-in-law, Mark Talney, married us. Mark was minister at Portage la Prairie at the time and came down to Brandon with my sister to marry us. And Stanley took my services at Weyburn while we were on our honeymoon.

> Where did you spend your honeymoon?

In Winnipeg. And when we came back to Weyburn, Stanley Knowles had a reception waiting for us at the station.

> Now, there are a lot of things in a minister's life besides preaching sermons. I mean you couldn't deal only with young people; there were the older people, the sick, and the business of counselling. Did people come to you for

secular and spiritual advice? Was this new to you, or
had you had previous experience in this kind of thing?

I had a good deal of experience, as far back as the fall of '24. I
always made a practice of fixing up a study in the church. People
don't like to come to your home. And they won't come to a place
where you're boarding, because other people might see them
coming and they'll wonder why people are coming to see you. I
would announce from the pulpit the hours I'd be glad to see
anybody who had a problem, or if they wanted, they could phone
to make a special appointment, and I'd be there.

Then you have to work out certain afternoons when you do
your visiting. You take the community and you map it out, and
you do a certain section on Monday and a certain section on
Tuesday, and so on, until you get around to see everybody in the
district. In the towns you just do your own members or adherents.
In the country you call on everybody, no matter who they are;
you just drop in and see them.

The minister is really the psychiatrist of the community.

That's right. This is why I've always maintained that if I had the
chance to set up a school for ministers I would throw out Hebrew
and Greek, on which I spent six years, and put in religious psychiatry, religious psychology, and the understanding of people.
We're not properly trained in these areas. It's being done now, but
it certainly wasn't in those days.

I can think of one rather humorous incident about my study.
I hadn't been there more than a year when one Monday morning
Magistrate Graham phoned me. He said, "I have eleven boys
coming up before me this morning for juvenile delinquency.
They're constant repeaters. I hate to send them to the Industrial
School in Regina — it's pretty grim there — but I don't know what
to do with them, and I haven't much choice unless somebody will
do something about it. I was wondering if you'd come down to
watch the proceedings." So I went down to the courtroom and
saw these boys. They were typical youngsters who lived in little
shacks on the outskirts of town. In some cases the parents were
mentally subnormal; one or two of the mothers had been in and

out of the mental hospital, and should really have been permanently placed in a home for mental defectives. Some children were illegitimate who lived with a grandmother, or a woman and her common-law husband. The youngsters just roamed the streets.

They'd been into almost every conceivable type of crime. They were dirty, wore cast-off clothing, needed haircuts, and were really scruffy. Maybe it was because it was Monday and I hadn't gotten over the Sunday sermon, but I ended up having the eleven of them committed to my care by the police magistrate. I wondered what on earth I was going to do with them.

I took them home. To march in with eleven ragamuffins was quite a sight, and my wife, to whom I'd been married for less than a year, just about went home to her mother. She was a good sport, though. We got them some lunch and then started to badger the members of the congregation for some decent clothes, got them haircuts, bathed them, and cleaned them up. A number of younger men in the church tried to get some of them jobs for after four o'clock, so they could earn a little money sweeping out a store, acting as an office boy, doing any kind of odd job, raking lawns or shovelling snow, or something of that sort. And then I made arrangements for them to come to the church every day after four, and I had some of the other boys from our own church young people's group come with me. Wally Stinson, who is now director of the Department of Education's Division of Fitness and Recreation, was one of the boys who came and played with these youngsters.

One of the first significant things we noticed was that these boys didn't know how to play. They could fight at the drop of a hat, and knew everything except the Marquess of Queensbury rules. They could pick a lock. They could get into a building and out again, and you'd never know how they got there. But they couldn't play games. And so these other boys who could play basketball and who could box, whom I had been training in athletics in so far as we had equipment, joined in and taught these boys how to play.

But the one day I would lose control of them would be Sunday, because I had the church service in the morning, and I had to go all the way to Stoughton in the afternoon to take the church service there and come back at night. Sunday afternoon was a bad time. I came back from Stoughton on one particular Sunday to get ready for the evening service, and found a very irate storekeeper waiting at the house. Having told my wife his story he then proceeded to tell it to me: the boys had broken into the store and had stolen boxes of chocolates and various other things, and he was going to lay a charge against them. I had a fairly good idea where the gang hung out, and finally located them. They were gorging themselves on chocolates and having a great time smoking the cigarettes they had stolen. So I pretended to be very cross and told them that I was going to have them all committed back to the magistrate. What they'd better do was be in my study after church that night as I hadn't time to talk to them at that moment.

So they were all at church that Sunday evening, and sat through the service, looking as innocent as angels; then after the service they trooped into the study, and I gave them my very best lecture. How they had let me down, had let down the other young people in the church who had worked with them and tried to help them, had let down Nurse Morton who had helped to get clothing for them, and that there was nothing else to do but turn them back to the police magistrate and let him send them to a corrective institution.

They began to sniff and cry, and the tears flowed. After we had a proper reconciliation, we all agreed that things would be different, that this wouldn't happen again. They'd brought with them what they hadn't consumed—there were quite a few things —and they decided to return them to the store in the morning, which they did.

After the lecture and the tears, they trooped out of the study one by one. The last boy I shall never forget, he was the toughest of the lot, he could pick a lock with a hairpin, he had all the aptitudes for a criminal, and was very courageous. He would fight anything, any size. He was thin and wiry; he looked like a terrier. He stopped, and he said, "Mr. Douglas, I'm terribly sorry for what we've done. I'm so sorry. I want to give you back your things." And he handed me back my watch, my penknife, my fountain pen, and a half a dozen other things he'd stolen off my desk while I was giving my ten-cent lecture.

The interesting sequel to the story is that he stayed, did quite well, got on in school, straightened up, and became one of the best youngsters I had around there. He moved away and I didn't see him again until 1945. I was getting off a plane at Nijmegen, Holland, where the brigadier met me and said, "We're putting you in charge of four of the provost corps who will act as a guard of honour for your car wherever you go, and the sergeant here will be in charge of looking after you and getting around." He introduced me to the sergeant, who was this same boy. The provost officer said to me that evening, "You know that sergeant — I noticed you talking to him. He's a marvel. These boys, no matter what they try, he's one jump ahead of them. I don't know one trick in the game that he's not wise to." I didn't tell him where he'd learned all the tricks.

Did many of the boys more or less turn out all right?

The ones I've followed up have. One of them is driving a taxi here in Regina, one of them went on to be a school teacher. Those I've been able to keep in touch with have done remarkably well. I've met them all across Canada.

A lot of them would go into the armed services.

Practically all of them were in the armed services.

About the work, can you tell us about some of the problems connected with being a minister?

It's always difficult when you've had a great loss. There's the problem not only of the person who is dying, but often more difficult, the problem of the family, who are heartbroken. This is a very difficult thing, particularly when children have died.

This period was probably more difficult than any other time to be the minister of a church. The economic depression started about October 1929. The drought began about the same time. By the time we got into 1931, 1932, and from then on until 1938, we went years without any rain and without any crops. But more than the matter of not having a crop, there was no water in the wells. There was no water for livestock, to keep chickens alive, for gardening. Many people were hauling water eighteen and twenty miles in a wagon with a tank on it. This meant that people did not have garden vegetables, chickens, cream, butter, and eggs that a farmer would normally have. It was more than just a loss of income; it was a loss of sustenance. And in the town, unemployment was growing by leaps and bounds. Not only did we have the general depression, but the farmers couldn't buy; ninety-five percent of the farmers in that area were on relief, and this made it very difficult for the business man. Many of them cut their staff, some of them went bankrupt, and others closed up.

Out in the country I performed funeral services. I remember burying a girl fourteen years of age who had died with a ruptured appendix and peritonitis. There isn't any doubt in my mind that it was just an inability to get her to a hospital. I buried a young man at Griffin, and another one at Pangman, both young men in their thirties with young small families, who died because there was no doctor readily available, and they hadn't the money to get proper care. They were buried in coffins made by the local people out of ordinary board. This boy at Griffin was buried on a hot day in August. The smell permeated the church. This is a difficult thing. What do you say to a woman whose family is on relief, whose husband has died because they couldn't get the kind of medical and hospital care he needed, a woman who has no prospects for the future and very little in the way of social welfare assistance? It is awfully hard to know what to say to people like that.

The other thing that always left a scar in my heart about that period was the number of young people who had finished high school and just couldn't go on and get further education. I remember one family: the father had been a comfortably well-off farmer. He put his oldest son through medicine and his second oldest child, a daughter, through university. They were brilliant students and did very well. But the next boy was exceedingly brilliant, more brilliant than the other two. He finished high school with an average up in the nineties and he wanted to go into medicine. Then the depression came. This boy and I did everything we could to see if we couldn't find some way of getting him into university. He shovelled snow, sawed wood, swept the poolroom, any kind of a job at all, even working on the streets at manual labour. But he just couldn't make enough — a few day's work at a dollar or two dollars a day — but not enough money to go to university. His father did everything he could, but instead of holding his own, he was getting behind. The little bit of money he had saved was going to pay taxes, and to pay for his seed and fuel to put in a crop. Each year he got nothing, so each year he would sink two or three thousand dollars more in the farm and get nothing back from it. This young man never did get to university. There were a great many like that. We tried to do what we could for them there. We had a group of young people, most of them between eighteen and twenty-five who had finished high school, couldn't get work, and were just sitting around at home. I set up classes in the basement of the church, and also arranged some classes at the collegiate after four o'clock and in the evening. They took their courses extra-murally from the university. There wasn't any hope that in writing off two or three subjects a year they'd ever get through university, but the idea was to keep their time occupied and keep their interest in study alive, so that if conditions got better, they could go on.

I have always felt bitter that society allowed these young people to go without an education, and deprived some very brilliant students of an opportunity to make some real contribution. When the war broke out they took the young men and made them pilots, navigators, and tank experts at the cost of twenty-five thousand dollars each. The young man who wanted to study medicine had a very brilliant career in the air force. If we'd spent the money that made him a pilot in 1932, '33, and '34, we'd probably have had a great scientist today. As it is, we've got an insurance salesman.

> At this time I detect a transition in your own life. I would like to quote you from this period:
>
>> The religion of tomorrow will be less concerned with dogmas of theology, and more concerned with the social welfare of humanity. When one sees the church spending its energies on the assertion of antiquated dogmas, but dumb as an oyster to the poverty and misery all around, we can't help recognize the need for a new interpretation of Christianity. We have come to see that the Kingdom of God is in our

midst if we have the vision to build it. The rising generation will tend to build a heaven on earth rather than live in misery in the hope of gaining some uncertain reward in the distant future.

I sense that you were rebelling against orthodoxy, or maybe this was part of the Baptist tradition. First, we had the typical Puritan origin, then second, we had all kinds of rebels in the Baptist church in North America, those who set up their own government and practiced pure democracy, religious liberty, and so on.

I think you're right in pointing out that the Baptist view lends itself to very progressive ideas about religion. It doesn't necessarily mean that all Baptists are progressive; we've only got to go to the southern United States and hear the debate over the present integration question to realize that these people are not all progressive. But the basic doctrine is that the New Testament is the foundation of the Christian church, and that there is no other church doctrine you must accept. This has made Baptists in many parts of the world quite progressive. In the history of Europe, Baptists have always been at the forefront of most socially progressive movements. In Great Britain and particularly in Wales, the Baptists are strong, the backbone of the British Labour movement. In the 1926 general strike, Baptist churches were thrown open to feed miners and their families. The Baptist, as well as the Methodist and some of the other nonconformist churches, have always had a great interest in social and economic questions. I'm not trying to suggest that they have any monopoly. When you think of Dr. Temple, the Archbishop of Canterbury, or some of the great leaders of the United Church, leaders of the Methodist church south of the line, these are very outstanding religious leaders who have taken very courageous positions on social and economic questions.

At this particular time, there was a great period of social misery and poverty. You're preaching in a pulpit, trying to do what you can in a spiritual way to look after the flock, but the conditions are becoming such that even the church is not grasping the fundamental problem. Is that it?

First of all, let's be very fair to the church. The people in the church were doing everything they could in a completely broken down economic system. In Weyburn when everybody was so hard up, people were coming to your door constantly — not only the hoboes going through, but often people from the town would come and see if there wasn't something you could help them out with. I'm sure we gave away a third of everything we earned in those days, or more. We were constantly handing out clothing. My wife was constantly buying things for people. I was constantly either giving my own money, or borrowing from other people, or getting other people to give me money to give to some of these folks.

I'll give you two examples. Our Ministerial Association of Protestant ministers in Weyburn made an appeal for help, and we sent word out to the churches in British Columbia and Ontario. We got carloads of apples and vegetables from British Columbia, where people had lots of apples and vegetables but couldn't sell them, and if you could pay the freight it was just as easy to ship them down to the prairies as it was to dump them. By taking up collections and that sort of thing they got enough money to pay the freight. I think the railways also gave them a special rate, and so we got carloads and carloads of apples and vegetables.

The other ministers and I stood from early morning till late at night with scoop shovels filling up people's sacks, baskets, barrels, anything they chose to bring, because the fruit just came in bulk. We would stand there for two or three days emptying these box-cars, and nobody asked who you were or what church you belonged to. People just queued up and got their winter's supply of apples, carrots, turnips, potatoes, and so on.

From Ontario we got great supplies of second-hand and new clothing that was a bit out of date. A lot of storekeepers would send us their old stock. We'd get button boots and derby hats, but also a lot of useful things. A lot of people made quilts, and sent whole bolts of flannelette. And we distributed these to the people. It wasn't good social welfare practice, but we didn't have any facilities for knowing what people needed. We assumed that anybody who asked was in need, and we gave them things. The women set up sewing groups, and took the bolts of flannelette and cotton and other materials, and they made layettes for babies and children's clothing, and whenever we knew that somebody was going to have a baby, we'd give them a layette. We made Christmas hampers. We worked closely with people like Nurse Morton, who was a relief officer and could tell us about people in need who wouldn't come to us.

There were a great many cases. I can remember a family of five or six children, and no one would have ever known they were in need. The mother came to church with a coat over her clothing so you wouldn't know whether she had a good dress or a poor dress. And they seldom ever said anything. But I knew they must be having a pretty tough time. The day before, I happened to get some very good bedding in a parcel, and so I said to this lady that morning when she was going out of church, "How're you fixed for bedding?" Her eyes filled up with tears and she said, "Mr. Douglas, I haven't got a decent sheet in the place. We've patched and patched and I just don't know how I'm going to get by." I asked, "How are the youngsters for clothing?" She could hardly talk. She said, "Well, they haven't any winter underwear, so I've been trying to make some out of flour sacks." I said, "Just stay behind and we'll fix it up." So we filled up the back of her car with bedding and clothes. Now these were once well-to-do, very respectable, very proud people. They'd never have asked. And today they're successful farmers, comfortably well off and the children have gone on to get an education. But during this particular period no matter how hard you worked, no matter how proud you were, it was through no fault of your own that you'd be in this very strafed condition.

This was going on all around us. The church was trying to do what it could about the effect, but what began to bother me was that we weren't doing anything about the cause. Why did this society break down? What was wrong with it? Why was it, that when you had a surplus of food and clothing and almost every known commodity produced by an advanced technological society, why were there people who couldn't get decent houses to live in, couldn't get clothing to wear, and who couldn't get enough to eat? What had broken down? This is what made us all start to think.

I had been in Chicago in the summer of 1931 to do some more work on my Ph.D. I worked under Arthur Erastus Holt, who was the head of the Department of Social Science at Chicago. He put me on a group who were doing case history work down in what was then called the jungle land in Chicago. They'd estimated that about seventy-five thousand men, mostly vagrants, were living in the paper shacks or little huts they'd made out of building materials, pieces of tin, anything they could get. They were lining up at the soup kitchens as long as the food lasted, begging, panhandling on the street, and stealing whenever they got the chance. We worked amongst them for two or three weeks taking case histories, which were most revealing. There were many professional hoboes who lived in the United States by riding the freights, going south for the winter and coming north for the summer, and some with no intention of working. But the great bulk of them had worked on the railroad and had had good jobs, were laid off, and lasted on their savings for six months or a year, and eventually ended up in jungle land. There were boys who had been bank clerks, medical students, and law students. I remember talking to one young fellow who told me his home was in Iowa. He went to university, then got and lost a job, did odd bits of work until his money ran out, moved from a poor boarding-house to a still poorer one, until finally he had no money at all. I said to him, "What is it that keeps you from stealing?" He said, "The only thing that keeps me from stealing is that my family don't know the condition I'm in. There's no use in my going home, I know they're on relief. But I don't want my name to appear in the newspaper for being in police court. That's all that keeps me from stealing, and if it gets any worse, I'll do even that."

When we finished about a week of this, we went over to probably the worst part of jungle town. We were winding up at about midnight or one o'clock in the morning, and a group of these fellows gathered around us, recognized that we were from the university, and asked for money and one thing or another. We told them that we didn't have any money, and that we were simply students trying to find out what conditions were like, and what we could do to help them. One old fellow who had been a railroader said something I've never forgotten, "Sonny, you can't do anything to help us, there's nothing you can do. But go back to this school of yours, and work, and see that this doesn't happen again."

This is when I began to read and think and inquire why we were in this mess. I recalled my background. It was true that I had known Mr. Woodsworth, and had been interested in the Labour party in Winnipeg, and my father had belonged to the Labour party in the old country, but I had never sat down seriously and asked what's wrong with this economic system of ours until it actually broke down. I was like a lot of other people who had taken only an academic interest in this question. We had a course in economics at university. I'd studied socialism and syndicalism and guild socialism, and communism and capitalism. But I'd never sat down and honestly asked myself what was wrong with the economic system. I think most people in the church were exactly the same. We'd taken it for granted. We'd accepted it. But here we were facing poverty, misery, want, lack of medical care, and lack of opportunity for a whole generation of young people who were frustrated and denied their right to live a normal decent life.

> About 1944, I had quite a discussion with Stanley Knowles. He said, "I finally determined that I could serve the Kingdom of God better in politics than in the pulpit." Did that occur to you the same way it did to Stanley Knowles at this particular time?

I hadn't got to the stage when I was thinking that the church was limited. I was trying to direct the attention of Christian people to the fact that we had to be concerned about people's daily problems. It wasn't enough to talk about pie in the sky; it wasn't enough to talk to people about some afterlife with no misery and sorrow and tears. We had to concern ourselves with the problems people had here and now. What I was trying to do, both in the church itself, and at church conventions when we met with other churches, and in meeting local organizations of various sorts, was to constantly remind people that Jesus said it was better for man that a millstone be hung about his neck and that he be cast into the depths of the sea, than that one of these little ones should perish. We have a concern for our brother, we have a concern for this child who's not getting an education or a proper diet and not being properly clad, and as Christians we can't be indifferent to how people live and what their daily problems are.

At one of the conventions when I moved a resolution along this line, I was attacked by a minister of a very prominent city church, who got up and said in all seriousness that the Bible told us that the poor we will always have with us and that God had made two classes of people, the rich and the poor. He made the rich so that they would learn the lesson of benevolence and charity. He made the poor so they would learn the lesson of gratitude, and that we were interfering with the will of God when we tried to abolish poverty. To me, this was sheer blasphemy. My concept was, and I go back to Dr. H.L. MacNeill, the idea of the Kingdom of righteousness and justice for every person in it. Every person in the Kingdom has a right to life, liberty, and the pursuit of happiness. In this Kingdom we are members of one another, and the strong must help to carry the burdens of the weak. I'm not a fit member of the Kingdom if someone else is undergoing misery or carrying burdens and I don't attempt to help that person.

For that time, it was a new approach, embraced by Rauschenbusch,[2] Harry Emerson Fosdick,[3] and a few other religious leaders. But at that time in religious circles this approach did not agree with the popular position, which was that the church had nothing to do with social and economic questions.

We ran into a good deal of conflict from the people, although not in my own local church, where the people were quite progressively minded. I used to argue at the conventions that we were blind in one eye, and that we thought only in terms of God. The Bible says: ["What doth it profit, my brethren, though a man say he hath faith, and have not works? Can faith save him? Even so, faith, if it hath not works, is dead, being alone." James 2:14,17] If any man say he loves God but hates his brother, he is a liar, because how can any man love God unless he also loves his brother? That was the question.

> I think you were also concerned that the church may have been concentrating on trivialities.

That's right. I was asked to address 1,500 Baptist young people of Ontario and Quebec at a great convention. This was in 1937 or 1938. We were still not out of an economic depression, there were a million people on relief, fascism was sweeping over a large part of the world, ordinary human rights — freedom of the press, freedom of religion, freedom of speech — were being taken away, the Jewish people were being persecuted, and leaders in Germany were being arrested and thrown into concentration camps. In the presence of these tremendous evil forces in the world, the best we could do for these young people was give a resolution condemning dancing and slot machines and close beer parlours an hour earlier.

I'm not quarrelling about whether or not these activities need to be controlled. But you can't afford to be concerned with trivialities at a time that the church needs to make a declaration, the kind made in Germany by the leader of the Confessional church, Martin Niemöller.[4] When I was in Germany in 1936, Niemöller nailed his thesis to the church door — the custom in Germany ever since Martin Luther's time — which said: "Believing as we do in the fatherhood of God and the brotherhood of man, we cannot accept and we will not accept the theory of the superiority of any one race over another." This is more important than arguing about closing the beer parlours an hour earlier.

> Did you make some kind of a definitive decision in your mind that here is all this misery, I want to do something greater than I'm doing at present? How did your desire to go into politics arise?

At no time did I make a definite decision to go into politics. It was a cumulative conclusion. Those case histories during the summer of 1931 at Chicago University really shook me. I lived for two or three weeks among 75,000 homeless transients, mostly decent boys who had come from the same kind of home I had. The only difference was that I had a job, and they didn't.

When I came back I began to read a good deal. I read books like Fred Henderson's *Case for Socialism*[5] and Rauschenbusch's *Christianity and the Social Crisis*, and some of Woodsworth's writings. I thought in terms of the church making some pronouncements on social and economic conditions, setting forth some goals for a better society. That was as far as I went. I thought that something practical could be done. Since I had no authority to issue pronouncements on social and economic theory, I could at least do something practical.

So when I came back in the fall of 1931, one of the first things I did was organize the unemployed. Lots of houses were empty, so City Council gave us an old house. We sawed wood and got a little bit of coal together, and turned it into a club room for the men. We also managed to get enough money to buy a telephone, and we set up an agency so that anybody who wanted a chair repaired, snow shovelled off their sidewalks, their lawn raked, their garden dug, or their basement cleaned could phone and we'd send a man and they might give him twenty-five cents an hour, or fifty cents for the whole day. At least we generated some work on an organized basis. We also put on some entertainment for these people. This was the hardest of all because there was nothing to do. We got special rates at the picture show, and special tickets so that the men could take their wives to a show once a month. We put on the odd concert, and the odd dance, at which you would get a lunch for ten cents. People would contribute the food. The unemployment association went on for some time.

> Who was in this unemployment association besides yourself? Did the other ministers collaborate?

No. The other ministers were all sympathetic, I think, but none of them wanted to get into it.

> Why?

I think some of them felt that this might cause friction with their congregation. You can understand what goes on in a small city. There is a group of people who are unemployed. They need relief, and part of the relief has to be paid by the city, part by the province, part by the federal government. If you pay them too much, it's going to raise taxes. The business man is worried about the taxes, and is hardly keeping his head above water. And so the feeling was against anybody organizing the unemployed and asking for higher relief schedules, milk for the children, and more shoes for the kiddies.

I had a lawyer in my own congregation, and I remember one morning I dropped in to see him in his office. He took issue with me about having any part in this unemployed association. I said, "You see people in your office who've got some money or they wouldn't be coming here. They're concerned about money matters, setting up their estate or buying or selling property. Have you ever actually seen the conditions in the poorer part of this city?" And he said, "I've lived in this city for twenty-five years; I lived here before you came here." And I said, "Yes, but you don't see it as it is now." So I took him around to some of the homes where there were children who couldn't go to school because they didn't have shoes or clothing, places where they had hardly enough coal, where they hadn't had milk for a week. I took him to the school nurse, and she repeated the story I'd given him. This man said, "I wouldn't have believed it. I know this might happen in the east side of London but for it to be happening in the town where I live, I'm ashamed that I don't know this."

This was the sort of thing that made people somewhat apprehensive about forming a stronger unemployed association. We had the highest relief schedule in Saskatchewan, but still it wasn't high by any standards of human requirements.

> Then you were becoming singled out during this period as one minister who had departed a little bit from the orthodox. Is that right?

I was labelled as a rather dangerous radical in the community, stirring up the unemployed to ask for more money and sticking my nose into places where it was none of my business. I had several very bad set-tos with the provincial relief officers, who would come down to meet the council and say, "You're spending too much money, you'd better cut this and that off." When I would go before them, armed with the school nurse's report citing cases of children needing milk and families needing coal, and children with no shoes or clothes to go to school, I was a nuisance. "Why didn't I get back into my pulpit and preach the gospel?" they would ask, whatever that may mean.

> Can you remember the first time when somebody said that you should be in politics?

Never at any definite time. When I had the unemployed association, the union people in the town, the railwaymen, a few carpenters, and some Labour people thought they ought to have an organization like the unemployed. They wanted some sort of labour movement. I said, "I don't think there's enough for a labour group, but why don't we take the unemployed, the trade union group, and any who are labouring people and form a Weyburn Labour Association to wipe out unemployment?" So we did.

Also, I was being drawn more and more to conditions in the country, because a lot of my congregation were in the rural area. I had one appointment at Stoughton. The United Farmers of Saskatchewan came to me frequently and asked if I would address some of their meetings. So I got drawn into going to some of their meetings, and on one or two occasions I went as the head of a delegation of farmers to meet Premier Anderson[6] and representatives of the provincial government regarding the terrible conditions among these farmers.

The conditions on farms just beggared description at that time. I saw a great many farm homes and the pitiful little bit of relief they were getting, the few apples and vegetables and things we were able to hand out to them. They were really hard up. It wasn't only a matter of the physical suffering, it was the hopelessness of the situation. There was a man in Weyburn comfortably well off, who prior to the depression had a good farm; he and his wife were hard workers. Not only did they do their own farm work producing a crop, but he also peddled butter and eggs and cream from door to door in Weyburn, and also chickens and turkeys that they killed and plucked and cleaned themselves. My wife always bought some things from them; he was a member of my church, and later became my campaign manager. One day, sitting in our kitchen we got talking about conditions. This man, who was a veteran of the First World War, broke down in the kitchen and just wept. He said, "When this depression came, I had a farm clear. Now I'm in debt, I've had to borrow money, and I'm going to lose my farm." Later he said, "I'm better off than most. I've managed to keep off relief. But I'm going to lose my farm, there's nothing surer than that."

Well, what do you do for people like this? Here are people

who, through no fault of their own, are going to lose the product of their life's work. They would lose their home and be out on the street. This was not a hypothetical fear. In those days, almost every week in the summer and fall, wagonloads of people were heading for the north country. They piled all their possessions into a wagon, with their cow walking behind, and started off for Loon Lake and Carragana and Sturgis, up into the north country. I had members of my congregation who finally just pulled up stakes and went up north with an axe and a cow to try and wrest a home for themselves out of the bush.

Farm groups were constantly involving me more and more in their problems. Finally some of the farm leaders in the community said to me, "Look they've got this labour group in town and we've got the farm group. We're trying to do the same thing, we're just different occupational groups, why don't we get together? Isn't there some way that we could work together? What do you think we should do?"

I had no experience in this field, so I said, "I'll think about it." I decided to write to Mr. Woodsworth, since I'd known him, and followed his work in Parliament and read Hansard avidly. I asked him what he thought ought to be done. I got a letter back saying how glad he was to hear from me again, and: "Strange to say, I got in the same mail a letter from Alderman Coldwell in the City of Regina along exactly the same lines. He is president of the Independent Labour party in Saskatchewan. He feels that the farmers' movement and the labour movement ought to join hands if they're going to be an effective force in Saskatchewan. I suggest you get in touch with him."

So I wrote Mr. Coldwell, and told him of our situation. I got a note back saying, "I can't come during the week, but I'll be free next Saturday, and I'll come down and see you." I can remember Mr. Coldwell coming into the study at the back of the church. That was the first time we met. I'd read about him in the paper. He told me that he thought the time had come to try to bring the farm and labour groups together. As the first step, our Weyburn Labour Association joined the Independent Labour party. We arranged a mass meeting at the Exhibition Grounds, and Mr. Coldwell addressed it on behalf of the Independent Labour party.

What was the date of this meeting?

In the early summer, May or June 1932. And then Mr. Coldwell and Mr. George Williams, president of the United Farmers of Saskatchewan, arranged a joint convention to be held on 27 July in Saskatoon.[7]

> I've always been interested in whether you paid much attention to the mental hospital in Weyburn at that time. Did you get the idea that Saskatchewan wasn't coping with the mentally ill?

I was interested in the mental hospital from two standpoints. First of all, the ministers took turns taking services there, and my turn came about every four or five weeks. My wife used to come with me and play the piano, and we would have sing-songs and I would talk to the patients. The amazing thing was that when you came back four or five weeks later, they would remember the sermon you had delivered and the main point of it, which was much better than most of my congregation downtown could do. And sometimes better than I could do. I remember once speaking to them on the word "watch" and taking a different word with each "watch": watch your words, watch your actions, watch your thoughts, watch your companions, watch your habits, or something simple like this. And they remembered it all when I came back. So I got to know a lot of these people through these church services.

Then you must remember that during this period, I was working on my master's thesis from McMaster University. I had decided to write my thesis on the problems of the subnormal family, under the general topic of Christian sociology. I had to do a good deal of case work, and there was no better place than the mental hospital. Dr. Campbell, the superintendent, was very kind to me, and made case histories available to me, and allowed me to work on the wards. I spent one or two afternoons a week on the wards, questioning various patients, following up their case histories, and trying to analyze and interpret the case histories. A good portion of my thesis dealt with the problem of mental health.

I had some interesting experiences at the hospital. In those days the staff worked on twelve-hour shifts. I was working on Ward B one day, and I knew that the staff changed at five o'clock, so I should be out before then, but I got very interested in something until past five o'clock. I found an attendant who was brand new on the night shift and said, "Well, I'm ready to go home." He replied, "That's fine, just go and sit down and supper will be ready in a little while." I said, "But I'm writing a master's thesis for the university and I'm just here doing some cases." He said, "That's fine, I'm sure the superintendent will be interested to know. You just go over there and keep on writing." It took me forty-five minutes to get off Ward B. Dr. Campbell never let me forget that they had tried to keep me in there, and he said it was proof that the attendant was a better psychiatrist than he was.

◻ I've always looked at Weyburn as a gloomy place. Do you regard it as home more or less? That's where you started your career.

Yes. That's where I spent some of the happiest years of my life, and my wife would feel the same. Weyburn was a depressed-looking place in the thirties. We went for eight years without a crop, buildings were unpainted, places were run down, and it looked quite grim. One of the reasons was that there was no water. The city had a couple of wells, yet there was never more than just enough water to meet the household needs. It has improved since, but there's still a lot to be done.

At this stage you were starting in politics. You were definitely in, come what may, weren't you?

After we formed the Independent Labour party (I.L.P.), I became the first district president in Weyburn. John Brown was vice-president. Then the next move was to amalgamate the Saskatchewan section of the United Farmers of Canada (U.F.C.) and the Independent Labour party.

Did you go to the convention in Calgary in 1932?

No, I didn't. We managed to get the Independent Labour party and the U.F.C. groups together and co-operating in Weyburn. That summer I was studying economics, which was required for my master's degree at McMaster, at the University of Manitoba. Other delegates went to the convention from Weyburn. Although I wasn't present, they named me as one of the representatives to the joint council. The council was made up of seven members from the Independent Labour party, seven from the U.F.C., and seven picked at large from the convention. I was one of the seven named from the Independent Labour party. This was the group who went to the national convention in 1933 to pass the Regina Manifesto and lay the foundation of the Co-operative Commonwealth Federation (C.C.F.).[8]

As a member of the council, you were interested in the organization of this new party. It wasn't officially called the C.C.F. until when?

Not until 1936. It was still called the Farmer-Labour party in Saskatchewan.

By now you are definitely in politics.

I was in politics in the sense that I was a member of the Farmer-Labour party from 1932 on. But at this time I had no intention of being a candidate. This goes back to my personal thesis. I felt that the church could not divorce itself from social and economic, and consequently, political involvement, and that just as I ought to be active in relief, in helping the unemployed, helping distribute milk, or active in any mental health association, so I ought to belong to a political party and try to do something about these economic conditions. I hadn't the most remote idea at this time and a long time after, that I would become a candidate or pursue a political career.

3

C.C.F. politician

☐ You worked as a council member during 1932, and there was a provincial election coming up in 1934. When did you start thinking about the provincial election?

In 1933 when the national convention was held in Regina, I arranged for Mr. Woodsworth to come and speak in the rink at Weyburn. The other man who came was later a Liberal Member of Parliament, Elmore Philpott. This was the first really big political rally we had apart from Mr. Coldwell's meeting in connection with the I.L.P. I felt that these farmers, the workers, and the unemployed people who had been coming to me had finally found a vehicle of their own, and that now I could drop out and get on with my work.

I didn't think about politics at all until the spring of 1934, when the new Farmer-Labour party was looking for a candidate.

There were two or three farmers and two or three men in town whom I thought would be suitable. But apparently nobody wanted to run. It was a fairly hopeless proposition. The Conservatives were in office, and everybody knew they were going to be beaten. The Liberals had already nominated Dr. Eaglesham, who had been practising in the area for forty years, who was almost sure to win even if the Liberals didn't sweep the province. He was a very fine old family doctor who had brought half the people in our community into the world. And so nobody wanted to run. It was purely an educational campaign to put the story of this new movement before the people. Finally it was put to me, "If you don't run, we haven't anybody to run. Nobody will take it, and this is a duty you have. You helped us get it launched, and you can't just walk out and leave it now." So I ran, purely with the idea that this was an education campaign.

Was there a nomination convention?

Oh, yes, there was a nominating convention.

I suppose the spirit would be rising just the same, wouldn't it?

The spirit was rising among the farmers, the more progressive farmers, among the labourers and unemployed. But it hadn't gotten through to the great majority of people. Most of the campaign was fought on the question of land policy. This new party, everybody thought, was going to socialize the land; people were going to lose their farms and their titles. Everybody went around waving a title, saying that this is the title of your land that is going to be taken away by the Farmer-Labour party. Already, the fact was that the number of people who owned their farms had dropped from 94 percent in 1926 down to about 63 percent in 1934. So they were already losing their farms. But nevertheless this sort of fear was engendered in people's minds. This was the danger facing every new political party. It doesn't fight the issue in the elections, it fights the issue by trying to combat misrepresentation.

[Martin Lipset has misled a whole generation of historians, political scientists, and political sociologists by claiming that the

Farmer-Labour party advocated the socialization of land.[1]
However, M.J. Coldwell, the leader of the party, at a conference
held in December 1933 to prepare for the forthcoming election,
stated categorically in the published report of the conference:
"We do not stand for the socialization of the land." Those farmers
who possessed absolute title to their farms (the Torrens title)
would continue to possess it. They could however exchange it for
a "use hold title" to be granted by the provincial government. The
greatest concern of the Saskatchewan farmer was security of
tenure of farm and home. Thousands of farmers had lost their
land to mortgage companies and banks and had become tenants.
Farmer-Labour party land policy sanctioned the voluntary surrender of a fee simple (Torrens title) to the government, which
would issue a "use hold title" and contribute to paying off the
mortgage or agreement of sale. The new title would guarantee
use and possession for as long as the farmer wished, and he could
will it or dispose of his interest in it to someone who would use it.
This was the land policy of the Farmer-Labour party Official
Manifesto of 1934.]

George Williams had made a trip to Russia. I see now that
the head of the Bank of Montreal and the head of Massey Harris
have also done that, but George's trip to Moscow and Russia at
that time proved that the party was made up of Communists and
atheists who were going to burn the churches and do away with
the family and that sort of thing. All things considered, seeing it in
perspective now, we really did much better than we had any right
to do, although we were disappointed at the outcome.

[George Williams (1894–1945) was elected president of the
U.F.C. (Saskatchewan) in 1928. He was the farm leader who, with
M.J. Coldwell, president of the Independent Labour party of Saskatchewan, promoted the formation of the Farmer-Labour party
in 1932. He succeeded Coldwell as leader of the party in 1936. In
1934 he was elected to the Legislative Assembly as the member for
Wadena, and became leader of the opposition—a post he held
until 1941 when he enlisted for overseas service. In 1931 he visited
Russia under U.F.C. auspices and on his return wrote *The Land
of the Soviets*, which led his political opponents to brand him as a
Communist. Williams was a sincere Democratic Socialist, but

humourless and uncompromising. He was an unusually able political organizer who sometimes aroused resentment among his colleagues because of his complete control of all aspects of the party apparatus.][2]

> Did you have a rough time or an easy time in the campaign?

It was my first campaign, and I conducted it like a university professor giving a course in sociology. I had charts and so on, and I'm sure half the people didn't know what I was talking about. But I think it did some good. It laid the foundation, and we began to get people who understood the basis of our present competitive capitalist society, its monopolistic nature and structure, its basic weaknesses, and the fact that it could never adequately solve the problems of distribution. A fairly good educational job was done. We mostly went to little schoolhouses. We had no campaign funds to set up a campaign office. Rod McLean, a friend of mine who ran a business college in Weyburn, let us use his office for campaign headquarters. Rod ran the office, and Jack E. Powers was my campaign manager. I drove around in an old car from schoolhouse to schoolhouse, talking to groups of farmers. In Weyburn we had little house meetings.

> Did you collect much?

There was nothing to collect. You'd be very fortunate if you got enough to pay your gas bill for the next meeting. I've seen many a collection in which there were more coppers than any other coins. Paper money was just unheard of.

> Did you get any heckling, any hostility?

Not at this stage. There was more the next campaign. In this campaign there were a lot of questions. The question period would go on until 12 midnight or one o'clock in the morning. A lot of the questions arose from the campaigns of our opponents. People asked if it was true we didn't believe in God and if it was true we were going to take the people's farms. Once, a woman with about five youngsters around her said to George Williams, "Is it true that you're going to take all the children?" George said,

"Certainly not." She said, "I thought it was too good to be true."

How about the vote?

We all thought we were going to win. This has been the blessing of the C.C.F., that we're perennial optimists; we always think we're going to do better than we do, and this keeps us going. Coldwell spoke to tremendous crowds, six and seven thousand people. People were hanging from the rafters to listen to him. If twenty-five percent of the people who turned out to the meetings had voted for us, we'd have swept the province. And so, in our naivety, we thought we would win. We had no organization, and half the polls didn't have scrutineers, but we did reasonably well. I'm depending entirely on memory, but I think that Mr. Leslie, the Conservative, got roughly 1,500, I got 1,300, and the Liberals got 2,200 votes.[3]

And out of that election the C.C.F. emerged. What was the representation in the Legislative Assembly that year?

The Tories were wiped out, we won five seats, and the Liberals won all the rest.

Who were your five, the quints?

George Williams, Louis Hantelman, Clarence Stork, Herman Kemper, and Andy Macaulay.[4]

If nothing else, this showed Saskatchewan people that this was a new political party. It became the official opposition in the Legislative Assembly.

That's right. Tommy Davis[5] said that it came with the depression and the grasshoppers, and it would disappear with the depression and the grasshoppers.

So what did you think about your defeat?

I thought that I'd done my duty, and now I'd get on with my business. I thought of staying in the church or going into university work. When in Chicago in 1931 I'd been offered a very attractive church in Milwaukee, a large church, with permission to have an assistant and continue my studies at Chicago; I was very tempted. When I came back, I half-intended to give the church my notice, and move to Chicago the next spring. But conditions were so bad, and they couldn't have gotten anybody to come out to Saskatchewan at that time, so I gave up that idea. But I still had in mind that I'd get back to Chicago and finish my doctor's degree. Subsequently, they offered me a chair in Christian and social ethics at the University of Chicago.

Even after I was later elected to Parliament, I thought I would only do one term, and then get back to my life's work.

> So after you'd thought it over did anything happen to change your mind?

When we finished the 1934 election, I went off to study again that summer. In the fall the question came up again: "You know we've got a federal election coming up next year — what are we going to do?" I told the people in the words of Sam Goldwyn, "You can 'include me out.' I've done my job, and there must be somebody else around here who can run."

The Weyburn federal seat was made up mainly of four provincial seats, and we lost all four of them. Weyburn was the only one in which we'd saved our deposit. So it wasn't a very promising area for a political campaign. Nobody was very keen about running. I stuck to the position that I wasn't going to run.

Two things happened almost simultaneously just before the nominating convention. The first was that I got a visit from the superintendent of the Baptist church for the West. He came to see me, visited around among the congregation, and found that the congregation was, with one or two exceptions, agreeable to my participation in the political campaign. He had come to admonish me, but decided not to. He said, "Your people don't mind it, and if they don't mind it, of course I'm not going to say anything about it, except this is to be the last. You're not to run again." Weyburn was a self-supporting church. We weren't getting money from anybody and we weren't a mission church under him. But he was the superintendent, and had considerable influence elsewhere. The day before he came, I received a call from the university church in Edmonton. The superintendent said, "I know that Strathcona Baptist Church in Edmonton has given you a call, and I suggest that you go there and carry on with your university work at the same time. This will let you clean up your doctor's degree. I think that's the best thing for you to do." I said, "Many people here have been pressing me to run again. I don't want to run. On the other hand, I've seen the party build up and I hate to walk out and leave it." He said, "Leave it." Then he made the great mistake, saying, "If you don't leave it, and if you don't stay out of politics, you'll never get another church in Canada, and I'll see to it. The board has given me authority." I replied, "You've just given the C.C.F. a candidate."

About two days later I got a letter from Stanley Knowles. He was the assistant minister in the First Baptist Church in Winnipeg. He said, "I've been wondering what you're going to do if a federal election came along. Many of us in the church (Stanley at this time had no thought of politics) are looking to you to speak for the church in the political field, and a lot of ministers here have spoken to me and asked me to write you. If you're asked to run, you've got to run. I've heard about your call to Strathcona in Edmonton, but you just can't run away from this situation." At home, my wife and I read the letter and talked it over, and we decided that with the threat on the one hand, the feeling that some of my friends in the church, the younger men, were counting on me to run was more important. I made up my mind.

There were other young men in the same position. Armand Stade was a Baptist minister at Shaunavon during this time, and was approached by the same superintendent, who told him the same thing he had told me. Armand made the same decision as I. He was defeated in the election, was struck off the rolls in the Baptist church, and joined the United church. He took a United church pastorate and then became minister, and is now general superintendent.

Did this also happen to Stanley Knowles?

No. Stanley didn't run. But it just shows that success is its own reward. After I was elected in 1935, the Baptist church wrote me and said that they would like to leave my name on the rolls as a minister in good standing. Each year they renew it. In tribute to the superintendent, Reverend A. Ward, he later came to my office in the House of Commons and said that he was delighted with the work I was doing, and that he had changed his views considerably. Unfortunately, he later became blind. Despite the fact that by this time he was in his fifties or early sixties, he learned Braille, worked for the Institute of the Blind, and went all over Canada lecturing and raising money for blind people.

> Before we leave the religious sphere, it has been suggested that you emphasize religion in politics in the manner of Aberhart and Manning. As I recall, you set yourself firmly against doing this, did you not?

Yes. I've always been strongly opposed to using religion as a gimmick for gaining political support. I believe in applying Christian principles to politics and to government. But I think one must remember that in a political party there are people of all religious beliefs, just as in every church there are people of different political points of view.

> Did you continue to preach after the nomination?

Yes. I was nominated in June of 1935. I offered my resignation to the church at Weyburn. They asked me not to press it, but to withdraw the resignation, continue to take the services on Sunday, and discharge my usual duties. It was agreed that I would have time off for the campaign throughout the summer of 1935. When I was elected I submitted my resignation once more, and it was accepted in time to allow me to go to Ottawa to attend the session.

> Now, about the preliminaries of the 1935 federal campaign. Between 1933 and 1935, the C.C.F. story is somewhat difficult and detailed. We have the great confusion that existed about Social Credit and C.C.F. Some wanted to merge. Others recognized the gulf between the two movements. Could you tell us any interesting details about the 1935 campaign?

It was a very interesting campaign. The 1934 election, when I ran as a Farmer-Labour candidate, had been a fairly dull affair. Most of the other candidates and I were complete novices, giving little lectures on elementary economics with charts and trying to explain a planned economy with not too much success.

When we got into the 1935 election a new note was introduced. At that time in Weyburn there was a member of the unemployed, D.C. Grant, who had done some campaigning in various parts of Canada, and had some experience. He offered his services as my chauffeur and did a good deal to brighten up the campaign. He helped with little things we hadn't done before, like decorating the hall and making sure there were ushers to get people into the front seats. When the questions weren't provocative enough, he asked some questions himself. When he found the campaign was getting too dull, he began to prod me, and tell me that I had to do something different. Those professorial speeches of mine were alright in college, but they certainly weren't good for a campaign.

We found, for instance, that Mr. E.J. Young,[6] the sitting Liberal member, was holding meetings and making wild and irresponsible statements about the C.C.F. So we started to place some of our people at the meetings to ask if he'd have a debate with me on these various questions. He persistently refused. If any of our meetings were close to where his were held, we would adjourn early, everybody would get in their cars, and we'd go to his meeting. At the psychological moment I would walk up the aisle. I would challenge him on some statement he had made and then we would have a bit of a debate. This enlivened the whole campaign because no one ever knew what was going to happen.

We finally did get him to agree to a debate. I think it was the biggest crowd we ever had in Weyburn for a political meeting. It was estimated that about seven thousand people jammed in the skating rink at Weyburn on a cold night in October. There isn't any doubt that the debate was the turning point in the campaign. Up to that time we'd been catching up on him, but I think he still had a good lead until the debate.

There were a number of other things. Mr. Young did some very foolish things, which with my inexperience I wouldn't have been able to exploit. But Dan Grant knew what to do immediately. For instance, there was an old printing plant that was lying empty. We went to the landlord and asked if we could use the printing plant if we paid him a small rent. He agreed and we got the old stove going, and one or two unemployed printers came in, and so we printed our literature there. This was the only way we could get literature. I prepared a special pamphlet, a copy of which was to go to every family in the constituency. At a number of meetings I said that when you get this pamphlet it'll tell you so and so. This got under Young's skin, and instead of letting it go at that, he got very curious. One night the printing plant was broken into and some copies of the pamphlet were taken. The cabinet where the pamphlets were kept was broken open, and it was very apparent the intruder was anxious only for some copies of this pamphlet. I wouldn't have paid any attention to it, but Grant insisted that we lay a break and entry complaint before the Mounted Police. On a hunch, Grant also demanded a search warrant for the premises of the president of the Liberal Society, who happened to be principal of a school at McTaggart.

We all drove out to McTaggart with the Mounted Police, went to the school, and found this principal. When we entered his home, we immediately saw some of the stolen pamphlets sitting on the table. Grant made a great fuss about it. To me it didn't matter at all, but to Grant, this was terrific: this man had broken and entered into private property and stolen a confidential pamphlet being prepared for the electors of Weyburn. While we didn't lay any charges, the publicity was considerable, and helped build up excitement for the debate. Mr. Young did another foolish thing when we got into the debate—he produced this pamphlet, said, "I don't know what all the fuss is about; there's nothing in this pamphlet, and it needn't bother anyone," and read parts of it to the audience. This gave me a perfect chance when closing the debate to say that there was nothing about the pamphlet I was ashamed of, but it was my personal property and was being sent out to the people of the constituency. I added that first of all, any man who would choose to steal my property wasn't fit to be president even of the Liberal Society, let alone principal of a school, and further, that any candidate who would condone such action wasn't suited to represent the good people of Weyburn in the Parliament of Canada. The people agreed.

It was a most colourful and interesting campaign, one of the liveliest I have ever seen. However, I think we benefitted mainly from the ineptitude of Mr. Young rather than the brilliance of our campaign. He did a number of very foolish things. First of all you remember that he had written a minority report on Stevens's investigation on mass buying and price spreads, in which he had used graphs straight from the annual reports of Canada Packers and Simpson's. Then, to make matters worse, Mr. C.E. Burton, president of Simpson's, speaking in Regina to one of the service clubs about a month before the election, made the unfortunate remark that we ought to put the unemployed in army camps and train them, very much like what Hitler was doing at that particular time in Germany. Mr. Young publicly agreed with this statement.

Your friend Grant was also a fortune-teller, is that right?

Yes, when he was unemployed, he used to do some teacup-reading and fortune-telling in the restaurants, both in Regina and Weyburn. This was part of his stock-in-trade.

Did he ever tell your fortune?

No. He knew that I hadn't any faith in his fortune-telling, palm-reading, or numerology. But Grant had a good political sense. I'll give you an example. Mr. C.M. Fines came to speak at our nominating convention in June 1935. Mr. Fines had always been a great student and a wide reader and kept good records, and so before coming to speak he had gone through his file in Hansard on the M.P. for the Weyburn constituency. In the course of his speech he tossed off the fact that on 9 February 1933, Mr. Young had said that the people of Canada must reconcile themselves to a lower standard of living. Grant saw the immense potential of this, and so all our literature was aimed at that one sentence, "The people of Canada must settle down to a lower standard of living." This was put on blotters, pamphlets, and every poster announcing a meeting.

Where did your friend Mr. Grant come from?

He had been in Weyburn. Prior to becoming unemployed he was in charge of the Labour Bureau for the Anderson administration. The provincial government kept a labour office, then after the

Liberals came in, in 1934, he was dismissed and without a job.

    Did he believe in his own fortune-telling, do you know?

Yes. It was strange, but he did. He had a mystic streak about him. He was always playing around with numbers and predicting when he was going to be ill, and when he would die. He died a few years later of cancer, and was quite convinced that he would die about that particular time.

    He took his own medicine, though.

Yes. And he was constantly trying to get me to give him figures that would help me to convince myself that we would win the election.

    But his type of publicity was effective. I saw it for the first time close to home. Mr. Bennett postponed the election, which everybody expected in July or August, because he had a heart attack. It was pushed back to October. So we campaigned all through the harvest season. I remember going out by Estlin, which was the northern end of the constituency, to visit a farmer who was harvesting. He was too preoccupied to talk to me. I asked him if he would come to the meetings. He said, "I can't come to any political meetings, I'm too busy." "Well," I said, "I hope you've given some thought as to who you're going to vote for." He said, "No, I haven't thought of who I'm going to vote for, but I know who I'm not going to vote for; I'm not going to vote for that fellow that said we've got to settle down to a lower standard of living." This proved to me the effectiveness of concentrated advertising.

    What did Grant look like?

He was short, rather sharp-faced, with sort of a pug nose. There were times when he looked like an undertaker — that's probably the best description. He used to wear a little Christie stiff hat and a very high collar. He was always smartly dressed.

    Did you know anything about his background?

Very little. When he had been in the provincial labour office in Weyburn, I used to have quite healthy battles with him over relief schedules and things of that sort. But it wasn't until the election that I got to know him quite well, and grew to be very fond of him.

> Do you believe that he was honestly interested in the
> C.C.F., in the party?

I think he was. I would say that he had a keen mind, but not a deep mind. I don't think he ever thought through the C.C.F. programme. But he, like everybody else, thought there was need for a change. Also I think he wanted some excitement, and the idea of taking part in a campaign rather pleased him.

> There was something else that was quite interesting about
> that campaign. Some time afterward I noticed that people
> called you a Social Crediter. I wonder if you would tell
> the story behind this.

I was never a Social Crediter. But in the spring of 1935, the Social Credit party swept Alberta for two reasons. First of all, it was a protest movement. Second, it had a very simple formula. People couldn't understand a planned economy or nationalization of a banking system, but could very easily understand twenty-five dollars a month. So after sweeping Alberta, it came here, and all over the province Social Credit candidates began to appear.

We had no objection until we found that the Liberal party was putting up dummy Social Credit candidates with a view to splitting the vote. This came to my attention when I was addressing a meeting near Minton, and I got a call from Mr. E.B. MacKay, who at that time was principal of the school in Radville. Mr. MacKay ran against me at the C.C.F. nominating convention, and was a very good friend of mine. But the Liberals naturally thought that since he had run against me, he would probably hold a grudge and could be used as a stooge. He phoned to tell that two members of the Liberal executive had been to see him, put $1,500 cash, which in those days was a lot of money, on his kitchen table and said, "This is for you to start with if you'll let your name go in as a Social Credit candidate. You'll have another $2,000 the day your nomination is filed."

He explained to them that he wasn't a Social Crediter, and they said, "We don't care about your being a Social Crediter, but you'll cut into Douglas's vote. This will ensure the Liberals of election." He, of course, wouldn't have anything to do with it, and immediately called me. He also told me that as they were going out the door, the two men said he was very foolish to turn it down because they had another fellow who was not as desirable, but prepared to run as a Social Credit candidate. They went to see him, and persuaded him to run. After the election was over, this fellow was immediately appointed to a job by the newly elected Liberal federal government, which would seem to give some credence to the fact that this Social Credit candidate was indeed a dummy Liberal stooge.

When MacKay phoned me with this news, I said it was a dirty trick, thanked him for calling, and would have let it go at that. But not my friend Grant. Dan Grant said that because they couldn't get MacKay they'd get somebody else, which was going to be very serious. He wanted to do something about it. Personally, I didn't see what we could do. He said, "I'm going to talk to Aberhart." So off he went. He told Aberhart that if the Social Credit wanted to run a candidate against me, that was their business and their privilege, but that he did object to the Social Credit party allowing its name to be used by the Liberal dummy candidate. Aberhart got quite indignant, said he certainly wouldn't stand for this, and asked, "Would Douglas run as Social Credit?" Grant said, "Certainly not." Then he said, "Are there any Social Crediters there at all?" Grant said, "There may be some, I think we could find them." "Well," said Aberhart, "would the Social Credit people there endorse this candidate? Because if they will, I will denounce this Liberal stooge as a fake."

So Grant came back to the Weyburn constituency and rounded up twenty or thirty people who proceeded to hold a Social Credit convention, at which they said there wasn't any Social Credit candidate running, and that they had written authority from Mr. Aberhart to say that the alleged Social Credit candidate wasn't Social Credit at all,[7] but was being financed by the Liberal party. They called on any Social Crediters in the constituency to support me. This was published and played up by the press that I was running as the C.C.F.-Social Credit candidate. But at no time was I ever in any way associated with the Social Credit party, except that I did accept their endorsement and their support, although there weren't actually many Social Crediters in the constituency.

> The way I heard, while the meeting was called a Social Credit nominating meeting, there weren't any Social Crediters there and they nominated you as their candidate.

No, they didn't nominate me, they simply endorsed my nomination. Their resolution said that since they were not running a candidate, they would endorse my nomination and call on the people of the constituency to support me.

> From that time on there was quite a lot of perturbation among the C.C.F. hierarchy, because at least one newspaper reported that you were in serious trouble from your ties with the Social Credit party. I presume they didn't know the story at all.

That's right, they didn't know the story. In those days we had no central organization. Every candidate ran on his own. We had little or no money for organizers or expense money to call candidates in to candidate schools. So it was a matter of every man for himself, and Mr. George Williams, who at that time was leader of the opposition in the Saskatchewan Legislature, became very much perturbed about these reports that I was running as a C.C.F.-Social Credit candidate, and at one time he wanted the executive to expel me. Mr. Coldwell, who was still provincial president and provincial leader of the C.C.F., would have no part of it until he heard my side of the story. When the election was over, and I laid all the facts before them, the copies of the resolution, and the other data, the whole matter was dropped.

> That's haunted you, though, hasn't it?

Oh, yes.

> I suppose that many people in Saskatchewan never really got the true story.

I'm sure most of them didn't know it.

> Also, there was a lot of misunderstanding about Social

> Credit in those days. On the surface it appeared to have the same aims, in some respects, as the C.C.F.

Yes, there was a great deal of confusion among our own people. One of the big difficulties we had at that time was trying to explain to people the difference between a Co-operative Commonwealth society, and this new theory of Social Credit. And as a matter of fact, the Social Crediters themselves were badly divided between Douglas and Aberhart.

> It was some time later that people realized they were as far apart as the poles in their ultimate philosophy. Was there any violence at this election? Your other campaign in 1934 was more or less academic.

I think in 1934 the Liberal party, which everyone knew was going to sweep back into office since the Anderson administration was completely discredited, really didn't take the Farmer-Labour party too seriously. They knew we had no organization. We were getting big crowds and people were listening to Mr. Coldwell's burning eloquence, but there was no poll organization, and I think they felt they could wave it aside.

But when we got into the federal election, and as the C.C.F. strength grew in the Weyburn constituency, the campaign became much more violent. Our opponents weren't averse to sending out groups of young fellows, who had had a few drinks and were prepared to make as much noise as possible, to the meetings to rough things up a bit.

One of the meetings that always sticks in my mind was at Odessa. I went with my campaign manager, Mr. E.T. Stinson, who was also chairman of my Deacon's Board, to the Odessa school auditorium. There was no back door; the only door was at the end of the hall and we were on the platform with no way out. The hall was packed, and there was a group of young fellows who listened very quietly until the time was ripe to start a commotion, and then they began to shout. When they couldn't get anywhere by heckling and interrupting, they made a rush for the platform. I looked around and saw Ted Stinson with his best deacon's manner taking off his coat and rolling up his sleeves. I was in the process of taking up the water jug and smashing it so as to have a good sharp edge, and telling them in printers' language that the first person who came over the footlights of the stage was going to get this in the face. Fortunately, about that time half a dozen of our own young fellows, who had heard there was going to be trouble, had driven over from Montmartre. When they walked down the aisle and across the front of the platform, the trouble quietened down very quickly.

When Grant and I were driving back to Weyburn, we got a flat tire, fortunately for us. Just by accident I put the flashlight on the front wheel when we got out to fix the tire, and we saw that the nuts had all been loosened from one of the wheels. Our car was tampered with several times.

Once or twice things were thrown at me, some fruit or the odd bad egg, but on the whole I think we probably created as much disturbance as we received. Not that we broke up anybody's meetings, but quite frequently we'd go to Mr. Young's meetings. When he got to the question period, and he gave what we thought was an incorrect answer, I would make for the platform and ask for permission to answer the question from my point of view. Usually people were fair, and said, "Sure, let him have a few minutes to answer."

Did you expect to win?

No, I never thought we would win until after the debate. The night of the debate, I thought that the tide had turned, although I wasn't absolutely sure even then. The night of the election we went to bed not knowing the outcome because the returns from the string of polls along the international boundary wouldn't come in until the next day. That night I knew that, although we were down a few votes, judging by the polls still to come in where we had good support, there was a very strong possibility we had won.

Who informed you that you had won?

The returning officer, the next morning. Mr. Stinson, Grant, and I went down to see him. We had a majority of 301 votes.

What was the C.C.F. philosophy about elected members?

Most of us in the C.C.F. had always shared the opinion that

members who were elected, particularly Members of Parliament, should give their whole time to the movement. The indemnity, which at that time was four thousand dollars a year, was adequate. That, with a railroad pass, would enable a man to give four or five months a year when Parliament wasn't sitting to campaigning in the rest of the country or looking after his own constituency.

> Am I wrong in assuming that C.C.F. members were almost required to donate a certain percentage of their indemnity?

Not until later did we put this rule in writing.

> This is most unusual for a political party. Federal members in Ottawa used to tell me that the C.C.F. had great difficulty in making ends meet.

Yes, and this is why we have followed this tradition religiously. As a matter of fact, I have given ten percent every year whether there was an election or not ever since I went into public life, which is quite a sacrifice. While four thousand dollars looked like a lot of money, you must realize that you had to keep a home in your constituency and one at Ottawa; in 1944 I wound up very much in debt.

> When did you go to Ottawa?

Parliament opened on 6 February 1936. Before that we went home to my people's place in Winnipeg for Christmas. My wife and I and my daughter Shirley, who at this time would be about eighteen months old, had a very happy Christmas. The following Christmas my father died of peritonitis and was buried on 6 January. He just lived long enough to see me elected to Parliament.

> He was very pleased, I presume.

Oh, he was very happy, yes.

> And your mother, too?

Yes. But particularly my father. He had always hoped that I

would go into politics. When the question came up about the possibility of my running, he didn't want to press it, but he hoped that I would run, and when I finally decided to let my name stand, he followed the campaign with great interest. I wasn't in Winnipeg at the time, but my friends told me that he was quite disturbed the night of the election, not knowing the results, and was delighted when he got the word I'd been elected.

The first thing he said when I saw him afterward was, "Now remember, laddie, the working people" (this was always his term for people in general who worked) "have put a lot of trust in you, you must never let them down." This was basically his attitude. He was very pleased, and it has always been a great source of comfort to me that he lived at least long enough to see me going to the House of Commons.

> When you went to Ottawa, did you take the family with you?

Yes, until Shirley was old enough to go to school. At that time my wife decided to take up residence in Weyburn and come down for Easter or once or twice during the session. After Shirley was six years of age, my wife didn't attend the session except for a short interval from then on.

> Had you been to Ottawa before?

No. I had never seen the Parliament Buildings, and knew very little about Parliament except from having read Hansard over the years. I was very excited. I was particularly excited about meeting men about whom I had read. I had met Woodsworth, Heaps,[8] and Coldwell but was yet to meet people like MacInnis. Coldwell and I later roomed together and were deskmates in the House.

> Did Mr. Woodsworth assign any special field for you because you were a new member?

No. We were a small group, just seven. Woodsworth used to quote Wordsworth to us: "We are seven," and so we had to cover a lot of fields. Mr. Coldwell and I were allocated agriculture first of all. Mr. Woodsworth, with a twinkle in his eye, used to refer to us, neither of whom had ever run a farm in our lives, as his agricultural experts. This was one of his pet jokes. Coldwell and I were the only two from Saskatchewan.

Was there someone from Manitoba?

Woodsworth was from Manitoba. But there was no one from Alberta, so agriculture was given to us: The Wheat Board, orderly marketing, and farm legislation, generally. We were also assigned most of the international field. I was given youth work, and worked with Grant MacNeill[9] on unemployment problems. Those were our main assignments.

In Ottawa you come in contact with Mr. Mackenzie King for the first time. What was your impression of him?

My first impression was that he was a rather wordy and evasive type of person. I always thought of Agnes McPhail's description of him as "a fat man full of words." He always gave you the impression that he was still in the days of Disraeli with the courteous gesture, parliamentary mannerisms, and long speeches. His speeches lasted four or four and a half hours. They wouldn't have seemed bad in normal times, but here I was coming from an area where ninety percent of the rural people were on relief, where in the towns and cities three out of every five young men were walking the streets or living at home. We'd just come through the Regina riot, and had this feeling of urgency that we ought to be doing something. And here I was, catapulted into the House of Commons and watching this stout, courteous, elderly gentleman talking for hours, mostly quoting statistics to prove that the tariffs had gone down, and at least that they hadn't gone up.

He quoted himself quite frequently.

Always, always.

In later years, did you develop a different impression?

Yes. As I sat in the House I could see another side to his character. But in those days of crisis, it was most irritating to see his vascillation and failure to give any leadership. At that particular time across the border, there was dynamic leadership from Roosevelt, who was rallying the people of the United States behind his great campaign against poverty, against a nation ill-fed, ill-clad, and ill-housed. Meanwhile, in Canada we were getting these monotonous speeches about the need for freer trade. There was nothing that would indicate to a young man that we were coming to grips with our problems.

> You also came into contact with the gentleman who used to be known as the boy orator, the boy with silver tongue, Mr. R.B. Bennett. He was then leader of the opposition. What did you think of him? Do you think he merited the title of statesman?

Yes. I changed my opinion about Bennett. Before I had gone to the House I had thought of Bennett as a blustering bully. But at the House of Commons, I realized two things. First he was probably one of the greatest orators and best parliamentarians the country ever had. In terms of carefully prepared statements that wouldn't commit yourself, Mr. King was better. In terms of an assessment of the situation and attempt to find an answer to it, Bennett was superior. Also, Bennett had a human side that he kept from the public. He was certainly very kind to Mr. Coldwell and me. He congratulated both of us on our maiden speeches, and asked if there was anything he could do to help. I pointed out that, not being a lawyer, I was at sea with parliamentary procedure; he came around to my office and brought some books. Periodically, if we were out walking through the grounds around the Parliament Buildings and he was sitting on a bench, he'd call me over and chat away about his opinion on general things. He'd reminisce about the years when he was head of the government in Canada. I think he was a man who hadn't had close contact with the people, and consequently, he didn't know people and was shy of them. In my opinion, he was a better Canadian than he was given credit for. He introduced the compulsory Wheat Board legislation, which the Liberals set aside by an Order-in-Council in 1936, as soon as they came into office. He set up the P.F.R.A. [Prairie Farm Rehabilitation Administration], and he attempted to bring in the Natural Products Marketing Act, which the courts later threw out. He brought in the Farmers' Creditors Arrangement Act to help the debt-ridden farmer. Then his New Deal legislation, while it was somewhat late in the day, was nevertheless a somewhat belated recognition that something had to be done — something his successors never did come to realize.

Then he faded from public life.

It was about 1939 that he finally left Canada and decided to go to England, and there took a peerage.

Somebody told the story that you saw him off.

Parliament was sitting at the time and there were only three of us, Howard Green of Vancouver South, Ernie Perley from Qu'-Appelle, and myself, who went to see him off at the train. The man who had been fawned and flattered by all the politicians for years was completely ignored when he left. He said he left Canada betrayed by his friends and deserted by his party. He felt very bitter about it, and I think it was a great pity. I think if he stayed in this country, he could have made quite a contribution. But Bennett never could stay on the stage unless he had the leading role. He was a very lonely old man. I saw him in England later. He asked me to come and visit him, but I couldn't because my train was leaving. When I talked to him on the long distance phone, he was really very lonely, just wanting somebody to talk to.

I suppose he was reasonably moved when the three of you came to say goodbye when everybody in Canada had forgotten him. He never did get back, did he?

No. He didn't return at all. In England, where I think he was under the impression he might cut a swath, he made no impression at all. Had he been willing to play the role of the elder statesman he could have been of tremendous value.

[Mr. Douglas's memory is at fault here. Bennett visited Canada and the United States in 1942. Meighen called a national leadership convention in that year to select his successor. The convention met in Winnipeg in December and was attended by Viscount Bennett. Like Meighen, Bennett favoured John Bracken, who won the election for leader.][10]

At your first session in Parliament, you were an inordinate talker for a young member who didn't know parliamentary procedure. You spoke sixty times according to Hansard. My own experience as a reporter has been that new members who have succeeded in limping through one speech consider themselves very good. You talked about agricultural implement prices, the address-in-reply, bilingual currency, the C.B.C., the Farm Loan Board, the budget, Cadet service, cattle, whisky (in favour I hope), the C.C.F., economic sanctions, Ethiopia, the German cruiser *Emden*, Indian soldiers' burial, insect pest destruction, the Italo-Ethiopian war, P.F.R.A., the Regina riot, unemployment relief, relief camps, and the Weyburn post office. Your maiden speech, I thought, was very outstanding. You gave your views on the League of Nations, war, peace, and anti-religious charges against the C.C.F., and so on.

Let's take your address-in-reply first, which was largely on Ethiopia. Do you recall that speech?

Yes. Just before the House of Commons met, Mussolini invaded Ethiopia. Dr. Riddell, who was the Canadian delegate to the League of Nations, advocated oil sanctions against Mussolini and subsequently in the memoirs of Marshall Badoglio, he admitted that if these oil sanctions had been implemented, Mussolini would have had to discontinue the war because they couldn't get enough oil through the Suez Canal. Riddell was repudiated by the Canadian government under Mackenzie King, and this ended the whole question of sanctions.

[Here, Mr. Douglas expresses a view widely held by Canadian nationalists and internationalists of the time. The statement of Badoglio does not appear, but is implied in his book, *The War in Abyssinia*, translated and published in London in 1937. The Riddell incident has been examined by a number of writers, but there is no unanimity of opinion, even today.][11]

This gave Chamberlain and his appeasers the perfect excuse, since Canada had withdrawn its delegate, to softpedal the oil sanctions. This made a lot of us very angry.

This was one of your most outstanding speeches. I think you agreed that the action of Canada in favouring sanc-

> tions was alright provided they were effective, but you also said that Italy can get along without Christmas trees, Christmas candles, and Teddy bears. You were probably one of the first to point out that Canada was indirectly shipping nickel to Italy, and that Italian planes were being flown on British oil. The main point was that you singled out the oil interests, with their eyes on profits, as having too much influence in those days. Can you see parallels between that and the Middle East situation today in the late 1950s?

Yes, I think it's exactly the same. I hadn't any doubt then and I've less doubt now that Standard Oil and a number of the international oil cartels were deliberately pressuring the government not to interfere in the matter of supplying oil to Mussolini. A few months later I visited Spain and saw exactly the same thing with reference to the German and Italian planes operating there, fueled by oil from the Middle East. At that very moment we were shipping tremendous quantities of nickel to Japan, which was then engaged in the rape of Manchuria. I said that the day would come when the nickel we were shipping would be used to kill Canadian boys. Some of my chums died in Hong Kong.

> In that same first speech you talked about people on relief, and in a retort to Mr. King, you said that they'd asked for bread and were given a stone. Your solution was the reorganization of the economic system to put purchasing power back into the pockets of the common people, to enable them to buy back the things they produced. Has your attitude changed at all?

When we talk about a planned economy, there is never overproduction, there is only underconsumption and maldistribution of purchasing power. The fact that we had surpluses then, and in some commodities have surpluses now, is simply due to the fact that there are large sections of our population who can't buy the things they need. I made a plea that if a public works programme was introduced and unemployed workers in Canada were given adequate purchasing power, our consumption of meat and dairy products would go up. This was greeted with great laughter. The

fact remains that when we got into the war, by 1941 the consumption per capita of beef in Canada had gone up from fifty-two
to seventy-three pounds.

> I want to show that these were the shape of things to come
> in your provincial government days. You also talked at
> some length on the chronic inability of people to pay
> medical, dental, and hospital bills. You debated about the
> C.C.F. and its principles. The opposition suggested that
> because the C.C.F. was anti-capitalistic, it was therefore
> atheistic and communistic. You stressed that capitalism
> and Christianity had not gone together, and that being a
> Christian didn't necessarily mean being a Capitalist. You
> quoted Pope Pius and the United Church of Canada as
> supporting those views. Your point of view was that if op-
> position to the 1936 brand of capitalism was atheistic and
> communistic, then some saintly people were Communists.
> You have more or less kept that attitude. In the provincial
> Legislature in 1947, when the opposition was again shriek-
> ing Communist to the government, do you remember
> what you said then?

I outlined the four points of difference between the Communist
philosophy and the C.C.F. or Socialist philosophy. One, we
believed in parliamentary government. Second, we were opposed
to any type of one-party government. There must always be a
place for opposition parties, and free opportunity for any group to
form a political party. The third difference was that the end did
not justify the means, and that means were tremendously important because they shaped ends. Using illegal or inhuman means to
attain an end would result in finding that the end was not the one
initially attempted to achieve. The final distinction was that as
Socialists, and particularly Christian Socialists, we did not believe
in a materialistic interpretation of life. Physical well-being and
material gain were not ends in themselves, but simply the means
to an end.

> These were the foundation policies as far as your public
> life was concerned. As I trace them one by one, they keep
> coming back again. I remember a young opposition mem-

> ber one night in the Legislature saying that it was too bad that you had once been a Baptist minister, and you had turned into a Socialist premier. You replied, "It's true that eighteen years ago I dedicated myself to serve the Kingdom of God, and if I didn't believe I was still doing that I would not be standing here today."

The position that Christian Socialists have taken from the days of Robert Owen, Dr. Temple, some of the Catholic popes, and many others is that Christianity far pre-dated capitalism. As Tawney points out in *Religion and the Rise of Capitalism*,[12] capitalism grew up in almost complete contradistinction to the Christian philosophy. The two have been in conflict ever since. If you had the application of Christian principles, you'd almost have to eliminate the whole form of Capitalist society and the Capitalist philosophy of life.

> Another important milestone was 4 February 1936, when you spoke on the Woodsworth resolution asking that industrial, commercial, and financial organizations failing to function in the general interest should be taken over by the appropriate public authorities, operated as a public service or a co-operative enterprise.

In the speech from this particular debate in 1936, in one of the last speeches I made in the federal Parliament in 1944, and also in the very first speech I made in the Saskatchewan Legislature in October 1944, I stressed the fact that we believe in a mixed economy. Public ownership, co-operative ownership, and private ownership should each operate in their respective fields.

> We hear even today that the C.C.F. intend to run everything as a government enterprise, which according to the record here, has never been the policy of the C.C.F. party at all.

A person has to be pretty unintelligent to think a government could run everything from a shoeshine parlour to a barber shop. The position is, as Mr. Woodsworth pointed out, that it was only necessary to take over those industries that were essential to planning the economy, so that it would function and put people to work. That might mean the Bank of Canada, which ultimately we did nationalize anyway. It might also mean taking over transportation and integrating a transportation system—whatever is necessary in order to put our economy on a planned basis rather than on the present hit-or-miss basis. We've taken the position repeatedly, for instance, that there's no need to nationalize banks and insurance companies as long as you have two things. One, the Bank of Canada must control the issue of currency and credit. Two, a national investment board should control where these funds are to be invested, so that they will be invested for socially useful projects. Then you don't need to nationalize them.

> On about 2 March 1936, there was a resolution calling on Canada to fulfil its obligations under the League of Nations. It said, until and unless there was sincere acceptance and application by member nations, and I quote: "Canada should refuse to participate in any foreign war no matter who the belligerents may be." Was this your resolution?

Yes, it was. I had quite a battle in our own camp before I got support, because in this resolution I stressed for the first time in the House of Commons that we ought to have an international police force, and have not only economic sanctions, but if necessary, military sanctions. Some of our own people were pacifists, and were a little reluctant to support the idea of military sanctions, although they could agree to economic sanctions. I took the position then that you couldn't set up an international body and ask them to make the international pirate behave if all they could wave in his face was an empty gun. Nations would ultimately have to give an international police force the power and authority to deal with an international bandit. This is important because it was the first time that Mr. Woodsworth, after a great deal of argument, finally moved to that position and was prepared to support it. Remember he was a pacifist, against all force and all use of force. But he was prepared to concede that force could be used to maintain international law and order. This was a big advance for us.

> Has the situation improved at all? We have a United
> Nations as we had a League of Nations, but whether it's
> done any better is open to question, isn't it?

There is one apparent difference, but I don't know whether it is
an improvement or not. In the 1930s we had a League of Nations
with the United States outside, and consequently it died from
futility and internal weakness, betrayed by its sponsors. Now we
have a United Nations supported by the United States, but to a
large extent probably dominated by the United States and used as
a weapon in its cold war against the Soviet Union rather than
being used to establish a genuine system of collective security.

> Would you say the Soviet Union also uses the United
> Nations?

There's no doubt about it. It has used the veto to promote its own
particular ends.

> Your contribution in your first session of Parliament also
> laid down some basic philosophies. The federal govern-
> ment had lowered tariffs on farm machinery, lowered the
> tax rate on gasoline, and increased corporation tax; you
> said these were all to the good, but you wanted a levy on
> wealth and undivided profits. In other words, you wanted
> to lessen inequalities of income by increased taxation on
> larger incomes, and reduce the national debt with the
> levy on huge accumulations of capital. Is that still your
> position or would you do this in some other way?

These are still the things we have to do to combat inflation or deflation. At that particular time we were in a period of deflation,
and our contention was that the government could use the Bank
of Canada to finance a great public works programme, and then
hold some of that money back from the people who had more
than they needed by means of excess profits tax and high steeply
graded income tax, a capital gains tax, and if necessary, a levy on
wealth. Now the situation is reversed. We still have inflation, but
what we need to do is pull money out of circulation, out of the
pockets of people who have more than they need, and leave more
money in the pockets of the people who can't purchase.

> There's just one other point about this 1936 session, whether or not you are a pacifist.

I've never been a pacifist. This is a matter to which I've given a great deal of thought and a great deal of study, and I've read the works of some of the greatest pacifists to settle my own philosophy on this matter.

First of all, I've a tremendous admiration for the pacifist, and during the war I appeared before the War Relations Board in defence of a number of conscientious objectors. Some of the boys in my boys' clubs later became conscientious objectors, and two whom I had great difficulty getting out of jail joined the international fire brigade and went to London; they were decorated for bravery, which shows that they weren't cowards but had conscientious objections to bearing arms or to killing another human being.

I had to settle this for myself. Having read the works of Ghandi and of other prominent pacifists and having a great admiration for Mr. Woodsworth, who was a pacifist, I found that, philosophically, I couldn't be a pacifist for a number of reasons. First of all, I think that any absolute creed is always an oversimplification. To say that force is always wrong seems to me a failure to recognize that different things have different values, and that you must have a sense of value. It is a terrible thing to take a man's life. But you have to weigh that against something else which may have greater value than a man's life. I think of a man going to set fire to a school in which there are five hundred children. You have to decide whether to kill this man in order to prevent him committing a terrible act of arson.

The second reason I am not a pacifist is that I think one not only has the rights but the responsibilities of a citizen. I think Robert Louis Stevenson once said, "I have a perfect right to turn my cheek if someone slaps me, but I've no right to turn my child's cheek because for my child I'm responsible." And so if I have responsibilities to defend my child, my home, and my wife, to protect my community and the weaker members of society, I can't abrogate this merely on the philosophical idea that force is never correct.

Third, if you accept the completely absolutist position of the

pacifist, then you are saying that you are prepared to allow someone else who has no such scruples to destroy all the values you've
built up. This is what I used to argue with Mr. Woodsworth. Say
you've spent most of your life helping to build up trade unions,
are you now prepared to say that if a government or a group of
employers uses force to destroy the unions, that you'll stand and
watch your life's work and a hundred years of social development
wiped out in a single night? This is what is happening in Germany. Personally, I wouldn't stand for it. We've made certain
gains, and if we say we will not use force to defend them, we could
have them all taken away from us. But there are values to be
defended, and in 1936 I saw in Germany and in Spain what was
happening to many of these values. I recognized then that if you
came to a choice between losing freedom of speech, religion,
association, thought, and all the things that make life worth living,
and resorting to force, you'd use force. What you have internationally is what you have within a nation. You must have law and
order, and you must have the necessary military means to enforce
that law and order. But force without justice is tyranny, and the
necessary machinery must exist so that if any nation feels ag-
grieved, it has peaceable means for adjusting its grievances.

>   You associated yourself with the last war, did you not?

Yes, I served in the Second Battalion of the South Saskatchewan
Regiment, and at one time was commissioned to go to Hong Kong
with the Winnipeg Grenadiers, but I was held back because of my
knee.

>   That almost completes the 1936 session, excepting the
>   debates on relief camps, railway camps, and the one
>   million and a half unemployed.

These were foremost in my mind. I had come fresh from the
prairies where there was drought, poverty, and unemployment,
and the Regina riot left an indelible impression on me. It was
natural that I should want to speak about these things. It was also
only natural, looking back now, that I should feel a bit impatient
with a government that seemed to be doing practically nothing
about these problems. One of Mr. King's promises was that he
would take the young men out of relief camps where Bennett had

put them on twenty cents a day. He took them out and turned them loose—now they didn't even get the twenty cents a day—and they wandered about the country on freight trains. Grant MacNeill, who was a C.C.F. member for one of the Vancouver seats, and I walked at the head of fifteen hundred of these young single transients who hadn't been in any one place long enough to qualify for relief. They couldn't even go back to their respective homes because they'd been away too long to qualify, which required two years' residence.

They were pitched from pillar to post, and the Mounted Police just pushed them onto the boxcars and they went to the next province and were pushed on again. We marched to Parliament Hill to get an interview with Mr. Mackenzie King. Instead we spoke to Mr. Rogers,[13] the Minister of Labour. He was appalled when he listened to their story. But the fact is that nothing was done about it.

> From this vantage point of 1958, do you think that such conditions could return?

Not in the same way, no. I think with Unemployment Insurance, and some of the built-in banking techniques for preventing rapid deflation, a situation as bad as that could not return. But I am rather disturbed at statements made in the last few days, that the United States have now settled down to a normal figure of anywhere from four to six percent unemployed. The Minister of Citizenship and Immigration from Canada, speaking in London the other day, said our unemployment figure is just about the normal figure you'd expect for Canada. I don't think 281,000 in the month of August is hardly acceptable as a normal figure. There seems to be a tendency now to accept a small percentage as desirable, because this keeps the fellow who has a job much quieter when he knows that there is somebody outside ready to take his place.

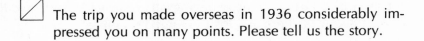 The trip you made overseas in 1936 considerably impressed you on many points. Please tell us the story.

It was a very interesting trip for me at that age. The Canadian Youth Congress was held in Ottawa, to which church groups, Y.M.C.A., Y.W.C.A., university groups, and political youth groups all sent delegates; from their number thirty-five were selected to go to the World Youth Congress in Geneva. Three Members of Parliament were selected to accompany them as chaperones. They chose three of the younger Members of Parliament: Paul Martin (later Minister of Health and Welfare) from the Liberal party; Denton Massey, the Conservative member from Greenwood-Toronto, who had the biggest Bible class in the world (two thousand members); and myself from the C.C.F. It was a very interesting experience to meet with young people from all over the world.

Before we returned, we got a cablegram from Mr. King asking us to sit in with the Canadian delegation at the League of Nations. We saw Anthony Eden, later Sir Anthony, who led the British delegation, and other interesting figures of international politics.

On my way back I visited Spain, where the revolution had broken out.[14] Some of the Spanish delegates to the World Youth Congress had asked a group of us to come and visit Spain, and with the help of some of the French Socialists in Paris, we were able to get there. On our return to Paris we met Mr. Léon Blum, at that time Premier of France.

> What did you see in Spain? There has always been a lot of controversy about that revolution.

There was no doubt in my mind, and I think it has been well documented since, that this was first a counter-revolution; it was financed mainly by Spanish capital, but also by money from other countries in an attempt to overthrow a properly and duly elected government. It was later described as a Communist government. I think there were one or two Communists in the government, but there were more Liberals who would be right of centre, as compared to the C.C.F. and the Socialist party, than there were left of centre. I talked to some of the cabinet ministers, and they certainly didn't impress me as having very radical ideas. We would have thought of them as Lloyd George Liberals.

When did you talk to them?

In Madrid and Barcelona and in Bilbao, where you could see the German and Italian planes overhead with their markings. I talked to priests in the government ranks, who were marching, carrying rifles and machine guns, and fighting along with the men. There isn't any doubt that without the financial aid from the big interests of Spain, surrounding countries, and even the United States, and without German and Italian planes, munition and tanks and troops and technicians, Franco never could have defeated the government of Spain. I think the great majority of the people were with the government.

The non-intervention policy was a disastrous thing. Hiding behind it were Mr. Chamberlain and Mr. Léon Blum, the Socialist leader of the Popular Front government in France. When we talked to him, Blum made no bones about Chamberlain's statement that if France got into war with Germany and Italy as a result of intervention in Spain, Britain would not support her. He would have to go alone if he interfered.[15]

It's strange how this non-intervention story was so easily sold to the public. When we got back to London, I went to Transport House, where Mr. Arthur Greenwood[16] was the only Labour leader there. The rest were all in Edinburgh.

Was that your first meeting with any leaders of the British Labour party?

Yes. We were appalled when Mr. Greenwood told us that the day before, the British Labour party conference in Edinburgh had just passed a resolution supporting the government's non-intervention policy. Here was a fantastic situation. The government of Spain had two million pounds in gold on deposit in London and couldn't buy a machine-gun with it. But the rebels were able to buy all the weapons they wanted from Germany and Italy. Here was a legitimate government properly elected, simply trying to maintain its authority and denied the right to buy weapons on the international market. The Labour party thought this was quite alright. This was going to keep us out of war!

Some of the Labour M.P.s with us on this trip asked me to go with them to Edinburgh to tell our story to the Labour leaders and eventually to the Labour conference, at which time they rescinded the resolution and called for support for Spain. As a matter of fact, they raised money at the convention to send to Spain; trade unions contributed money for ambulances, and for supplying whatever could be purchased.

You were in Europe for how long?

About three months. We went from Switzerland to Nuremberg, because I wanted to see the great annual fesitivity Hitler put on each year there. It was frightful. I came back and warned my friends about the great German bombers roaring over the parade of self-propelled guns and tanks, Hitler standing there giving his salute, with Göring and the rest of the Nazi bigwigs by his side. There was no doubt then that Hitler was simply using Spain as a dress rehearsal for an attack on other nations.

It was with very great difficulty that people were able to appreciate the anti-Semitism that was going on in Germany. Did you yourself see any examples of it?

I didn't see any. Most of it was over by the time I got there. But I know that this was the time that the nonconformists, many of the Baptist ministers to whom I had letters of introduction, had already been arrested. The Reverend Martin Neimöller[17] and some of his group were being picked up. Hitler was playing the old game. First of all he'd picked up the Jews. A few people objected to that, but it didn't worry the rest too much. The next attack was on the Communists, then the Socialists. The next victims were a few university professors. They always took groups one at a time. By this time he was beginning to tackle the smaller church groups. He hadn't got around to the Lutheran church or the Roman Catholic church. Their turn was to be later, after he had liquidated the rest.

You can probably find the press accounts of the lectures I gave when I got back in the fall of 1936. I made the statement then, that unless we were prepared to use a system of collective security, I was convinced we'd either have to go to war or sacrifice Czechoslovakia within two years, in which case we'd only postpone the war for another one or two years. I was a better prophet than I realized. I started to tour the province; the C.C.F. was badly in need of money and George Williams suggested I might do some lectures to raise funds. So I went around the province, and to some other provinces, too, speaking about my trip. I got some warnings from the Deutscher Bund in Saskatchewan, a German organization that was quite pro-Nazi.[18] When the German consul officer was there, they displayed the swastika. I had some pictures taken of some of these picnics because some prominent Saskatchewan Liberals attended these gatherings.

The warnings from the Deutscher people said I had better stop talking like I was or I'd be in trouble. In my own constituency, I had some fairly strong German communities who were very incensed at what I said about Hitler.

I've said it ever since, that there is not a great deal of difference except in degree between the brownshirts and the dress shirts. You can get either form of fascism.

> In the fall of 1936, there was another C.C.F. National Convention.

It was held in Winnipeg. At the convention I became national president of the C.C.Y.M., the Co-operative Commonwealth Youth Movement. I would be almost thirty-two.

> Did you have much to do with policy making then?

Mr. Coldwell and I were on the National Council, which means we were elected from the floor or from our province.

> This was the time that Mr. Woodsworth made a declaration that he would have no truck with any other party. Was that an issue at the convention?

One of the big issues was the cry for a united front. The Communists were following the same policy all over the world. They'd got a united or popular front in France, and they were calling for a united front of all progressive left-wing groups, with the Communist party, of course, as the core. It had a fair amount of appeal in a country where a million and a half people were on relief and business was stagnant. Mr. Woodsworth was a vehement opponent of the Communists. He'd fought them all his life. He had seen them betray the working people at almost every turn, and he was a very outspoken foe of any united front.

> I think he also was opposed to the C.C.F. party linking up with any other party, including the Social Credit. He said, "I'll never associate with a Capitalist party."

Yes, that's true, although the Social Credit never made any overt approaches to the C.C.F. There may have been among the ranks some talk of amalgamating, but the Social Credit party realized that their main strength lay in appealing to the upper middle classes of Canada, saying that they were the one party that could save them from the C.C.F.

I have a little anecdote about the Social Credit. In our first session of Parliament, Mr. Coldwell and I were asked to lunch by Lord Tweedsmuir. The governor-general had all members over to his place once a session, sometimes for a cup of coffee in the morning, or for lunch. Lord Tweedsmuir was also John Buchan, the famous author, and an independent Member of Parliament for the Scottish university. He was a fascinating character. As a boy living in Glasgow I had read all the books of O. Douglas, and on talking to him this particular day I found out that O. Douglas was his sister.[19]

He had a great time chatting with us, and chided Mr. Coldwell and myself. "You know," he said, "I am not allowed to come and sit in the House of Commons, but I read Hansard avidly; and so you two call yourselves Socialists. My friend, Jimmy Maxton,[20] would have nothing but contempt for such dishwater socialism as yours. You're just left-wing Tories."

He decided to quiz us about our impressions of the political scene in Canada. He said, "Mr. Coldwell, what do you think of this Social Credit party?" Mr. Coldwell said, "It's a flash in the pan, twenty-five dollars a month; in two years it'll be all gone." Lord Tweedsmuir then made the most penetrating observation, which I've always remembered. He said, "Mr. Coldwell, don't be too sure of that. Social Credit is a Conservative's idea of a revolution." When you stop to think it over, this is true. This gives the Conservatives the feeling of having a revolution without having to pay the price of a revolution. You can be a radical by doing terrible things to the banking system, but this won't cost you a five-cent piece. You won't pay more taxes, you won't have any of your profits taken away, you can keep on exploiting your neighbours, and you can pay low wages. And you can keep on getting twenty-five dollars a month.

Was 1937 or 1938 distinguished by anything you can remember offhand?

In 1938 I introduced a private bill to amend the Farmers' Creditors Arrangement Act.[21] Dunning accepted my amendments to the Farmers' Creditors Arrangement Act, and incorporated them in a bill of his own. But as I recall, '37 and '38 were mainly concerned with agricultural legislation.

This period was one of tremendous discontent here in the prairies. I remember Mr. Coldwell and myself attending mass protest meetings called by farmers' organizations because the Wheat Board wasn't in operation and because there was no crop insurance programme.

All our politics have stemmed from the price of wheat, in Saskatchewan particularly.

That is true. In those days eighty percent of our total income in Saskatchewan came from agriculture, and the major part of that from wheat. It was by far the largest single commodity we sold. There were more people dependent on the return from wheat than any other commodity.

Your other concern at that time must have been the continuing drought and poverty on the prairies.

Yes, 1937 was probably the worst year in our history. Our entire provincial income dropped to 171 million dollars. Our crop that year was about 36 million bushels, we hadn't enough feed, and a lot of the cattle had to be sold for a cent a pound on the hoof.

I remember a meeting at Carlyle, which was in Mr. Gardiner's constituency.[22] I stood at the back of the hall, while Mr. Gardiner gave solemn assurance that there would be feed coming in two weeks to take care of the cattle. The weeks went by and the feed didn't come, and a lot of the farmers had to sell their livestock. A few were able to make arrangements to send them to Manitoba. But the result was that thousands of farmers lost their herds.

I went after Mr. Gardiner in the '38 session about this as soon as Parliament met. I recounted his promise in Carlyle, and the feed that didn't come. Mr. Gardiner interrupted me to deny it, and I said, "I was there; I heard you make the statement and give those people your solemn assurance." Mr. Gardiner shot back from his seat, and said, "I don't think you were there; I didn't see you!" I said that was quite possible; like the Minister of Agriculture I'm not very conspicuous even when I'm standing up. This delighted Mr. Bennett. He was no friend of Mr. Gardiner.

> I remember a terrific stormy encounter in the House of Commons one night when the agricultural estimates were being discussed. There was quite an exchange between you and Mr. Gardiner about whose feet touched the floor. Do you remember that?

No, it wasn't disagreement on that. I was endeavouring to make a speech on his estimates; there were a lot of Liberals in the House — 186 members — and the ones from Saskatchewan were particularly adept at keeping up a constant barrage of interruptions. Mr. Gardiner led the orchestra. Finally I stopped him and said, "I don't want any more interruptions. If the Minister of Agriculture will sit up in his chair and dangle his feet, I'll go on with what I have to say." For this he never forgave me. This also delighted Mr. Bennett.

Before we leave the Wheat Board, perhaps we could briefly count the steps. In 1935 Mr. Bennett brought down the Wheat Board Act. In his original draft all farmers in western Canada had to deliver their wheat to the Wheat Board. It was a compulsory marketing plan, approved by the farmers. The Grain Exchange hired Colonel Ralston, later Minister of Finance and Minister of

Defence, as their counsel. The secretary of the Grain Exchange, Mr. Murray, headed the delegation. They put on a terrific battle before the parliamentary committee to whom this bill had been referred. They fought so long, all during July and on into August, that Bennett, who had suffered a heart attack, had to direct the battle from his bed part of the time, and finally agreed to a compromise. The agreement was that the farmer could deliver his wheat to the Wheat Board or to the private grain trade. This was at least a partial victory for Ralston and Murray and the Winnipeg Grain Exchange.

When the Liberals were elected, one of the first things they did was virtually to set aside the whole act by Order-in-Council in a very neat way. They simply prescribed that the Wheat Board would still be in operation, but could not accept delivery of wheat as long as the price stayed above ninety cents. As long as wheat was above ninety cents, farmers had to deliver it on the open market. This continued right through until the war.

The Grain Exchange made sure that the price stayed above ninety cents. Mr. Bennett and Mr. Coldwell made the best speeches I ever heard on this subject, and fought over a long period of time, attacking the government on the ground that they had set aside an Act of Parliament. This was a most unconstitutional and undemocratic practice. Farmers protested this action all over the prairies. But the Wheat Board remained inoperative for most of the Liberal government's first term of office.

It always amuses me now when I hear Mr. Gardiner pretending to be a friend of the Wheat Board. I remember that he was the Minister of Agriculture and Dunning[23] was Minister of Finance in all those years when the Wheat Board was inactive.

> In the Speech from the Throne later, was there not something to the effect that government had decided to return to the open market?

Yes, it was before the war that they were quite prepared to return to the open market. Ironically, prior to the war they refused to operate the Wheat Board to prevent the price of wheat from going down, but as soon as war was declared, they reopened the Wheat Board to keep the price of wheat from going up.

In 1942 the farmers trekked to Ottawa. Several trainloads of them, organized by the three prairie pools and the various farm organizations, stayed in Ottawa for three days. They made a very strong case in the railway committee room before the cabinet and Members of Parliament, and asked for an initial payment of a dollar a bushel, delivery at Fort William. They finally got ninety cents, and raised the price a dime a bushel.

In 1940 I was attacking them on the grounds that they were making the Wheat Board operative only to hold the prices down, and had now introduced a maximum price to be put in by legislation. Now the Wheat Board had no authority to raise prices, and in 1943 they raised it this miserable ten cents per bushel when the world price for wheat was very much higher. This was the sabotage of the principle of orderly marketing, where the farmers' wheat would be fed onto the world market so that we would get the best price we could and pay it back to the farmer. He'd get his initial payment, then his secondary payment, and even a third payment if the amount of money received from the sale of wheat warranted it.

> This led to some promises by Mr. Mackenzie King, did it not, that since the farmers had taken these sacrifices during the war, they were to be rewarded afterward with fair prices?

He didn't deny the fact that the farmers were growing wheat for a price much below that of the world market, and promised that when the war was over they would get their fair share of the national income. As a result, he brought in the Agricultural Prices Support Act with a fund of some 200 million dollars. The preamble to the act was very interesting. It said the money was to guarantee farmers a fair share of the national income and that the price they received bore a fair relationship to the remuneration received by other segments of the economy. When the Liberals left office in 1957, at least two-thirds of the 200-million-dollar fund hadn't even been touched, and most farm commodities derived no benefit from it whatsoever. Part of the money was used to remedy the foot and mouth disease problem and some potato crop failures in the East. But as far as putting price supports under agricultural products, very little was done.

> Today in 1958, the Liberal government has gone into the
> shadows for a while, and we have a Conservative govern-
> ment. Has this pledge of Mr. Mackenzie King's to wheat
> farmers ever been implemented?

The very opposite has happened. Since 1949 the cost of producing a bushel of wheat has gone up 50.3 percent. Since 1949 the
price for a bushel of wheat has gone down 20.7 percent, barley
down 27 percent, and oats down 36 percent. I saw some interesting figures the other day compiled by the Wheat Pool: in 1946 you
could buy a small tractor for a boxcar of wheat; today it would
take two and a quarter carloads. It represents a contrast between
1,875 bushels and 3,960 bushels.

> In your opinion, is the Wheat Board legislation the only
> piece of legislation passed since settlement days that
> recognizes the farmers' poor bargaining position?

Yes, but it has only been allowed to operate when it has suited the
government's purpose.

> In other words, it's in a state of impermanence at the
> present time, only extended for five years. Mr. Gardiner
> continually warned farmers that if they screamed about it,
> they'd probably lose it.

The favourite line of Mr. Gardiner and his forces over the years
has been that anybody who criticized the government's handling
of the Wheat Board was indirectly going to cause the farmers to
lose it because any criticism would cause such a storm of protest
in the East that the legislation would be dropped.

My argument always was that this was as silly as if I complained to the station-master that the train was late, and the railway company pulled up the tracks and stopped running the train
altogether.

 Now I would like to ask about the dramatic events in the
> parliamentary period from 1938 to 1944. First, the Bren
> gun inquiry—this was a question of corruption, humor-

> ously expressed in a cartoon in *Maclean's* magazine. The caption was, "The boys did nothing wrong but they mustn't do it again."

The details of the case can be found in the many articles written at the time. The whole thing was precipitated by an article written [in 1938] in *Maclean's* magazine by Colonel George Drew,[24] who at that time was leader of the Conservative opposition in the Ontario Legislature. The Bren gun was manufactured in Britain. A few Bren guns had been sent to the Department of Defence in Ottawa, and Major General LaFleche, who was Deputy Minister, called in some people from Toronto and showed them the Bren gun, allowed them to take it home with them. They came back in a few days with a proposition for him and Mr. Ian MacKenzie, the Minister of Defence, that they could get the old John Inglis factory in Toronto, open it, and produce Bren guns. They somehow managed to get the Canadian government to give them a very large sum of money in advance to equip the plant. Then the government issued a very fat contract to manufacture Bren guns.

And Colonel Drew very properly pointed out the scores of plants in Canada who would have been prepared to bid on the order to make Bren guns, improve their own plant, and put up their own equipment. But this company was given very special consideration. They didn't have to bid, they received a fat contract on a cost-plus basis, and got all this money to assemble equipment and so on for the new plant.

Drew wrote a series of very penetrating and scathing articles, for which both he and *Maclean's* were sued. Then it was taken up in the House in the Fifth Session, early in 1939.[25] There was a very long and bitter debate.[26] The two main leaders in the debate were Mr. Howard Green, who at that time was a member for Vancouver South and is now the Minister of Public Works in the Diefenbaker government, a very able lawyer, and the other was Grant MacNeill[27] of the C.C.F. group, member for Vancouver North. Grant MacNeill had been secretary-treasurer for some ten or twelve years of the War Veterans' Association of Canada. He had a first-class mind.

In the debate, the Minister of Defence, Mr. Ian Mackenzie, didn't help himself at all by losing his temper, thumping his desk, and offering to knock the damn head off anybody who accused him of corruption or misappropriation of funds. The government put three of their most clever lawyers in the debate and also in the Bren gun committee. They were Gerry McGeer, a former mayor of Vancouver, the member for Vancouver-Burrard;[28] Arthur Slack, a great Toronto corporation and jury lawyer, a member for Owen Sound; and Peter Bercovitch, probably the best lawyer in the city of Montreal, who represented Montreal-Cartier.

Those three carried the ball pretty well for the government, for Mackenzie was more of a liability than an asset. Gerry McGeer was easily the best spokesman for the government because of his Irish wit, the fact that he never lost his temper, and his great capacity for hard work. I remember he followed Dr. Manion, leader of the Conservative party and leader of the opposition, after the departure of Mr. Bennett to the House of Lords. Manion was an Irishman, like Gerry McGeer, whom they used to call "gattling gun Manion" in his younger days because of his rapidity of speech. When McGeer got up to follow him, the atmosphere in the House was tense.

The galleries were packed, and Gerry McGeer opened his speech by saying, "Mr. Speaker, it's very difficult to follow Irish suspicion travelling at two hundred words a minute." McGeer did a superb job, but he couldn't whitewash this very tawdry and shoddy business deal. When it got to the committee, Howard Green, Grant MacNeill, and myself, the main committee members, called Colonel George Drew as a witness.

What kind of a committee was this?

This was a special committee of Parliament to look into this matter of the Bren gun contract. An unusual event happened; the chairman took ill in the last few days, and I was made chairman. I don't know whether this was to keep me quiet, or because by this time everybody had become so bone weary that I was the only one left. We never were allowed to finish the investigation or submit a report. We were sitting in the committee examining witnesses, and somebody walked in and said, "Well, boys, you can all go home, the House has been prorogued."

The star of the show undoubtedly was Drew. I had never been particularly warm to Drew—he'd always been in a different social set, somewhat pompous, certainly reserved and dignified— who was a lawyer with the typical Toronto approach to the rest of Canada, looking down on the West and the Maritimes, thinking mainly of Ontario and of the upper classes. Drew had never been a particular favourite of any of us. But he was examined for at least a week, and was by far the most outstanding speaker in the hearings.

They threw everything they had at him. He was being sued in court, and anything he said before the committee, while it might be privileged, would certainly have an influence on the court decision. He came carefully briefed, with all his data at his fingertips. He stood a constant barrage from McGeer, Slack, Bercovitch, and everyone the Liberals could bring in. He had an answer every time.

McGeer tried everything. First of all he tried ridiculing Drew, catching him off base. He tried questioning facts on which Drew couldn't be budged because he had made a very close analysis of the whole thing. Finally, McGeer resorted to abuse. He practically told Drew he knew he was lying. Drew looked him straight in the eye and said, "Mr. McGeer, I wouldn't repeat that if I were you." McGeer stopped at that point. My estimation of Drew went up a hundred percent as a result of these inquiries.

I got to know him later when he was Premier of Ontario, and met him at federal-provincial conferences. Although we had a good many fights, as we naturally would have, because he was heading a have province and I was associated with a have-not province, the fact remains that Drew, like Bennett, was a much misunderstood man. He had the sort of stuffed-shirt qualities that come from being a corporation lawyer from Toronto. But basically he was a very genuine person, and a very honourable man, with a high idea of what public service entails.

Were you very active in that committee?

I spent a lot of time examining all the data that came in and cross-examining the witnesses. We had Mackenzie and Major General LaFleche on the stand.

They were prime targets, I suppose?

Oh, yes. Then we had the John Inglis people as witnesses. It was a great experience, and I think the investigation was fully justified. The contracts were revised, and although the company continued to make Bren guns all through the war, a good deal more safeguards were included for the benefit of the Canadian treasury. By this time people realized that we weren't out gunning for the Liberal party, but we were really trying to do a service to the country, and get to the bottom of this. I don't think the government had anything much to do with the scandal. I think department officials were the culprits.

Later on I became a member of the War Expenditures Committee. We voted about five billion dollars a year for defence, which was ten times the peace-time budget for the whole country.

Some of this five billion dollars was made up in huge amounts like fifteen hundred million dollars for the army, two billion dollars for the air force. The Minister of Defence couldn't say which planes they were going to buy or how much they were going to pay for each one. This would risk giving the information to the enemy. Instead, we followed the practice of the British government: a committee was given complete access to all the information, saw the plans, knew cost per unit, visited factories, and made any type of investigation they desired. However, none of the committee reports were made public. If the members from each of the parties were satisfied, detailed questions were not asked when the estimates were passed.

Someone in the Bren gun committee was supposed to have said, "I wish that preacher would shut up." Did you say that if this gentleman wasn't satisfied verbally, you could settle it in physical combat?

It was Taylor, the Liberal whip, really a very nice person. I was whip for our group at this particular time, and so we worked together quite closely and we were as good friends as people can be who haven't much in common.

As whip, he had the awful job of trying to keep the Liberal members together in committee and at their job when they were getting a bad shellacking. He was getting out of patience and I was probably riding some of their witnesses fairly hard. He kept telling me to quit talking and I finally said, "If you think you can make me shut up, why don't you try it?" The press interpreted this as a challenge for a fight, which really wasn't what I had in mind.

> There is a whole history of western politicians in the good and bad old days who, whenever a heckler became too vociferous, would settle the dispute with a fight. I have on record several who did. Did you have any experiences like that?

No, I never got in any fisticuffs. On a couple of occasions I was annoyed enough to tell a heckler that if he didn't keep quiet, I would come down and personally put him out. But I never had to do it, for which I'm very thankful.

> Have you ever been challenged from the floor?

No, nobody's ever offered, and now I'm much more careful as to who I offer to put out.

> Mr. Gardiner told me that such incidents were exaggerated. Is that true in your case?

Yes. One of the things I've always tried to avoid is taunting people into fighting. When I trained boys in boxing, I always said that if I taught them to box, they weren't ever to use it against somebody who couldn't box. Any man who knows boxing or judo can kill another man with his hands if he really makes up his mind to do it. He knows where and how hard to hit.

> After the house was prorogued, did you prepare a report?

No. There never was a report. The committee died when the House died.

4

War years in Parliament

At the beginning of the Second World War, there was a special war session of the federal Parliament in 1939. Starting with the dramatic incident in the House, where Mr. Woodsworth stood alone with his convictions, what were your impressions?

Prior to our being called to this special session of Parliament, Mr. Woodsworth suffered a mild stroke. It was not generally known that he came to this session almost blind, with one side slightly paralyzed.

Britain declared war on 3 September, and Parliament was called on 7 September because King had always taken the position, quite properly, that we were not at war merely because Great Britain was, and that the Canadian Parliament alone could declare our nation to be at war.

This put the C.C.F. in a very difficult position because Mr. Woodsworth and a few others were outright pacifists. The rest of us were in favour of a system of collective security. We'd even managed to get Mr. Woodsworth to agree to a motion that I introduced in the House of Commons calling for an international police force under the jurisdiction of the League of Nations. All of the members of the League of Nations should be willing to surrender their national sovereignty to the point where the League of Nations would have the authority to impose either economic or military sanctions against an aggressor.

Mr. Woodsworth went along with that in theory, but he was still basically a pacifist. He was opposed to force in any shape or form. We had long private discussions about this, and although we respected his point of view, philosophically we couldn't accept it. We took the position that using force was preferable to seeing those things we cherished destroyed: our democratic processes, all social institutions such as trade unions and co-operatives, free churches, freedom of speech, freedom of assembly, rights of collective bargaining for labour, and so on. So a conference was called of C.C.F. M.P.s, C.C.F. provincial leaders, and the C.C.F. national council in Ottawa for two or three days prior to the special momentous session of Parliament.

Where was the debate?

Either in one of the rooms of the Chateau Laurier or in the C.C.F. National Office. Mr. Woodsworth took no part in the discussions as they went along.

Why?

First, because of his stroke, but also because he had already made up his mind as to what position he was going to take. He felt he shouldn't try to influence the party because his was a personal position, rising out of his deep religious convictions.

He died not very long after that; I suppose he felt that his days were numbered.

With his stroke, he felt that it probably wouldn't be too long until he'd have to quit political life. He'd already mentioned to several of us that he would soon have to drop the leadership, and he hoped that Mr. Coldwell would take it over even if he were able to continue as a Member of Parliament.

The discussion went on for two or three days, and with the exception of a few forthright pacifists, everyone was agreed that we had no choice but to support the war. We had criticized Chamberlain for the Munich appeasement policy, and now that Chamberlain, with the support of the British Labour party, was going to stand up to Hitler, we had to take our position beside him. We did agree, however, that if there was going to be a war and we were going to be in it, then we must have equality of sacrifice. If there was going to be any type of conscription, it must be conscription of everything, not only of manpower, but wealth and resources and machinery for producing the weapons of war.

Mr. Woodsworth then said to the group that he had refrained from taking part in the debate because he didn't want to embarrass or influence us too much. He didn't want us to make decisions on the basis of our personal regard for him. He said, "War is morally wrong, and the taking of human life is always wrong no matter by what name you may call it. I'm not going to support this, but I don't want to influence the rest of you. I hope you will select Mr. Coldwell to speak for the group in Parliament."

Although it may have looked like a split in the C.C.F. to the general public, it was one of the most amicable divisions you ever saw. We all admired Woodsworth, and after he made his speech, there was not a dry eye in the room. Everybody loved and respected him, but in the realistic position in which we found ourselves, we felt that we couldn't go along with him. This was not a piece of political expediency, either. We could have gotten a lot of support in Quebec, and from the German communities, and other groups throughout Canada who would have been very glad that we were against the war. In my own constituency, I had lost support in quite a number of areas because I voted for the war.

It was a case of conflict of ideologies. One believed in collective security and the rule of law in an attempt to protect and preserve certain values. The other position was that of the pacifists, who took an absolutist stance against the use of force.

Mr. King then presented the case, and stated why the

government felt that we should declare war. Dr. Manion, the leader of the Conservative party, made the usual type of Conservative speech, "Ready, aye, ready," and criticized the government for taking so long to get to the issue, indicating that they should have declared war without bothering to call Parliament. Mr. Coldwell made the statement for our group, and then Mr. Woodsworth rose. In one of the most moving scenes in Parliament, just before he rose to his feet, Mr. King asked for permission to say a word.[1] He said that in view of the fact that Mr. Coldwell had spoken, he took it for granted that Mr. Woodsworth was going to take a position different from the rest of the House. He hoped there would be no untoward demonstration, nothing said of an unkind nature, because Mr. Woodsworth had been the conscience of the Canadian Parliament for a quarter of a century; men of his calibre were an ornament to any Parliament and he hoped Mr. Woodsworth would be listened to accordingly. It was a magnanimous tribute from a political opponent, and showed us the depth of Mackenzie King's character in a time of great crisis.

When Mr. Woodsworth rose to speak,[2] few people knew his physical condition. I moved down to sit beside him. Normally this seat was occupied by H.H. Stevens, who had left the Conservative party to become the Reconstruction party leader.[3]

His wife had written out his notes with a crayon in great big letters, an inch or two inches high. He had several sheets of these notes, each with just a few words to remind him of what he was going to say. He could hardly see them, and I passed them up to him one by one. I never admired him more than I did that day.

He made his great declaration of faith, that some day men would learn to settle their differences without resorting to force, and that in the long run, end determines means. When we take the wrong end, this destroys the means, and when we take the wrong means, this destroys the end that we have in view. While we might think we were fighting to preserve democracy, the fact that we were now going to engage in wholesale butchery would destroy the very democracy that we were seeking to preserve.

It was a fine speech. When he first started, two or three Conservative members shouted, "Shame." I knew one or two of the men who were shouting. They had never seen a shot fired in anger in their lives, had never taken a stand for any unpopular issue, and were completely incapable of understanding a man like Mr. Woodsworth.

But in the main, the House gave him a most respectful hearing, and when he sat down I'm sure there was hardly a member in the House who didn't admire him, even though they recognized that his position just wasn't practicable in a world where the horrible Nazi philosophy was slowly creeping over Europe. We felt that if Hitler had triumphed in Europe, we would have had the black night of barbarism for centuries to come. Hitler had to be stopped even though it meant war and the loss of life.

So we supported the war. I didn't speak in that particular debate; only Mr. Coldwell and Mr. Woodsworth spoke, But I did take part in a subsequent debate, which I think had great significance. At the previous session in 1939, Mr. Howe brought in a bill for a Defence Supply Department to prepare munitions of war. I introduced an amendment to provide that no company manufacturing armaments for the Government of Canada should be allowed a profit of more than five percent. Mr. Howe accepted, and this amendment was in the act.

After we declared war against Nazi Germany, we started the task of prosecuting the war. On the Saturday night we went into committee of the whole for fifteen minutes, and in that time we created through the Bank of Canada fifteen hundred million dollars to prosecute the war. This took me back to the days in 1936, '37, and '38, when we had introduced motion after motion asking the government to issue money for the work and wages programme, and had asked for the trifling sum of five hundred million dollars. Mr. Dunning, Minister of Finance, had looked across at me and said, "I'd like to tell my young friend that money doesn't grow on gooseberry bushes." I now had the satisfaction of watching Mr. Dunning find the gooseberry bush.

When we came to the defence production act, Mr. Howe now wanted to take out the five-percent profit limitation clause. I asked why, and Howe, who was no parliamentarian, but a blunt, forthright business man, said, "I have done everything in my power. I have appealed to the patriotism of the manufacturers, I have used every form of persuasion of which I'm capable, and they have refused to produce the instruments of war unless we remove the five-percent profit limitation clause." This to me is what people have lost sight of, and I tried again and again throughout the war to draw people's attention to it: when we were wailing about men not wanting to go to war, and having to be conscripted and forced into the army, we had a strike by the arms manufacturers who wouldn't be held to a five-percent profit margin.

When we began the 1940 session, Mr. King brought in the well-known national resources mobilization bill. It was very carefully drafted, and allowed the government to conscript manpower for home defence or overseas service on any basis it chose; it gave them power to conscript wealth, industry, and labour, clerical, and managerial services of any type. It was a good bill in words, but it was pure window-dressing because it didn't say that this was mandatory; also, the government could conscript in one area or a few areas and not in others as it pleased. We had quite a debate on it.

I had been called back to join my unit, and I was leaving the next day to go under canvas with the Second Battalion of the South Saskatchewan Regiment, so there was a good deal of interest in the House of Commons as to what position I would take. Some of the government members and Mr. King thought that there wasn't any doubt that I would support the bill. But as far as I knew, I might not be back in the House of Commons, because my regiment might be going overseas.

I opposed the bill. I would have been perfectly prepared to support the legislation if it said that the government was now going to conscript manpower, wealth, war industries, and managerial capacity on a mandatory basis. Because the bill simply gave cabinet the power to conscript whatever it wanted, it was perfectly apparent to me that what would be conscripted would be manpower. I had no objection to conscription of manpower; this was the fairest way in which to select manpower. But I would not vote for the bill unless the government conscripted manpower at the same time they invoked the other sections of the bill. If they left wealth in the hands of private individuals, and left arms manufacturers the right to make profits without the five-percent limitation clause, I wasn't having any part of the bill whatsoever.

Most of the C.C.F. group voted against it. One or two French-Canadian members voted against it, too. We were subjected to a good deal of criticism because the public very easily fell for the window-dressing. Because the bill said it covered conscription of all forms of wealth, manpower, and services, they thought that this would be conscripted. But subsequent events proved that our demands were justified. Only conscription of manpower was invoked; the other parts of the bill were never exercised.

> This was your first session as a young parliamentarian. Did Mr. Woodsworth have any advice for you at the time?

Mr. Woodsworth was a very complex person. Biographers[4] tend to stress his gentleness, but he was also very firm. He had the complexity of a Methodist minister. Strict with his family, but not tyrannical, strict with himself, he was quite a disciplinarian, but nevertheless very kindly. When I went to Parliament after I'd made my first speech, he took me up to the Hansard room to show me how to check my speech and make sure the quotations were correct and so on.

He advised me to make my first speech fairly early in the debate. He said, "Don't wait for months until you get such cold feet you never have the nerve to try it. And after you've made your first speech, don't get in too often until you know what you're talking about. Take time to find out how the House is run. The important thing is to gain the ear of the House. A lot of men make speeches almost every other day, but nobody listens to them, partly because they don't know what they're talking about, and partly because their material isn't well prepared. Once you have the ear of the House, then you can speak on almost anything that comes up and you'll get a hearing."

His advice was very useful to me throughout the years. As he got older and we got to know him better, he would take a little time out to talk. In the first years, he was so busy that he would read the newspaper standing up so he wouldn't waste any time. He only allowed himself so many minutes to read a newspaper. He wouldn't waste time reading a lot of nonsense. He was always working.

But after he'd been there a few years, and especially after that first stroke, he'd go back over some of his experiences and give you the benefit of his advice. He was the kind of person who drove himself very hard.

You might be interested in the winter election of 1940. Only a few of us knew that he'd had this stroke, and we decided to try to keep him out of the 1940 election. We passed the word around to various provincial offices that he would not be available as a speaker, he was going to confine himself mostly to his own constituency, and do a little radio speaking. Otherwise he wouldn't be available. Because we couldn't tell them the reason, some people thought that the office was being merely arbitrary and went to him directly to ask if he would come to a big meeting in Massey Hall, which he gladly agreed to do. When we found out, we got in touch with the Ontario people and finally explained that he'd had this stroke, and we were very concerned about his health.

They felt sorry about it, but they couldn't cancel. They did the next best thing. They got him a compartment on the train, so he could sleep in bed all the way down to Ontario, and all the way back to Winnipeg. He accepted. He addressed the meeting, had a great time, and after he got back to Winnipeg the railway sent the Ontario people a cheque for the money for the compartment. He had turned the compartment ticket in, and had travelled there and back on the day coach with a little box lunch his wife had put up for him, so that he wouldn't cause any unnecessary expenditures by going to the dining room or using the compartment. I was a little cross when I spoke with him about it. He said, "Tommy, I just couldn't travel in a compartment thinking of all the people who are hungry and homeless, and all the people who don't enjoy that kind of luxury. It would just be against my conscience."

That dramatic debate in the special session of 1939 was probably his last major public appearance. When we came back to the regular session in 1940, after the election of 26 March, he reappeared in the House, but had had another stroke in the meantime. From then on he was in and out of the House, most of the time in bed. My wife and I called on him toward the very end of his life, and he was still courageous. We'd just won a by-election in

Toronto.[5] He said to me, "I haven't got very long, but it will be up to you people to carry on, and remember that time is on our side, and that the things we've worked for and struggled for are bound to come to pass."

That was the last time I saw him. He was so ill that he had to stay in a roomette on the train out to the Coast. On the way, he stopped in Winnipeg. Stan Knowles met him at the station, and Woodsworth told some of the Winnipeg people he hoped Knowles would consent to run in Winnipeg North-Centre. When he got to the Coast, he died there, and his ashes were scattered over the Pacific Coast he loved so well.

He had been a missionary there.

Yes, at Gibsons Landing, where he'd spent some of the happiest years of his life. After he was kicked out of the church in the First World War for his stand as a conscientious objector, he worked as a long-shoreman. Here was a preacher looking for work, quite a frail man, who weighed about 135 pounds and stood about 5 feet 7 inches. He wasn't a very robust character to be a stevedore. But he got the job because he knew Harold Winch's father, old Ernie Winch, who was president of the stevedores' union. When the flu broke out, he nursed a lot of people at night, and worked all day. He always kept the hook that he used for lifting the bags of sugar hanging in his office. [Harold Edward Winch came to Vancouver from England in 1910 when he was three years old and later became an electrician in Vancouver. He was an organizer of the C.C.F. in British Columbia and was the provincial leader from 1938 to 1953. First elected to the House of Commons in 1953, he was re-elected in 1957, 1958, 1962, 1963, and 1965.] Woodsworth stayed there for months, and later became secretary of the long-shoremen's union.

Memorial services were held for him all across the country. I came all the way from Ottawa to take a memorial service for him at Westminster United Church in Regina. It was packed with friends of his from all over. It was the end of a great Canadian, whose influence will undoubtedly live long after many of the men who sat on the treasury benches have been forgotten.

◻ Another important event was the Hong Kong inquiry. You had a personal interest in the Hong Kong disaster because you lost comrades there. Could you talk about your own military service?

My part in the military service was exceedingly small. When war was declared, the First Battalion South Saskatchewan Regiment was formed. I tried to get into that without success. It was filled up quickly with younger men; I was about thirty-five years of age. I managed to get into the Second Battalion, which was a training group for the First Battalion. The commanding officer was Colonel Hart, now a lawyer practicing at Oxbow, Saskatchewan, a very good leader.

I went through the officers' training courses and became a corporal, then a second lieutenant, then first lieutenant, and later reached the rank of captain.

Some of our officers were forwarded to replace men in the First Battalion, some were forwarded to other regiments, and others were taken out as training officers. I was used as a training officer at Weyburn, where we had a winter training camp.

Then the word came that they were looking for officers to go to the Winnipeg Grenadiers. We didn't know that the Winnipeg Grenadiers were on their way to Hong Kong. Practically all of our group volunteered to go, and six were selected. When we got to Winnipeg, I was held back. The Weyburn doctor and the Regina doctor passed me with some reluctance, but the Winnipeg doctor turned me down. Although I'd had a bad history with my leg, at this time it wasn't bothering me.

You were able to do route marches?

I did all kinds of route marches. My buddy, one of my platoon commanders, was Blake Harper from Weyburn. He and I were very good friends, and being about the same age, we knocked around and had done a little hunting together when we lived in Weyburn. He was the manager of a wholesale grocery. Often after a half day's work, he just couldn't take an afternoon of marching. I'd put him in the quartermaster's stores lining up equipment for the next day, and I'd take his platoon out.

Ironically, he was accepted, and I was turned down. I was disappointed at the time. Looking back on it now, I can see that I would have spent the rest of the war in a Japanese prison camp, like the rest of these fellows. Harper got killed in Hong Kong.

The Hong Kong incident caused a terrific furore,[6] and was the topic of one of the major speeches I made in Parliament.[7] The information we dug up was most damning.

> Where did you find this information? In the committee or in the House?

From getting in touch with men in the services. We saw the officers who went from our own battalion to the Winnipeg Grenadiers and came back on leave. We knew what training they'd had. In the Winnipeg Grenadiers, some of the companies had fired thirty rounds on the rifle range; some hadn't even done that. None of them had ever handled a mortar, and only about a third of the companies had handled a Bren gun.

We also knew that when they were sent, they went on a troop ship doing about sixteen knots an hour, and all their equipment, Bren gun carriers, mortars, mortar ammunition, was put on a freighter travelling eight knots an hour. Of course, it never did get to them. The freighter was captured by the Japanese. So these men went into action without any training and without any equipment. Here were men with rifles, no mortars, no knowledge how to handle them if they had them, going into action against seasoned, trained Japanese troops. It was just a little short of murder.

> After you debated this in the House, there was an inquiry.

We'd been pressing for a debate for many days, and for various reasons the government tried to put if off. Finally, I got a motion, and the debate was to take place on a Monday at three o'clock. On Monday morning I got a call from the prime minister's office asking if I would come over to see him. I told the secretary that I didn't make a practice of going to the prime minister's office without someone accompanying me and so Mr. Coldwell and I went.

The prime minister brought out all the bulletins and the cablegrams he had received from the British War Office and from British Intelligence. I think the prime minister believed what they said: that troops required for Hong Kong would be garrison troops, with no prospect whatsoever of their being in combat, that an outbreak of war with Japan was a very remote possibility, and that everything indicated the Japanese had no intention of starting war. Therefore semi-trained troops would be fine, and could be trained while they were waiting in Hong Kong. He'd accepted this in good faith, and had allowed these untrained, ill-equipped troops to leave for Hong Kong.

Then Pearl Harbour was bombed on 7 December, and Hong Kong was captured on Christmas Day, 1941. This debate was during the session of 1942, a couple of months later.

The prime minister said, "This is going to be very embarrassing if I have to get up in the House and tell you that we acted on the report of British Intelligence. This will destroy public confidence in British Naval Intelligence, who gave us most of this information, and the British Foreign Office, and yet I don't see how I can do otherwise. If you press this debate, I've either got to keep silent, or I've got to betray the fact that the British were completely misinformed on this whole international situation." I said, "Mr. Prime Minister, this is a decision you have to make. You have to decide whether you want to be a bomb-proof shelter for the British Foreign Office and the British War Office. As far as I'm concerned, all I know as a Member of Parliament is that constituents of mine were sent out to take part in a war ill-trained, ill-prepared, and ill-equipped, and it's my duty to request that the matter be fully investigated. Those who are responsible must be properly punished so that this doesn't happen again."

So the debate went on. But here was an example of behind-the-scenes pressure to prevent investigations during the war on the grounds that you were doing a disservice to your country and were giving comfort to the enemy.

> You didn't make a practice of going to the prime minister without having someone with you. Is that common among opposition parties when they're in discussion with premiers and prime ministers?

Usually when the prime minister at the beginning of the session, for instance, wants to discuss the business of the session, he would ask the leaders of each of the groups to meet him and to bring their whips with them in order that there might be no misunderstanding. You made sure you were always safe with Mr. King; you always took somebody with you.

> If there weren't reliable witnesses around, there might have been confusion. Do opposition parties generally follow that practice?

Oh, yes. It's not customary to ask a private member in to see the prime minister. The proper procedure would have been to talk to Mr. Coldwell. I think Mr. King thought I would be tremendously impressed to see all these private dispatches, and that I would immediately agree to withdraw the motion.

> It's always puzzled me that an opposition member is sometimes shown correspondence of that description, but it doesn't deter them from bringing it up in the House. They want the information to be public.

It's very bad actually, to agree to be shown anything in confidence, unless you make it clear beforehand that you'll not allow this to tie your hands.

Following the debate, Mr. King decided that it would be best to have a Royal Commission investigate the Hong Kong affair. He didn't want another Bren gun inquiry before a parliamentary committee. I agree that this was probably the best course to take. Parliamentary committees seldom, if ever, settle anything, because the members divide on party lines in most cases. So a Royal Commission was set up headed by Sir Lyman Duff, the Chief Justice of Canada.

Mr. George Drew, who had made a great many charges in printed articles, was again a witness. I was called as a witness because of statements I made, but I had no military information to give them. All I could tell was my conversations with some of the officers of the Winnipeg Grenadiers, who told me about their training. It was subsequently proven from the training records, which the Chief Justice demanded from the army, that the amount of training was exactly as had been related to me by the officers themselves.

> When you appeared before this committee, did you still hold a commission in the army?

Yes, I held my commission in the militia, which I still hold today.

> This didn't inhibit you in any way?

To some extent. I had to be quite careful not to use any inside information that I had as a training officer for political purposes. I had to be much more careful than if I'd been an outside observer. The Chief Justice asked why I wanted to give this evidence, and I said, "I have only one object — not to embarrass the government or make any personal political gain — I knew these men. I knew from personal conversation with them how unprepared they were when they left, and I thought the country had a right to know." The military authorities who were responsible certainly ought to have been disciplined.

> Was the Duff Commission open?

Only parts of it were.

> Very little evidence was ever allowed out.

Yes, because in some cases they gave information about kinds of equipment, training programmes, and training syllabuses. Most of it was done *in camera*.

> Did you come under fire for taking the attitudes you did?

Oh, yes. Both in this and in the Dieppe affair, there were a good many people who took the position you often get during wartime: we're at war, so you mustn't criticize the government and the commander-in-chief. I thought that if we had inefficiency and incompetency, it's little comfort to the enemy to tell them about it — they already know it. It is much better for the public to know, and to replace inefficient people with competent people. The shake-up in army command after Hong Kong was very considerable.

> You've always subscribed to the theory that wars are too serious to leave to generals.

It's almost incomprehensible now that you could send out men, who had little else than week-end training, to an empire outpost four or five thousand miles away without knowing that, even if there was no immediate prospect of war, there was always the possibility. We had thousands of trained men, both in Britain and here, who could have been sent instead.

You just mentioned another milestone, or landmark, the question of Dieppe.[8] You'd have quite a sympathy for and an understanding of this because the South Saskatchewan Regiment was involved. There was an inquiry into Dieppe in the Commons.

That's right. I raised the matter in the House of Commons, and precipitated the debate on the whole thing, and Colonel Ralston defended the action. I didn't get too much support in the House. Even the Conservatives, who were usually prepared to back a good issue against the government, thought this was a good thing to leave alone. After all, it had been approved by the commander-in-chief, General McNaughton, by Montgomery, and all the other commanders of the British and allied forces.

Where is the genesis of your interest, apart from the South Saskatchewan Regiment? Where did you get your information about Dieppe on which you based your attack?

There were many reports available by way of letters from men who had taken part in it, conversations with officers who'd been sent back to carry on a training programme, a few odd disconnected press reports[9] you could piece together, and some statements by Mr. Churchill and various people who tried to justify it. When you put them together, you saw that they contradicted each other. So it looked like something to ask questions about. We started with some queries on Mr. Ralston's estimates, and then promoted a full-scale debate.

Did Mr. Ralston try to prevent any debate on this?

He wasn't keen about the debate. Here was the question that automatically came to one's mind: What was the purpose of what happened at Dieppe? It was certainly apparent that it was no attempt at a landing, because all plans were made before it was started to bring them off the mainland and to bring them back to England. So what was it? It wasn't a commando raid, because it involved thousands of men, so later it was designated as a reconnaissance in force. What were they trying to do? This is the one thing we wanted to know.

Secondly, if it was a reconnaissance in force, why wasn't it more successful? None of our tanks got off the beach. Mr. Churchill hastened to tell the British House of Commons that the sea-wall was not demolished with block-busters, as it was supposed to have been, for some reason he didn't explain. The air raid and the naval bombardment were called off at the last minute.[10]

I had visited Dieppe back in '36 and later in '45, and went over this battleground with Colonel Allan Chambers, formerly a Liberal Member of Parliament in Ottawa, and then the military attaché to the Canadian High Commissioner in London. This sea-wall was six or eight to ten feet high, and in some places twelve feet high. The plan was that with a naval bombardment and by dropping block-busters, this was to be completely demolished. Why wasn't it demolished? Knowing that it wasn't, why were fifty tanks landed on the beach to lie there and be blown to bits? There are many of them still lying there, deep in the sand, every man in them killed. Why were none of the artillery placements demolished? Why had the air raid and the naval bombardment been called off?

The story was that the weather was unsuitable. Then why wasn't it postponed? The answer we were given was that they had postponed three times and the men were getting out of hand, so they had to go ahead with it. But you don't go ahead just because men are a little impatient for action, when you know perfectly well that the first part of the plan, demolishing of the artillery placements and removing the sea-wall, hadn't been completed. Who ever gave the order to proceed with landing infantry in the face of this fire?

In '45 I went through the German fortifications, which still stand there. Pourville, where the South Saskatchewan Regiment landed, is a very good illustration of the whole situation. It's a crescent-shaped beach with a huge headland at each tip of the crescent. That whole headland of solid rock had been honey-combed by the Germans with corridors, artillery, and heavy machine-guns with their distances pegged so that they knew the exact range for every spot on the beach, and with cross-fire so that they could make sure that nothing lived on that beach for more than two or three minutes. Nothing or no one could get off the beach except by climbing over the sea-wall. The only hope was to get in close to the sea-wall and lie down where you might have some protection, but for a tank even this was hopeless because they couldn't get through the sand.

The marvel is that anybody lived at all. That we lost all our tanks and a third of our personnel is quite understandable.

I think most military authorities now agree that it was a terribly mismanaged affair. It showed what the German reaction was; they immediately began to move up armour. But any military strategist would have known they would move up armour. It showed that the German fortifications were well manned and alert. But apart from this, it 's very dubious as to what lessons we learned. You can't land armour and troops unless you had a saturation bombardment from the air and the sea — this anybody would have known without Dieppe.

> Then you went into the debate. What was the government's defence?

Mr. King was always defending and protecting the British War Office. Ralston, who was a pretty blunt type of individual when we were pressing him back step by step, finally slipped open a manila folder, which I noticed he had on his desk all day, and said, "If you really want the information on this, let me read." Mr. King got hold of his coat-tails and pulled him down. We were quite convinced that he was prepared to read some of the dispatches. I don't think Ralston was at all happy about the entire thing. I doubt if General McNaughton was too happy about it. I think this was the brainwave of somebody higher up. Mountbatten, who was in charge of commando operations, has been suggested;

it was somebody who wanted a certain type of information, or wanted to try a certain type of military manoevre.

Was there any sequel to the debate?

No, except that Ralston assured us that the Canadian government would be kept more closely informed regarding the use of Canadian troops on major operations of this sort. A struggle was going on behind the scenes; McNaughton was losing command of his own troops. When he wanted to land in Italy to have a look at his troops, Montgomery told him that if he landed, he would be arrested. This is the battle every Canadian government has had. In the First World War, Borden constantly had to fight to keep Canadian troops under the command of Sir Arthur Curry. In the last war we had the same problem keeping the troops under the command of General McNaughton. They were taken from him completely, and I doubt if he knew anything about the use to which they were being put.

5

Provincial leader

◻ What were the circumstances that led to your selection as provincial leader of the C.C.F. in Saskatchewan? Was there any friction in the party during those years that you can recall?

No, there was no overt friction. There's always been a coolness between Mr. Coldwell and Mr. Williams, and so when Mr. Williams was elected House leader, Coldwell, who was provincial leader, made way for him. Williams became the provincial leader as well as being House leader, and Coldwell went to Ottawa. They were operating in different spheres, and the misunderstandings cleared up.[1] Mr. Coldwell became national secretary of the C.C.F. when Williams was provincial leader here in Saskatchewan.

Then there was a provincial election in 1938. That was a terrible schemozzle from our standpoint. George Williams got the idea that the government would be almost impossible to defeat, and that to prevent the C.C.F. from being annihilated, he should enter into an arrangement with the Conservatives and the Social Crediters to saw off seats. The result was that we only ran thirty-one candidates.

Consequently our total vote fell from about 105,000 in 1934 to about 83,000 votes in 1938. We went up from five seats in 1934 to ten seats in 1938, but our popular vote had dropped. To some extent, I think our prestige dropped because of these deals. I know there were constituencies where people who had fought hard in the C.C.F. were being asked by the C.C.F. to vote for a Tory or a Social Credit candidate. This went against the grain, so some of them voted Liberal because they had voted Liberal before.

> That was Mr. Williams's idea.

Maybe I shouldn't put the blame on him. It was the provincial executives' idea; I assume that as provincial leader, he probably was the main instigator.

> I think the C.C.F. reached a crisis when they realized the voters weren't altogether rational people, that they were looking for immediate gains. That was Mr. Williams's idea. I think that's why Mr. Woodsworth and Mr. Cold-well were so strongly opposed to any affiliation of that kind.

It was a disastrous move, because you remember that the Liberals came out with great big posters saying, "Are you going to vote for a mulligan stew?" and had pictures of these three or four parties all trying. People are always suspicious of a government made up of bits and pieces.

> Did Mr. Williams cause any antagonism toward himself among members of the party?

I don't think so. It caused a bit of friction between the federal men in Ottawa and the provincial people here in Saskatchewan. But Mr. Williams had the provincial people behind him in this policy. Certainly the members of the legislature executive supported him.

It was never attempted again though, was it?

No.

You were not involved in that discussion?

No. I wasn't on either the provincial council or the provincial executive. I was national president of the C.C.Y.M., the youth movement, and I was going across Canada trying to get youth groups going.

I suppose you were more or less regarded as a young man in the party. They were all older than you.

That's true. Also, I was devoting two or three months to my own constituency. I used to spend a day in each poll, writing letters for people, dealing with their problems, holding a meeting at night, and visiting among people during the day. In addition, there had been that coolness between Mr. Williams and Mr. Coldwell, and I was very close to Mr. Coldwell. I was looked on with a little bit of suspicion as being Coldwell's man.

When did you enter the provincial picture?

Not until about 1940 or 1941, when I was literally dragged into it because the organization was failing here so badly. We dropped to the lowest membership we'd had for years, and after Mr. Williams went overseas the whole organization seemed to go dormant.

Where was the convention held?

In Saskatoon.

By this time Mr. Williams was out of the picture but did he not more or less endorse or ask the convention to endorse another person? Also, was Mr. Williams at odds with other members of the party on the issue of con-scription at that time?

No, there was no difference of opinion between George Williams and the rest of the group on the question of conscription. All of the party had taken the same line[2] at the outbreak of the war, with the exception of Mr. Woodsworth. Mr. Williams, along with Mr. Coldwell, Angus MacInnis, myself, and others at the council meeting prior to the declaration of war, were unanimous on that question. When it came to the matter of conscription, Mr. Williams took the same position as the rest of us, namely that any conscription of manpower should be accompanied by a conscription of wealth.

Soon after war was declared Mr. Williams and myself both joined the militia. I was with the Second Battalion, South Saskatchewan Regiment, and Mr. Williams with the Twenty-second Light Horse Regiment commanded by Colonel Van Allan. He was allowed to go overseas with them as a quartermaster. He had a bad ankle from the First World War, so he couldn't go as a combat officer. I was still in the House of Commons, although spending a good deal of time in training with the militia as a training officer. There was a general feeling, with the Saskatchewan leader absent, that it was necessary to take fairly aggressive measures to pick up the party's fortunes. In '41 at the leadership convention, we had to decide whether or not Mr. Williams was going to continue to lead the party in the event of an election *in absentia*, or whether someone else would lead the party.

I was selected both as provincial president and provincial leader. Mr. Williams was overseas with the Twenty-second Regiment.

Mr. Brockelbank was also a nominee, was he not?

My recollection is that he was nominated, but instead he withdrew and nominated Mr. Williams. The contest was between myself, and Mr. Williams *in absentia*.[3]

Did you hear from Mr. Williams after the convention?

Yes, we carried on considerable correspondence all the time that he was overseas. When he was invalided home because of a heart attack, I urged him to run in his home constituency of Wadena. He got back in time for the election of 1944. When selecting a cabinet I gave him the choice of any portfolio he wanted, and so he became the Minister of Agriculture in the first C.C.F. government.

So far as you and Mr. Williams were concerned, there was no bad blood, was there?

No, he and I had no personal animosity toward one another.

> When you assumed the leadership, the C.C.F. gained
> confidence. Did you notice any trends? Did you have any
> indication that they might win in 1944?

When I agreed to accept the leadership in the province, it was
with a good deal of hesitancy. In 1939, before the outbreak of war,
I had already discussed with my constituency executive the possibility of their releasing me, and not running in the next federal
election. I had already made some tentative arrangements to go
back to university and finish my Ph.D. The war changed my
plans, and when I couldn't go overseas, the question of coming
back to the province was raised. I wasn't keen about it. My
interest at that time was mainly in federal matters, international
affairs, and national programmes. I came back because of a good
deal of pressure mostly from farmers and people whom I knew
very well, who said, "It's going to be a long time before we can ever
form a federal government, but there are things you could do
here provincially to give us a certain amount of protection, particularly to farmers who were losing their farms, and also in the area
of basic health and welfare, and educational reforms. You owe it
to the movement to come back into the provincial field and try to
pull things together."

It would be honest, looking back on it now, to say I didn't
think there was any prospect of forming a government at the next
election when I accepted the leadership. But I thought it might
be possible to give the movement a shot in the arm and to see it
through the next election.

However, as the campaign continued, the prospects continued to brighten. The Liberals made a very serious mistake in
postponing the election. If they'd had the election in 1942, which
would have been the logical time, they'd probably have been
returned. It antagonized the public. Second, it gave us another
year in which to perfect an organization that by this time was
becoming quite active and fairly efficient.

> It has been suggested that you were able to unite the fac-
> tions and bring an end to the petty warfare that was going
> on within the ranks. In other words, unity grew after that.

I think that is true. I felt that the little coldness between the two groups who seemed to be fighting about nothing else except personal jealousies had been holding us back. The second problem was that it had been a one-man show, and we had a lot of capable people who hadn't been given an opportunity to do a first-class job.

> By a one-man show, sir, what do you mean?

Mr. Williams had largely kept the control of the party and all the different jobs in his own hands. He was provincial leader, provincial organizer, and in charge of publicity. He did all the work himself. No matter how capable a man is, even Williams, who was a first-class organizer and had a very keen mind, no one man can do all these jobs.

One of the first things I did when I became provincial president was to set up a shadow cabinet. Each member of the executive became in charge of a committee: finance, organization, political education, publicity, and youth activity. Mr. Fines, who was vice-president, was in charge of office administration and general efficiency of the organization. I said, "I don't propose to be tied up with all these day-to-day matters, I want to be free to do two things. One, I still have to carry on my duties as a Member of Parliament, and the moment I'm free from that, I want to go out into the country and set the heather on fire."

When I became provincial leader I carried the same principle, and set up a shadow cabinet of elected members. I set up committees with at least one Member of the Legislature as chairman, and maybe one or two other members, but also some outsiders, so that there would be a committee on development of natural resources. Mr. Joe Phelps was chairman of that committee, and later became Minister of Resources. Mr. O.W. Valleau was chairman of a committee on welfare programmes, and later became Minister of Social Welfare. Mr. Brockelbank, who was the leader of the opposition, was also in charge of agriculture and municipal government, and later became Minister of Municipal Affairs. Mr. Fines headed a committee on the financial problems, and later became Provincial Treasurer. Mr. Lloyd, who at that time was secretary of the Teachers' Federation, became chairman of the committee on education along with Dr. Carlyle King of the university, and Mr. Lloyd later became Minister of Education. There was no promise that if they headed a committee they would some day become cabinet ministers, but about half of them did. It was a good way to test them, and also a good way to give them a little responsibility. When they found they were being given a free hand, they worked hard.

I did the same thing with the M.L.A.s. I divided the province into small groups of constituencies, and got M.L.A.s to look after that particular group of constituencies. If possible, the group of constituencies would include their own, but in some cases a man like Mr. Peter Howe, who was the member for Kelvington, was given three constituencies in the southwest corner of the province a long way from where he lived. We had no sitting M.L.A. there, and he took over these three constituencies, nursed them along, and we won all three of them in the subsequent election.

This way we got a lot of people working, which is the secret of any successful campaign or organization. I think there were two reasons why we managed to pull things together. The first was that I personally had no enemies, really, and I was able to deal with everybody on a friendly basis. Second, I refused to carry any old enmities into the reorganization. I was criticized by some of my friends for taking some of Mr. Williams's supporters and Mr. Williams himself into the cabinet. I was seeking people who had ability, who could serve the C.C.F. movement and the people of the province, and it made little or no difference to me whether they'd been one of Mr. Williams's friends, or one of Mr. Coldwell's friends. My main job was to get everybody working together, pointing out that the party was like a symphony orchestra; my part was to beat the time and keep everybody playing on the same score.

This unity seems to have carried through to today in 1958, has it not? There's never been a major break.

We've never had a major break, but there have been people like Mr. Jake Benson who left us. He was one of the people who felt that because he had been a very loyal supporter of Mr. Coldwell and a bitter enemy of Mr. Williams, that he should immediately be eligible for a cabinet post. Instead, I felt that he must be measured in terms of his ability and the contribution he had made to the movement.

An election was called in Saskatchewan, so you put in your resignation from the House, which was read by the Speaker in the usual way on 1 June 1944. You came back to Saskatchewan feeling fit and confident. In Ottawa you used to spend some of your time in the Y.M.C.A., and you were always physically fit or at least appeared to be. I met you just as you were leaving, and you told me you'd never felt better in your life, and that you were pretty confident you were going to lick the Liberals. What grounds did you have for that statement?

It was mainly the reaction I'd found as I'd gone across the country. When I became provincial leader, and organized the work so that the M.L.A.s were chairmen of committees, preparing programmes and policies, this left me feeling comparatively free. When Parliament wasn't sitting and when I wasn't in the military training camp, I would go out and campaign in the country.[4] I found quite a change of sentiment, probably because of the 1942 and '43 treks to Ottawa to get the dollar a bushel for wheat and the disappointment of the farmers when they got only ninety cents.

The growing realization was that the Liberal party, who had talked so much about doing something for them, had let them down badly. Also, the Liberal government in Saskatchewan had become almost completely static. There were no new programmes. It was true that during the war, there was some difficulty in handling programmes, but there was no sign of any awareness that these programmes were even possible. Some of the cabinet ministers were getting quite old, and there was no sign of new blood coming in or even any planning for what would happen when the war was over. By 1944, the end of the war was only a year or so away.

Was it also a case of reaping the whirlwind?

That's true. In 1938, for instance, when the Liberals won the provincial election, there was a good deal of pressure on the voters from relief officers. My own constituency elected a Liberal M.L.A. even though I was sitting in the federal House. All the provincial ridings in my federal riding were won by the Liberals, and the C.C.F. suffered a very major setback.

The Liberal machine was well known. Mr. Gardiner built it up first when he was Minister of Highways in the Dunning government. It's a well-known fact that Mr. Dunning had intended his mantle to fall on Mr. Hamilton, who was his Minister of Agriculture, and the member for Weyburn. Mr. Hamilton went to the convention expecting to come out as leader of the Liberal party and premier of the province, but when the dust had cleared away, Mr. Gardiner and his well-organized and well-oiled machine had captured the convention. That was when the term "the highwaymen" was coined to describe Mr. Gardiner and his highway inspectors.

From the time Mr. Gardiner became leader of the Liberal party and premier of the province, he began building his system. It was described later by the man who is now Canadian Ambassador to India, Escott Reid, in the 1936 *Canadian Journal of Economics and Political Science*.[5] No one has ever successfully refuted the charges made in that article, a definitive work on the Gardiner machine. The fact that Mr. King kept Reid on in the Department of External Affairs despite the article indicates that no one seriously thought he was doing other than an objective political analysis.

The Gardiner machine continued even after Mr. Gardiner went to Ottawa. In 1938, it was well organized, had key men in every constituency, worked a great deal among municipal secretaries, reeves, councillors, and inspectors — highway inspectors, relief inspectors, and almost all government employees on the road as field men, who were part of the machine. In my area and in the rural areas, ninety percent of the people were on relief, and people were told very frankly that if this poll doesn't carry, their relief would be cut off, and as an added inducement, those who were willing to go out and campaign got an extra relief order. Everyone who lived through that time knew it.

In 1937, we had the worst drought in our history and in 1938 we were in very bad shape, because we had to get relief seed, relief feed, and enough food from the government to keep the average family going until the crop came off in the fall of 1938.

> Did that condition have an effect on people's attitudes in the 1944 election?

By the 1944 election, several things had happened. One, the Liberal party concentrated all its effort on this political machine, and was so confident that the machine would carry them through, that they had totally disregarded any attempt at a programme or progressive policy for after the war.

This would have been alright if the conditions of 1938 still existed. But in 1944, after five years of war, farmers were able to pay off their debts by raising hogs and cattle, for which there was a demand during the war. There were still a lot of unpaid mortgages, but the farmers were off relief and the economic conditions were slightly improved. Farm wives and dependent parents were getting army pay from those serving overseas. Economic conditions now made people less vulnerable to the type of political blackmail to which they had succumbed in the previous election.

> The Liberal party actually lacked organization, because it was controlled by the few who had axes to grind. It wasn't a democratic political organization. How did a person become a member of the C.C.F.? What is the policy?

C.C.F. memberships are open to any person who pays the small fee required, and signs a declaration that he is not a supporter of any other political party and that he will support the programme and policies of the C.C.F. as laid down by the democratically elected convention from time to time.

Each member is entitled to go to the poll meeting. The polls are entitled to send three delegates to a constituency convention. Constituency conventions are in complete control of the affairs of that constituency. They elect their own executive. The convention elects delegates, ten from each provincial constituency, and the provincial convention sets down the policy. Rather than the elected members or the candidates, the convention makes the policy, and elects the executive and the provincial council, which acts during the year when the convention is not sitting.

The council in turn elects some of the executive, but also a legislative advisory committee, which has two main functions. One is to confer with the political leader in the matter of selecting a cabinet, making changes in the cabinet, or in any matters of major importance of a political nature; it also sits in with the caucus when the caucus is preparing legislation, and reports back to the provincial council from time to time on what legislation has been discussed, and whether or not it agreed with the caucus on preparing that legislation. Prior to the legislature opening, we have made it a practice every year to have the provincial council meet and discuss with the provincial cabinet all the major legislation, particularly that which is likely to be controversial.

The annual convention also elects the political leader for a term of one year. Each year he must come back to the convention and give an account of his stewardship and seek re-election, whether he's in the opposition or leading the government.

> If he were rejected by that convention, even if he were a premier, he would be automatically dismissed from the leadership.

I've often said, I'm the only premier in Canada who must seek re-election once a year before my own supporters. Any time that the convention is dissatisfied with my conduct, or the conduct of my associates in the government, all they have to do is to nominate and elect someone else, whereby I would have no choice but to go to the lieutenant-governor, submit my resignation, ask my colleagues to allow the newly elected leader to form a government, and ask the lieutenant-governor to swear in the new government.

> Was this in effect in 1944?

Yes. Practically all our candidates had been elected at democratic conventions. Because an election had been anticipated as far back as 1942, some constituencies had held conventions and elected candidates. Because there was no great political activity in 1942, the conventions were poorly attended, and at least six or seven candidates elected ranged in age from seventy-one to seventy-eight. I had the very unpleasant task of suggesting to these men that since the election had been deferred, and in view of their age, they really ought to ask for another convention, submit their resignations, and permit an opportunity to select younger representatives.

> In the earlier days of the party, there was a principle of recall. Did that ever go into effect?

Yes. It was never laid down as part of our constitution, but among many of the conventions including my own, the principle of recall was in effect. When I was first nominated back in '34 and at each subsequent convention, I signed a resignation addressed to the Speaker of the House of Commons and later to the Speaker of the Legislative Assembly, and placed it in the hands of my executive with the written authority to submit to a democratic convention in my constituency. If the convention passed a resolution saying that I was no longer competent, the resignation would be forwarded to the Speaker.

It wasn't done all the time, and was a matter of individual choice, but I would say that great majority did it. [The recall had been a popular idea among reformers in the four western provinces from 1913 to 1923 and was associated with the initiative and the referendum of the Direct Legislation movement.[6] Saskatchewan was the first province where the government was induced to accept the initiative and the referendum principle, but the 1913 bill did not come into effect, and the recall was never the subject of legislation. In Alberta, some U.F.A. candidates in the early 1920s accepted the recall policy, but it was never enacted until the advent of Social Credit when a majority passed the legislation in 1936. But the act was repealed the following year when a petition to recall Aberhart was being organized in his constituency. In brief, the recall remained an informal voluntary arrangement between a candidate and his party organization.]

> Do you remember any incidents where recall was exercised?

No. The other agreement was that elected candidates would give a percentage of their indemnities to the movement each year. I think the percentage was ten percent in an election year and five percent in each of the years between elections.

> Can you remember any serious or humorous anecdotes about the campaign? When did you begin to feel that you had got the Liberals on the run?

The organization of the campaign was prepared before I left for Ottawa to attend the '44 session. Mr. C.M. Fines was the provincial president, and he would go to the office each day to help line up itineraries, supervise advertising, and so on. We had an advertising man. The campaign was ready to go the moment it was announced.

It was a fairly rough campaign because the Liberals had by this time begun to smell defeat in the air. Their attacks became almost frenzied. We had now ceased to be Communists, which we had been called in previous elections, because the Communists had become respectable. Several Liberal M.L.A.s attended a meeting with Tim Buck[7] of the Anglo-Soviet Friendship League at city hall. I was invited but refused to go. We were very angry with the Soviet Union over the murder of a couple of Polish Socialists. People were toasting Churchill, Roosevelt, and Stalin, and overnight we were classified as National Socialists and Nazis.

We, who for years had opposed Hitler when other people were saying he wasn't a bad fellow, were now classified as National Socialists. They made wild assertions that we were going to take farms, confiscate businesses, and drive all the industries out of the province. The attacks became more hysterical with every passing day, and in that sense it was a rough campaign.

There was tremendous interest in the campaign. We had big meetings. Our people in the country were working as they had never worked before, talking to their neighbours and friends, and canvassing house to house. As usual, we were fighting with very little money for advertising, broadcasts, or literature. But we made very good use of the small amount we had.

During this campaign I had my first debate with Walter Tucker[8] at Watrous in a rink filled with four or five thousand people. He was a Member of Parliament for Rosthern. The debate gave me an excellent opportunity to deal with some of these fantastic charges the Liberal party had been using. He very foolishly tried to use them on a public platform, where I could give my reply.

At that time, hadn't big business gotten a little wary?

Big business began to take some notice of us because of two or three events. First, we had won two out of three federal by-elections in succession, one in Toronto, and Humboldt in Saskatchewan. We elected Scotty (William) Bryce in Manitoba. And in Ontario we had become the official opposition, with over thirty members. This really shook Bay Street.

The Gallup poll broke down support for the three political parties on this basis: 29 percent for the C.C.F., 28 percent for the Liberals, and 27 percent for the Conservatives. This was the only time that the C.C.F. had any leg in the national Gallup Poll. So all across Canada we were being subjected to a stiff attack.

There was a lot of money poured into that attack.

Oh, yes. Here in Saskatchewan the mortgage companies and lending institutions openly took part in the 1944 election. In my own constituency, land agents for mortgage and trust companies were contacting debt-ridden farmers and telling them that terrible things would happen if they dared to elect a C.C.F. government.

You heard that they were going to take action even before you were elected, and you had to warn them that there'd be a good deal of trouble if they did.

That's right. They made a statement that if a C.C.F. government were elected, before we could pass any legislation, they would foreclose on several farmers' mortgages. In this event, we would take an emergency action by putting a blanket moratorium across the province in order to protect the farmers.

I don't think people realize how much security of land tenure was a factor in this election. Because of this feeling of apprehension, I promised that we would have farm security legislation on the statute books before the snow fell.

Did you have secretarial help during the campaign?

No. I wrote a lot of broadcasts at night until two or three o'clock in the morning in the hotels after a meeting was over. Then I would rush in and do a broadcast, and get on the road again. Many times I'd ride half the night, get a few hours sleep, write a broadcast, record it, and then get on the road. We were operating under the War Emergency Measures, which required that all radio speeches must first be submitted in manuscript form and passed by the censor either twenty-four or forty-eight hours before they were to be delivered. In previous elections, you could ad lib a speech, or finish writing it half an hour before and then go on and read it live, but during the war speeches had to be in ahead of time, which was a real hardship.

I had no private secretarial help but the secretaries at the C.C.F. provincial office would type my scribbled manuscripts at almost any hour of day or night.

Did you do any open air speeches?

Quite a few: picnics in the afternoon, and meetings in halls and rinks at night. I couldn't go out in the street and shake hands with people very much. The distances were so great. I'd have a picnic at Indian Head in the afternoon, and go to Yorkton for a meeting at night; there was no time to stop.

Did you get a rest during the day at all?

No, none at all and not too much sleep at night, because after finishing a meeting at eleven o'clock, I'd be invited to have a cup of coffee, shake hands with two or three hundred people, get to my hotel room at midnight, and attend to my broadcast speeches.

People would want to feed you at every place you went, and you had to make the gesture, I suppose.

This is the politician's heaviest cross. He needs sleep, not food, and everyone wants to feed him rather than let him sleep.

There was also an active newspaper campaign with full-page editorials. Some papers devoted the whole editorial page to attacks on the C.C.F. Did you regard that as a very good omen or not?

I thought it was a good sign. I still believe in the verse in the Bible that says: "Woe unto you, when all men shall speak well of you" [Luke 6:26]. The moment they start to tramp on your toes, it's apparent that you are giving them trouble.

It will show in our story that this continued for a long time afterward. It still hasn't died down.

It reached a crescendo in 1944. In the same year, Roosevelt was re-elected despite the fact that almost all the press in the United States was against him. We were elected here without a single friendly newspaper, and the following year in 1945, the British Labour government was elected while everyone confidently predicted that Churchill's government would be re-elected. This indicates to me that there is a time when newspaper editorials haven't very much effect on the public mind.

What kind of a day was Election Day, 15 June 1944?

It was a lovely, typical June day. We always watch Election Day with great anxiety, because our support lay then and still lies mainly in the rural poll. Small towns made up of the bank manager and the lawyer and one or two implement agents are usually on the other side. If the rural polls can't get out to vote, our vote is cut down. This is what happened in the winter election of 1940, when a blizzard swept across the province and the rural people couldn't get out. When the roads are really bad, the men will get out by walking or driving the tractor, but the women and the old people won't take a chance of being stranded on the road at night, cutting the rural vote in half.

On this day, we had one of the biggest votes in the history of the province.

Where were you?

I was at my own headquarters in Weyburn.

Did you have a home in Weyburn at that time?

Oh, yes. My wife and daughter, Shirley, were in Weyburn. Ever since Shirley was old enough to go to school, my wife and Shirley had made their home in a little cottage in Weyburn. When I went

Premier T.C. Douglas, daughter Shirley, and Mrs. Douglas at home in Weyburn the day after the 1944 election.

to Ottawa, I stayed at the Y.M.C.A. or boarded somewhere, and my wife came when she could to make a visit.

You probably had little sleep the night before.

I finished the campaign at Stoughton, and got back at one o'clock in the morning, but I was up early checking the polls. We visited the various polls in the constituency to make sure that our scrutineers were on the job, and in Weyburn to make sure that our organization was functioning.

Were you in the committee room that night when the results came in?

Actually, I was at home. I went home to wash up, shave, and have supper. The first returns were coming in while I was still at home, and they indicated a complete landslide for us. In the end, out of fifty-two seats, we won forty-seven.

> I suppose there was quite a celebration in Weyburn that night.

There was a parade and speeches and phone calls and wires, not only from all over the province but from all over Canada. Everyone was wildly enthusiastic.

> Did you leave Weyburn that night?

No. There wasn't much point in coming to Regina, because in those days it would have taken a couple of hours, and by that time the celebration here would have been over.

> What was your first step afterward?

The next morning, I called the provincial office in Regina to check on final figures, and see who had been elected; you can't always rely on newspaper and radio reports. Then I suggested to Mr. Fines that he contact Premier Patterson[9] to set up a meeting about taking over the government.

> What's the protocol?

At the meeting with the head of the retiring government, he indicates how much time he and his ministers need to wind up their affairs and clean out their files — there are always some personal letters in the files they are entitled to take out — so that things are left in reasonably good shape for the people succeeding them.

Then we make arrangements for the swearing in. We made sure that the lieutenant-governor would be on hand, and that the clerk of the executive council had the names of ministers to be sworn in, and for what portfolios.

> Was there any great evidence of bitterness after the election? Were the Liberals good losers?

I'd always like to say that they were, but some were not at all good losers. From my experience in sports, I'd always taken for granted that you chat with the fellow who had lost on a friendly basis, but it wasn't easy in this case. I remember meeting Dr. Urich and saying, "Have you got any suggestions for a man taking over the

Department of Public Health?" He said, "You made all the promises, you know all the answers — go ahead and see what you can
do." I said, "That is precisely what we intend to do, Doctor. I'll just
give you a tip that we plan to do more in the next four years than
you've done in the last twenty-five."

> In places like Ottawa it was a tremendous shock to some,
> although the people working in the campaign knew that
> the Liberals were going under. How long was it before
> you took over?

Mr. Patterson suggested that his government would need a considerable amount of time. The usual is a couple of weeks, but he
wanted about four weeks. It was his prerogative, so we agreed that
a cabinet would be ready to be sworn in on 10 July.

6

First months of office

☐ What was necessary for you to do after the victory?

First, I had to get some sleep. My wife and youngsters [besides Shirley, Douglas also had a younger daughter, Joan] and myself went to our little cottage at Carlyle Lake, and I spent about the next five days just sleeping and eating, and thinking about how we would go about setting up a government.

> How did you determine the members of your cabinet? Did you make this decision alone or with the help of advisory groups?

Before I left Regina to go to Carlyle Lake, I asked for a meeting of the legislative advisory committee, and then a meeting of all the elected members and members of the provincial executive.

Our constitution says that the provincial leader shall discuss with the legislative advisory committee the cabinet ministers he wishes to have serve under him, but that the final decision shall rest with him. In most cases I already had very definite recommendations to make for each portfolio, and the advisory committee were wholeheartedly in favour of the names I submitted to them. [The premier himself chose the public health portfolio, which he held from 1944 to 1949.]

> In the broadcast,[1] you mentioned that no one had been promised a cabinet post, nor had they been picked by any geographical division, but instead, for sheer ability.

I have always felt that if a man is appointed to administer a department, he is required to have a certain administrative ability, drive, and skill as a politician so that he can explain his programme, not only to his own constituency, but to all the people of the province.

Not only have I never promised anyone before an election that he'd be a cabinet minister, but I've never yet had anyone ask me before the election if he could be a cabinet minister.

> Is it true that Mr. Jacob Benson was offered the post of Speaker and turned it down?

Yes. When the caucus met following the meeting of the legislative advisory committee, the caucus members didn't know who the cabinet ministers were, and the first thing I said was that I was gong to add some new departments, the Department of Labour, the Department of Co-operatives, and the Department of Social Welfare. This would mean new ministers, although in other cases we would double up some departments. It meant a slight increase in cabinet ministers — one or two extra. It would mean increasing the amount of money for cabinet ministers' salaries, and if they thought it was necessary I would be willing to reduce cabinet ministers' salaries. They voted that we reduce the cabinet ministers' salaries from seven thousand to five thousand dollars. This way, the total amount paid for cabinet ministers' salaries would not be any greater than what the previous government paid. Since nobody knew who the cabinet ministers were to be, every person could vote without bias.

I'm not sure it was such a smart idea. I think we left some

Swearing-in ceremonies, 10 July 1944, in the Legislative Assembly Chamber. Seated to the right of Douglas is Lieutenant-Governor McNab. Standing and administering oaths is Chief Justice W.M. Martin.

ministers who had to move their families and buy houses in a tight financial position. But we took the position that they were primarily interested in serving, and that this is what they should be willing to do.

Then I told the caucus whom I had selected. Then Mr. Benson was suggested for Speaker, and he indicated that he wouldn't accept the position if it were offered to him.

Did you have any other problems organizing the new cabinet?

None at all. The caucus nominated Mr. Tom Johnston as Speaker and Mr. I.C. Nollet as Deputy Speaker. Mr. Nollet only held the Deputy Speakership for a short time, until the death of George Williams,[2] and then Mr. Nollet became the Minister of Agriculture.

Douglas with his secretary, Miss E. McKinnon, 1961.

I suppose the premier is always in a lonely position on
these matters.

It's a very difficult position because you're dealing with people
you like, with whom you're very close personal friends. You may
pass a man by, not because you don't want him or because you
don't like him, but because there's a more compelling reason why
someone else should be selected. Some other man may have
better ability, and sometimes geography is a factor. For example,
if you have two men for Minister of Agriculture, and one was
from the outskirts of Regina, where you already have two
members, and the other was from the northwestern corner of the
province, where you haven't got a member, then I think it would
be wise to take the man from the northwest.

Once the cabinet was formed, we met on a number of matters. We had our annual provincial convention coming up, and arrangements had to be made. We also wanted, for the first time in the history of the province, the swearing in of the cabinet to be a public function rather than a private one. We decided to have it in the Legislative Assembly, and on film; we probably had a thousand people attending the swearing in ceremony of the first C.C.F. government in Canada. The moment the swearing in was completed and the photographers had gone, we left the Legislative Assembly and held our first cabinet meeting in the Executive Council Chambers.

As soon as the cabinet meeting was over, I immediately moved in to my office.

Did you make any changes in the office?

I didn't change anything. I had to requisition for a penholder for my desk, but apart from that, everything carried on as it was.

I also had to look around for secretarial help, because Mr. Patterson took his own secretaries into the government service.

You chose Miss Eleanor McKinnon, who has been your secretary now for over fourteen years.

Yes. Miss McKinnon had been secretary to the superintendent of the Weyburn Mental Hospital, Dr. Campbell.

Many ministers have told me that it's a tremendous help to have a good secretary when you are a public man.

No one can estimate what it means to have someone who can intelligently deal with your mail, people who come to the office, and calls on the telephone.

I suppose you were flooded with people wanting to see you on those first days.

Oh, yes. I would never again want to go through that period from 10 July to 19 October when we began our special session. There was a constant flow of people and we had half a dozen crises on our hands. Looking back on it now I don't know how we did it, but we prepared over seventy pieces of legislation during that period. Some of those were monumental tasks of draftsmanship, for example, the Farm Security Act, the Trade Union Act, and the Crown Corporations Act. We would shudder now to attempt that amount of work in a year.

> There was a story in Ottawa that loads of government paper were carried away from here.

Yes. I was astounded to find that the filing cabinets were completely empty. Every outgoing premier is allowed to take his own private correspondence with him, but there is a portion of departmental correspondence that is absolutely necessary in order to pick up where somebody else has left off. The filing cabinet was completely barren.[3] Preliminary arrangements had already begun for holding a Federal-Provincial Conference on Reconstruction in 1945. I wrote to Prime Minister Mackenzie King asking if I could have a copy of the agenda; he wrote back to say he had already sent one to Mr. Patterson and to look it up in the files. Sometime later when I was talking to Mr. King in a social way, he said, "You didn't really mean that when you said the files were all empty." I said, "I've never been more serious in my life. Every filing cabinet in the place was absolutely empty." He said he had never heard anything like it before.

> It would certainly put a cloud of suspicion, I imagine, over the people who cleaned out the files. Why would it have been done?

I don't know, but we found one or two files which inadvertently hadn't been destroyed, but had been passed down to the Deputy Minister's office. One of them was instructions from a senior official to one of the land men in the country on how to carry on political activities, who he was to see, what he should tell the people about what would happen to them if they didn't vote right or didn't behave themselves.

The other letter was a part of correspondence having to do with the purple dye arrangement. We investigated the letter, and were able to piece the file together. We found that for years a dummy company had been acting as the go-between in selling purple dye. The dye had gone directly from the manufacturer to the Government of Saskatchewan at a mark-up from about $2.35

to $6.50 or $7.00. The dummy company, called the Acme Dye Company, existed only on paper and was making a very large margin on dye. This was one of the methods of financing the Liberal party. I'm not suggesting that the money was going into anyone's pocket, but it was clearly a way in which the Liberals built up a political treasury.

> There was a tremendous amount of political activity among civil servants. What attitude did you take toward them when you came into office?

I outlined my position in a radio broadcast I made just a few days after we took office, and also in a broadcast before the election. We were not going to embark on the usual policy of patronage, either in hiring people or in awarding government business. If an employee was doing a job in an efficient and competent and honest manner, the job would be perfectly safe. We thought people should be hired for what they knew, not for whom they knew. People who had been part of the Liberal machine, who used their position, government cars, and government expense money to carry on a political campaign would be dealt with.

[In this important broadcast of 12 July 1944, Mr. Douglas describes the various policies of the new government:

> The first pledge we will proceed to fulfil is that we will take the civil service out of politics and establish it upon a basis of merit. This does not mean that we can retain the services of all those who are now employed by the government. There are positions which we consider unneccessary and there are employees who are either incompetent or are merely political appointees. But I want to assure you that where there are vacancies they will be filled on a non-political basis. I haven't worked all these years merely to get the power to put Liberal partisans out of office and put C.C.F. partisans in their place. Wherever there are vacancies we will seek to have them filled from the civil service by the men and women who have been doing the work while, very often, someone else was drawing the salary.
>
> I want to assure all civil servants who are listening to me

tonight that no person who has done his or her job efficiently and has refrained from political meddling need be afraid of losing their jobs. Also I want to say to the public that if you want honest government it must begin with you. There will be no patronage committees set up throughout the country—do not expect us to hand out jobs on the basis of political favouritism. The Public Service Commission will handle all applications for employment and every person will be measured by their ability irrespective of their politics, race, or religion.][4]

Our people didn't embark on a large-scale firing operation.[5] We let go of some people over the next few years. One or two of them quit before we even got in, because they knew they were well documented. The same was true with reference to government business. We immediately set up a government purchasing agency, and all purchases were made by calling for public tenders. This saved us a lot of money—a million to a million and a half dollars per year—because people bid against each other. We were always sure of getting the best price, not only with what we bought but with what we sold. We auctioned second-hand cars and second-hand tractors we had no use for.

> Would you also tell us about your Public Service Commission, which brought civil servants together?

In the past, the Conservatives under J.T.M. Anderson fired all the Gardiner inspectors and the Gardiner machine, and when the Liberals came back in 1934 the wholesale slaughter was repeated.

We felt that the best thing that could happen to the civil service was to improve standards of efficiency and give them independence from the government. As soon as our Trade Union Act was passed, we invited representatives of the civil servants to my office. I said, "Under the Trade Union Act, you can bargain collectively if you form a union. You should apply to the Labour Relations Board to decide which congress (the Trades and Labour Congress or the Canadian Congress of Labour) you want to name as your bargaining agent. If you are supported by at least fifty-one percent of the civil servants, then you'll have a union and we'll bargain collectively regarding wages, hours of work, and conditions of labour." When we passed the Trade Union Act, we deliberately refrained from excluding the crown, as has been done in other provinces under other jurisdictions.

The result was that the civil servants, most of them somewhat aghast, formed a civil service union, which represented most of the civil servants. The mental hospital staff decided to form a separate union. The Civil Service Association became affiliated with the Trades and Labour Congress, whereas the mental hospital employees and some crown corporation employees, decided to affiliate with the Canadian Congress of Labour. In each case, they went before the Labour Relations Board and were certified. We worked out collective bargaining agreements and have continued to do that from year to year.

This gave them certain basic rights. In the meantime we had called in an organization from Chicago, which specialized in public administration and personnel problems, to classify our service. We decided we would set up standards and academic qualifications for each position.

Anytime the union is not satisfied, they can ask for a joint council, which is a board of arbitration. We've had cases where we've had to take back men we've dismissed because, in light of the investigation, the facts didn't warrant our right to dismiss them.

> In addition to employee rights, you also gave the civil service political freedom.

The old Public Service Act said that no civil servant could participate in politics. In my opinion, this was the most rank piece of hypocrisy that has ever been put on the statute books, because most of the employees, or a great many of them, were absolutely required to take part in politics. They had to canvass when they were supposed to be doing government work.

We amended the act. We followed the clause that the Labour party in New Zealand had put on their statute books, which said that any civil servant could not take part in politics during government hours, while earning government pay, or when driving a government car, but that on his own time he had the same rights as any other citizen. He could attend public meetings and run as a candidate, providing he got leave of absence and wasn't drawing pay. If he wanted to run as a candidate against the government, this would be his privilege.

> Were there any specific announcements between 10 July and the opening of the special session on 19 October?

At the provincial convention in July, because of rumours I'd heard, I repeated my position to the mortgage companies. If I heard of any further threat to foreclose mortgages, we would take very drastic action and would declare a blanket moratorium over the province.

> There was a tremendous amount of new legislation that you were ready to put to the people, including the following: the three new government departments of Social Welfare, Labour, and Co-operatives; the economic advisory board; collective bargaining; labour legislation including paid vacations; socialized health services; free hospitalization and care for the mentally incompetent; free medical care for old age pensioners; co-operative farms for soldier settlers; larger school units; increased minimum salaries for teachers; crop failure legislation; a government purchasing agency; rural electrification; farm legislation preventing eviction; and a bill to allow government to enter the insurance business.
>
> In the House there were some other bills passed: the Farm Security Act, annual holiday with pay, and the Trade Union Act.

It was a rather heavy programme. In the debate in reply to the Speech from the Throne, I outlined again what I had said in Ottawa only a couple of months earlier. When we talked about a co-operative commonwealth, we had in mind a mixed economy combining public ownership, co-operative ownership, and private ownership. In our opinion, those industries that were vital to the life of the community, and were monopolistic in character, ought to be publicly owned. Both producers and consumers should be encouraged to establish co-operatives. We felt that if twenty to thirty percent of the economy was co-operatively owned and operated, this would act as an effective balance wheel to maintain a free economy. The balance of the economy ought to be privately owned, because there should always be opportunity for initiative, for people to start new services; these services are competitive with one another, and prevent exploitation of the community.

I made the statement that the only freedom we were taking away was the freedom to exploit somebody else. I noticed that Mr. Lipset, in the last chapter of his book, *Agrarian Socialism*,[6] actually fell for the propaganda printed in the newspapers, after being away from Saskatchewan for a year.

The newspapers said we were going to socialize everything, that the government would own the farms, the corner store, the barber-shop, and the beauty parlour, and that everybody would be working for the state. When that didn't happen, they had to give some explanation. So the explanation was that we had betrayed our principles, we were no longer Socialists, we were reactionaries and had departed from our original ideals. In effect, we were now traitors, because we didn't do the horrible things they promised we would. They had built up a straw man and now they were knocking it down.

When people say, "You have become more mellow, less socialistic now than before you took office," this is absolute nonsense. I'm more of a radical than when I took office for one very obvious reason. In 1944 I thought these things could be done, and today I know they can be done. I've seen health insurance become a reality. I've seen public ownership of power and natural gas. I've seen a bus transportation system. I've seen compulsory car insurance. All these things are now accepted as part of our way of life in this province. We've become convinced that these things, which were once thought to be radical, aren't radical at all; they're just plain common sense applied to the economic and social problems of our times.

> Many other governments, who thought these programmes were awfully socialistic in 1944, have since adopted them.

In subsequent elections, the very parties who in 1944 and '45 voted against these measures, were promising in '48 and '52 that if they were elected, they would certainly not abolish them, but improve them.

> You have almost set out your long-range programme here.

Yes. This was the period when we would lay the foundation of our plans. I remember saying, "We recognize that under the British North America Act there is a distinct limit to the powers of a provincial government; we do not have the power to create an entirely new society. But we have the power within our provincial jurisdiction to lay the foundations of a new society. Someday we hope to see a federal government elected that will build a superstructure upon the foundation that we are now engaged in laying."

In the speech I made in the opening of the special session of 1944, I said, "We recognize that no one can build an island of socialism in a sea of capitalism. Within the limited jurisdiction of a provincial government, we can lay the foundations of a cooperative commonwealth and begin to set up public, co-operative, and private ownership in our provincial society."

We started on the first of January. We passed legislation so that commencing 1 January 1945, old age pensioners, blind pensioners, mother's allowance cases, and all wards of the government would receive a blue card entitling them to medical care, hospital care, dental care, eye care, glasses, and drugs. We also implemented legislation that the Liberals had passed, but not implemented, providing for free care and treatment for all cancer patients.

> In the first special session, you were accused of welshing on the seed grain agreement of 1938 by Mr. Patterson. It was quite a fight, probably one of the biggest, in which the federal government threatened to stop funds.

They not only threatened, they did. This is one of the worries about that period of 10 July to 19 October. I was seldom out of my office before one o'clock in the morning, yet back here before eight o'clock the same morning. My family was at the lake or at

Weyburn, and so I had nothing else to do but work. I think few people realized that not a single member of the cabinet ever sat on the treasury benches, or that only about half the members had ever sat in the Legislature or Parliament; they were completely inexperienced, although two or three of them had been mayors of cities and on councils.

On top of all this, we had the constant worry about this seed grain situation. The previous government had an arrangement with Ottawa whereby they gave seed grain to the farmers in the spring of 1938. It was a terrible schemozzle, because there was grain in the elevators in 1937. As a Member of Parliament I had pleaded with both the federal and provincial governments to hold some of that grain in Saskatchewan when I saw the elevators being emptied, but it was all shipped out, the elevators were cleaned out completely, and the next spring they shipped the grain all the way back. Grain for which the farmers could get seventy cents a bushel, basis Fort William, and about fifty cents on the farm now came back and they had to sign a note for it at $1.47 a bushel.

This money was advanced by the banks, with a provincial guarantee and a federal guarantee. By 1944, with the interest added, the grain cost over $2.00 per bushel.

In addition, wasn't there a crop failure, too?

Yes, they sowed the grain but they got no crop. The moment that we took office, the banks demanded their money, over twenty-five million dollars. The banks hadn't been able to collect from the farmers. They hadn't pressed the previous government for the money, but they immediately put the pressure on us. We said that the farmers should not have to pay the entire amount. We were only prepared to collect fifty percent of the principal.

You also considered this a national disaster of great magnitude.

Yes, something equivalent to a great flood or a tornado, in which case the federal government would have put up all the money. In presentations to the Rowell Commission, T.C. Davis said that there was no nation in the civilized world that had received such a disastrous economic blow as did Saskatchewan in 1937.

The banks asked the federal government to implement its guarantee and pay them, which they did. Mr. Ilsley, the federal finance minister, paid the banks and then said, "If you don't pay us for the fifty percent we guaranteed to the banks, then we will seize your payments under the tax-rental agreement." In 1941 during the war, the tax-rental agreement allowed the federal government to collect income, corporation, and inheritance taxes in return for paying the province a rental per year. We maintained that they had no right. A commission was set up, but we lost the decision.

So here we were without this federal money, which we badly needed. Subsequently we worked out an agreement with Mr. Ilsley so that we gave him non-interest Treasury bills for the balance of the eighteen million over a period of years. The last of it was paid off in 1957.

Interestingly, Mr. Ilsley was a Baptist, and had a conscience he wrestled with constantly. He was worried that he had gone a little far in keeping the subsidy, even though he'd gotten a favourable decision from the commission. I can remember him pacing up and down his office and saying to Dr. Clark, his deputy, "Is there any other way we could solve this? These debts are old, the provincial government will never collect from the farmers, and we have some responsibility. What do you think?" Dr. Clark was a former Saskatchewan man, tough when it came to dealing with finances, but he finally said, "I would go along with it if you think you can persuade your colleagues." So Mr. Ilsley took it to the cabinet, but he was unsuccessful. We didn't propose to surrender our subsidy at that point, and I told him we'd take it to the Supreme Court.

He said, "Hold off until tomorrow. I think I can get another cabinet meeting tomorrow morning. I know one minister is going out of town, and maybe we can get it through tomorrow."

The next day he called to say, "You'll be glad to know that the cabinet has accepted your proposal of giving them non-interest-bearing Treasury bills." I made some slight inquiries, and the only cabinet minister who left town that evening to my knowledge was Mr. J.G. Gardiner, who was supposed to be representing the people of Saskatchewan on the federal cabinet.

Between this and the next year, we had another worry hanging over our heads like the sword of Damocles. The federal government was requested to disallow the Farm Security Act and the Local Government Board Special Powers Act by the mortgage companies and some of the lending institutions. Also, they'd been asked by the C.P.R., the Hudson's Bay Company, and a number of other companies with large properties of mineral rights to disallow the Mineral Taxation Act.

For quite a while it looked as though the federal government would go ahead with the requests. They had already disallowed some Alberta legislation. But it had been conceded for years that the province had the right to step between a debtor and a creditor, between a creditor and a municipality in financial difficulties, and that the province had the claim to mineral rights.

In response, I did a broadcast, which began, "There comes a time in every man's life when he can either stand up and fight or crawl on his belly for the rest of his days." I explained that the government had been elected with a clear-cut mandate to have power of moratorium to protect debt-ridden farmers, to protect municipalities with financial difficulties, and to impose taxes on large companies like the C.P.R., which held millions of acres of mineral rights in Saskatchewan that were not being developed. The people of the province had elected us for these reasons, and the federal government was about to use its arbitrary powers to disallow this legislation.

The broadcast had some effect, because a good many Liberals, some of them very prominent lawyers, wrote or phoned me and said, "I didn't support you in the election and I'm not sure I agree with what you're doing, but you are quite right — the people voted for you and no government in Ottawa has the right to prevent you from implementing legislation. Let the courts decide whether it is *ultra vires*. It's not an action for federal cabinet, and I'm writing the federal government accordingly." Federal ministers were also deluged with letters and wires from people in this province.

Mr. Corman, our attorney-general, presented our case, which I was told by some of the federal cabinet ministers was a masterpiece of lucidity. He summed up in about twenty or twenty-five minutes, while the previous speakers had talked for two or three hours. The committee recommended to cabinet that the legislation be left alone, and so the legislation was not disallowed.

> Would you describe the purpose of the Local Government Board, which was to adjust bonds?

The Local Government Special Powers Act allowed the provincial government to step in when a municipality was in financial difficulty. The Local Government Board could ask the bond holders to make an arrangement for payment rather than foreclosing on the debtors and seizing their assets. When Moose Jaw, Prince Albert, and the town of Melville were in trouble in the past, the Local Government Board lacked the authority necessary to solve their debt problems.

> The Farm Security Act protected the homestead, didn't it?

There were two concessions in the act. One was that the 160 acres upon which the farm home was located, generally called the home quarter-section or the homestead, could not be foreclosed at all. A farmer might have foreclosure proceedings taken against the balance of his land but this quarter-section was forever exempt from foreclosure and eviction.

Second, while foreclosure proceedings could be taken, the court order of foreclosure could not be put into effect unless the Saskatchewan Mediation Board gave its consent. In other words, the Saskatchewan Mediation Board could intervene and prevent foreclosure, and if they thought it necessary, they could even recommend that cabinet, by Order-in-Council (which we have done many times), declare a moratorium over that particular piece of land until such time as we felt the farmer was able to meet his obligations.

I made it clear that we were differentiating between the farmer who couldn't pay and the farmer who wouldn't pay. We had no intention of having debt legislation to protect the deadbeat, the man who had resources and could meet his obligations but was simply trying to hide behind the legislation. But the farmer who couldn't pay, through no fault of his own, would have adequate protection until such time as he was able to meet his obligations. In a broadcast, I said, "Let me remind you once more that we have always taken the stand that those who can pay their debts should do so. We do not propose to protect those who are seeking to avoid the payment of their just obligations. But we do intend to protect those who cannot pay their debts, or those who have already paid them once or twice over." By that, of course, I was referring to the exorbitant interest rate that many of them had paid. We had interest rates as high as twelve percent.

> At the very first session, there were steps taken to institute the welfare state. It was under the slogan of "Humanity first."

We set up the Department of Social Welfare to give our people a greater measure of social security. Again we divided people into two classes. We were not interested in paying able-bodied people merely because they weren't able to find work. We proposed social aid, instead of the old term, relief, for people who were unable to work because they were crippled, aged, or mentally ill. Those who were able to work would participate in public works projects. We have worked out work and wages programmes with municipalities for a variety of jobs: brushing off the sides of roads, fencing pastures, painting schools, installing telephone lines, working up community pastures, or any type of project which a community feels would be useful.

> The Saskatchewan government spent an enormous part of its budget in the first few years on welfare and health.

This was a criticism levelled at us both by Mr. Patterson, who was the financial critic for the opposition, and Mr. Culliton,[7] who later became the financial critic for the opposition. They said we placed too great an emphasis on health, welfare, and education. Between sixty and seventy percent of our total budget went toward these three departments. The argument was that our economy wouldn't carry such a heavy welfare programme, and that if we suffered an economic recession, we would have to cut back and discontinue the programme.

If one were dealing with an economic situation in a vacuum, this criticism was valid. If we lived in a police state, where people's desires didn't matter, and where the government did not have to consider public opinion, we probably would have put most or all of our money into industrial development and geological, magnetometer, and seismograph surveys to stimulate new industries. These industries would have produced more wealth and given us the money to carry on our health, welfare, and educational programme.

However, we recognized that we were trying to do the two things simultaneously, so we set up an economic planning board to spend money to give our people at least a minimum sense of welfare security, and at the same time use some of our money for industrial and natural resources development. Even in the event of an economic recession, these programmes would have produced sufficient money so that we'd still be able to carry on.

This has been proven. In 1954 a frost destroyed 250 million dollars' worth of wheat in one night, but we didn't have to reduce a single part of our welfare programme. Instead, that year we increased it by $7 million for health, welfare, and education, because by this time our development programme was bringing in such good returns. When we took office we were getting less than $1.5 million from royalties and natural resources development; last year we received $25 million.

> Would you give your reasons for founding the crown corporations?

There were three primary purposes. One was to process our primary products, the second was to create employment, and the third was to raise the wealth production of the province, and consequently the provincial revenue of the province.

> In the first session you probably came in for your biggest fireworks; you were called totalitarian. The Canadian Manufacturers' Association said, among other things, that you were ruining the principle of free enterprise. There

Miss Diane Lloyd, on behalf of the National Federation of Canadian
University Students, presenting T.C. Douglas with bursary proposals for
students at the University of Saskatchewan in 1961. *Left to right:* W.S.
Lloyd, Provincial Treasurer; Diane Lloyd; Murray Swanson, Students'
Council President, University of Saskatchewan; T.C. Douglas; Dr. W.A.
Riddell, Dean of Regina College; A.E. Blakeney, Minister of Education.

was a story that the C.C.F. government was expropriating
industries all along the line. Practically everything was
taken over.

The Crown Corporation Act had a clause in it giving us the power
to expropriate any industry.

But none was ever expropriated.

Not under that clause. The only expropriation was a box factory
to settle a labour dispute. We felt we had to have the expropriation clause because five or six power companies had lines criss-
crossing each other, duplicating services, and sometimes one

company was generating power and another company was distributing it. Unless we could develop an integrated system, we had no hope of reducing power costs for our rural electrification programme.

The box factory story is very simple. The workers in this box factory at Prince Albert were working for about twenty-five cents an hour. They sought to form a union by getting signatures. Then they went to the Labour Relations Board to be certified, and the board ordered the employer to bargain collectively. He put it off for almost a year. Finally, he was issued a court order. When he still didn't react, I called the owner and asked him to meet the cabinet. I didn't want to do anything until he had a chance to tell us what his problem was. He said he couldn't come for two or three weeks, in which time he transferred all his assets to his sister. The court order no longer applied to him, and we had to start all over again.

In the meantime—this was about October or the beginning of November—he fired every man in the place. Here was a group of men thrown on the street with winter coming on, and the owner of the factory was simply defying the government, the court, and the Labour Relations Board. So we expropriated his plant. We immediately sat down and negotiated an agreement with the men, in compliance with the order of the Labour Relations Board. The men went back to work and operated the plant, and we offered to return the plant to the owner. He said, "I don't want it back. I'm going to go to court and have the court decide what you have to pay me for it," and the court decided we had to pay him I think about twice the worth of the factory, about seventy thousand dollars.

But we owned the plant—not because we wanted a broken-down box factory—but because it was the only way to enforce the Trade Union Act. If this man had been allowed to defy the Labour Relations Board, scores of other employers might have followed his example, torn up their collective bargaining agreements, and thrown their employees on the streets.

◻ In the election, did the Saskatchewan people vote for or
against socialism? The Gardiner machine? Was it a general
reaction to the war? Are they the same as now?

I've felt all along that the war caused a good deal of change in the
way people thought. Wars always have an unsettling effect. Old
orders are broken and new orders come into being. In 1944 and '45
Mr. King was loudly promising that we weren't fighting a war just
against nazism, we were fighting for a new social order. There was
a great deal of ferment in the country, a widespread feeling that
we didn't want to go back to the soup-kitchens, the breadlines,
riding the rods, poverty, and unemployment when this war was
over.

This was true in the United States and the United Kingdom
as well as in Canada. We won by-elections, and one Gallup poll,
the only one in the history of the C.C.F., where we were actually
one point ahead of the old-line parties. I think this contributed to
the victory in 1944.

That contributed, but your tremendous programme
would have also been responsible for the election results,
would it not?

Yes. Saskatchewan was particularly backward in almost every
field of welfare, education, roads, industrial development, and
farm security. The government then showed no sign of having
any progressive philosophy, and so a party with an imaginative
programme, who looked earnest about it, could command
support at the polls.

There was always a radical ferment in Saskatchewan that
could be awakened.

We had that tradition from the days of the Non-Partisan League,
the Patrons of Industry, the United Grain Growers, and later the
Wheat Pool and the Progressive Party. Practically all of the agrarian revolutionary movements on the prairies had found their
origin in Saskatchewan, or very close by.

[The grievances of the Saskatchewan farmers that prompted
the formation of the above organizations included: high freight

rates on grain exports and on goods imported from Ontario and Quebec; the exactions of private elevator companies; the inadequacy of the terminal elevator facilities at the Lakehead and the long-delayed action on providing alternative export facilities by constructing a railway to Hudson Bay; the domination of wheat sales by the members of the Winnipeg Grain Exchange; tariffs permitting central Canadian industries to charge higher prices for farm machinery and other products than those prevailing south of the border; and the exactions of central Canadian banks and mortgage companies, and monopolies in the meat-packing industry. Above all, the westerner felt isolated from the centre of Canada political and economic power in Ottawa, Toronto, and Montreal.]

> Perhaps more than any other province, there was a certain antagonism toward Ottawa in Saskatchewan. Even the Saskatchewan Liberal party had dissociated itself from the federal Liberal party.

Saskatchewan felt neglected, like the step-child of Confederation. The war had demonstrated the validity of many of the arguments the C.C.F. had tried to advance before the war. From 1936 to 1939 we pleaded for a work and wages programme and for money to give the farmers a fair price. Mr. Dunning had said, "Money doesn't grow on gooseberry bushes." We always said that if we needed the money to fight a war there would be no difficulty in finding the bush, and people demonstrated this. When we got into the war, we found suddenly that the Bank of Canada issued money, people were put to work, and unemployed men were given all the security and care they had been denied in civilian life by joining the military service. With a million people taken out of production and put in to the service, we were still able to feed and clothe the entire nation better than it had been fed and clothed in peace-time, take care of a million people in the service, and fight a war. To a lot of people, this exploded the old myth that there was no money to implement the programmes the C.C.F. was talking about. We went from a budget of $5 hundred million to $5 thousand million and yet the economy remained solid. The old reactionary cries that the C.C.F. would bankrupt the nation didn't have the same terror for people in 1944 as they had in 1934.

> Could you comment on the ideological aspect of the rev-
> olutionary or radical element in Saskatchewan? People
> like Partridge and others had advocated a certain form of
> socialism.

Partridge's book was called *A War on Poverty* in which he used the
term co-operative commonwealth.

[Edward Alexander Partridge (1861–1931) was born in Ontario
and homesteaded at Sintaluta, Saskatchewan, where he also
taught school briefly. Later he was associated with the organization of the Territorial Grain Growers' Association in 1901, and was
the founder of the Grain Growers' Grain Co. (1906), of which he
was the first president. He was the first editor (1908) of *The Grain
Growers' Guide*, founder and organizer of the Canadian Council
of Agriculture, and an active member of the Progressive party. *A
War on Poverty* (Winnipeg: Wallingford Press Ltd., n.d. [1926])
advocated the establishment of a co-operative commonwealth in
Western Canada. He was strongly influenced by the social ideals
of John Ruskin, social Darwinism, and Christian socialism.]

> People here were perhaps not so frightened of socialistic
> or co-operative ventures. I notice that the crown corpora-
> tions receive tremendous diatribes, but the Liberals have
> also formed some themselves: municipal hail insurance,
> the briquette plant, and there was some talk about nation-
> alizing the coal-mines.

They set up a Power Commission, which was at least a bow in the
direction of public ownership, in order to appease the public
holler.

> So it was logical that the province voted the way it did.

That's right. People often ask, "How can a form of socialism in
Canada start in an agricultural province?" It has usually been the
opposite. Agricultural people have been the conservatively
minded people and the industrial workers have been the radical
thinkers. Here in Canada the position was reversed. The explanation you have given is, in my opinion, the accurate one. We have a

long tradition of radical thinking in Saskatchewan. This came from two main sources. One, with our heterogeneous population, we had many people from the old lands. Many Social Democrats from Germany found their way to this country; Scandinavian people and many people from the United Kingdom brought with them the traditions of their forebears. In 1934 and '35, I would say that eighty percent of my key campaign workers were either Scandinavian or ex-Labour party members from the old country, people like my friend Tom Johnston, the ex-Speaker of the Legislature, and Bob Harris, who was my campaign manager and the president of my organization for many years. Bob was a member of the Labour party in Birmingham, and came out to Canada to work on the railroad. The Scandinavians had belonged to the Socialist party in their respective countries; the Belgians had belonged to the Belgian Socialist party; and some came from the radical parties of the United States. In the southern part of Saskatchewan there are many Americans. Many of these people had old contacts with the now defunct Socialist parties, the Non-Partisan League, and the Patrons of Industry in the Dakotas. Many had come from Minnesota and were very strong supporters of the Farmer-Labour party, which elected Governor Olson in the thirties.

Also, I think westerners generally have less veneration for the sacred cows that you find in eastern Canada. The C.P.R. and Hudson's Bay Company, the great banks, mortgage companies, and lending institutions, and the Winnipeg Grain Exchange don't get the same reverence, and are greeted with less than enthusiasm out on the prairies. This is why we had the ideal setting for a fairly radical movement. On the one hand, people came from traditions in which socialism wasn't a bad word, and second, a mixed group of people hadn't yet settled into a new tradition in which certain things were sacrosanct and unquestionable.

> When you were describing the hectic first days of office, you omitted an added burden, the Kamsack cyclone. Could you tell us something about that?

Well, in the midst of our own cyclone, installing a new government with inexperienced ministers, trying to prepare over seventy pieces of legislation, another cyclone hit us and blew away the town of Kamsack. We turned my office and the Executive Council Chamber into an emergency headquarters and operated very much like a general staff.

I put Charlie Williams, Minister of Labour and Minister of Telephones, in charge of communications. He used to be a telegrapher on the C.N.R., and he worked night and day. He slept on a couch in the office. He found some trainloads of brick and building materials on the way to the Pacific Coast, and got permission to have them turned around and shipped back. We had the army send a motorized detachment carrying supplies, construction equipment, and men from the engineering corps. We had the Red Cross and Salvation Army, and all the charitable organizations we could contact, taking care of the people. It was really a first-class job of organization.

We also immediately set up a committee headed by the Chief Justice, Mr. Martin, also a former premier of the province,[8] who went on the air and appealed for funds. Although the war was on, and money was scarce, we raised enough so that we could not only rebuild all the homes that were destroyed and refurnish them, but we actually had some money over. An Act of the Legislature subsequently granted the money to the University of Saskatchewan for research. Later we used the same techniques when we helped the Manitoba people with the Red River flood, and the floods around Swift Current and other parts of Saskatchewan later on. This is the kind of thing that the civil defence can now do so well. It meant that for three or four days some of us just slept here in the office until we got the situation under control.

Did you feel like retiring at any moment during all this?

I rather enjoyed it.

What kind of men constituted your Legislature?

We had about six men who could be classified as Labour men,

Douglas and his first Saskatchewan cabinet members at Matador Co-op Farm.

members of trade unions. Most of them were railroaders, Alex Connon from North Battleford, Jim Arthur from Melville, Arthur Stone and Charlie Williams, Dempster Heming and Harry Gibbs. Then there were two or three merchants, Arthur Swallow, the member for Yorkton, and Daniels, the member for Canora. There were teachers: C.M. Fines, Woodrow Lloyd, Jack Sturdy, and Herschel Howell, the member for Meadow Lake. All the rest were farmers. Out of the forty-seven members I would say about thirty-five were farmers. The same was true in the cabinet. At least half of the ministers were farmers.

> I suppose a typical farmer member would be a man who would be a former Wheat Pool delegate, a reeve or a councillor. There were quite a few with the background of a rural public man.

All of the members had come up through the co-operative movement; Peter Howe had been a Wheat Pool delegate for years and
Allan Brown had been a Wheat Pool delegate. Others had had a
good deal of experience in municipal affairs, both rural and
urban. We had two former mayors, Charlie Williams of Regina,
and Jack Corman of Moose Jaw; and Clarence Fines had been an
alderman. While they didn't have parliamentary experience, they
had a good deal of experience in business matters, particularly in
co-operative and municipal business affairs.

> Were there Progressives among them?

Oh, yes. Clarence Fines had not only been secretary of the
Labour party, but before the Independent Labour party had been
formed, he had been secretary for the Progressives when Mr.
Coldwell ran as a Progressive candidate in 1925 or '26. Jack
Corman had run for the Progressives, and so had Tom Johnston,
who also later ran for the Farmer-Labour party and for the C.C.F.
in both federal and provincial elections.

> Would it be safe to say, too, that a fair percentage of them
> would have been Liberals where there was no Progres-
> sive party available?

A good percentage of them would have voted Liberal although
most of them hadn't since 1921 or '25. The first Progressive was
elected to the House of Commons in 1921. Sixty-five Progressives
were elected from the west. Practically all of these people had
voted Progressive at that time. From that time on there had been
a Progressive, a Farmer-Labour candidate, or a C.C.F. candidate
to vote for. In my own case, when I came to Weyburn in 1930,
there was a Liberal, a Conservative, and a Progressive in the
election that year. The Progressive didn't get a big support, but he
was somebody whom we could vote for—Dr. McManus, a veteri-
narian from Colgate, Saskatchewan—a good friend and supporter
of mine until he died.

> You could almost say that the Liberal party, which both
> here and in Quebec had been regarded as the top poli-
> tical party, started to decline around about the twenties.

Yes. The Liberal party suffered a terrific defeat on the prairies in 1921 when the Progressives came to the fore. It's also true that the Progressive party was led down the primrose path by Crerar and Forke, who led it into the Liberal party by the subtlety of Mr. Mackenzie King. But while they led the leadership, and while they had the majority of the voters, a hard core opposition had been established in 1921 that has never been completely eliminated. I don't think it ever will be.

I glanced through some of the broadcasts you made in 1943, 1944, and 1945. The first item is a report of a speech published in *The Commonwealth* of 15 November 1943. It deals with the attitude of the Roman Catholic church toward the C.C.F. All church attitudes toward the party are mentioned indirectly in this speech. Do you want to comment, sir?

Yes, I do. While we ourselves had kept strictly away from any religious issues, the closer we got to being elected the more desperate our opponents became. So in the last twelve months before the 1944 election, the campaign moved from a discussion of political and economic issues to a more emotional type of issue. They used every appeal to prejudice and to basic fears—that people were going to lose their farms, that we were going to socialize all the children and put them into institutions, and that we lacked patriotism. We were National Socialists who had opposed the war, and the flag was waved as usual. We discovered, as one always does in a progressive party, that not only is patriotism the last refuge of the scoundrel, so is religion.

I tried to point out that some of the people most concerned about the C.C.F. destroying religion hadn't, in my opinion, formerly been supporters or proponents of religion; their concern for religion was newly acquired. In French-Canadian and in some of the central European areas, where there was a genuine fear of communism and naturally a very genuine regard for their church,

186 The Making of a Socialist

our opponents played on those fears to their utmost. It's rather significant that the Roman Catholic church, the Anglican church, and the United church—the three largest groups in Canada—had repeatedly placed themselves on record as finding nothing contrary to Christian doctrine in the philosophy and principles of the C.C.F. This helped to allay some fears, still found in isolated pockets now, but with time, the argument has become quite ridiculous.

> There is a broadcast that deals with the Ontario election results, communism, and in particular, the Saskatchewan Liberal government's extension of its own life.

Again, the purpose was to answer some of these absurd charges. The other great institution to whose defence the Liberals suddenly came was democracy. The purpose of this broadcast was to show that this concern for democracy came strangely from a party that had defied democracy by extending its own life. While the laws of the province said a government was elected for five years, they passed a motion extending their term to six years. If they could extend it for six years, they might try to extend it for sixty years.

> The Kerr broadcast was very important. William Kerr was a former editor of the *Morning Leader* in Regina and a minister in the Liberal government at the time. He alleged, among other things, that you were challenged to enter the army, but that you or the party decided you should stay. You also replied to a Liberal charge that Victory Bonds, savings, and life insurance would vanish if Canada ever got a C.C.F. government.

The Liberals said that if the C.C.F. came in, all the Victory Bonds people bought out of patriotic duty would be worthless. So the Liberal party stayed in federal office from that period until 1957, in which, by their complete failure to grapple with the problem of inflation, the purchasing power of war bonds, insurance policies, and annuities was cut in half.

> In another broadcast made during the 1944 campaign,

you made an important pledge that your government
would resign if any family in Saskatchewan was compelled to give up title to their home.

This was in answer to the oft-repeated accusations that the
C.C.F. would socialize all the farms. I said that if a C.C.F. government headed by me took any action to deprive any person of their
home, I, for one, would resign. This was later interpreted by some
of our opponents as a pledge to resign if any person lost their
home for any reason whatsoever — because they didn't pay their
taxes, or because they signed a quit claim deed in order to make a
new agreement.

In 1944 you went overseas. What was the purpose of this
trip?

During the hectic period getting ready for a special session of the
Legislature called for 19 October, I had planned to visit Saskatchewan units on the Continent and in Britain as soon as the session
was over. I wanted to make a round of the hospitals and see if any
Saskatchewan personnel were there. So the day after the Legislature finished, I left to go overseas. I received excellent co-
operation from the Minister of National Defence, Colonel Ralston, and later from General McNaughton. Not many premiers or
cabinet ministers had gone over, and it was felt this would be of
some value to help the men overseas feel that those back home
hadn't forgotten them.

The doctors never really figured out what happened —
whether it was this terrific grind getting ready for the session and
the strain of going through it — but my resistance was down, and I
was extremely sick on the train. I was running a temperature of
about 103 to 104 and was terribly bloated and almost delirious. By
the time I got to Ottawa, my temperature was up to 105, and they
decided to take me off the train there and immediately had me
taken to the Civic Hospital. They called in one of the best intern-

ists in the country, Dr. Plunkett. I think the only thing that saved me was that just the week before, penicillin, which had been only on the military list, had been released by the army for civilian use.

They used to give penicillin by the drip method, which meant that about six needles were placed down the length of your leg, all held together by little tubes, and a bowl suspended through which it dripped. Your leg was strapped on a board so you wouldn't move. Every six hours they'd take those needles out and stick them on the other leg. Of course, now they simply give you one good shot in the buttocks, and you've got your penicillin.

Because there is a tendency of penicillin to speed up the coagulation of the blood, there was a risk I'd get an embolism, which I did. I had to be kept completely immobile, lest the blood clot moved and got into the lungs or the brain.

When I was ready to come out of hospital, my hospital bill was just under a thousand dollars. This gives you some idea of why hospital insurance certainly appealed to me. I didn't have a thousand dollars. I had to borrow the money.

Mr. Mackenzie King had sent a car to take me to my hotel, and also requested that I have dinner with him that night.

So that evening Mr. King showed me around Laurier House: the statues, the cups he'd been presented with, the degrees he had received, and all the things of a historical significance he had collected over the years. He'd also told me that he kept every single card, programme, or menu of any place where he had spoken or event in which he had taken part. He had hundreds of boxes of newspaper clippings. That's why they're having such a terrific job now sorting out his papers.

We had a very delightful meal, and when we'd finished I made ready to go. But he wanted me to stay, so we went to the private elevator he'd just installed, one of his chief joys, and we went up to his den on the third floor. We sat in front of the fireplace and he fed Pat, his dog, biscuits and chatted.

Bruce Hutchison makes the comment in *The Incredible Canadian*[9] that Mr. King was a most complex individual. He could be so secretive with his colleagues, yet most open with somebody he hardly knew. I was a good example. I'd never been close to Mr. King, and had only met him on parliamentary business. I also saw him when he came and reviewed the troops, and later asked for Mr. Tucker and myself—we were both in training—and had his picture taken with us. I often thought that if Hitler had ever seen the picture, it would certainly have encouraged him greatly about his prospects of winning the war, with Mr. Tucker and myself supporting Mr. King, and neither of us looking very soldierly. But apart from these incidents, I'd never had any contact with Mr. King.

First of all he showed me the sanctuary—I would almost call it an altar—on which he kept a Bible, an everlasting light that burned night and day, and above it a picture of his mother with long hair. He told me that every day he came and read a chapter of the Bible, looking at his mother's picture. He apparently had very deep family feelings. He said, "You know, Douglas" (he had the English habit Woodsworth also had of calling people by their surname), "I've watched you a lot from across the House, and you probably don't know why I'm so interested in you, and why I've a strong feeling for you. You're the spitting image of my brother who studied for medicine and who died." He dug out the family album and the picture of his brother. I couldn't see any resemblance; we both probably had a high forehead, but that was all.

So then we sat down and he began to talk. He was a charming host, exceedingly courteous, with the old Victorian manner of being very meticulous, and a very good conversationalist. It was fascinating to get inside this man's mind for a couple of hours and to see things as he saw them.

He discussed a wide variety of subjects. One was the political situation, and he said, "Douglas, you've got a very brilliant career before you. I regret very much that you couldn't have found your career inside the Liberal party." I told Mr. King that I didn't think I could have done any of the things I wanted to do in the Liberal party. He said, "But I think you're wrong. I was for many years a member of the Fabian Society, along with H.G. Wells and George Bernard Shaw, and many of the other originals. Sydney and Beatrice Webb are very close personal friends of mine, and I carry on correspondence with them. The Liberal party is broad enough to take in a lot of people who believe in progress and reform," and went on to quote Gladstone and Lloyd George, and so on. I said, "But the Liberal party as we've seen it in the last few years has been moving steadily right." I cited some of the incidents of Mr. Howe, and the Gardiner machine. Mr. King was almost brutally frank: "These are the excrescences that have hung onto the Liberal party. As far as the Liberal party in Saskatchewan is concerned, I think they've lost sight of liberalism. As a matter of fact, I warned them several times that they ought not to extend their own life, that they should have gone to the province when their time was up."

I gathered that he hadn't too much confidence in the leadership of the Liberal party in Saskatchewan. The one man he had the greatest confidence in was Judge Martin, with whom he corresponded a great deal, and from whom he received advice on the western situation. He said, "I think you made progress in Saskatchewan partly on your own effort, but also partly on the mistakes and blunders those people out there made." His reference to "those people," as though they belonged to another party altogether, was rather significant to me.

> Mr. Justice Martin is now head of the Saskatchewan Court of Appeal.

He's Chief Justice of the Province of Saskatchewan, and was Liberal premier for six years. He was mentioned in 1919 as a possible leader for the Liberal party, and I think he withdrew in Mr. King's favour.

Mackenzie King had political antennae stretched out all over Canada. He didn't depend on newspaper reports. He was a real professional politician. He had friends here and there in whose judgement he had confidence. History has proven that probably no man had a better political pulse and timing than he had.

We went on to the conscription issue. In *The Incredible Canadian*, Bruce Hutchinson leaves a gap and finds it difficult to explain why, at one moment, King was fighting tooth and nail against conscription—he lost Colonel Ralston over it, he almost lost Macdonald and Ilsley and Mackenzie—and then, suddenly, he brought in the Order-in-Council sending sixteen thousand conscripts overseas, and as a consequence lost Cardin and

Power.[10] He reviewed his problem, and said, "You know, all my life I have tried to follow a policy of unity in Canada. I have never gotten over the great lesson of what happened to Laurier when the country was split down the middle, first of all on the British naval bill and the fight between Laurier and Bourassa, and then later on the conscription issue of 1917. This split the Liberal party and the country down the middle, and the sores and the scars are still there. All my political life, this has been my one tenet of faith: you must at all costs retain this unity no matter what else you have to sacrifice. I've been obstinate on this conscription issue, and as a result I've lost some support among my friends and colleagues."

I told Mr. King that while I greatly admired Colonel Ralston, I didn't think he was a great loss as a minister, although he was a great loss as a man. I never considered him a first-class administrator; I think he spent too much time on detail. But I couldn't understand why he let Mr. Power go. He then made this revealing statement: "Ah, Douglas, you don't understand my political strategy. We lost Ralston when he came back from Italy after having visited the troops there, convinced that a lot of untrained and semi-trained men were being sent up the line. He came back determined that there was only one answer, to send these conscripts who were already well trained, had been trained for a couple of years, and put them into action. We debated it in the cabinet for three days. I didn't say a word. I let everybody express their opinion. It was apparent to me that the French-Canadian members would never agree to conscription, that if Ralston had his way, we would lose the French-Canadian members, we would arouse all the old antagonisms we had in the past, and we might even have to take the Conservatives into a national government in order to stay in power. This to me would have been a repetition of 1917, with the Anglo-Saxon Canadians on one side, and the French Canadians on the other. After this had gone on for three days, I simply said, 'Colonel Ralston, some time ago you offered me your resignation in relation to another matter; I'm now prepared to accept that resignation'." Mr. King said, with a bit of a chuckle, "Ralston's jaw fell, and then he got up and walked around the room and shook hands with everyone except me and walked out of the room." Macdonald started after him, but Mackenzie and Ilsley grabbed his coat-tail and pulled him back into his seat. "So, that saved that crisis, but this put me into the arms of the French Canadians. And my place has always been in the middle of the road. So I then got the idea of the Order-in-Council, not for total conscription, but just to send these sixteen thousand men over. This was a token gesture. I had some reason to believe," and I thought he smiled here, I don't think he expected me to believe this, "that the army was planning sort of a coup d'etat, and I explained this to Mr. St. Laurent and Mr. Mackenzie and a number of the other ministers, and in the light of that imminent and possible military coup d'etat, I called the cabinet together, and presented this Order-in-Council. They agreed to pass it. Well, Douglas, this put me right back into the middle of the road. All the conscriptionists who were crying for my blood because I was against conscription, now began to feel that I had agreed to some conscription. When Power and Cardin resigned, this was perfect, because this now made the conscriptionists say, 'King can't be so bad, otherwise Power and Cardin wouldn't have resigned'."

I asked Mr. King if he told this story about the coup d'etat to Mr. Power. He said he certainly wouldn't have done that. I could only assume one of two things. He must have known that Chubby Power was too smart and too much of a realist to believe it. Looking back now, I don't think anyone would believe that a military coup d'etat was almost attempted in Canada. It's so ridiculous that I don't know how he expected Mr. St. Laurent to believe it. I'm amazed that Mr. St. Laurent gave it any credence. He must have deliberately refrained from telling Power and Cardin of his intention to present the Order-in-Council at the meeting; all the other ministers came, some of them having been phoned at six o'clock in the morning, and told about this so-called imminent coup d'etat. They came prepared to vote for it. Power and Cardin, not knowing why there was this sudden change of opinion, not knowing why this Order-in-Council was being presented, when only three days before Ralston was fired for wanting to send these men overseas, could only resign. They'd had no explanation whatsoever and they were astonished to find all their colleagues agreeing with Mr. King.

Chubby Power had saved Mr. King in the Quebec elections of 1940. He was the one who said, "There's only one way to beat Duplessis and that is by saying that if Duplessis is elected in Quebec, all French-Canadian cabinet ministers will resign from the federal cabinet, and you will be left all through the war without any Quebec representation in the federal cabinet." Chubby Power forced that strategy through and carried most of the campaign. And here King deliberately manoevred Power and Cardin into resigning to put himself back into the good graces of the Anglo-Saxon Canadians across the rest of Canada, who were irate about Ralston having been shoved out of office.

And so, he leaned back, relaxed, fed Pat another dog biscuit, and said, "You see, Mr. Douglas, it put me right back where I belong, in the middle of the road. The conscriptionists were angry because I had fired Ralston, but they were mollified because Cardin and Power had resigned. The anti-conscriptionists were displeased about the sixteen thousand, but they felt that I must be on their side, since I had let Ralston go and had refused to accede to his requests."

Another interesting story fits in with this. Sometime before, when I was in Ottawa as a member of the War Expenditures Committee, I often had occasion to go to Ralston's office. He came in this particular day from a cabinet meeting, slammed his books down, and said, "You know, Tommy, King would rather be with French Canada than be right." I said, "What's the trouble?" He said, "He just won't do anything about this troop question. By the way, you know Edgar Bailey, don't you?" I said, "Yes, I went to college with Edgar Bailey, I think he was a year behind me at Brandon College." Edgar Bailey was a Baptist minister who later went to Tabernacle Baptist Church in Winnipeg until the outbreak of the war, and then went overseas as chaplain for the Royal Edmonton Regiment. He continued, "Bailey put me on the spot. He wrote me some months ago." He told me the story of Bailey's correspondence. After the war, I got the other side of the story from Bailey. He told of a patrol that had gone out to cover an advance and seize a small house. When they got near the house the sergeant in charge of the patrol said, "Keep the house under fire with your Brens, and the other men and myself will try to slip down and come from behind and flush these fellows out with grenades." The men said, "But we can't fire a Bren gun." The sergeant answered, "If you can't fire a Bren gun you'd better get back to the company as fast as you can." They were killed on the way back. When Edgar Bailey came to bury these fellows, the sergeant told him the story, and he went back through their records himself and found it was true that they'd had no Bren gun training.

For months Bailey kept a record of men who had been put in to handle a gun in a tank and had never fired one, who had been sent up the line to operate a Bren gun and didn't even know how to load a Bren gun. Any able-bodied man was being shoved up the line and put into duty without any adequate training. When he had collected enough evidence of this he sent it directly to Ralston.

So Ralston told me the story, which later Bailey corroborated. "You know, Bailey sent me this stuff," he said. "I felt terrible about it and wrote him that he could be court-martialled for this, but that I knew him to be a man of honour and was prepared to look into this matter—if he were wrong I'd have him court-martialled, and if he were right, I'd do something about it." He said, "That's why I went to Italy. Everything he said was true, and much more." He said, "Our casualties were twice as great as we expected in Italy and we just hadn't the replacements. We were picking up hospital orderlies, clerks, fellows who had been pounding typewriters, butchers, fellows driving trucks and shoving them up the line as infantry reinforcements. It was just murder. I came back resolved that either we're going to send the conscripts overseas as reinforcements, or I was going to resign as Minister of Defence."

Ralston was one of the finest men I ever knew. I said that I don't think he was a good administrator. He killed himself with hard work. When you asked him about something, instead of doing as Chubby Power would by asking his secretary to get me the information, and then forget about it, Ralston would make a laborious note in his own handwriting. Then you'd get a long memo from him corrected by himself with words written in, and then he'd phone you up and give you some more of the information by telephone. He made a big production when he didn't need to. Everything was done by himself. He told me that he even wrote the orders going out to his military districts in longhand and then corrected them — there'd be about three copies before they finally went out — instead of calling in an orderly or one of his staff officers, and saying, "I want this sent out. You phrase it, and see that these points are properly set down" and then forgetting about it. He'd been a corporation lawyer too long, where he had to give attention to all the little details; he couldn't get the overall picture. But he was one of the finest men I ever knew. The suggestion in some quarters that this conscription issue was a grandstand play to push him forward is sheer nonsense. As a matter of fact, the night he resigned, I was in the House of Commons, and if he had wanted to topple the government that night he could have done it. The Conservatives certainly would have joined with two-thirds of the Liberal party in forming a national government with Ralston as prime minister.

Instead, Ralston got up, gave King one of the worst castigations that I ever heard one man give another, not so much by what he said, but with the complete contempt for this man who had so apparently double-crossed him.

7

Saskatchewan government reforms

◩ In the 1945 regular session, there were three soldier members in the Legislature.

That's right. Dobie, representing troops in Canada, Delmar Valleau, representing troops in the United Kingdom and in western Europe, and Colonel Embury, representing the Mediterranean areas.

There was also some talk about the lieutenant-governor's residence.

When we came into office, the Honourable Archie McNab was lieutenant-governor. Archie was a very colourful figure. He was as poor as a church mouse, and had gone through politics spending all that he had earned, donating to almost every charitable cause, buying roller-skates for youngsters, and ice-skates for boys' hockey.

When I first went to see him to give him the list of new ministers who were to be sworn in, knowing he had been a former Liberal member and Minister of Public Works, I approached him with due dignity and said, "Your Honour, I now have the names I would like to submit." He tapped me on the arm and said, "Just call me Archie." So from then on we got along famously.

You've got stories about him?

In 1948 I was attending the parliamentary conference in London, England, as a guest of the United Kingdom Parliamentary Association. We had travelled for six weeks through the United Kingdom, Germany, Holland, Belgium, and France and wound up for a week's study in London of the various matters on the agenda of the conference. The last day of the conference was the opening of the House of Commons by His Majesty, King George VI, to be followed by a buffet dinner at Buckingham Palace.

There was a tremendous crowd there, and we were milling around at this buffet dinner, when a powdered footman came up and asked if I was the Premier of Saskatchewan. I said, "Yes," and he said, "The King would like to see you." I said, "I think you have probably made a mistake." He said, "No, the King wants to see you." So I followed him to where the King and Queen were standing in a corner receiving people, and the King shook my hand and the first thing he said was, "How is my friend Archie McNab?" This was 1948 and the King had been in Saskatchewan in 1939 almost ten years before. I told him that unfortunately Archie had passed away. He said, "You know, the two people I remember most on the Canadian visit were Archie McNab and Camillien Houde of Montreal." [Houde (1889–1958) was mayor of Montreal from 1928 to 1954, and was interned from 1940 to 1944.] He said, "How is Camillien Houde?" "Well," I said, "for some time he enjoyed Your Majesty's hospitality as a guest in one of your institutions." He had been a prisoner, or at least in an internment camp, during the war. Then the King turned to those who were standing around him and began to tell some of his experiences with Archie. He said that when he and the Queen arrived in Regina in 1939, great crowds of people were there, and Archie was standing beside the train. The moment the King and Queen stepped down he came forward and shook hands. The King said, "We have a wonderful day, haven't we?'" and Archie said, "Yes, it's a wonderful day and we have a tremendous crowd, but if you'd brought the kids there'd have been twice as many." The King enjoyed this.

The other story that the Queen said the King had been telling everybody who would listen for all the years since he'd visited Saskatchewan, was about a state dinner in Government House. It was very hot, and after everyone had gone home, the King and Queen and Archie and Mrs. McNab and some of the staff were having a cup of coffee and a cigarette before going to bed, and Archie said to the King, "It's hot, you better take off your coat." The King very blissfully agreed with this, although it wasn't part of usual court etiquette, and took off his coat, which the footman immediately proceeded to pick up, take away, and hang up. After they had chatted for a while, the King said, "I'll think it's time that the Queen and I retired." So Archie hurried off to find the King's coat. The King followed him, but Archie wasn't aware that the King was behind him. Archie said to the footman. "Where in hell's the King's coat? The bugger wants to go to bed." The Queen said this had been the King's favourite after-dinner story to his inside cronies for years.

> The first thing Archie McNab did when he took over Government House was to open it to all the kids. Can we describe him for people in the future? He was a short, stout, rotund man, and very unpretentious. He wore a bowler hat, which he sort of pushed half-way over his head, and he had quite a jolly round face, and nobody would have taken him to be a lieutenant-governor in any circumstances. Somebody once said that he looked very much like a retired London cab driver.

He had the same type of humour and offhandedness, and the same wit. When he passed away, a new lieutenant-governor was going to be appointed. We had to decide whether or not we would continue this very costly item of maintaining a Government House for Saskatchewan. Ontario had already dispensed with theirs.

There was not only the tremendous cost of maintaining a huge staff of footmen and butlers and gardeners and maids and cooks for the few state occasions they were required, but also the building was in a very bad state of disrepair, and would require over seventy thousand dollars to put it in decent shape. It needed a new roof, and there were some structural defects that had to be remedied. We felt Government House was completely unnecessary in our type of frontier society. So we announced that some other use would be made of the building. Subsequently, we leased it to the Department of Veterans' Affairs for the sum of one dollar. They spent a very large sum of money reconditioning it and used it as a veteran's home right up until we moved the veterans into the new geriatric centre we built last year on the legislative grounds.

The lieutenant-governor's residence has now been turned into a building called Saskatchewan House, a centre for continuous learning, and is used by the Adult Education Division of the Department of Education. We have 1,000 to 1,500 people a week making use of that building for evening classes covering almost every subject from French and German to philosophy and economic theory. During the day and week-ends it is used for all sorts of conferences.

> From time to time, you and other premiers in Saskatchewan over the last two decades have variously expressed yourselves about the usefulness of the lieutenant-governor's office. What has been the general view?

When Mr. McNab died in 1945, I contacted Mr. King by wire and letter, and suggested to him that in our opinion all the duties discharged by the lieutenant-governor could easily be handled by the Chief Justice. They consist mainly of reading the Speech from the Throne at the opening of the Legislature, coming at the close of the Legislature and giving assent to bills, signing Orders-in-Council a couple of times a week, and attending a few public functions where the Queen's representative should be present.

Mr. King, I suppose very properly, put us in our place by saying that this is a prerogative of the federal government, which would be dealt with on the basis of their best judgement, and in their opinion, someone should be appointed as lieutenant-governor.

> You also raised the question that the lieutenant-governor had always been a Liberal appointee.

When a governor-general is appointed for Canada, the British government has never, to my knowledge, made an appointment without consulting the Government of Canada. By the same token, it seemed to us that the provincial government ought to be consulted by the federal government in making an appointment. We believed that it ought not to be just a reward for political services to the party in office, but a position given to someone who has carried on a long useful service to his community, an honour in recognition of that service.

One of the people whom I had hoped would be appointed in this province, and he's certainly not a member of the C.C.F., was Dr. Ferguson, the man who had started the anti-tuberculosis programme in Saskatchewan. He was the type of man who would have been an excellent non-political appointment. He had the high regard of everyone concerned. There could be no question of political influence, and it would have been a fine climax to a great career of twenty-five years' service to the people of Saskatchewan.

> I don't think it happened in Saskatchewan, but there have been lieutenant-governors who participated in politics somewhat beyond their vice regal limits. The lieutenant-governor of Manitoba interfered, but presumably had the right to do what he did. Do you regard the office as being in any way dangerous?

Yes, it can be. In Alberta the lieutenant-governor reserved certain bills for the consideration of the governor-general.[1] I disagreed with the Alberta banking legislation and the newspaper censorship legislation. To me they were anti-democratic and certainly unconstitutional insofar as the powers of a provincial Legislature

are concerned. But that's not the point. If they were unconstitutional, it was a very simple matter to refer the matter to the
court or to the Department of Justice.

Another problem can be a bad relationship between the government and the lieutenant-governor. We've never had it in this
province; we've been extremely fortunate. Mr. Reg Parker was
one of the kindliest men we could have ever had. He was Minister
of Municipal Affairs in the Liberal administration. When Mr. W.J.
Patterson, who was the former premier of the province and leader
of the opposition when I became premier, became lieutenant-
governor, we co-operated and worked together very harmoniously. Our present lieutenant-governor, Mr. Bastedo, has been
quite pleasant to work with.

> Do you think that if existing provincial governments were
> allowed to have some say in choosing a lieutenant-
> governor, and provided they chose a man of eminence
> with a background in his province, he could be of great
> assistance to a premier?

Yes, he could. I've never been a provincial rightist; I've never
believed that provinces are sovereign powers, and I completely re-
pudiate the compact theory of Confederation. But the provinces
have certain sovereign rights within their own field of jurisdiction,
and the federal government has sovereign rights within a much
wider field. If a federal system is to function harmoniously, there
must be a certain amount of consultation, and the wishes and
views of provinces should be recognized. This is true with reference to the lieutenant-governor. It might also enhance the dignity
of the position by appointing people with less political connection, rather than people who generally received this appointment as a political reward.

I would not only carry this into the field of the lieutenant-
governor, but into the realm of the Senate, and more importantly,
into the Supreme Court. A few years ago the governments of Ontario and Quebec, Saskatchewan, Alberta, and British Columbia
were all non-Liberal, yet the Supreme Court and the members of
the Senate continued to be appointed by a Liberal government.
Now what did this mean? It means that when the provincial legis-

lation is referred to the Supreme Court as to its constitutionality, it is heard by the old-line parties, usually by the government that's been in power, as in the case of the Liberal government, which had been in power for twenty-two years.

The same is true of the Senate. Supposing the Senate deals with a piece of legislation that the federal parliament has passed, and that legislation in some way affects the rights and privileges of certain provinces, or certain groups of people. Saskatchewan, Alberta, and British Columbia all have non-Liberal and non-Conservative governments, yet we haven't got a single person in the Senate who can present our point of view. I think the time has come that appointments for lieutenant-governor, senators, or members of the Supreme Court ought to be a matter for either joint appointment or at least the basis for consultation.

> During the February 1945 session, the main work done was the implementation of the legislation from the last session.

We began the process of buying up the various power utilities operating in the province. The purpose was to integrate them into a single integrated power system.[2] The power companies were relatively small, and there was a considerable duplication. None of them were big enough to generate power economically. None of them were large enough to undertake a rural electrification programme. Each had to carry a certain amount of surplus capacity, and if they were integrated, one amount of surplus capacity would do for all. Rates were also extraordinarily high. People tend to forget that. In the little towns in my constituency people were paying as high as twenty-five cents per kilowatt-hour for electric power, and in many cases power came on only in the evening, and one forenoon a week so that the women could do their washing. It wasn't twenty-four hour service.

> This integration was very necessary to this rural electrification programme you were about to start.

We couldn't start until we had an integrated system, and until we had increased the generating capacity. It took about four or five years before we were actually ready to begin rural electrification on any big scale.

A good deal of fuss has been made in the press, particularly in other parts of Canada, about the fact that in the Crown Corporations Act there was a clause giving the government the right to expropriate any industry. In 1957 this clause was taken out of the Crown Corporations Act. Some people thought this was a surrender. The sole purpose for putting that clause into the act was so that we could deal with the power question. In the end, we didn't once use the power of expropriation to deal with the power companies. In each case we were able to reach a satisfactory price by negotiation. But we had that power in reserve because the whole programme of power integration and rural electrification could be set adrift merely because one company refused to sell to us, irrespective of how generous our financial offer might be.

> People of this province think that the word "expropriation" is something new on the statute books of Canada. Yet Ontario has more expropriation legislation on its books than Saskatchewan ever had; all Legislatures and the Dominion Parliament have it and exercise it.

There's not a federal or provincial government in Canada that hasn't got expropriation powers. Before we came in, there were at least seven or eight acts in Saskatchewan that gave powers of expropriation.

> In this session, there was the eighteen-year-old vote, a crown corporation operated a bus line, and equal pay for equal work in the public service.

Both of the old-line parties were against the eighteen-year-old vote. When I introduced it, I made the statement that if we had a right to conscript men, put them into uniform, and send them out to fight for a country at eighteen years of age, then automatically they had the right to have something to say about how the country should be governed. I pointed out that young men of eighteen, nineteen, and twenty were flying bombers worth two or three million dollars, and if they were old enough to do that, they surely had sufficient intelligence to know how to cast a ballot. It's rather significant that in subsequent elections, the old-line parties who had voted against the legislation spent a good deal of their time making a special appeal to the young people. I constantly reminded young people of the fact that the Liberals had voted against the legislation, and I reminded them of the editorial in the Liberal press, where a statement was made by the leader of the opposition that people of eighteen to twenty-one were the chocolate-bar vote, and didn't have sufficient intelligence to know how to exercise a franchise.

Following the session of 1945, I did what I had been prevented from doing following the emergency session—I went to Europe. General McNaughton was Minister of Defence, and he had made all the arrangements for me to go overseas. I went over on the *Aquitania*. There were about 9,600 personnel on board, mostly air force, some army, but mostly pilots and navigators, and only six civilians. Five were British technicians who'd been brought over to do special jobs in Canadian factories, and the sixth was myself. The captain of the ship was Sir Thomas Bassett. He was the captain of the *Queen Mary*, which was tied up in dry dock in New York getting scraped off, and they had sent him to take the *Aquitania* across. During the war he had transported thousands upon thousands of troops. He was one of the best merchant captains in the whole British mercantile navy, and a fascinating person.

He had some of us up for dinner in his cabin, and gave us the comforting news that we had lifeboats and rafts for 2,400 people. There were about 9,600 on board. We were sleeping in three-tiered bunks. He added that the six civilians were at the bottom of the list of the 9,600, and said, "I wouldn't bother struggling to get up on deck if one of the submarines hit us because you've got the lowest priority possible with the exception of myself."

It was a bad trip. Hitler had activated all his submarines, and they were everywhere. When we got close to the Irish Sea, the captain had some of us up for a cup of tea before going to bed and said, "If you want to see something really interesting, I'll have the steward call you tomorrow morning about 4:30; we'll be passing right through one of the big convoys that's had a rough time." There had been a pack of submarines following it and snapping away at it for days. He said, "We have to go through it but we can't stop. We've been switching our course and we've been away north; now we've got to slip south because if we keep on north they'll be waiting for us."

And so we got up the next morning and went through this convoy. There'd been about 106 ships in it when it started but it was down to about 70 or 80 by this time. There were at least half a dozen oil tankers on fire, burning from end to end and men jumping into the water, and other ships keeping on going. It was the most heart-rending thing I ever saw. The little destroyers were like sheep-dogs herding sheep together, nipping at the behinds of the ships, keeping them going. Everybody was holding at eight knots an hour, although many of them could do twelve or fifteen knots. They had to stay at eight knots, the pace of the slowest. They were creeping along, trying to keep in line, trying to close up the gaps. There were a couple of destroyers and the rest were corvettes. We plowed right through. We were doing about thirty-three knots an hour [*sic*].[3] We swung away south and came up to London through the Bay of Biscay.

We were not allowed to stop in London or Southampton or Liverpool, so we went north to Scotland. There were a lot of ships being sunk around these harbours. When we left from Halifax, there were three other ships leaving at the same time, the *Pretoria*, the *Saturnia*, and the *Grampion*, and Sir Thomas Bassett told me that two of them were sunk five miles out of Halifax harbour. I got off the ship at Greenock, and the rest went on to Glasgow.

Colonel Abolt from Winnipeg, who used to be with the *Country Guide*, met me at the ship, for which I shall always be grateful. It was rather odd; I'd been the only civilian among so many army personnel, so nobody paid much attention to me, naturally. But when I docked, a little launch came out with all these people with red bands on their hats, and somebody said, "There must be some bigwig the boys are coming out for," and I said, "Yes, probably some of the top staff officers are going to be taken off." These fellows marched up onto the quarter deck and then the loudspeaking system started calling for me to come up. Some fellow asked, "Where's your luggage?" I only had a haversack. "And where are your staff—your secretaries and your aide-de-camps?" I didn't have anybody. They whisked me off to Glasgow, and we caught the night train to London. I had told Canada House to arrange a room for me, but they sent me to the Savoy. At the Savoy I had a room about as big as this Executive Council Chamber, a living room, a huge bedroom, and a sunken bath with black marble steps. It was fit for a maharaja. When I asked what the room cost, I was told, "Only ten guineas a day." And when I asked, "Haven't you got anything less palatial?" the receptionist said, "But the premier of ———— was here last week, and he used it." I said, "Yes, but he's got about six times as many people to pay for it as I have." He couldn't get me anything else, so I phoned the Park Lane and I got a little room for twenty-eight shillings.

Then I went to the Canadian C.M.H.Q., the Canadian headquarters, and found one of my old friends from the South Saskatchewan Regiment on the staff there, Major William Beta, who is now manager of the Weyburn mental hospital. I saw the head of general staff, and everything was lined up for me to go to the Continent.

I flew in a military transport plane to Brussels, and then got on a plane that was mostly filled by paratroopers and small cans of petrol and ammunition, and we flew into Germany. For the next two or three months I toured Germany, Holland, Belgium, and France, and then went back to the United Kingdom. Then I started to visit the hospitals and the airports. It was an exceedingly interesting experience. I happened to get into Batingsville hospital, for instance, the day that the wounded arrived by plane from near the Rhine at Uden. One whole bank of the Rhine had been sown with these little mines about the size of an apple pie. If you stepped on one it was just enough to blow your foot off, and most of these fellows had lost their foot or somewhere between the ankle and the knee. Some of them had lost both feet.

I was amazed at the excellent medical service the Canadian army had developed. Our losses of wounded men were less than half of one percent. If they could get a man to a dressing station quickly, and unless he was mortally wounded, he could be treated with penicillin, and sulphanilamide.

How far did you get to the fighting?

I visited all of them.

How far did you get to the fighting?

I went to see the Loyal Edmontons, who were up the line in Holland fighting to get into Rotterdam. The night I stayed there, I slept in General Foster's trailer. The line by this time was getting quite fluid, and during the night there was a terrific amount of gunfire right near us, so I dashed out of the trailer, and met about fifty Germans who had wandered into the camp. They said they'd lost their way, but it was perfectly apparent they couldn't, as all the irrigation canals ran in one direction. It was a moonlit night and you could easily tell your direction. I think they were just trying to surrender.

In Germany I got up to the Second Division, and there I was fortunate to run in to Sandy McPherson, a son of M.A. McPherson, former provincial treasurer and attorney-general of Saskatchewan. He was very good to me and arranged for me to get as close as I could to the South Saskatchewan Regiment. I met young Les England, who was a lieutenant with the South Saskatchewan Regiment, and he agreed to take me up the line and let me visit with some of the boys. Coming back, they were fighting their way up toward Durenhoffen.

Was it a trench war?

No, purely open. There was no trench warfare. They were moving motorized infantry and tanks and armoured cars almost entirely. I flew over the battlefield before I went up, and could see the troops moving along roads, and when they'd hit resistance they'd spread out into the fields. The rest of the time they travelled on Hitler's very good roads. Those roads he built for moving troops in were a great help to an invading army; they were the best roads in Europe.

Coming back we were hit by a big American truck. It was our

own fault — we were supposed to keep in line — and once we broke out of the line, we were sideswiped by this truck. It threw both Les and myself into the ditch, and I hit my knee. While I knew it was sore at the time, and black and blue, I didn't take it too seriously. But this started my old osteomylitis again and I've had the knee operated on about every year or two since.

When the truck was smashed, Les was in trouble because I wasn't supposed to be there, so I said to Les, "Can you get out of this alright if I'm not here?" "Oh, yes," he said, "I can have this thing hauled back and simply report an accident." So he gave me general directions on how to get back to the billet, where I was supposed to be staying in the officers' mess. It wasn't until after I had left him that I suddenly realized I was in civilian dress in a foreign country where everybody was trigger-happy, and it took me quite a long while to get back.

What were you wearing?

A trench coat, a khaki shirt. I had been living out of a haversack for weeks, and had an electric razor and a change of socks and underwear. Otherwise I wore the same thing all the time.

How far were you from the enemy?

About forty miles.

Did you run into any trouble?

The nearest I ever got to trouble was in Holland, where I was also out poking around, visiting Saskatchewan lads. I was with one of the companies of the Loyal Edmonton, and coming back to camp I lost my way. I knew I wasn't supposed to be there, I was supposed to be in bed back at the division headquarters. That same afternoon I was with a motorcycle escort, and as we were riding along we saw some Dutch underground partisans with the four-inch band on their arms. They were bringing in a collaborator. Suddenly, he broke away from them and started across the field; they just levelled off with these Sten guns and cut him in half.

Here I was at about two o'clock in the morning, wandering around Holland, and I began to think about the collaborator and the Sten guns, and how I would explain that I wasn't a German spy or a collaborator. So I went up to a farmhouse and pounded on the door. Finally somebody upstairs threw a window open and a fellow stuck his head out and asked what I wanted. I tried to say, "I am an Englishman." I couldn't get Canadian, and I certainly couldn't get Scotchman, and I wondered what my father would have said if he came back to life and could hear me standing on the doorstep of a Dutch house and claiming to be an Englishman. The fellow was very good. He came down in his clogs, I can still hear them rattling on the steps as he came, opened the door and came out, and he walked with me and put me on the right road. The next day before I left the camp, I wheeled down to his house with my little motorcade and gave him a couple of boxes of chocolates and some bars of soap; the soap, of course, was the most welcome of all. I certainly was never so relieved in my life as when he helped me get on that road. That was much more dangerous in many ways than being up the line. The place was seething everywhere with raw trigger-happy partisans.

How long were you on the Continent?

Until about three or four days before V.E. day. I was back in London the day that it was almost certain that an armistice was being signed. I remember there was a bit of a mix-up: it was announced and then it was withdrawn, and not officially announced until the next day. I was at the co-operative headquarters in Manchester when the cablegram came. All the day before the people had been celebrating; I had seen the tremendous crowds in Trafalgar Square. That day in Manchester, nobody worked, everybody assumed they were going to have a holiday, and there was a great celebration that night.

I suppose you talked to many young privates when you were overseas. What sort of impression did you get from them? Were they fed up with the war? Did they give you any indication what they wanted to happen in the post-war world?

I would say that morale was very high. There was no indication of being fed up. This might have been more so when they were garrisoned in England. But there had been plenty of action, and

Douglas discussing rehabilitation with members of the First Canadian Division, 1945.

they'd been on the move and seen new country, and by this time it was very apparent that Hitler was folding up.

Almost every place I went, Ostend, for instance, there were 22,000 men on parade. Ostend was a retraining depot, occupied by men who had been wounded or convalescent, who were retrained prior to being sent back to action. Most of them were veterans going back again. I said a few words to them formally over the public address system, and then I said to the officer in charge, "I wonder if you'd have the men just break off, I don't want to weary them with making a speech, and those who want can go about their business, and some can stay around and just chat." It was just a human sea; they broke off ranks and stood or sat around on whatever was handy, and they shot questions to me standing on this truck.

The same thing happened more than a score of other places

in smaller groups running anywhere from a hundred to a thousand men. Always the questions were the same: "What's it going to be like when we come back?" Almost every place I went I found I knew people. Boys came up to me and said, "You won't know me, but my dad is a farmer and always goes to your C.C.F. meetings," or "I heard you speak at a picnic." One fellow said, "One night in Brandon you were on the way down to Parliament, where they were going to declare war, and I was on my way to Winnipeg to join the P.P.C.L.I. [Princess Patricia's Canadian Light Infantry]. You saw me getting off the freight train, took me in to dinner, and gave me a dollar or something, and I later joined the P.P.C.L.I. and have been all through this show."

I remember three of them came up to me and said, "You know, we three have been together all through the war, and we marched behind you once." I said, "Were you ever in the South Saskatchewan Regiment?" and they said, "No." I said, "Then you didn't march behind me." They said, "Yes, we did, in 1937. You and Grant MacNeill marched ahead of us—there were 1,500 of us—and we marched up Parliament Hill. We were among the single unemployed, and you were trying to see if we couldn't get some status, because we had none at all at that time."

I found this was the story all over. Here were boys who had been on the breadlines, who had ridden on the boxcars, and had been working on farms for five dollars a month. And now, in the war, they had found security, prestige, and a feeling of belonging. Suddenly they were afraid of peace, much more than they had been afraid of war. This is what I was discussing last Tuesday with a group of veterans on Remembrance Day: "What do you say to boys in those circumstances?" You have to be honest. Finally, I said, "Frankly, I don't know what you're going back to. I know what I'd like to have you going back to, and I know what has been said you're going back to. The Prime Minister of Britain and the President of the United States said we're fighting for four things: freedom of speech, freedom of religion, freedom from fear, and freedom from want. This is the kind of world they say we're going to build. The Prime Minister of Canada has said we're not just fighting the war against nazism, we're also fighting a war for a better way of life. I can't guarantee that you're coming back to a better way of life, but all I can say is that if enough of us make up our minds to find a better way of life, then we can have it." I pointed out to them that during the war, with a million soldiers in uniform, the rest of the economy had produced more goods and services than we had ever produced in peace-time. If we could do that during wartime, surely we could produce all the goods for a better life when a million people came back and entered industry and agriculture.

When I look back, I am troubled because I just don't think we've kept faith with these people.

> A lot of these boys would have been in the Regina riot, the Estevan riot, and the march to Ottawa. Those would probably be just the type that would be in the front lines.

I'll never forget what happened at Ostend. I said to the officer in charge: "Sir, you don't need to wait around, I want to talk to these boys and I have nothing to do until dinner time tonight, and I can see you then." He said, "No, I'd like to stay. I'm interested in what you're saying." When we had finished and were going back to dinner, he said to me, "Mr. Douglas, you're a very lucky man. Anyone who's got as many friends among these boys as you have — I've watched these boys coming up and talking to you — is a pretty lucky person." I thought this was true. A politician has a lot of compensations after all. He won't make any money, he won't build up much security, but among those troops I found hundreds of boys, that at some time or in some way, whose lives had been touched by mine. I felt that I had been of some use to them.

> Were they worried about what was happening at home?

They weren't worried about people back home, except that the farm boys knew their dads were working too hard, working long hours, raising pigs and doing all the things we were supposed to do to win the war. They were anxious to get back and take some of the load off them again. But apart from that, and the terrific homesickness, they had a tendency to feel that they had been forgotten. That's why I was very glad that I went. I was a bit worried about the trip, because from my experience in the army, I knew that soldiers don't like V.I.P.s coming around, parading in front of them, and making a little speech about how much people appreciate what they're doing, fighting for King and country and all those things.

But I found that they did appreciate somebody coming around to see them—especially the boys from Saskatchewan—and this was particularly true in the hospitals. I must give credit to the C.M.H.Q. of the Canadian army. When I got to a hospital, a complete map was available, with every bed marked where Saskatchewan men lay. If they were ambulatory, they were all brought to a central place and I spent an hour or so with maybe twenty or thirty of them. Then I would make the rounds from ward to ward, visiting the Saskatchewan men. I walked miles every day down hospital corridors. These boys' faces would just light up to think that somebody from back home had come to see them.

I suppose you heard all the home towns mentioned?

Oh, yes. At one of the hospitals the matron said, "We've got one ward where all of the boys have been blinded. They were in tank actions where they were burned badly. They're pretty low. Maybe you could come in and just say a few words to them." It was about the toughest assignment I ever had in my life. What do you say to fellows who are lying flat on their backs, blinded? They have lost their ears, and are going to be disfigured for life. The newspapermen were trailing me around, but I'd sort of lost the feeling they were there. I stepped inside this ward and the nurses were all standing beside the beds. I was dog-tired and just sort of groping for something to say, "Well, fellows, it's nice to be here, and I can certainly understand why you like this hospital. All the prettiest girls in Canda must have been shipped over here to look after you." This went over the press wires. And when I got back to Regina I got the chilliest reception you ever saw—almost the first thing that was said to me was, "It's true, is it? All the prettiest girls in Canada are over in England looking after the troops and just us homely women are left here?" My wife never allows me to forget this foot-in-the-mouth statement of mine.

How did you approach the men? Did you start by asking them where they were from?

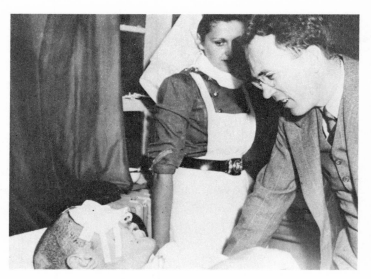

On his trip overseas in 1945, Douglas visited Saskatchewan men in Canadian army hospitals.

Yes. There was no problem with the fellows who were in uniform and in action, because after all, while I hadn't done any fighting, I'd been two years in the reserve army and I knew about their weapons. I asked them where they were from, how things were going, and what the grub was like, when they last got leave, how they liked the German girls or the Dutch girls or the Belgian girls: the usual army line. That was no problem.

The difficulty was with the wounded men, the chaps who were crippled. I remember one boy they took me especially to see — he wasn't from Saskatchewan — who had lost both arms and legs. It was terrible. What can you say to a man who the rest of his life is going to be completely helpless, will have to depend on someone else to feed and clothe him? But what amazed me was that many of these people were more cheerful and had more courage than a lot of other people back home with nothing the matter with them.

You couldn't sympathize with them?

No, you didn't dare. All you can say is, "You've had a bad break, but you'll never know how much the rest of us appreciate what you've done, and we want to try to make it up to you, and believe me we will." This is about the best you can do. You can help a fellow by saying, "After all, everybody gets bad breaks, and if you never go to war you get bad breaks. It's not so much the bad break you have, as how you meet it. If a man has the courage and the faith, in the long run it may do things for him. The important thing is not to let it get you down."

Do you think that men were inclined to turn toward religion?

Oh, yes, I think so. Somebody said that there were no atheists in the foxholes. I think when men come face to face with the grim realities of life, when any moment may be their last, they lose some of the flippancy and the cynicism they normally have. They begin to think about life in realistic terms. There isn't any doubt in my mind that people can't live through wartime, or even go through some bad breaks during peace-time, unless they've got some sort of a basic faith.

Then you went back across the Channel and you were in Manchester on Armistice Day.

I spent a day with the Scottish Co-operative Board of Directors in Glasgow. They asked me to lunch. I was sitting next to Donald Gow, now the president of the Scottish Co-operative Wholesale Society, and Donald said, "Have you ever been in Glasgow before, Mr. Douglas?" I said, "Yes, I went to school here at the Scotland Street School." He said, "You're not wee Tommy Douglas that played inside left for our football team?" and it turned out that he had played centre and that we had gone to school together. I didn't recognize him and he didn't recognize me. It was marvellous.

I was due to fly back because of the general election that had been called in Canada in the meantime. I came back on a Lancaster bomber, one of those old unheated bombers in which you sat with an oxygen mask on your face once you got above eighteen thousand feet. It was dreadfully cold. The passenger list was made up almost entirely of men who were going back to run as candidates. I got back just in time to get into the general election of 1945.

> Had anything happened provincially between then and the Dominion-Provincial Conference?

In July or August 1945, Mr. King called the Dominion-Provincial Conference on Reconstruction, and at that time he presented his green book proposals [sic]. [4]

The economic advisors to the government were quite convinced that once we returned to a peace-time basis, we were going to be faced again with the problems of over-production, unemployment, and surpluses. So the green book proposals were designed, and I quote, "to maintain full employment and a healthy level of national income." I think the green book was probably one of the most comprehensive pieces of work that has ever been done in Canadian history — in laying out a blueprint for establishing the beginning of a planned economy in Canada. It dealt with agriculture, industry, social welfare, a complete programme of national health insurance and public works. The general idea was that in times of prosperity we should be pulling money out of circulation, and in times of depression we should be pumping money into circulation. On the basis of the shelf theory, both the provincial and federal governments should have a whole series of public works projects on the shelf — already drafted with all the specific details — which could be taken off the shelf at any time that unemployment began to reach menacing proportions, so that people could be put to work.

In addition, the Bank of Canada would be involved, so that whatever was physically possible could be made financially possible. It was a great forward step. It was a tragedy that it was all ditched. None of it in its broad concept was ever implemented, either by Mr. King's government or Mr. St. Laurent's, and there is no sign that it's likely to be implemented by Mr. Diefenbaker.

At that conference, Mr. King arose one afternoon and said, "I have just received an important cablegram from Washington. The President of the United States has just announced that atomic bombs have been dropped on Hiroshima, and that the empire of Japan is doomed to defeat." The conference coincided with the end of the war in the Far East.

> Those were the famous Green Book proposals that you endorsed for Saskatchewan?

Yes. We were the first province to support this approach to the period of transition from war to peace. At the conference, I said that the Saskatchewan government was prepared to support these proposals in total and to co-operate to make them a success.

> Could you tell us what the fiscal arrangements were at that time?

Because the federal government was going to invade the field of direct taxes so enormously in order to finance the war, and more particularly to keep down purchasing power since there weren't enough consumer goods available, in 1941 it was suggested to the provinces that the federal government would collect all the income, corporation, and inheritance taxes and would pay a set sum each year to the provinces. The provinces agreed.

But when the war was over, we wondered if we were going to continue with this fiscal arrangement. Ontario and Quebec wanted no part of it; they wanted to go back and collect their own direct taxes. The rest of us, sometimes called the have-not provinces (although Saskatchewan is not in that position now), said we wanted this pooling of the revenue from these three tax fields for the very obvious reason that there are a great many corporations that make their money in our provinces but don't pay corporation taxes, income taxes, or inheritance taxes in our province. The banks, the insurance companies, the implement companies, the oil companies, and scores of others that do a tremendous amount of business in our areas don't pay any of these three direct taxes in our province. We have a right to part of this tax revenue. If the Massey Harris Company does fifty percent of its business in the prairie provinces, but doesn't pay any taxes here, then surely the western provinces have some right to part of that taxation and there's no reason why Ontario and Quebec should be allowed to take that tax revenue on money that was not earned in their provinces. We have a claim on it.

A tax-rental agreement finally came in 1947, which was later superceded by the tax-sharing arrangement. To me this is the kernel of the whole problem of dominion-provincial relations. I think we've wasted a lot of time in Canada arguing about federal grants for education, highways, and development of natural resources. The moment you do this, you run into constitutional questions. Quebec says, "If we accept money for education, then eventually we'll be asked to give up some of the control of our curriculum and the type of material that will go into our educational system, and we can't take a chance." Personally, I don't agree. I think they should be able to accept money without any strings attached.

I think we could get around all those constitutional arguments by simply making a fair division of these three tax revenues. Under our constitution, these three tax fields are open jointly to both federal and provincial governments. Provincial governments and the municipalities were the sole occupants of some of these tax fields prior to 1917. The federal government levied no income tax until 1917, which continued for twenty years and was considered a wartime measure only; and it was thought that after the war the federal government would get out of the income tax field, and leave it to the provinces and municipalities. The figures for 1957 show that out of every five dollars the federal government has collected from these three fields of revenue, they have kept four dollars and given the provinces one dollar. The federal government must be prepared to share this field, or at least divide it on the basis of sixty-forty, and there's a good case for it being divided fifty-fifty. It must be remembered that when the Fathers of Confederation divided the field of revenue, they divided the fields of responsibility. Those they gave to the provinces and municipalities were relatively unimportant, but today health, welfare, and education are now provincial and municipal responsibilities, and represent sixty percent of our total expenditures. They have become extremely important. But the sources of revenue have not kept pace with the increasing responsibilities laid on our doorstep.

◹ During the 1946 February session, House broadcasting was started.

We were the first province in Canada to start broadcasting parts of the legislative proceedings. It wasn't a new idea in the Commonwealth; New Zealand had House broadcasting since 1935, Australia also had it.

We started on an experimental basis for the first few weeks of the session. The radio people assured me that two weeks would be plenty; people wouldn't be interested. At the end of the two weeks, the outcry from the public was so favourable that the radio people phoned me frantically, and said that they would continue the broadcast for nothing if we would let them; they were being accused of all sorts of things for shutting off the broadcast.

They were extremely popular. People may have got used to them by now. But certainly in the initial stages they were quite a novelty.

What would you say was the primary purpose of these broadcasts?

The purpose was twofold. The first was to keep the people acquainted with public affairs, which is difficult when half the people in the province don't live in towns or villages or cities, and don't receive a daily newspaper. They get the daily news over the radio, but that may only be fifteen minutes long, and has to cover everything from international affairs, federal and provincial matters to deaths, murders, and traffic accidents. The amount of time given in news broadcasts to provincial affairs is very small. If we're going to have an intelligent electorate, they ought to know how their business is being conducted, how their money is being spent, and they should be aware of the programme of the government and the alternative proposals of the opposition.

This closer contact with the Legislative Assembly enables people on these far-flung prairies to know where their members stand on the various questions. I've been asked by many people, "Has it ruined the conduct of the House?" There's no use denying that it has required some changes in the conduct of the business of the House, but I don't think these are serious changes. Indeed, when the broadcasting is on you try to choose legislation that will cause some debate, which will demonstrate different points of view. For example, you wouldn't spend an hour and a half of broadcast time arguing whether municipal voting should be at 3 P.M. or 4 P.M.

My considered opinion is that the broadcasts have raised the standard of debate. In our Legislature we have no time limit, as they have elsewhere. Consequently, there's a great temptation for a member to throw a lot of documents and papers together and ramble all over the place for one or two hours with no particular clear-cut statement of policy. But with this vast radio audience he's got to organize his material better, and speak to the point. He can't have long periods of silence while hunting up more quotes from a newspaper file. He must have everything ready, and try to make his speech as effective as possible.

However, I admit that broadcasting has tended to make members speak to the country rather than to the House. But after all, what is the function of Parliament or a Legislature if it not to speak to the country? Why are two people arguing in Parliament? Surely they are not trying to convince each other. Is the government trying to convince the opposition or is the opposition trying to convince the government? If that's the purpose, then Parliaments and Legislatures have wasted their time for centuries.

Members in the Legislature are speaking to the people they represent. They are trying to give their reasons for or against a certain measure. Why shouldn't the people hear it? I argued all along that the radio is an extension of the gallery of the Legislature. Just as the people in the capital city can come and sit in the gallery, by radio we've made it possible for a person three hundred miles away in Lac La Ronge to sit in the gallery and to hear members speak.

If there is criticism in the House about it, it's that some of the members feel they don't get enough time.

Yes.

The Automobile Accident Insurance Act was the first of its kind anywhere in the world. It was violently opposed by the insurance companies.

The Automobile Accident Insurance Act was introduced by the Minister of Social Welfare. It was really not a commercial venture so much as a social welfare measure in its early stages. The reason for it was obvious. We came across pitiful cases of people who had been maimed as a result of automobile accidents. Many of those who were responsible for these accidents had no financial means, so there was little value in getting a judgement against them because they didn't have anything that could be seized. We also came across an increasingly large number of people lying in hospitals with broken legs or backs, people who were permanently disabled with no means of getting any financial assistance from the people who were responsible. In many other instances, the father, the bread-winner of the family, had been killed in an automobile accident.

We proceeded with the Automobile Accident Insurance Act on the principle that when you give a licence to drive a car to an individual, you are handing over a lethal weapon. Surely we have the right to provide that the motorist shall make some financial contribution to take care of the people he might injure, and at least some minimum compensation for the people who are left destitute as a result of a fatality. This does not preclude the injured party from going to the court and getting further remuneration, but it at least guarantees that there will be a fund from which these people can get some financial reimbursement. In a good many cases when people did go to court, sometimes forty percent of the money paid was already spent in lawyer's fees and court costs.

The insurance fee was six dollars, which was put into the fund. Any person injured riding in a car, driving a car, walking, on a bicycle, in a buggy, or on a hayrack or wagon, could draw money on this fund for doctor and hospital benefits — twenty-five dollars a week up to a maximum of thirty months while they were incapacitated. Death benefits were up to ten thousand dollars for a widow and her children. At this time we made no provision for other types of insurance such as collision or public liability or property damage insurance. We only sought to provide insurance for the people who were injured as a purely social welfare measure. Mr. Procter, the former Minister of Highways, who was in the opposition at this time in 1946, said that this act was the greatest hoax that had ever been perpetrated on the people of Saskatchewan in the guise of insurance.

Subsequent events have proven that it wasn't a hoax. People began to see the benefits. Later on we covered property insurance, public liability, collision insurance, and theft. Now we have a five-point insurance policy that people get completely at cost. I made the pledge that never would one dollar of the money paid for automobile insurance go into the provincial treasury. At the same time, I said that the people can determine what the premium will be. If accidents increase, then they will have to pay more for insurance. If people drive more carefully, then accidents will decrease, and the premiums will be reduced.

> Insurance companies naturally raised a row because it turned out that the government rates were considerably less than anywhere else in the world.

As far as they were concerned, they had to stop selling car insurance because they could not compete with our rates.

> Even in general insurance, the insurance companies dropped their rates tremendously, which showed that they could exist and still make gains.

The Government Insurance Office, which is a commercial organization, doesn't get any money out of this Automobile Accident Insurance fund. The Government Insurance Office sells automobile insurance over and above the compulsory insurance, so that anyone who wants to take additional protection can take out a package policy, and they were in direct competition with the insurance companies. The insurance companies were progressively compelled to reduce their insurance rates, not only on automobile insurance, but also on fire insurance, casualty insurance, bond insurance—almost all forms of insurance. The last rate book issued by the Dominion Underwriters Association carries a notation that these rates included apply to the four western provinces except Saskatchewan, where premiums are discounted twenty percent. This is part of the reason why insurance companies have been so venomous in their attacks on the Saskatchewan government.

> There are movements in places like Ontario, although they might not materialize, to follow the system to some extent of Saskatchewan, although another faction is anxious that the private insurance companies handle it.

They follow the typical free enterprise reaction to the kind of situation I have described. But they also recognize that some provision should be made. So what do they do? They say they'll protect the person who is injured, or the dependents of those who are killed, by making car insurance mandatory. But when they say you must take out insurance—in some provinces you can't get a licence until you produce your pink slip—it doesn't matter what the rate is, you have to pay. Instead of coming down, insurance rates went up in those places.

> At this same time, the government wanted to buy a radio station. A crown corporation was set up for that purpose.

The radio station C.H.A.B. in Moose Jaw was for sale, and we negotiated with them and got an option to purchase it. We were prepared to set up a crown corporation in order to have a provincial radio station that could give our people not only entertainment but a good deal of information regarding various departments, information for farmers from the agriculture representatives, news from the Health Department, Welfare Department, and the Labour Department that should be passed on to the public.

When we made application to operate this radio station, we were denied. The reason given was that it would cause complications if a provincial government had a radio station when radio stations normally came under the federal government. Ironically, it hadn't caused any complications for Mr. Duplessis to have two or three, or the Manitoba government to have two, or for the Alberta government to have one. But when the Saskatchewan government wanted a radio station, it was decided that it would cause complications.

> I don't think the C.C.F. could depend upon the existing media for any kind of a satisfactory relation.

It is almost impossible to get an objective statement of our policy, or even an adequate description of any piece of legislation, printed in the daily press. We can hand the press a statement and either it won't be printed at all or it will be run in such distorted form that it looks almost meaningless and would appear among the classified ads, while the criticism of the legislation would be plainly visible on the front page with a two-inch headline.

We felt that the radio station would have been very useful to explain to the public exactly what we were doing and why we were doing it—and not simply exist as a political propaganda agency. How does the average person go about applying for an old age pension, how does an old age pensioner go about getting his health services card, what requirements are there for getting natural gas in your house? These are all important pieces of information to pass on to people. We try to tell farmers about better farm practice, better land use, how to combat grasshoppers and cutworms, and new methods of tillage to conserve moisture. How do you get this information to people? We send out pamphlets, but not many people sit down and read pamphlets, whereas it is quite convenient for most people to listen to radio broadcasts.

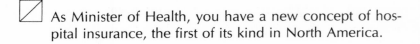 As Minister of Health, you have a new concept of hospital insurance, the first of its kind in North America.

In Britain, they started in 1948, but they were already studying it in 1946.[5] The Scandinavian countries were ahead on hospital insurance. We in this province had something on municipal plans so we had a precedent on a municipal basis. We had a tuberculosis programme, and in 1944 we had launched the cancer programme, which covered hospital, medical, and surgical care. We had already set up complete health services for old age pensioners, blind pensioners, and mother's allowance cases in 1945. But there had been no attempt anywhere for an overall inclusive plan.

> This rather vast scheme seemed to be something that no province could even tackle. Where did the thought originate?

We had campaigned on proceeding with a system of complete health care. Each election year we issued a small pocket-sized card that outlined our programme. Here's our 1944 platform. It read,

> The C.C.F. government in Saskatchewan gives: 1. Security in your home; 2. Real debt reduction; 3. Increased old age pensions; 4. Medical, dental, and hospital services irrespective of the ability of the individual to pay; 5. Equal educational opportunity for every child in the province; 6. Increased mother's allowance, maternity grants, and care for the disabled; 7. Freedom of speech and freedom of religion; 8. Right of collective bargaining; 9. Encouragement to the co-operative movement.

Number four, medical, dental, and hospital services irrespective of the ability of the individual to pay, was the plank we had been working on. We said quite frankly that we would not be able to establish a complete system of health services in four years, but we could make a start.

We began with free cancer treatment and hospitalization, free care the mentally ill, and free care for those suffering from venereal disease. Starting January 1945, we extended free care and treatment to old age pensioners, mother's allowance cases, blind pensioners, and wards of the government.

At the opening of the University Hospital, Saskatoon, in 1955.

But we were now beginning to come to grips with the overall programme. We thought we should start with hospitalization. We didn't feel then, and I don't feel now, that you can set up a complete health insurance programme covering every aspect of health services all at once. The federal government might do it, although I'm not even sure that even a federal government ought to do it all at once. The Labour party in Britain (I said this to Mr. Bevan when I discussed it with him[6]) would have been better to have gone step by step. There are several advantages in doing this: first of all, you get your machinery established. You get one problem, you solve it, you get it running smoothly, and you move on to the next. But in trying to set up six programmes at once, the possibility for confusion and inefficiency and incompetence is almost certain.

So our feeling was that we should first tackle the general

hospital insurance programme. We couldn't proceed at once because we didn't have hospital accommodation. In the fall of 1944, we set up a commission headed by Dr. Sigerist, Professor of Social and Preventive Medicine at Johns Hopkins University, to make a complete survey of the health facilities in the province.[7] Dr. Sigerist pointed out that we had a good deal of preliminary work to do before we could implement medical or hospital insurance.

After we took office, we were the first province in Canada to pay construction grants to communities to build hospitals. When we suggested to the federal government that they might contribute, they replied that the request was completely unconstitutional. Then in 1948 the federal government said they would give a thousand dollars per bed providing our government would match it. This was one of the instances in which you had to pay a price for being too progressive, because the plan wasn't retroactive, so all the money we had paid out to the municipalities from 1944 to 1948 wasn't recognized. Many municipalities would have received twice as much money if they had waited.

But I'm just as glad we didn't wait. It was necessary to go ahead. We spent a million dollars during that period on hospital construction grants. Many new hospitals were built, while many existing hospitals built additions. There were about thirty-three hospitals in the province that were closed; we opened them by giving grants for re-equipping and renovating the buildings. By 1946 we felt that we were moving toward the goal we had set for ourselves, which was seven and a half beds per thousand of the population. I think by 1947 we had probably reached about 6.8 beds per thousand.

In 1946 we brought in legislation that people had to pay a per capita tax of five dollars to a family maximum of thirty dollars into a hospital insurance plan. In addition, we levied one percent sales tax on certain commodities. When we took office there already was a two percent sales tax on everything. We released foodstuffs and grocery products, drugs, school books, farm implements, fertilizers, weed sprays, chemicals, and farm fuels from the sales tax. Today, about half of the commodities sold carry a sales tax. My theory on financing total health care is that all of it ought not to be financed on a per capita basis. This means each family pays the same tax irrespective of whether their income is two thousand or a hundred thousand dollars a year, which to me is retrogression of the worst sort. Some day I would like to see a nominal per capita tax of five or ten dollars a family, five for the husband, five for the wife, and ten dollars maximum for the family.

I think people appreciate something if they've paid for it. If you give people a card from Santa Claus entitling them to free hospital services, it is not good psychology. But the amount should be sufficiently small that it doesn't impose financial burdens on anybody.

The balance of the money, in my opinion, ought to come out of general revenue. A province can't collect income tax, so we have to collect from the sales tax. Last year, 1957, about forty percent of the cost of paying people's hospital bills came out of the per capita tax, and about twenty percent came from sales tax. While sales tax is not as equitable as an income tax, it bears some relationship to the ability to pay. The people buying luxury items pay more. The remaining forty percent of the cost has come out of the royalties received from the development of our resources: oil, uranium, copper, lead, zinc, sodium sulphate, potash, coal, timber, fish, and fur.

Social Crediters have talked a great deal about paying dividends. Mr. Manning tried this idea of giving everybody twenty-five dollars for two years, irrespective of whether they needed it or not. If you were an old age pensioner you got the same as if you were a millionaire. It seems to me that this is not the proper way to pay people social dividends. You pay dividends on the basis of need. Forty cents of every dollar for hospital bills last year were paid out of this social dividend fund from the sale of the resources that belong to them. People who weren't sick didn't receive anything.

There was tremendous opposition to our plan, unexpectedly so. Now, everybody's in favour and everybody wants to get in on the act. Mr. Tucker, who spoke before the Women's Liberal Club here in Regina, and Mrs. Parker, president of the club, both said that the municipal plan was far better, far less expensive, and that our plan was a great centralized bureaucracy in which half the money would go for administration. Our administrative costs are about four percent, the lowest on the continent. Blue Cross plans run anywhere from sixteen to twenty-one percent in administrative costs.

Doctors were very much opposed, not because they objected to the idea of hospital insurance, but because they felt this was the beginning of socialized medicine. The hospital people weren't too happy about it, and about three weeks before the plan was to go into effect the entire executive of the Saskatchewan Hospital Association marched into my office and said, they were not prepared to co-operate with our legislation dated to become valid in January 1947. Their objections were on the grounds that the government would virtually take over the hospitals. Since we were going to pay all the bills, it was only natural that we would control the hospitals. We would be appointing auditors and managers, and we would take control of municipal hospitals, and what was even worse, we would take control of the private hospitals, particularly those run by the churches. I explained that our intention was to centralize finance and de-centralize administration. We would collect the money and then pay the hospitals for the care given to the people protected under our plan. As far as we were concerned, the running of the hospital would continue to be in the hands of hospital administrators. But I told them that if they couldn't run the hospitals under this plan then on 1 January, we would take over the hospitals. I suggested that they think it over and return later to give me their decision. They decided to go along but they were most reluctant; they were quite prepared to begin protesting the moment we took over the hospitals.

It's rather significant that today the hospitals are the strongest advocates of the plan. Many hospitals were unable to collect between thirty and sixty percent, in the bad years, of their accounts. Many had the unpleasant task of refusing to admit people unless they paid a week in advance. They couldn't run a hospital on thin air. Now they have no problem about accounts. They don't have to wait. On the first and fifteenth days of each month they get a cheque covering the cost of their operation. A hospital that used to run deficits of anywhere from seventy to a hundred thousand dollars a year has no deficits today. Many of the Catholic hospitals, because they get paid for sisters on staff whom they don't pay, have been able to build up reserve funds for improving their hospital facilities.

In addition to these other opposers, my own people in the department, bless their hearts, almost went on strike on me. I've never told this story. We had gathered some very able people: Dr. Mindel Sheps and Dr. Cecil Sheps, a husband and wife team, came to us in 1945 and helped us with a good deal of planning. Dr. Sigerist suggested that the ablest man on the continent to implement the plan was Dr. F.R. Mott. His father was John R. Mott of the Y.M.C.A., a world figure and a Nobel Prize winner.[8]

Dr. Fred Mott was in the army at this time, and I arranged to meet him and discuss the situation. He was very interested but couldn't get away unless the American government would release him. [In this connection Dr. Mott states: "I was a commissioned officer of the U.S. Public Health Service, still on active duty in the spring of 1946 (Senior Surgeon in rank). The person releasing me from active duty was the internationally known Surgeon General of the Public Health Service, Dr. Thomas Parran. The position I was released to fill was that of Chairman, Saskatchewan Health Services Planning Commission. In 1949 I became Acting Deputy Minister of Public Health, and in 1951, Deputy Minister."][9] He brought Dr. Len Rosenfeld with him, a charming person, now working with Dr. Mott in Detroit running a health scheme for the United Automobile Workers under Walter Reuther.

So we had this fine team: Dr. Cecil Sheps and his wife Dr. Mindel Sheps, Dr. Len Rosenfeld, and Dr. Fred Mott. The first week in November, just a month before the hospital people called on me, my own people came in to see me. They had been working night and day. You can imagine the task of trying to register almost a million people in Saskatchewan, set up records, establish a uniform bookkeeping system in hospitals so that auditors could estimate accounts, and develop a uniform auditing and cost-accounting system. It was a Herculean task, and they had been working on it for about a year or year and a half. We took offices wherever we could get them downtown, we had temporary staff, and everybody was working at top pitch. They were tired, and like everybody who's been working hard, they were somewhat dis-

Presentation of the first Saskatchewan hospitalization card, 1946. *Left to right:* T.G. McNall, Dr. Hames, T.C. Douglas, unidentified, Dr. F.R. Mott.

couraged, and said to me that day: "We're afraid we've got bad news for you. We can't be ready before 1 January 1948." After listening to all their arguments, I said: "I told the people from the beginning that we'll be making some mistakes because we're blazing a new trail, but one mistake that we will not make is the mistake of doing nothing. So we're going to start." They were somewhat solemn when they went out and back to their task, but let it be said to their everlasting credit that they had that plan in good shape by 1 January 1947. We all met at my home on New Year's Eve, waited for midnight, and then went out to the hospital to see the first patient taken in under the new Saskatchewan Hospital Plan. Our Economic Planning Board did an excellent job of graphing the anticipated hospital population. They estimated that our increase in population would be about twenty-six percent. Experience proved that they were only two decimal points out.

So it was New Year's Eve when the first patient arrived.

The first patient admitted under the plan at the General Hospital was a woman coming in to have her baby.

◹ You took up residence in Regina after the 1944 election. Did you rent or buy a house?

We bought a house on 217 Angus Crescent. We already had a little cottage in Weyburn, and after the election I made arrangements to sell that house and purchase the house in which we're now living.

How much did you pay for it?

My recollection is $6,000 for the house and $150 for a little garage at the back, a total of $6,150. I had $2,000 from the sale of the bungalow in Weyburn, and I borrowed the balance of the money to pay for the house.

You weren't loaded, in other words.

I was very badly in debt as a matter of fact. In 1940, going to attend that session of Parliament, I thought, as everyone did, that it would be a regular session. So I went to the bank and borrowed a thousand dollars to see me through until the session took place and I got an indemnity. In that 1940 session, we sat for one day. Mr. King sent us home on 26 January to hold a winter election on 26 March 1947, which meant that we got twenty-five dollars for our work. I think that was the only election in Canada in which my bank manager was praying every night that at least one C.C.F. member would get re-elected.

I was in much the same position in the 1944 election. We were on an indemnity of four thousand dollars a year in those days. Income tax was quite high, and there were also compulsory savings. I was looking after my wife and daughter in Weyburn and I was boarding in Ottawa, which meant that I had two homes to keep up and a good deal of travelling to do all on four thousand dollars. I was in fairly strained financial circumstances.

> When you bought the house you weren't yet drawing any salary, were you?

Salary began the moment we took office, which was 10 July 1944.

> How much was your salary?

My salary was $6,500 and cabinet ministers were paid $5,000.

> You once attempted an excursion into big business with your friend and colleague Clarence Fines. You started a mink ranch, did you not?

Yes. It wasn't really started as a business venture. The doctors who looked after me in 1945 after I hurt my leg in Germany began talking to my wife and to Clarence Fines, saying that I was working too hard, spending too much time at the office, and that I should have some sort of a hobby. I've never had a hobby. More recently I've started to play golf, but only about two games a year. The idea was to get me outside, and so Clarence Fines got the bright idea that he and I would start a little mink ranch on the outskirts of Regina. We only had a dozen or twenty mink, and we found someone who had a mink ranch of his own to look after ours. But we would go out and knock together cages, whitewash the fence, and move the mink around from cage to cage. We spent a good many evenings out there, and sometimes a Saturday and part of a Sunday during the breeding season. The old mink ranchers of the province always tell about the time Fines and I tried for four solid hours to breed a mink by putting two males in the same cage!

> The story goes that some distinguished visitor came to town, and you were so busy shingling that you forgot about him.

Yes, and I looked much more like the hired man than the premier of the province.

> You weren't highly successful as a mink rancher?

We were a bit unfortunate. The fellow who was looking after our
mink seemed to have considerable difficulty keeping our mink
separate from his own and we finally decided to give up the venture. We got out with a total loss of maybe fifteen hundred
dollars.

> Your other excursion into business was your share in a
> drive-in theatre.

Yes. Again, that wasn't supposed to be a business venture. Phil
Bodnoff, whom I'd only met because he was running a cafe
downtown, told me that the only drive-in theatres were owned by
the chains and the Famous Players, but he and some of his friends
were starting a drive-in theatre that was to be owned entirely by
local people. They planned to put on local boxing bouts some
evenings before the show started, and other evenings they'd get
Regina and Saskatchewan artists to perform. This could become
a very good community affair, and he wanted me to go into it. I
explained that I didn't have any money to go into a business venture, but, he insisted, "Put in a little bit." So I put in five hundred
dollars, with the option to buy more shares if and when I got any
extra money.

Subsequently this was blown up into quite an affair, because
Bodnoff, in connection with a totally different deal altogether,
had borrowed some money from the Government Insurance
Office on a theatre he owned in Weyburn. The two cases had no
relationship whatsoever. I wasn't even aware when I agreed to go in
with Bodnoff that he had ever borrowed from the Saskatchewan
Government Insurance Office.

Later on, Mr. Danielson from Arm River kept referring to
the Premier's Passion Pit. I had to admit I never attended one
show there. I think the theatre was used for church services on
Sundays, and a great many people came and saw religious films.
In those days, before television, drive-in theatres represented a
real saving for young married couples. They could put the youngsters in the back seat and go and see a show, where otherwise
they'd have to get a babysitter.

But this taught me a lesson that as a politician you just can't
do the things you would normally do as a citizen, because some-

body will try and make a mountain out of a molehill. I made up my mind that I would never at any time try to dabble in any kind of business, because inevitably any business will have something, directly or indirectly, to do with the government. There'll always be the suspicion that somehow special concessions were granted by the government because you happened to be a shareholder in that company.

> You're not connected with any companies?

Not at all. I think young men going into politics must realize this. People talk a great deal about the sacrifices men make going into public life, but there are a good many compensations, too: the people you meet, the chance you have to make some useful contribution to society. But there are sacrifices: you're away from home a good deal, there's practically no home life, and you certainly have no privacy. People feel free to call on you, and you have to accept that as part of the price you pay.

A great many people don't realize the extent to which you have to limit your business affairs. Mr. Fines and I on several occasions have had excellent opportunities to have invested in business deals. When propane gas first came to the province, you could go to any refinery and get propane gas for a fraction of a cent a gallon. They almost let you take it away; it was a by-product. We could have had an exclusive franchise for distribution for the whole of Saskatchewan. The people who took it over, of course, made a fortune. It would have meant either trying to look after it in our spare time and having a very good general manager, or both of us resigning and giving our full time to it. I don't think there's any doubt we'd have made a million dollars quite comfortably. But I came to the conclusion then, and I hold to it even more tenaciously now, that any man who is in public life is wise to sever himself from any business connections for his own sake, for the sake of his party, and above all for the sake of his colleagues.

> If possible, a politician, provided he's serious about making this his life work, should have some provision to keep him independent.

That's why we introduced superannuation, or pensions for members. The federal House had already done so, and so had Nova Scotia, but theirs only applied to cabinet ministers. We pay five or six percent, not just on our indemnity as the federal members do, but on our indemnity and salary. Somebody worked it out for me once: if I were to pay this percentage of my salary and indemnity[10] into a fund, I would earn about sixty percent more than I'm getting under this plan, because we have a three thousand dollar annual limitation to our plan. But this gives some type of security for men who are giving their full time to public life. While it doesn't mean wealth, it does mean that they will not become beggars.

> We had a terrible example of one man, a former premier, who was reduced to taking direct relief in this province.

We've had two. For example, one premier was actually paid relief in the City of Saskatoon until the C.C.F. government came in, and we put him in charge of the School for the Deaf. We gave him employment, because he was a very capable man in the field of education. In this last session we passed a special act giving to a former premier and lieutenant-governor a pension for the rest of his life.

> Otherwise they'd have nothing.

They'd have nothing, and this isn't good when a man has spent thirty to fifty years of his life devoted to public service.

> About your hobbies, you tell me that you're a good golfer, and we know that you like to read as much as you can. But when you first came to Regina, you had a most unusual hobby—you organized a group of underprivileged boys, did you not?

No, the boys I had were from the Sunday school. I got roped into it.

> What Sunday school was it?

The First Baptist Church. Shirley came home from Sunday school one day and said, "The Superintendent was making a great plea for a teacher to look after boys. There aren't enough boys coming to the Sunday school, and they were very anxious to get someone. Daddy, why don't you do it?" I thought it was very diffi- cult to persuade a youngster to go to Sunday school and do her duty in the church work if I refused to do it. So I offered my services, and I was given eight boys between twelve and fourteen years old. We later had over forty boys; I'm sure I taught this class for eight or ten years. We met about three times a week: on Sun- day morning at Sunday school, on Saturday afternoons for bowling, and one night a week we went out to the R.C.M.P. barracks to swim, play basketball, and box. I got a great deal of pleasure working with these boys. I was able to advise some of them in the matter of picking their courses, and going for further education. I was also able to help some of them get jobs.

> It must have been relaxing for you to some extent because the pressures of your work must have been dreadful.

I was exercising, and thinking young, instead of thinking always in terms of my own age group. There's nothing to puncture your pomposity, your self-complacency, quite so much as a group of boys asking you questions.

◸ When you studied languages at Brandon College, you were one of a class in which there were five rabbis and one Baptist. Could you tell us what happened there?

One of the standing jokes at college was the fact that in this Hebrew class, there were five Jewish rabbis and a Scotchman. At the end of the year, the Scotchman got the scholarship. In all fair- ness it wasn't because I knew more Hebrew than the rabbis, but I could probably get it into English better than they could.

> You've preached in Jewish synagogues, haven't you?

Yes, on several occasions. I've always had a tremendous admiration for the Jewish people, and for their history and religion. They have a highly ethical content in their religion. I've always been particularly interested in their prophets. I don't think any religion in the world has ever reached a higher concept of social justice and social righteousness than the great prophets, particularly Micah and Amos. I've always welcomed any opportunity to speak in a Jewish synagogue, or at a Jewish gathering.

> Do you actually follow the Jewish form of service when you do that?

I can still follow the Jewish form of service fairly well — of course both my Greek and my Hebrew are pretty rusty — but periodically I go back and brush up some quotations from the Hebrew prophets, and the same with my Greek. I spent six years studying Greek, and I can still read parts of the New Testament in Greek. I can't do so well on the classical Greek now. It's a much more difficult form of Greek, and I haven't had much time to read the Greek playwrights. It sometimes surprises my Jewish friends to find a gentile able to quote the Hebrew prophets, and take part in the service.

> Do you remember what took place when you were debating at Halvorgate?

The Halvorgate debate was with Mr. Rupert Ramsay,[11] who at that time was leader of the Conservative party in the province. He was running in a by-election in the Morse constituency, and we had a debate at Halvorgate. There is a story told about this outdoor debate, at which there were a couple of thousand people. They had arranged for a manure spreader to serve as the platform, and Rupert Ramsay and myself spoke up on this manure spreader. Trying to be a bit facetious and getting the debate underway on the lighter vein, I said this was the first time I'd ever spoken from a Liberal platform. One of the farmers yelled out and said, "Trip the lever, Tommy, she'll never have a bigger load," which proves that it isn't wise to open your mouth, or somebody will put their foot in it.

There were two debates following the election of Mr. Walter Tucker as leader of the Liberal party. Mr. Patterson, who had been premier of the province, had been leader of the opposition following the 1944 election. In preparation for the 1948 election, the Liberal party decided to appoint a new leader. They had a convention at which Mr. Culliton, who is now Mr. Justice Culliton of the Appellate Court, contended for the leadership with Mr. Tucker. Mr. Gardiner and his organization threw their weight to Mr. Tucker, who at that time was federal M.P. for Rosthern. Mr. Tucker was elected as Liberal leader.

He began to go around the province drumming up support for the Liberal party for the coming provincial election. Very early in the campaign, our supporters and Mr. Tucker's supporters around the Canora constituency began talking about a debate.

We had been in the habit each year of holding a big picnic at Crystal Lake, north of Canora, and so it was decided that we would have a debate at the same time as we usually had this picnic. It was quite an affair. We had about 1,500 people who sat around on the grass and in the shade of the trees.

One of the interesting things of this debate was the little exchange that took place between Mr. Tucker and myself, for which I was thoroughly and roundly criticized by the Regina *Leader-Post* because of the undignified language I used. You have to understand that the people in the Canora area are largely Ukrainian, and they're not quite as sensitive and touchy about talking of their stomachs as Anglo-Saxons are. In the course of his remarks Mr. Tucker talked about "When Mr. Douglas was a small boy he was so and so."

He said, "He's not very big yet." Mr. Tucker stood about 6 feet 1 and weighed about 250 pounds or more. He continued, "As a matter of fact, I can swallow him." So when I wound up the debate I agreed with Mr. Tucker; he was much bigger than I and he could swallow me without any difficulty, and "If he ever were to do that he would become a biological monstrosity; he'd have more brains in his stomach than he has in his head." The Ukrainians loved this, but apparently *The Leader-Post* thought it was a most undignified way in which to carry on a discussion of public affairs.

You had known Mr. Tucker before, had you?

Oh, yes. Mr. Tucker and I both entered Parliament in the election of 1935 and I had known him very well in the House, and then he and I were in the Reserve Army together and I knew him there. We had our picture taken with Mackenzie King, an awe-inspiring trio!

◻ In July 1945 you were invited to become an Indian chief. Could you tell us about that?

The Assiniboine tribe, east of Regina at Sintaluta, Piapot Reserve, and at Carlyle Lake, invited me to become an honorary Indian chief. The ceremony was held on the Piapot Reserve. I said in my remarks of acceptance that I didn't want this to be looked upon merely as an empty honour, that I would really like to be one of their own number trying to deal with their problems. I must say that they have availed themselves of that invitation. They come here with their various band problems constantly, and I've taken up their grievances with the Department of Indian Affairs on numerous occasions.

In 1948 I called a conference of Indians, trying to persuade them that they ought to have the provincial franchise, that this was the first step toward getting a federal franchise, and that getting the franchise was the first step toward getting politicians to take some notice of them and deal with their grievances. When they have the vote, politicians are going to try to woo them, and in wooing them will have to make some concessions to them. I'm sorry to say that in 1948 we got nowhere. The Indians were frightened at the idea of enfranchisement. They thought this meant, as the term had been used in the past, that they would lose their treaty rights and would have to leave the reserve, or that they couldn't go back to the reserve if they left it, and so they turned it down. You can't force these things on people. I've always felt that to compel people to take a privilege is very bad psychology. They should want it, they should understand what they're asking for, and they should take it with a full sense of the obligations pertaining thereto.

We have just had another conference with the Indians at Fort Qu'Appelle a few weeks ago. I put two questions before them again: the matter of the vote that we were quite prepared to give them, and also the matter of equality in liquor legislation. This time we had more success. They asked us not to take immediate action, but they have set up a federation of Indian bands and tribes in the province. They have now one organization to speak for them.

> Bootlegging has caused considerable misery; many Indans have been thrown into jail. What can you foresee?

I think the Indians should have equality in the matter of liquor legislation. There are two main reasons. The first is that undoubtedly they're getting liquor anyway, from bootleggers, or by making all sorts of home-brew. The other day our air ambulance plane brought in a woman who was beaten up by her husband at a party and subsequently died, and it transpires that the concoction they were drinking was made up of six bottles of vanilla extract, some wine they had gotten from a bootlegger, some home-brew they had made with raisins and hops, and a mixture of other things. It would have taken the lining off a steel boiler, let alone drive human beings crazy. It doesn't seem that you can solve their problems by denying them liquor.

Second, when you have different laws for Indians than you have for other citizens, you're making them second-class citizens. In effect, you are saying that liquor is good for a white man, but because another man's skin has a different pigmentation, liquor is bad for him. Liquor is either bad for both of them, or it's alright for both of them, or people should have the right to choose for themselves whether or not they think liquor is good or bad. The Indians have the same right to make that decision as white men.

Mr. and Mrs. Douglas welcoming new Canadians during official opening of the Saskatchewan Legislature in 1959.

This is probably the black mark in Canadian history, the way we've dealt with our Indians. Do you think it is possible to assimilate them? Is it necessary? What sort of prognosis have you got for these people both in Canada generally and in Saskatchewan?

I agree that the story of our treatment of the Indians is the blackest page in our history. I don't think there's any doubt, whether deliberately or subconsciously, that during the latter part of the nineteenth century, the common view was that the Indians would die off naturally and that this troublesome problem would disappear if we just let them alone. We herded them onto reserves that couldn't possibly have sustained them. The white man's diseases, particularly smallpox, tuberculosis, and venereal disease, were killing them off at a shocking rate.

In the last fifty years however, the Indian has begun to

develop an immunity to the white man's diseases. The population of the reserves is expanding. We must recognize now that they're here to stay, and that we've got to face up to the position of the Indian. This growing population creates a tremendous problem. First of all, these little postage-stamp reserves will not support the growing number of families who are living on them. In the far north, the people who have been living on either trapping or fishing are finding that there aren't sufficient trapping grounds or fishing areas to support the growing population. If you have twenty families on a lake and that's all the lake will support, and you add five more families who have to be supported, either they've got to over-fish the lake, or they've got to reduce everyone's catch. The result is that many young Indians are leaving the north country, leaving the reserves, and coming to our cities. We recently had a conference on Indians and Métis people in Regina sponsored by the the Regina Welfare Council. We find that over eight hundred Indians or Métis are living in Regina.

We've got to do several things. First of all, I'd like to see the care of Indians and Métis turned over to the provincial governments by the federal government. We would be prepared to accept this burden, providing the federal government would make some financial commitment and pay us an allowance per head for a given number of years until we can rehabilitate our native people. This would remove the anomalous situation of the federal government looking after Indians, and us looking after Métis people. At what particular time does a man cease to be an Indian and become Métis? They should all be citizens of the province and have all the rights and privileges of being citizens of the province.

We need to train these people so that they can take their place in our society: teach the boys to drive a truck and operate tractors, learn trades, become schoolteachers or doctors or lawyers; teach girls so that they can work as waitresses in restaurants, stenographers, nurses, or schoolteachers. Many of them will want to work in their own community. Some will become lawyers. We have a young Indian lawyer working in the Saskatchewan Government Insurance Office, a very competent person. There is no doubt at all about the intellectual capacity of Indians. They can do anything that we do, with proper training.

When we talk about the Americans indulging in this horrible segregation, we should realize that we have followed a policy of segregation that is even worse. We have not only segregated them in our own communities, but we've segregated them off into back concessions where they can't be seen, and where their misery and poverty won't offend us. I feel that the Indian must now be taught to be a member of our community, and that he must have all the privileges and the obligations of being a citizen. He should have the same right to go to our schools and hospitals, and to become a Canadian citizen and a citizen of Saskatchewan.

Compare our treatment of the Indians to the way New Zealanders have treated the Maoris. Very similar to the Indians, with about the same standard of social development, the Maoris have very successfully integrated into the economy of New Zealand. They've elected their own members to Parliament, they've graduated from universities, they've gone into the professions, into the business world, into the various trades and occupations, and they are a very proud people, still looking back with pride to their old culture, and yet part of the economy and the society of New Zealand. There is no reason why we can't do that here.

Complete assimilation could ultimately happen.

Over a long period of time, it's quite possible. Not physical assimilation, but social assimilation is absolutely vital. We have Chinese people in our community who run restaurants and various kinds of businesses, and are highly respected, but this doesn't mean that they intermarry or that we assimilate them biologically.

Do you see any objection to intermarriage?

I see no objection at all to intermarriage. If I were looking at a prospective son-in-law, I'd be much more concerned about his honesty, his integrity, and his kindliness, and his sense of responsibility as a husband and a father than I would be to whether he was red, white, or any other colour. The only problem that intermarriage presents is children. The child of mixed blood has problems growing up because he doesn't belong to either culture. He could be very lonely and may have a difficult period of maladjustment, but this depends entirely on the society in which he lives.

8

The 1948 election

Before the 1948 election, Mr. Tucker was in the federal Parliament. Do you recall what his line was when he came back? What was he going to do to defeat the C.C.F.?

Mr. Tucker took the position that we were fastening a Socialist dictatorship upon the people of Saskatchewan. We were establishing what he called compulsion and regimentation by setting up crown corporations and imposing regulations. Automobile insurance was an example. A person had to pay their hospital tax and have hospital insurance whether they wanted it or not. We had imposed regulations in the north country for conservation of fish and game. All this was played up as part of a terrible totalitarian form of society we were imposing on the good people of Saskatchewan. He started his campaign with the slogan, "Tucker or Tyranny."

I remember a few voters put up one of these huge "Tucker or Tyranny" signs, and one poor fellow came away shaking his head and saying, "I'm not going to vote for Tucker in any case, and I don't even know of this fellow Tyranny."

At this stage, what was your impression? Had they sent a man who was a considerable giant, or did you consider that Liberals could have done better?

When Mr. Culliton and Mr. Tucker were put before the Liberal convention, I must confess that secretly I was hoping Mr. Tucker would be elected. Mr. Culliton, while not such a fire-eater, was a much more dangerous opponent in my opinion. He had a keen intellect, met people well, had a sense of humour that gave him a sense of balance, and he knew better than to overstate his case. Whatever you might say about the C.C.F. programme, nobody thought for one second that we had established tyranny in Saskatchewan. The case was overstated, and Culliton wouldn't have approached us this way. I always had very high regard for Mr. Culliton. Later, when he finally resigned from the Liberal party and wanted to go on the bench, I made the statement that I thought the Liberal party had blown out its brains.

Mr. Tucker had been able to get support through the years by constantly reminding the ethnic groups, particularly the Mennonites — many of whom had relatives in Russia and were terribly afraid of communism, with great justification — of fighting this bogey man of communism. Mr. Tucker thought he could transplant this into a provincial campaign. You might be able to frighten people who've got relatives in Russia, and who naturally are very apprehensive of the Communists, but you're not going to be able to persuade the people of Saskatchewan who knew the C.C.F. leaders and worked with them in the Wheat Pool and the co-operative movement and the trade unions and on city councils. To say suddenly that the C.C.F. were going to impose a Communist dictatorship was so silly that it insulted the intelligence of the people in the province. Mr. Tucker would have been much better to have taken a pragmatic approach to the problem, rather than this far-fetched ideological approach.

A small man has a disadvantage in public life, but a big man also has a disadvantage; in the concept of David and Goliath, sympathy isn't with the big man. The big man must use his big size with considerable discretion or it acts against him.

> It is generally agreed that Mr. Tucker was undoubtedly Mr. Gardiner's choice.

Mr. Gardiner has always tried to select a man he can handle as leader of the Liberal party in Saskatchewan.

> The C.C.F. party decided that the best time to call an election is within a four-year period.

We gave a solemn pledge in 1944. One of the pet arguments the Liberal party proffered during the 1944 election was that if the C.C.F. were elected there would be no more elections. It would just be like Russia; they would abolish the Legislature, they would end elections, and this would be the end of democracy.

It's very difficult to answer a charge like that, which was not made openly, but from door to door and at little schoolhouse meetings. You can prove what you have or haven't done, but you can't prove what you won't do. The only answer I could make was that if the C.C.F. were elected, I would undertake to guarantee that there will be an election, not at the end of five years when our term would expire under the Legislative Assembly Act, but in four years. I pointed out that the Liberal party, who had been making this accusation that there would be no more elections, had not only gone five years but had extended their own life and stayed in office six years.

In 1948 we pledged to continue the extension of our programme on welfare, health, and education. The new things we would undertake were the rural electrification programme, and our development programme. Until that time we had been doing the preliminary work of geological surveys, and we were ready to start industrial development and the development of natural resources.

We recognized that from 1944 to 1948 we were putting the cart before the horse. Saskatchewan had had such a low standard of health, welfare, and education services, and such terrible roads, both provincial and municipal, that we had to expend very large sums of money to attack these problems. Mr. Culliton, when he came back as financial critic for the Liberal party in 1948, condemned the budget on the grounds that over sixty percent of our total revenue was being spent on health, welfare, and education. He said this was top-heavy. He didn't think we could maintain the standard of services, and that we were spending too much on areas that were not economically productive. This criticism was in part justified. Properly speaking, if you had an unlimited amount of time, and if you were prepared to see people suffer, in the first years you ought to put your money into developing resources so that mineral, oil, and forestry revenue would flow in quickly. You would put all your money into attracting industries, building only those roads that would serve the industries, doing everything to improve the economic conditions of the province, raise productivity, and then in subsequent years, you could use that revenue to give people health, welfare, and educational services.

This is the logical economic sequence, but politically you couldn't do it. People were not prepared to sit back and wait ten years for the things they thought they were entitled to. Second, on humane grounds, you couldn't say to old age pensioners, mother's allowance cases, cancer patients, and people who needed to go to hospital that some day we will give you the kind of things we can't give you right now. These people faced an immediate situation. They weren't living ten or fifteen years from now; they were faced with a crisis. Therefore, in our first four years we deliberately spent (and we're probably still doing it) a disproportionate part of our budget on health, welfare, education, and roads. We made no apology for it, and we still make no apology for it. Our motto was "Humanity first," human considerations before economic considerations.

Nevertheless we knew that we couldn't raise ourselves by pulling at our own boot straps. Constantly raising health, welfare, and education standards without raising the economic base to pay for these would be folly. So we decided at the start of our second term that we would slow down the tempo of social services spending for the next four years, and devote ourselves increasingly to raising the productivity of the province. This meant generating more power. Every time we get power on the farms, we're giving the farmer another hired man and giving his wife a hired girl. This would increase agricultural productivity, particularly for dairy and poultry farmers and mixed farmers.

This is exactly what happened. In 1948 we began a very intensive programme of industrial and natural resources development, and the results speak for themselves. When we took office we were getting a little over $1.5 million from resources, and last year we got about $25 million. This was revenue we were able to spend on welfare programmes.

> When a reform party is in office, the critical period for that party is the second election. Most reform parties exist for one Legislature or one Parliament, and then that is the end. The forces against you were somewhat appalling.

The 1948 election was the toughest we ever fought. In 1944 our opponents didn't really give us much chance of a win, but in 1948, they had no illusions at all. They knew that we had a big majority. They knew we meant business. We passed legislation interfering with debtor-creditor relationships and bond holders, the Local Government Special Powers Act, and we had introduced legislation taking over a number of power companies to integrate the power system. It was very apparent that we intended to carry out our programme. So the reactionary forces decided we were in earnest and should be stopped.

Two things were done. A great deal of outside financial assistance was brought into the province. The most noted of these was the Canadian Insurance Underwriters Association. I don't know how much money they poured in here, but I know that they brought in their public relations firm and all their public relations experts, set up their office in the Saskatchewan Hotel,[1] and prepared radio broadcasts, advertisements for the radio and newspapers, and big posters. They organized four or five thousand insurance agents in the province to begin door-to-door canvassing. In my own constituency they came in in droves from Regina: insurance agents with cars told the people that the Socialist government had regimented them. It was a well-organized and well-financed campaign. The insurance companies had a vested interest in defeating us. We had done two things to them that were almost blasphemous. One, we set up the Government Insurance Office, which was selling all forms of insurance except life insurance, and we supported co-op life insurance. We had provided very strong competition for them. They had to cut their rates to stay in business or get any share of the business. Second, we implemented compulsory automobile insurance, which pushed them completely out of the automobile insurance field. What was even more dangerous, we set a precedent for the rest of Canada, and other provinces were beginning to look at this compulsory automobile insurance plan with some envy.

Mortgage companies had a similar attitude. There was a concerted effort to put us out.

For the first time the Liberals and Conservatives managed to work out a fairly effective coalition, which made the campaign even more difficult. The parties didn't go together at the top — the two leaders kept announcing that there was no coalition — but there were a number of constituencies with joint candidates. In my own constituency of Weyburn they put up a Liberal-Progressive Conservative. McDonald himself, who is now leader of the Liberal party,[2] was elected as a Liberal-Progressive Conservative. While in some seats there was only a Liberal candidate and in others only a Conservative candidate, in quite a number of the key seats there were joint candidates.

> It shows well for the Liberal strategy that most of those elected were Liberals. They manned the candidate, and the Conservatives provided the vote.

This is what I kept saying — these joint candidates were simply subterfuge.

> This continued in subsequent years, until finally the Conservatives realized they stood to gain nothing by it.

We lost quite a few seats because of the coalition. We dropped from forty-seven to thirty-one seats. But, in many of these seats we lost in '48, we received more votes than we did in '44. The difference was that the opposing votes were combined.

The campaign itself was rough, wasn't it?

Oh, it was the roughest campaign I think I ever went through. In addition to our other problems, our own people had always fought the campaign as the opposition. They found themselves on the defensive for the first time, and they weren't used to fighting an election this way.

> Also, a lot of the C.C.F. politicians weren't hardened to the kind of thing that the Liberals, with their stops out, could do so well. They said you were setting up a dictatorship, and that in a very short time we'd have a totalitarian state.

They made it very difficult to deny. One of their favourite stories, we happen to know on good authority, was that the government had a drafted blueprint that would completely eliminate personal liberties and freedom of movement, and as soon as the election was over, it was going to be put into effect.

You can say that there isn't any such blueprint and that you have no intention of doing this, but suspicion, once aroused, never slumbers again. You can never catch up with that sort of thing.

> We also had another fantastic newspaper campaign against the C.C.F., day in and day out, with no opportunity to reply. You had radio broadcasts, but as for editorial support, I don't think there was one newspaper in this whole country that supported you, was there?

There were a few weekly papers, the *Grenfell Sun* and the *Wolseley News*, but about ninety-five percent of the weeklies were against us, and all of the daily papers. It wasn't merely the fact that the editorial page was attacking and misrepresenting us, but the news stories were slanted, and even when you issued a denial, the news story would argue it all the way through. The story would say, "Premier Douglas today denied so and so," and then in parenthesis, "(it should be noted however that Mr. Coldwell on such and such a date said so and so)" and the debate would go on all through the newspaper story, with the newspaper editor interplaying his counter arguments with anything you said. If your story wasn't punctured with these editorial observations, it was usually hashed and rehashed until it was almost unreadable. Also, the attack on you by the opposition would be on the front page with banner headlines, and your reply would be cut down to three paragraphs, on page 17 with the classified ads. If it hadn't been for the radio and public meetings, we would never have been able to get any type of answer to the public.

> I heard several experts comment that it was these very excesses that actually helped to elect the C.C.F. party. A prominent Liberal told me that this particular newspaper is killing the Liberals, all they're doing is just becoming unbelievable, and they're associating it with the Liberal party. I should remind you that on election night Mr. Fines went to the editor of the Regina *Leader-Post* and congratulated him on winning the election for the C.C.F. There are numerous examples in history where this has proven the point. It seems awfully dangerous for the party being attacked at the time, but the results can boomerang.

I remember a few years ago, the Canadian Press Association had an annual meeting in Regina. Mr. Rogers, the editor of *The Leader-Post*, was on the executive, and asked me to address the luncheon. I reviewed this question of the extent to which irresponsible journalism eventually discredits itself. My point was that there comes a time when newspapers, if they don't exercise proper restraint, insult the intelligence of the public until the public no longer believes anything they say. That is certainly what the Liberal press has done in this province, and I think in many other parts of Canada. I have no objection to a man who owns a newspaper expressing his views on the editorial page — that's why he owns the newspaper — he's got a perfect right to use the editorial column to express his point of view. But when he slants the news and omits news about the other side of the question, he loses public confidence and support. When I go to Toronto and tell the C.C.F. side of the story on a public platform, the newspaper curtain falls around me, and I don't get any publicity.

> I was talking to you one night during the course of that campaign when you were feeling somewhat low, which is most unusual for you. You told me that it had almost made you believe the best thing was to leave public life entirely. At that particular time you'd been offered a post in southern California, a chair of Christian Philosophy or Christian Ethics. Do you recall that?

Yes, oh, yes. These newspaper attacks depress you, because you get the impression, although you ought to know better, that this represents a very considerable point of view, and that thousands of people are reading this and they're bound to be influenced by it. I've learned that the best thing that can ever happen to you if you feel this way is to go out to the country, and find out how little people are affected by these newspaper articles. One of the greatest blessings to progressive movements like ours is the radio; it gives us a counter-stroke against the newspapers. Also, the public platform is effective for a small number of people.

> The attacks were extremely bitter as far as some individuals were concerned—you were one of them. I suppose, how ever harmed a politician may be, he gets disturbed not for himself so much, but for his family. Is that true?

That's right. The canvassers are not above spreading any kind of story at all. I remember one of the few times that I really got angry, they were peddling stories around the east part of Regina about my daughter, who was a young teenager and shouldn't have been in the election campaign at all. But this sort of thing was traditional of the sort of muck the Liberal party peddled from door to door. In the last election in 1956, the story was that I had made three million dollars selling a brick plant to the provincial government. The brick plant belonged to Dr. McCusker and a group of his friends in Regina who were Liberals. We may have paid too much for it, and we may not have. It was assessed by a professor at the University of Saskatchewan who is a specialist in ceramics. We accepted his evaluation and so did they. I had nothing to do with it. But there was this story around my constituency that I had made money out of these various sales and had put it away in a safety deposit box in the United States, and that I was all ready to retire a millionaire. It's funny when the election's over, but at the time it can get to be pretty annoying.

Especially to a man's family.

They've got to move around in different circles, and particularly your children feel it when people look at them out of the corner of their eye and say, "I hear your father is a crook." I've often said to my family and to my friends that I don't ever expect to leave them much of this world's goods for the simple reason that both my occupations have not been remunerative, and I don't think they expect me to leave them very much. I have tried to give my children a good education, a start in life, and a comfortable home, but when they get out on their own, they're on their own resources, and they don't expect me to leave them an inheritance. But the one thing I do want to leave them is a good name, that they can say their father was in public life for so many years, and in all that time he never took a dollar that didn't belong to him, he never bribed or intimidated, and at no time did he ever conduct himself in such a way that any investigation was embarrassing. It's not easy for the children of a public man when they think their friends believe these untrue stories; they are under a cloud of suspicion.

In the 1948 campaign, Mr. Tucker was engaged in an attack on the C.C.F. He said that no industry would ever come to Saskatchewan and that there would never be an oil well drilled in Saskatchewan while a C.C.F. government was in office.

I think his exact words were, "There'll never be a barrel of oil produced in Saskatchewan as long as you have a C.C.F. government," and we are now producing better than 125,000 barrels a day. I think we now have about 3,600 oil wells in production or capable of production.

Mr. Tucker was slightly off beat at that time.

He was out on so many other things. He said then, and has said in subsequent elections, that prime industry would bypass Saskatchewan as long as there was a C.C.F. government; investors wouldn't put their money in this province because of the political climate. The fact remains that year after year we've been running around six hundred million dollars a year in public and private investment in the province, and we've been running about six to ten percent above the national average in terms of capital investment.

> We've reached the climactic point, Election Day. I don't think in my fairly long experience as a political reporter that I've ever known such bitterness hanging in the air as there was on that occasion.

I thought that it was going to be very close. I could see that the coalition was going to make it very difficult. I also knew that the row I'd had with Mr. Tucker that resulted in the libel suit[3] dragged me down a bit in the mud with them, and I regretted that but I couldn't see how I could have avoided it. I didn't think we'd be beaten, but of course you never think you're going to be beaten.

> You couldn't be positive.

No. A politician is actually the last person to ask how an election campaign is going. He's travelling over a lot of country and sees his own people and has wildly enthusiastic meetings. But he tends to forget that five hundred or a thousand people represent a very small fraction of the total number of voters in that area. If you get five or six thousand enthusiastic people at a meeting in Regina this doesn't mean you've won the city of Regina.

I thought we would win, but frankly, I didn't think we'd lose as many seats as we did. But looking back, I can see that we did remarkably well with the opposition we had.

After the election I got a letter from Professor Cassidy, Dean of the School of Social Welfare at the University of Toronto. Mr. Cassidy is not a C.C.F.er, he is an outstanding social scientist and a great humanitarian, and I always had a great admiration for him. He said he wanted to extend his congratulations and said, "You may be a bit disappointed that you lost some seats, but the miracle is not that you lost seats, but that you were re-elected at

Douglas at the National C.C.F. Convention, August 1948, in Winnipeg.

all. Most people think that if a government starts a lot of new things they are assured of re-election. But you can't do new things that need to be done without stepping on somebody's toes. No matter how good a programme is, no matter how much it helps people, it's bound to step on somebody's toes, and if you have a number of programmes and you step on a lot of people's toes and you add them all together they constitute a considerable number of people. It's true that the number of people you help are immeasurably larger than the number of people whose toes you stepped on, but the trouble is that the people you've helped forget what you've done for them, and the people whose toes you've stepped on never forget. From my study of political science, I think it's a miracle that you were re-elected, with the extensive reforms that you've introduced in the last four years."

> In brief, if you were in danger, it wasn't because you'd done too little, but too much. I think you tell a story about that, don't you?

This is actually Churchill's story. He told of a Tory candidate running for office who went around to visit an old friend and neighbour of his and said, "As you know, I'm running in this election, and I hope you're going to vote for me." And the fellow said, "I haven't made up my mind yet." He said, "Good heavens, man, look at all the things I've done for you. When we were boys together and we went skating and you fell through the ice, I pulled you out and saved your life. Later on when you wanted to get married I loaned you a couple of hundred dollars. Remember later on, your house burned down, and I went on your note, so you could get your house rebuilt. When your child needed an operation I gave you some money so you could look after the youngster's medical expenses." The fellow said, "That's all true, but what have you done for me lately?"

We were in the same position. We knew that we were probably doing too much. After all, when you look over that programme from 1944 to 1948, we had moved into almost every realm. Take for instance the hospital plan. There were a lot of people who weren't sick, had never been sick, and resented the fact that they had to pay a premium. One of our supporters, a big redheaded Irishman from south of Moose Jaw, wrote me the most abusive letter, which said, among other things, "You're just a Mussolini and Hitler rolled into one." He said, "I've never been sick, and I'm nearly sixty years of age. I've never spent a day in hospital, and you make me pay five dollars." I wrote back and tried to explain to him that while he had never been sick, he should be glad to contribute to the people who are sick, and at the same time he was paying for insurance against the event that he might be sick. About six or seven years later, I got a letter and a card from him at Christmas, which said, "I've just come out of the Providence Hospital after six months." His bill was almost a thousand dollars. "I could never have paid this, and I see the benefit of it now." But he still voted against us in 1948.

> In that election you weighed up your casualties. Joe Phelps lost out.[4]

Joe Phelps was one of the most volatile and virile speakers in Saskatchewan political history. He was a real loss to us. We also lost Valleau.[5] In all, we'd lost some sixteen members. At the time I was disappointed. Now I see that we did remarkably well to weather the storm.

> At the start of the new session, the C.C.F. had thirty-one seats.

And the Liberals had twenty-one. There are fifty-two seats.

> Did this mean any internal changes in government?

It meant some reorganization. We had to fill the vacancies brought about by the defeat of Mr. Valleau and Mr. Phelps.

> One feature of this election was the famous libel and slander case brought against you by Mr. Tucker. What are the events as you remember them?

Probably a year before the election, a woman complained to me that her father and mother, who couldn't write, had been deprived of their land in the Rosthern district by the Rosthern Mortgage Company. I sent her down to the Mediation Board. They looked into it, and the whole transaction looked very suspicious because the father and mother could neither read nor write. The man who had acted as translator for them and had persuaded them to sign a quit claim deed on the promise they'd be allowed to stay on their land was the very man to whom the Rosthern Mortgage Company sold the land that was taken from these people. Since it had happened some years before, there was nothing that we could do to rectify the situation. The woman had a lawyer in Saskatoon, and he had filed a statement of claim, and it was all part of the record in the Saskatoon Court House, but she hadn't the money to proceed with the case. I noticed, in reading over this statement of claim, that Mr. Tucker was the secretary of the Rosthern Mortgage Company, and I made photocopies of the statement of claim and of the mortgage and of the various legal documents in connection with the case. I must say in all sincerity I had no intention of using these; I simply had them because we were following up the case to see if there was any way we could get some restitution for this woman's parents.

This was completely out of my mind, but when we were in the midst of this very bitter campaign, Mr. Tucker referred to the old campaign issue of 1944, saying that the government is only biding its time to take away the farms. This had been told before, and I thought they wouldn't dare trot it out again in '48, since the C.C.F. government had passed the Farm Security Act to keep people from losing their farms. But he trotted that out again, and said the government is not showing its hand, but you are all going to lose the title to your farms. Naturally, I was a bit cross, but I didn't pursue the argument. But at Caron, just west of Moose Jaw, we had a meeting on behalf of Mr. Gibson, the C.C.F. member, and somebody got up at the question period and said, "Mr. Douglas, Mr. Tucker said that the C.C.F. government is going to take away our farms and that we are going to lose our farms if the C.C.F. gets back in. What have you got to say to that?"

I reviewed the situation and pointed out what legislation we had passed; instead of losing their farms, people had more security than they had ever had. Then, perhaps injudiciously, although it was a perfectly fair comment, I said, "After all, it isn't the government that you're in danger of losing your farms to, the danger lies in mortgage companies like the Rosthern Mortgage Company of which Mr. Tucker is secretary. He took people's farms up in the Rosthern district under very suspicious circumstances." That was all I said about it. I didn't mention the case or any names. I thought the matter would drop there.

However, Mr. Tucker saw the statement in the press, and immediately gave a categorical denial that the Rosthern Mortgage Company had ever taken anybody's farm. Of course, this left me no alternative but to reply. But I didn't reply immediately. I waited until I got to Rosthern where everybody knew the story. I took the documents along with me. I carefully tabulated the information that was there, all fully corroborated, and I made my statement in Rosthern on 11 June. I gave the names of this couple, whom everybody knew, and told how that subsequently this land had been sold to the very man who had acted as translator. The Rosthern Mortgage Company, in my opinion, had deprived these people of their land and I didn't think they had proper information as to what they were signing.

On 12 June Mr. Tucker filed a slander and libel suit against me for one hundred thousand dollars. It was unfortunate that this personal element was injected into the campaign, but the fact remains that throughout the entire examination before and during the trial, neither Mr. Tucker nor his counsel ever attempted to disprove a single statement I'd made. They were all documented, and my own counsel pointed this out to the jury, that I hadn't made a single statement they had disproved. Nor had they claimed in their suit that I had misrepresented the fact. Instead they claimed that I stated these facts purely out of malice, in order to hurt the political reputation of Mr. Tucker.

> If we look back through the early history of Saskatchewan, it was quite commonplace to have a dozen libel actions filed in the political arena. Usually, you never heard another word about them after an election.

I felt, like you, that chances were that they would drop the thing. However, when I got back from Rosthern and following the public announcement that Mr. Tucker had filed suit, my wife met me at the door and said, "Where in heaven's name are we going to get a hundred thousand dollars?"

The trial was held in Prince Albert before Mr. Justice G.E. Taylor.[6] I think it was a very well-conducted trial. When Mr. Tucker was under examinaton by my counsel, they took him step by step through the statements I had made, then finally Mr. Leslie[7] said to him, "These statements are true, then." He said, "Yes." And Mr. Leslie said, "Then why did you object to Mr. Douglas making these statements in a community where everybody knew whether or not they were true? Don't you think the people of Rosthern knew about this?" He said, "Not too many of them knew, and this is not the kind of thing that you want broadcast around." I thought at this particular point the jury reached its verdict. The decision on 15 January 1948 was against the suit.

Mr. Tucker appealed the decision, on the ground that the judge had misdirected the jury, and it went to the Appeal Court of Saskatchewan.[8] The Appeal Court said that on the question of libel the case should be reheard, and it was referred back to the court at Prince Albert.

We appealed from the decision of the Appeal Court to the Supreme Court of Canada. The Supreme Court agreed with the decision of the Appeal Court.[9] There was no question about the truthfulness of the statement; the question was whether or not I was justified in making it. The Supreme Court said that justification was proper ground for argument.

But Mr. Tucker dropped the case.

Yes. But there's no question that he could have proceeded at any time.

Did this cost you any money?

Yes, it cost me quite a bit of money and kept me broke for quite a while.

There was quite a rumpus here because the C.C.F. party wanted to pay the costs.

They did offer to help me. The factum in any case appealed before the Supreme Court of Canada has to be printed. Some of my friends got together and paid the printing bill without my knowing. It helped a great deal because by this time the financial burden was getting pretty heavy.

It caused you a lot of worry, didn't it?

Yes, I was quite worried that I had inadvertently, and with my unfortunately quick temper, got the C.C.F. into an issue which was undignified, and pulled them down in the gutter.

With your background and your ancestry, you were probably worried about the effect on people you'd been associated with.

The Scottish way of thinking is, if you're in court, there's something wrong. Decent people stay out of court.

9

At home and abroad

I've covered a lot of politics in my time, but I don't think
I've ever seen a Legislature to compare with the 1948
Legislature for this reason: it seemed that the chamber
was full of hate at this time. As you know so well from
your own parliamentary experience, you can raise hell
with a man, call him everything under creation, yet meet
him the next day in a friendly way. I remember Allan Embury had been raising supreme hell with Charlie Williams. They both walked out of the chamber, and he said,
"Charlie, how about giving me a ride home?" Charlie
said, "Sure, get in the car." That atmosphere of friendli-
ness is usual, but here for some reason it seemed to be
missing entirely. It seemed to emanate from Mr. Tucker.
This business between you and him seemed to be very
deep and personal as far as he was concerned. Can you
think on that for a moment?

What you say is quite correct. In the session of 1948 to 1952 there was a personal vindictiveness throughout all the deliberations of the Legislative Assembly, which was most unfortunate. I'm not sure that it's unusual to Saskatchewan. The Liberal party has always adopted the attitude in this province, and only in this province, that if you are against them politically, you are against them, period. This is also true with the Conservatives. I can remember when I came to this province in the fall of '29 and I took up permanent residence in Weyburn in 1930; Liberals, members of my congregation and many of them fine Christian people, would tell me the most awful things about Conservative cabinet ministers, J.T.M. Anderson, the Minister of Public Works, and J.F. Bryant. They had illegitimate children, they were scamps and scallywags, they were crooks. I used to say to them, "Surely you don't believe that. I can understand you differing with their political views, and I don't agree with some of the things myself, but surely the things you are saying about them are not charitable or kind. They have never been substantiated. They're the kind of street-corner gossip that decent people shouldn't listen to and certainly shouldn't pass on." But this was the atmosphere; I think this was part of the tradition of the Gardiner machine. If somebody's against you politically, you break them. You get him fired from his job, or you boycott his store, or you make life so miserable that he gets out.

It's not proper to say that because politicians are friendly when they're out of Parliament that their whole debate is phoney. I've always held, and I think most people in public life hold, that you can have a difference with a man about his economic theories or about his principles of fiscal policy or political administration and jurisdiction without having a personal dislike for him.

One of the first years I was in Parliament, Mr. Coldwell and I shared a room together in the House of Commons. Someone came in, a well-known Liberal, and started to berate Mr. M.A. McPherson, who had been an Attorney-General in Saskatchewan, and who had run against Mr. Coldwell in 1934. Mr. Coldwell turned on him like a lion. He said, "Mr. McPherson is a political opponent, but he's one of the finest Christian gentlemen I've ever known and I will not allow anyone in this room to make comments like that about him. If this is all you have to say, will you please go away?"

This doesn't mean that Mr. Coldwell's political differences with Mr. McPherson weren't genuine, but it means that he had enough sense to know that differences of opinion don't mean personal dislike or personal animosity, and that he certainly ought not to stoop to vilification and character assassination. The Liberal party has never understood this.

Part of the British tradition is that you recognize your honest differences but yet respect a man's integrity and his rights as a human being. This problem has degraded public life in Saskatchewan. I'm not saying that the C.C.F. haven't contributed to it — we certainly tried not to — but no one is without blame. But I do think a large part of the responsibility for this must fall on the Gardiner machine and the political outlook the Liberals have developed over the years.

> From 1948 to 1952, the Legislative Chamber was in an almost continuous state of bedlam. Mr. Tucker, along with Mr. Justice Procter, has the distinction of not only calling you a skunk, but "a stinking skunk and a dirty little thing."

I certainly resent that "little."

> You probably took him apart a little from time to time, but then he'd get so emotional that he was absolutely quivering with rage. There were never any positive tones or anything constructive.

During that period the Liberals started attacking the government by innuendo and insinuations. They'd been complaining that nobody would come into the province, but when people started to come in fairly large numbers to develop our oil and mineral resources, particularly uranium, their technique was to suggest that these people were getting some special favours from the government for which they were greasing somebody's palm, and that government cabinet ministers were getting some share in these companies.

> At the beginning of our oil days, when a man made
> money at it, the reaction was to link up with yourself,
> Clarence Fines, or somebody else in the government.

I remember going to address a meeting in Melville in 1949 on behalf of a C.C.F. federal candidate. Mr. M.A. McPherson, who was
the lawyer for the Tidewater people, said that they wanted to see
me right away; they couldn't wait until I got back to Regina. They
said, "We're prepared to do exploration and it's going to cost a lot
of money. We want some assurance that if we go ahead, the government won't expropriate. We've heard a lot of stories about the
Socialist government." I assured them, as I have assured other oil
companies, both privately and publicly, that this was not a field
for public ownership. It was a field for risk capital. No taxpayer
would for a moment agree to have the government spending
millions of dollars drilling for oil that might not be there. If they
privately risked their money and found oil, it would be their oil.
They would have to pay their royalties, and there were certain
crown reserves that would become the property of the crown.
Otherwise there'd be no interference. So they signed an agreement.

They took over exploration of nine million acres. At the next
session this was held out as a great gift to these people, who were
only paying a few cents an acre. It didn't matter what they paid
per acre, but that they were drilling. The moment they found oil
they became subject to a production tax and royalties. This company spent $27 million in exploration, and took back about $4.5
million in oil. But this didn't stop them from being maligned for
making a great deal of money out of the people of Saskatchewan.
At the rate they're going, it will take thirty or forty years to get
their money back, unless they hit something much better than
they've struck to date.

> Because they could never prove anything, the Liberals
> made themselves completely unbelievable when they
> started this scandal. They always overplayed their hand.

I've insisted that the ministers refrain from engaging in any type of business activity or partnership with any firm or any person doing business with the government. I won't even buy shares, even on the open market, on an enterprise operating in Saskatchewan, because it might be interpreted that this company got a special concession because I or my colleagues had shares or intended to buy shares.

A minister can buy government bonds, can't he?

Yes, he can buy government bonds on the open market if he wants. I hope Saskatchewan people buy Saskatchewan bonds rather than bonds from another province.

You made a trip to Europe, did you not, in 1948, after the provincial election?

In the fall of '48 I was invited to go as a guest of the United Kingdom Parliamentary Association to a Commonwealth parliamentary conference in London. There were other representatives from Canada, but Sir Howard D'Egville[1] had asked me particularly if I would go, not as a part of the Canadian group, but as a guest of the United Kingdom. There were delegates from every part of the Commonwealth. We met in London and spent two or three days working out an agenda, and as a preparation for this week of discussion, we went on a trip. We went to Scotland, where we took a plane directly to Frankfurt, and some of us went into Berlin, which at that time was blockaded by the Communists. There was an airlift. We landed at Templehof Airdrome in Berlin, and were met by the Canadian and British military commanders there. We also sat in at the Constitutional Assembly in Frankfurt. While we were there, General Lucius Clay had vetoed part of the constitution that provided for the new German Democratic Republic to have publicly owned railways, chemical industries, and a number of other provisions. The Assembly was almost unanimous in having public ownership of these great industries.

It was also interesting that the American representative should veto this. All the talk of democracy, and yet here were the Americans against it. When we met with Lucius Clay, Mr. Coldwell and I quizzed him about his action in this regard, and he said, "As a military commander here I have to take my instructions from the State Department. I have informed my government that we might just as well reconcile ourselves to the fact that in Europe they're going to have socialism. We can either have democratic socialism or totalitarian socialism. But I don't fool myself into thinking that free enterprise as we understand it in the United States is going to be acceptable here." I thought that was a rather remarkable statement for a military commander representing the United States in West Germany.

I sat with the Social Democratic group listening to the debates. Schumacher at that time was in hospital having his leg amputated. He'd been mangled in a Nazi concentration camp, and subsequently died following this operation. The other Social Democratic leaders were there, and it was very interesting to meet many of the Social Democrats in Germany. While these people thoroughly distrusted the American and British military leaders, they distrusted the Russians much more. We were able to talk very frankly with the Social Democrats and the trade unionists without the British and American military representatives present.

They told me of the elections, in which the Social Democrats had swept the board, and the Communists had won less than 20 out of 118 seats in Berlin. But the moment the election was over, the Russian military commander said, "We won't recognize this election." The same thing happened to the election of shop stewards in industry. The Russian military commander appointed his own members to the city council. The old refrain about the Russians protecting democracy was just eyewash. But on the other hand, the Social Democrats told me, as soon as I got back to England and saw Mr. Attlee and Mr. Morrison[2] and Mr. Bevin[3] (who was the Foreign Secretary), to ask why a Labour government in Britain is represented in Germany by about as reactionary a group as it would be possible to find in the whole Foreign Office. Mr. Coldwell and I posed this question very pointedly when we met the leaders of the British Labour party. Ernie Bevin admitted that under the pressure of work he just hadn't had time to screen very carefully the people who were representing Britain in Germany at that time.

[Ernest Bevin (1881–1951), the most influential trade unionist of his generation in Britain, was born in poverty and started work at age eleven, and later became a drayman in Bristol. He adopted socialism as a consequence of a nonconformist religious upbringing. Founder of a carters' branch of the Dockers' Union in 1910, by the end of World War I he was assistant general secretary of the union. From the early 1920s he was involved as an initiator or officer of the major trade union organizations of the next two decades, including the Transport and General Workers, the world's largest union. He assisted in the organization of the general strike of 1926, and subsequently fought many battles for the dockers, transport workers, and sailors. Elected chairman of the Trade Union Congress in 1937, widely respected for his knowledge, experience, and forceful personality, he was chosen by Churchill to become Minister of Labour and National Service in the coalition government of 1940–45. His activities played a large part in the successful British war effort. Foreign secretary in the Labour government from 1945 to 1951, he was deeply involved in all of the post-war co-operative European economic projects, and was one of the chief organizers of N.A.T.O. and the Colombo Plan for southeast Asia.]

It was a very interesting trip. We were all through Germany, Holland, Belgium, and France, and then we came back to Scotland, and went over to Ireland. Then we flew back to Wales, and visited the provinces in England. We were back in London after about a month of journeying. We debated the topics of current interest: international affairs, defence, trade, immigration, Commonwealth problems, the new countries that had come into the Commonwealth. At that time India, Pakistan, and Ceylon had just been given their Dominion status as independent members of the Commonwealth. They were most vociferous, and Nehru did a brilliant job, although his own supporters were a bit obstreperous and somewhat brash. They had been fighting against the British rule in India for years. Some like Mr. Nehru had spent years in British jails, and now they were feeling their independence. At almost every meeting they'd begin the discussion with, "We'll not be in the Commonwealth very long, we really should be a republic and will be leaving any time, but before we leave we'd like to say so and so."

The British handled themselves very well. The largest part of the British delegation were from the Labour party, and the opposition was also represented. The British took the position that any time you want to leave, go ahead, but in the meantime let's sit and talk things over. Nehru finally slapped down his own people. He gave one of the finest addresses I ever heard. He said, "No one will think I am subservient to the British. I've spent nine years out of eighteen in a British jail, but we owe much to Britain: our system of justice, our incorruptible civil service, our standards of fair play, and great economic benefits from hydroelectric power and irrigation. We must say this about the British, that when we pushed them out the front door they came around to the back door and offered to wash the dishes."

Where did you go from London?

We wound up the week's conference by attending the opening of the House of Commons in the fall of 1948, when His Majesty King George VI read the Speech from the Throne. He called for the nationalization of the steel industry and carrying on with the Labour party's programme. At the buffet supper at Buckingham Palace afterward, Mr. Coldwell and I had a little private audience with the King. He said, "What did you think of my speech today? I'm worried, I think it's going too fast. I think nationalization has to come, but I'm afraid they're going too fast." Mr. Coldwell and I decided we wouldn't tell Mr. Attlee or Mr. Morrison or Sir Stafford Cripps about what we thought was the King's indiscretion in discussing his opinion of his ministers' Speech from the Throne.

You have some very good impressions of the British Labour leaders at this time.

I have been very fortunate at various times in meeting them. In '36, when I came back from Europe, I met Arthur Greenwood,[4] who told me the story about Spain; he said that I should go immediately to Edinburgh and put the facts before the Labour Party Convention. I met some of the Labour leaders then. I met them again in '45 when I was visiting overseas. At that time they were all in the national government; it was just before the election that brought them to office. Then I met them again in 1948, and I have met them frequently since when they have visited us.

I might start with Mr. Attlee, of whom Churchill said, "There goes a sheep in wolf's clothing." Although Churchill gets the credit, Sheridan said it first in the British House of Commons around 1780. Churchill saw Cripps going by one day and said, "There but for the grace of God, goes God." That quotation also belongs to Sheridan.

Attlee wasn't the mousy little man people thought he was. A quiet, rather self-effacing individual, with all the toughness and tenacity of the cockney, he never pushed himself forward. I recall an incident when the Labour government had been going at a terrific pace — nobody will ever know the job they had taking over after the war with 15,000 factories destroyed, and a million people's homes wiped out — and doing a magnificent job. If they made any mistakes, they made the same mistake we did; they were trying to do so much in such a short space of time. They introduced a complete health programme at a time when the country was still staggering under the impact of the war. Morrison had a heart attack, Cripps was in hospital with colitis, Ernie Bevin was flat on his back with an angina pectoris, and Attlee was handling all the departments at once, puffing on his pipe and serenely confident of what he was doing. He had an incredible toughness inside.

[Actually, Clement Richard Attlee (1883–1967) was not a cockney; he was born in Putney, southwest London, the son of a solicitor. He was educated at Oxford, and called to the bar in 1906. He practiced law for three years before teaching at Ruskin College and later at the London School of Economics from 1913 to 1923. He had a distinguished war record and was a member of the Fabian Society. In 1919 he became the first Labour mayor of Stepney, and from 1922 to 1955 he was a Labour Member of Parliament. He held various cabinet posts in the Ramsay MacDonald ministry, was leader of the opposition from 1935 to 1940, and was deputy prime minister in the national government from 1942 to 1945. Prime Minister from 1945 to 1951, he was the recipient of many honorary degrees and the author of seven books.]

One day in '45, I had lunch with Anthony Eden, Foreign Secretary, and we got to talking about different people. I mentioned Mr. Attlee. He said, "Amazing man, Attlee, people get the wrong impression of him, but he's really a great little man; nobody will ever know how much we owe to him. All through the war he was deputy prime minister. He presided at cabinet meetings and Churchill did the talking, but Attlee did the committee work. Attlee kept the committees working and reporting to him, and he fed the material to Churchill. If we had a cabinet meeting with Churchill presiding, we didn't get any work done, but we got a marvellous résumé on military strategy for two hours. When Attlee was presiding, we heard very little about military strategy, but we got the agenda all cleaned up."

He hadn't much colour, and was given to understatement, but that's what the British like. But he knew at all times where he was going. In 1953, when I was in England attending the Coronation, a conference of the Labour and Socialist parties of the Commonwealth was held in Westminster Hall. Prior to the conference there was a small sub-committee, of which I was the only representative from Canada, to prepare the agenda. It was interesting to watch these discussions. Here were very brilliant men, particularly Nash[5] of New Zealand, who would get into a terrific argument with Aneurin Bevan. Attlee would just sit at the head of the table, doodling. I know he used to do the same thing when he was sitting in the House of Commons. When everybody had expressed their opinion he would summarize, clarify, and untangle the main points in half a dozen sentences. His mind worked with clear-cut precision. He was the ideal committee chairman. He certainly didn't give you any of the impression of greatness in the sense that Churchill did, but there isn't any doubt that he was the kind of man who could have held the Labour party together probably better than anyone else.

He said something strange one day: "You know, this man Coldwell of yours, if he hadn't left England and gone off to Canada he could have been prime minister. He'd have made a better prime minister than I have been." I think it's true. Watching these men, and working with them, able as they are, I still don't think there was anyone superior intellectually or with a better capacity for communication than Coldwell.

Of the other men, Gaitskell[6] impressed me tremendously. A bit donnish, still the Oxford [*sic*] professor, but very keen and yet very humble, a very able man. Morrison, I had always admired. Morrison was the organizer and the politician of the group, and had a very warm personality. He was a cockney, as tough as they make them, but he had more warmth.

Jim Griffiths[7] was a Welshman and former miner, and a lovable character, one of the best loved men in the Labour party. It was marvellous to watch the delegates from every part of Asia; the moment they saw Jim Griffiths their faces would light up. He had been Colonial Secretary, and had presided at meetings that led to their independence. He was the ideal person to do it. He had the warmth of the Welshman, the eloquence they loved, and they trusted him.

The controversial figure was Aneurin Bevan, a strange character. He's always been very good to me. Whenever I've been in London, he's invited me over to have dinner with himself and his wife, Jennie Lee.[8] He was very good to Shirley and when she was in London he invited her over to the House of Commons. Bevan was a brilliant man; there's no mistaking his brilliance. What he lacked was judgement and a certain stability of character. When I saw him in the fall of '52, I remember saying to him, "If you don't mind someone saying so who likes you and admires you, I think the leadership will fall into your hands if you don't try so hard, but if the Labour party ever senses that you're prepared to wreck the party just in order to gratify your personal ambitions, you'll defeat yourself." I think this was precisely what happened. But I believe he has settled down a lot more now that he has got older. I think he's reconciled to the fact that he's not going to lead the Labour party, and I think his great ambition now is to be Foreign Secretary, to establish peace by being a bridge between the United States and the Soviet Union. I think he can do it.

[Aneurin Bevan (1897–1960) was born in Tredegar, Wales, the son of a coal-miner. He became a miner in 1910, but had to leave the mines after a few years because of an eye disease. He was an active trade unionist and spent two years at the Central Labour College. Elected to the House of Commons in 1929 as a Labour member, he married Jennie Lee, another Labour M.P. An authority on mining affairs and a critic of the government during World War II, he served as Minister of Health in Attlee's Labour government formed in 1945. He was the architect of the national health service and became Minister of Labour in 1951, but resigned in the same year as a protest against health service changes. He became a controversial figure in the party as the leading spokesman for the left wing. He was defeated by Hugh Gaitskell in the contest for party leadership in 1955. In his last years he was elected deputy leader of the party in 1959.]

What was he like as an orator, a parliamentarian?

He stands in the great tradition of British orators. I think that time will put him with Burke and Fox and Gladstone and Disraeli, Lloyd George and Churchill. He was the only man in the House of Commons who could really stand up to Churchill at his best. I remember the first debate in which I heard him; the war was still on and Churchill was prime minister. Although the Labour party were in the coalition, it didn't stop Bevan from critizing the government. He put a motion on the order paper criticizing them because of a shortage of fish and coal. He opened the debate, not with a welter of statistics, as we would do in this country, but with one penetrating sentence. He said, "Mr. Speaker, this country is a lump of coal set in a sea teeming with fish, and only a man with the organizing genius of Mr. Churchill could arrange to have a shortage of both of them at the same time."

He had all the Welshman's attributes: a poetic, beautiful command of language, a musical voice, a great depth of feeling, and a priceless sense of humour. Old Welshmen tell me that he's on par with Lloyd George, and that's saying something. I heard Lloyd George myself when I was a boy in 1918, when he was at his peak, speaking in St. Andrew's Hall in Glasgow. He had the crowd in the palm of his hand. Aneurin Bevan is certainly in that tradition.

Could it be said that he was a bitter man? He was self-educated, wasn't he?

That's right. He was in the pits when he was a boy. He became secretary of his local union. His own members pledged a penny a week out of their pay to put into a fund to send him away to college. He didn't go to any of the great universities, but to an ordinary college. He was a self-educated, widely read man with a penetrating mind. I don't think he was bitter so much as he was personally ambitious, but I think part of this was due to the prodding he got from his wife. Jennie was very ambitious for Aneurin, and I got the impression that she and Barbara Castle[9] and some of the others in the Labour party were constantly pushing him to fight with the old guard even when he wasn't particularly anxious to fight. He had to stand out as being left of centre in the Labour party. In a way this has been a good thing for the party, to have a voice that was left of centre, providing always that it was a responsible voice that didn't destroy the unity of the party. When the Labour party was pushed out of office, it was largely due to a split from within. The voter never likes to vote for a government that spends all its energies on fighting among themselves. They like to elect a party that has at least been able to reconcile it's own difficulties and differences of opinion, and devote itself to the affairs of the country. More than any other person, Bevan was responsible for the defeat of the Labour party.

How about Sir Stafford Cripps?

Cripps was J.S. Woodsworth without a beard. He had the prim schoolmaster look about him, but people forget his background. He was the greatest corporation lawyer in Britain, with an income of 75,000 to 100,000 pounds a year. Long before he became a lawyer, he was an authority in chemistry and physics. There's one chemical law to which his name and that of another prominent Oxford scientist is attached. He studied law, particularly patents. With his mind and training in science, he made the ideal corporation lawyer. His father was Lord Parmoor, and he could very easily have spent the rest of his life in luxury and comfort, making tremendous fees at the bar. He used to say, "I make my money all day out of capitalists and go out in the evening and help to build a society to get rid of them."

He had tremendous personal integrity. And whether he was in opposition or whether he was in government, he never bent his views to suit the crowd. This meant that he wasn't always too popular in his own party. He said hard things that needed to be said. When he was Chancellor of the Exchequer, he carried out an austerity programme that nobody but the British could have put up with. But during those years from 1945 to 1952 when countries like France and Belgium were spending a part of their produce on buying luxuries from the United States — silk stockings and electrical appliances — Sir Stafford was saying, "Tighten your belts. We're still wearing cotton stockings and getting along with utility goods." He poured the money into rebuilding factories and re-equipping and electrifying the coal-mines; unless you raise the productive capacity of a nation, it can't afford luxuries. If Britain is in good shape today, I'm sure that history will prove that a large part of it is owing to those very necessary sacrifices the British people accepted from Sir Stafford Cripps.

[Richard Stafford Cripps (1889–1952), son of a distinguished lawyer, was a nephew of Beatrice Webb. He attended the University of London, specializing in chemistry. Called to the bar in 1913, he practiced patent law after the war, and was the youngest K.C. in 1927. In 1929 he joined the Labour party and was appointed Solicitor General by Ramsay MacDonald, and knighted. Elected to the House of Commons 1931, during the 1930s his relations with the Labour party were stormy because of conflicts over foreign policy and co-operation with the Communists (which he favoured). Appointed ambassador to Moscow by Churchill, he subsequently became Minister of Aircraft Production. Cripps held all of the various portfolios relating to economic affairs at various times. In 1946 he headed a cabinet delegation to India to negotiate terms of independence. In 1947 became Chancellor of the Exchequer and known as "austerity Cripps" for the rigidity of his policies affecting the balance of payments, inflation, and economic growth, which were highly successful. He was forced to retire in 1950 because of illness.]

He was very austere. The people close to him, people like

David Lewis[10] and Graham Spry,[11] would deny this immediately. Graham Spry was his personal assistant all through the war when he was Minister of Aircraft Production and later Chancellor of the Exchequer. Graham would deny that he was cold. To his immediate friends he was kindly, rather humble, and self-effacing. But in his public demeanour he was austere and rigid and uncompromising.

He had always been interested in India and was quite important in bringing about India's independence. He subsequently died after a long ailment in 1952.

> Was there anything else that happened on your trip to Europe in 1948?

Following the meeting of the Commonwealth parliamentary association in 1948, I went to France to pay a commitment I'd made some time before. I had always been interested in the famous Dieppe raid, in which the South Saskatchewan Regiment took part. Whether one agrees that the benefits of that reconnaissance in force made the losses worthwhile or not, the fact still remains that people were tremendously proud of the heroism and courage displayed by the Canadian troops. Naturally I was interested in the part that the South Saskatchewan Regiment had played. I made arrangements through Agent General Graham Spry, and we had a plaque made, which we were going to put up at Pourville, the village where the South Saskatchewan Regiment landed. Everything was set up for a great celebration over a weekend, and so Mr. Graham Spry and Bill Boss of the Canadian Press and I set out for Dieppe. When we got there, the mayor of Dieppe and his council, wearing their sashes, met us at the boat, and we had quite a formal celebration. At six o'clock in the morning I went inland to a little church where a special mass was being said, and where I was to decorate the grave of the Right Honourable J.G. Gardiner's son, who was killed during the Dieppe raid. He was with the R.C.A.F. and his plane was brought down just outside Dieppe. There was a tremendous crowd of people and the church was filled.

Then I went to Pourville. Colonel Allan Chambers of the Canadian Highland Light Infantry, a former Liberal member of the House of Commons, was with me. In 1948 he was military attaché with Canada House in London, and thank heaven he was sent along, because there was a rail strike in France, and if it hadn't been for him I would never have been able to get around. Colonel Chambers and the rest of us made a tour of the whole situation. Pourville is a little village nestling in a crescent-shaped beach and at either side of the crescent there's a big rock headland. We went through all the tunnels that had been hewn out of the rock, gun emplacements for heavy .50 calibre machine-guns. From these two headlands, they had complete control by enfilade fire of the beach. These were all manned by German troops, who had complete protection from fifty feet of rock above them. How any man ever lived on that beach is nothing short of a miracle.

We saw the places they had landed, and some of the rusty tanks still stuck in the sand. We saw the bridge across which Colonel Cecil Merritt led the regiment and won the Victoria Cross. He led them up a road that ran in a kitty-corner direction across the beach and up the headland, inland, and toward Dieppe. They got to the junction of a road leading into Dieppe when the signal came to retire.

There were a number of interesting things about the place. We had a wonderful luncheon with the mayor and the town council of the village. Then we had a celebration at which I uncovered a plaque to the South Saskatchewan Regiment, right at the place where they had landed. The people of Dieppe and Pourville and the little surrounding villages were greatly interested in Canada, because it was from Dieppe and Pourville that the ships first set out with Frenchmen and Bretons three hundred years ago to colonize Canada, and during the war, the Canadians came back to rescue them. They felt an affinity with Canada, and particularly with French Canadians. The returned veterans' organizations with their berets, white and black troops, and Scouts and Guides were all there. I made a little presentation. The mayor of Pourville had a little boy called William, who was born the night of the raid. Canadian troops got to within about a hundred yards of the house in which the mayor and his wife were. When the little boy was being born they heard the shots being fired and the noise, but of course they didn't venture outside. William, having been born the night the Canadians landed, was tremendously interested in meeting Canadians, and had one desire in the world, to get a cowboy suit and a pistol.

The Legion in Saskatchewan provided the cowboy suit, and I took it over on behalf of the veterans of the South Saskatchewan Regiment. It was a very well-tailored suit, custom-made for him, with the toy pistol and with the lariat and the chaps and the cowboy hat. He was just wild with delight, and so were the people, and everybody insisted he put the cowboy suit on right there. I later learned that he wouldn't take it off at night when he went to bed, spurs included, which did considerable damage to his mother's bedding.

I tried to make a little speech to these people, part of it translated and part of it in terrible French, but Bill Boss helped me out, and so did the Canadian military attaché in Paris. They took me up to the cemetery, about a mile and a half or two miles in from Pourville up on the headlands. I never saw a better kept cemetery. In it lay the Canadians from the South Saskatchewan Regiment, the Cameron Highlanders from Winnipeg, some of the French-Canadian Regiment, some American Rangers, some Commandos, and quite a few R.C.A.F. pilots. When I commented to the mayor that I'd never seen such a well-tended cemetery, he said that the people of this community had accepted the responsibility of maintaining this cemetery as part of their tribute to these people who tried to liberate them. They have a schedule; every week some organization accepts the responsibility of looking after the cemetery. When you think of the poor care that we give to our own cemeteries, how much we sometimes neglect the cenotaph that we put up, and think how these people care for a cemetery of men who are not even their own people, it's quite magnificent.

At this cemetery they brought up a little wizened old man, and introduced him as "the hero of Pourville." He looked anything but a hero. They told me that he was a teamster. All that day when the battle was raging, over the radio and loudspeakers everyone was warned to stay indoors, and that any person on the street would be instantly shot. This kept up even after the Canadian troops had been withdrawn. Men were lying dead on the beach, others were wounded and crying for water, others had fallen in the water, their bodies washed back and forth by the tide, but nobody dared come out. But finally this old man took his team and his wagon and he started down the beach, putting the bodies of the dead men on his wagon. When the people looked out and saw this old man, they felt a bit ashamed. They flooded out of their homes and came down and helped him load the bodies. Up the steep hill they went, and set out this little cemetery and started to dig graves. All night long, all the next day, and all the next night, they took turns digging graves and burying the dead.

The next place they took me was the Catholic convent. There I met the Mother Superior, the heroine of Dieppe. Late that afternoon of the raid, the men received orders to withdraw, and they had to leave their dead and wounded behind them. The orders to civilians were still that no one was to come outside, no one was to appear on the streets, or they would be shot instantly. Mother Superior heard men crying right outside this convent door, and she ordered the big doors to be opened and with the other sisters, she came out to get the wounded. A couple of them were shot, but they just kept right on going, until finally the people of the town came out to tend the wounded. They set up a temporary hospital for the men in the convent. The Canadian Government, in appreciation, turned over their fine hospital at Dieppe to these sisters. Of all the people in the community, the heroes weren't the mayor or those you would expect to give leadership, it was a teamster and a sister in a convent. These are the people, who, when the chips were down, had the courage to be humane.

I made my little speech ending with "Vive la France" or "Vive la Canada." We were supposed to go to Dunkirk and catch the night train back to Britain. But because of the general strike, we started to motor to Dunkirk. We hadn't gone five miles when a block and a group of strikers appeared across the road. Six-foot Allen Chambers got out of the car in his Highland uniform, and a French-Canadian colonel got out of the other side. The moment they saw the Canadian uniforms, and we explained to them that we had just participated in celebrations commemorating the

Canadian troops, the barricade was moved. We got to one little town, and the colonel and Allan were thirsty, so we went into a little cafe. You never saw a tougher looking crew of railwaymen and coal-miners, with their berets stuck on one side, in your life, and they certainly didn't want company. The whole mood of the country during the general strike was most sinister. But as soon as they found out we were Canadians, the whole atmosphere changed. We couldn't pay for anything, we were les Canadiens, and we were sent on our way rejoicing. Finally we got to Dunkirk, on the boat to Dover, and back to London the next day.

This demonstrated the tremendous impression Canadians had made on the French people, and the high regard the French have for the French Canadians. It demonstrated that the memory of the French people is still green, le Boche is still the great danger. Some of these people had been invaded three times in their lives, and they hadn't forgotten it, nor had they lost a tremendous sense of gratitude for the people who came and helped them.

◿ You came back to Saskatchewan at the end of 1948, facing a series of sessions. Your focus was industrialization in Saskatchewan to balance the one-crop economy. When did that start to develop?

The Dominion census of 1941 showed that about eighty percent of the provincial income came from agriculture and less than twenty percent came from non-agricultural sources. This meant we were vulnerable to the weather, which could cause a crop failure in a single night, as on 6 August 1954 when a frost wiped out 250 million dollars' worth of crop. Grasshoppers or drought or rust could have the same effect. We were also vulnerable to world market conditions. Irrespective of prices in Canada, we had to sell on a world market, and if there were surpluses of wheat in different parts of the world and prices were depressed, our prices would go down.

Dominion-Provincial Conference on the constitution amendment in Quebec City, 1950. *Back row, left to right:* E.C. Manning (Alberta); J. Walter Jones (P.E.I.); M. Campbell (Manitoba); T.C. Douglas (Sask.); Joe Smallwood (Nfld.). *Front row, left to right:* J.B. McNair (N.B.); M. Duplessis (Quebec); Louis St. Laurent (Prime Minister); Viscount Alexander (Governor-General); Leslie M. Frost (Ontario); A.L. MacDonald (N.S.); B.L. Johnson (B.C.).

With a one-crop economy, we were completely at the mercy of the weather and the world export markets. We had to do something about the development of our other resources. Also, ever since about 1930 there had been technological development for the mechanization of farming, which meant the end of the small quarter-section mixed farm. These were replaced by the half-section, the one-section, the two-section, and even larger farms. Every time these farms got larger, people were displaced by machinery. That's why from 1936 to 1946 Saskatchewan lost about a quarter of a million people. This would undoubtedly go on unless something was done to provide employment for these people. The average man with three or four sons, who formerly could give them each a quarter-section of land and set them up in farming, now turned the farm of one or two sections over to the eldest son, and the other boys had to get out and shift for themselves, which meant going to eastern Canada or to the Coast or to the United States.

While we recognized that this was our top priority, we also had other commitments to meet. Improving health and welfare and educational services and highways and roads had to be done because we had made promises, and also because people weren't going to wait forever until an industrial development programme could give us the money to do these things. But almost as soon as we took office, we began the job of laying a base for an industrial development programme.

> Were you taking the first step of establishing some industries where there was no hope of other people doing it? Did you deal with crown corporations?

We had to set a tentative time table and some order of priority for ourselves. Some things were basic to developing new industries. The first was that we had to have power, so we set up the Saskatchewan Power Corporation. To have any kind of industry you've got to have better communications, and our telephone services had to be expanded. We had very poor long-distance service, and we weren't tied in to a full extent with the other big industrial centres. We had a waiting list of over fifteen thousand applications for telephones when we took office. We also set ourselves the objective of tying all the cities of Saskatchewan together with black-top highways, because distribution of goods by truck was an important part of production costs.

We set up the Saskatchewan Bus Transportation Company because we had the same problem there. The Greyhound people operated only between the main cities, and refused to go to the smaller areas because they were marginal markets. We felt that we needed a publicly owned bus transportation company that would take whatever profits it made from the trade of the major cities and use it to serve the smaller areas. We've deliberately kept the Saskatchewan Bus Transportation Company's profits down to less than $100,000 consistently. This doesn't mean we run bus

Douglas at the
opening of a bus
depot in 1950.

routes where there are three or four passengers a day, but if the
surpluses from the inter-city trade warrant it, we use that money
to keep the marginal lines in operation.

Let me remind you that we believe in a mixed economy of
public ownership, co-operative ownership, and private ownership. The problem was deciding which businesses belong to each
category. There were some things we did, not because they
belonged in the public ownership category, but because there was
no one else to do them. For instance, we had large deposits of
sodium sulphate at Chaplin. There was a huge alkaline lake left
unused, which was considered a nuisance. Even the livestock
wouldn't drink the water. Yet this was a very valuable commodity;
at that time sodium sulphate was selling at around twenty-two
dollars a ton. So we put up a million-dollar plant and produced
sodium sulphate, and just the other day we celebrated the tenth

With Mr. Holland
inspecting sodium
sulphate plant at
official opening, 9
June 1948.

anniversary of that plant. It has paid for itself two or three times
over, and from it we made enough money to buy another plant at
Bishopric. This wasn't necessarily a field for public ownership,
but it was a field in which we had wealth that needed to be developed. If there wasn't a private entrepreneur who was prepared to
invest his money, then we felt that the people were justified in doing this on their own.

The same happened with our clay deposits. Near the end of
the war, everybody knew there would be a terrific building boom,
and yet we were buying our brick from Alberta. Both Manitoba
and ourselves needed brick, and we had the clay. There was an
old brickyard at Estevan that had been closed for years with no
prospect of being opened, and so we bought it. It has been said
that we paid too much for it, but we brought a professor of ceramics and an industrialist to look it over, and we paid less than

their estimated price to the owners of the brickyard. All over Saskatchewan today you see buildings built with Estevan brick. I just came back from Winnipeg a couple of days ago, where Estevan brick is considered the number one brick. It is far better than any other brick they can get, and there's a great demand and a very good sale for it. Our brick is even going to Fort William and Port Arthur and Toronto. But again, by default the brick company went to public ownership.

We set up a timber board; in our opinion that did belong to public ownership. We felt that the forests belonged to the people of the province. Instead of turning these great timber berths over to be denuded and ruined, the only solution was to have a timber board, which gave people contracts to cut timber and paid them for cutting the timber just as you would pay a man to cut your crop, but the timber still belonged to the people of the province. We set up a forestry commission because we were told that unless we took some steps to discontinue the wholesale denuding of our forests, in some parts of the province we would have only eight years' supply left, and in even the best areas there was not more than eighteen or twenty years of forests remaining. So the Timber Board was established for the purpose of forest conservation.

Then we set up a Fur Marketing Service. This and the Fish Marketing Service and the Trading Posts are three crown corporations about which there's been some criticism. Properly speaking, and we've said this again and again, if the people of the north had been as well advanced in terms of social development as the people in the south, the logical approach would have been to have their fish and their fur marketed on a co-operative basis, and to have co-operative stores. But a very large percentage of the people in the far north are Indians and Métis, they are widely separated, and have very little inter-communication. When we moved into the north there was no communication except by canoe and by caterpillar train. We developed the Saskatchewan Government Air Service to provide them with plane communication. We sent them about two hundred two-way radio sets, and now we're building roads into the north country, to Buffalo Narrows and Ile à la Crosse and Cumberland House. Power has now

Co-op store in La Loche officially opened by Douglas in 1959.

reached Cumberland House. The road will be extended to La Loche, and another road from Lac La Ronge will finally reach Uranium City. But in 1944 there was nothing. There was no way these people from all over northern Saskatchewan could get together at any central point. Here were twelve or fifteen thousand people inhabiting a hundred thousand square miles of wilderness, without any means of either communication or transportation. There was only one thing to do to save them from the exploitation by the Hudson's Bay Company. The Company would stake these fishermen and trappers, buy their supplies, and then take delivery of their product. When the trappers sold their furs they took whatever price the Hudson's Bay chose to pay them, and it was applied on their debt, and they seldom if ever were able to meet the debt. They were always in debt and always getting advances.

The private fish dealers in the north used the same methods. The price was always down when fish was plentiful. The fishermen would get a good price once in a while, when there was a Jewish holiday or some special demand for fish, but most of the time when the catch was good, the price was low. It was always applied against the advances they had.

So the government did three things to alleviate this problem. We set up a Fur Marketing Service, which cleaned, stored and polished furs, and auctioned them off. The service took a five-percent commission and the trappers got the rest in two instalment payments. Many people said, "This is ridiculous; there's never been an auction out here. Auctions are in New York and San Francisco and Chicago." Joe Phelps must get credit for his statement: "If you have good fur they'll come here," and he was right. We have four and five auctions a year, and consistently the fur dealers come, even from London, England, to buy furs here. This has greatly improved the price and profits for our trappers.

The Fish Marketing Service works the same way. We contracted to market fish on a commission basis. In a few places we built fish filleting plants. The reason for this was that our fish, particularly our whitefish in certain lakes, had been infested with cysts. The federal government quite properly labelled these lakes as "B" lakes and would not permit us to export the fish from these lakes because they would ruin the reputation of Canadian fish on the American market. If we want to ship fish from "B" lakes, we must fillet them and remove the cysts.

Poor Indians and halfbreeds had no money to build fish filleting plants, so we did it for them rather than put these people on social aid and keep them in idleness. In this way we were able to market fish from grade "B" lakes that otherwise would have been unsaleable.

We did the same thing with the stores. In some of these communities the people were paying atrocious prices for their goods, and what was worse, they were not getting cash for the furs they sold, but simply getting credit against which they could buy goods at any price that the storekeeper chose to charge them. So the government set up trading stores, in which we sold supplies to the natives as close to cost as possible. We have never shown a surplus

Douglas with Joe Phelps at opening of the Saskatchewan Fur Marketing Service in 1946.

in any year of more than ten or twenty thousand dollars, and some years less than that. This was an attempt to balance the cost against the receipts.

This year we have finally reached the stage where we're ready to turn the Fish Marketing Service and the Trading Stores over to the co-operatives, and we think the day will come when we'll be able to do the same with the Fur Marketing Service. It'll take time, but the natives have demonstrated at Ile à la Crosse and at Buffalo Narrows and one or two other places, and at Cumberland House and at Montreal Lake, that they can handle co-operatives. We've trained one or two native store managers, who have worked out very well. Now we can begin to turn these government operations over to the people to run on a co-operative basis. This is not a departure from public ownership, which was never envisaged as anything more than a temporary measure until such time as these people could be trained and helped and be ready and willing to take them over. We've appointed an interim board of well-known co-operators and some native people; as these operations proceed their dividends will be applied on equity capital, and as they pay out the government equity they will, bit by bit, take over all the operations of both the stores and the Fish Marketing Service entirely by themselves.

At the same time we developed these services, we recognized that there was a great area of economic development in Saskatchewan into which the government couldn't possibly go. We drew the line between public and private ownership on this basis: public ownership should deal mainly with monopolistic industries that had a fairly guaranteed return, such as power and telephone services, Saskatchewan Government Airways, and insurance; but we recognized that to develop our natural resources, a great deal of risk capital would be necessary, which would have to come from private ownership.

This field of risk capital for natural resources development is left to private enterprise, providing that we receive a good royalty to compensate the people for the resources being depleted, and that we checkerboard the area and every second square on the checkerboard is kept as crown reserves.

From 1945 to 1948 we encouraged magnetometer surveys and seismograph surveys. We did some ourselves while trying to get private companies to explore the mineral potential of Saskatchewan. In 1947 Alberta hit its famous Leduc field, followed by the Redwater field, and later the Pembina field. Everybody with a drilling rig rushed off to Alberta, which was only natural. It was said that we chased them out of the province, but this was sheer nonsense. Six months before they discovered Leduc, the president of Imperial Oil said in my office: "We're coming into Saskatchewan in a big way. We've worked for three years on Leduc and before that B.A. worked for three years, and before that Shell worked for three years. We've spent, between the three of us, close to two hundred million dollars, and we still haven't come up with any oil." As we were going out the door, he said, "I've got one geologist called Red, who says he's going to quit if I don't let him stay in Leduc, so I'm going to let him stay with one drilling rig, but

I'm pulling everybody else out." Red found the oil, a quarter of a mile from a dry hole, and started the great rush. It was only natural that oilmen rushed to Alberta.[12]

By 1948 and 1949 we were interesting oil companies in coming to Saskatchewan. We also located uranium in the northwestern part of the province around Beaver Lodge Lake, where Uranium City is now located. Eldorado, a federal crown corporation, was followed by a number of private companies. In the northeastern corner of the province the Hudson's Bay Mining and Smelting Company was more and more moving into Saskatchewan, and we increased their royalties very considerably. At one time they had been paying as low as less than one hundred thousand dollars; last year they paid two and a quarter million dollars. After we had done the preliminary ground work, we had sufficient geological information to present the prospects to companies. We made maps available at a dollar each and encouraged companies to come in and talk business with us. In '48 and '49 I spent a good deal of my time while in London, and later in New York, Toronto, Montreal, and Chicago, interviewing heads of oil companies, geological consultants for banks and lending institutions, and presenting our information to them. The result was that from 1949 on, we saw a steadily increasing flood of companies interested in developing these basic resources coming into the province.

That was the turning point. We were convinced that if we could get the primary industries started, we would also attract secondary and tertiary industries. We had oil, gas, uranium, copper, zinc, salt, and potash industries in operation. From 1948 to 1955 our primary emphasis was on these basic industries, and there's been a good deal of success. In 1945 our total production from minerals was 22 million dollars, last year it was about 160 million, and this year I think it will be in the neighbourhood of 200 million dollars. When we came into office we were getting about a million and a half dollars a year from resources, which didn't do any more than pay the cost of running the Natural Resources Department.

It has been a spectacular development. We haven't hit anything of the magnitude of Leduc, Alberta, but people forget

T.M. Ware, president of International Minerals and Chemicals
Corporation, and T.C. Douglas holding the final bolt placed in the
350-foot cast-iron lining of the potash mine shaft twelve miles northeast of
Esterhazy, Saskatchewan, in 1961.

that the first oil in Alberta was discovered in Turner Valley in
1913. From 1921 to 1947 they brought in nothing new until they hit
Leduc. We have made progress much faster than that, and geography is in our favour. We're four hundred miles closer to the
market for oil than Alberta, and this year with the Americans
putting a quota on oil, Alberta oil has actually dropped in production, while ours has continued to increase. It has not increased as
rapidly as it has in the past, but it is still increasing, and we're now
producing about 130,000 barrels of oil per day with 3,600 oil wells
in production.

Uranium development has accelerated by leaps and bounds.
For a while it was doubling each year over the previous year. In
1956 we produced 27 million dollars' worth, and last year uranium
revenue was 39 million dollars.

What was your second aim?

We can't have artificial secondary industries. This is a mistake that some of the South American countries made, and perhaps the same mistake that Newfoundland made. They thought that if they could entice people by giving them subsidies, buying factories, or giving them cheap labour, they could start to make cotton goods or something of this sort. We made errors on a few arrangements we tried, and make no apologies except to say that it was something we tried. These efforts represent less than one-tenth of one percent of our total government investment in crown corporations, but they've had ninety-nine percent of the publicity. I refer to the woollen mill and the shoe factory. We had sheep, and thought we could make woollen cloth; and we have lots of leather to make leather goods. We set up both businesses on a trial basis. They could have been made to succeed if we had been prepared to put in large sums of money and expand our market. We were making work boots, but the average storekeeper wouldn't buy work boots unless he was getting other lines from us, because the shoe companies refused to sell shoes to them if they bought work boots from the government plant.

> There has been considerable criticism in Canada and elsewhere, but you have no apologies because these enterprises employed people.

That's right. They did create employment. If we had the chance to do it over again, we probably wouldn't go ahead, but on the other hand, nobody was active in these businesses and we had to find out whether or not we could produce cloth and leather products. The simple fact is that there isn't a big enough market here to produce on a big scale, and with freight rates as they are we couldn't hope to penetrate either the British Columbia or Ontario market. They have the same problem in Alberta. A woollen mill is closing there, too. You have to build secondary industries around primary industries, and our experiment proved that.

When the oil and gas industry developed, there was a need for a number of other industries. Because oil and gas requires large quantities of cement, it made a cement industry possible, which has done very well. Pipelines and steel pipe were in demand. Now we're shipping our steel pipe throughout Saskatchewan and also in Manitoba and Alberta. There's lots of scrap iron in the province and now a steel mill is under construction [by the Inter-Provincial Steel and Pipe Corporation], and should be in operation by the fall of 1959. This in turn might make it possible for us to use the iron ore deposits in Choiceland. We discovered these in an aerial magnetometer survey some years ago. A company became interested, drilled down into the deposit, and was very satisfied with it both in terms of quantity and availability. It was in a good area near highways and rural roads, and probably one of the biggest deposits in Canada. But there was no use for the iron ore. With the steel industry, it has now become a definite possibility.

The same thing was true with our power programme. Our power load increases by over twenty percent per year, which is one of the largest increases of any power system in Canada. This produced a need for more poles; we needed wire and insulators, and we have firms here creosoting poles. The Timber Board sells them the poles, they creosote them, and they sell them to the Power Corporation. We have a plant in Regina manufacturing insulators, and one in Weyburn making wire cable and telephone cable, and plastic pipe for the gas industry. Secondary industries, if they're to be a success, must be based on supplying the needs of a primary industry. This is the great lesson we've learned.

> Income from non-agricultural resources has been larger, has it not, in recent years?

Yes. Last year, 1957, of 1,400 million dollars of wealth production in Saskatchewan, nearly 900 million dollars and almost 65 percent came from non-agricultural sources. But agriculture hasn't become less important. We're farming a million more acres than we did in 1941, and we're producing more food per acre, but agriculture represents now only some 35 percent of our total wealth production. We think that we'll have a much more stable economy when only a third of our wealth production is vulnerable to climate and world market conditions.

In your opinion, did the Regina Manifesto and the publicity or the criticism made by the opposition to these small crown corporations, which were only eight percent of the whole, do any harm politically?

They certainly did make it difficult for us. There's no doubt about that. In Saskatchewan, no one was particularly worried about these crown corporations. They recognized that we were trying. In the 1944 election I said we will make mistakes in judgement, but the one mistake we will not make is that of doing nothing for fear of making a mistake.

Newspapermen here sent their articles to other papers, where they were copied. *The Globe and Mail, The Wall Street Journal,* and *Barron's Financial Weekly News* gave quite a distorted picture. But these writers were guilty of fouling their own nest. I remember in 1947, visiting one of the big industrialists in New York and trying to interest him in coming to invest in oil development, which he subsequently did, and very successfully. But at first he said, "I don't think I want to do any business with anyone who shows as little business judgement as you people. I'm referring to the government plant you've got producing horsemeat," and he brandished an article which appeared in *Barron's Financial Weekly News* by Harold Kreutzweiser, in which it was said that the Saskatchewan government had spent the people's money on a plant to produce horsemeat, when everybody knew that nobody ate horsemeat in this country, and that this was just another example of the foolish Socialists that had gone mad. I said to this man, "Do you want to hear the whole story, or shall we just say goodbye?" He said he'd listen. I told him that in the fall of 1945, forty ranchers descended on my office and told me that they had a great problem on their hands. During the war nobody had done anything about horses. At the beginning of the war everybody thought that horses would be in demand as they had been during the First World War for cavalry and for hauling supplies, but the mechanized age had removed the need for horses. The horses had been running wild, and the estimate was that there were over a million horses on the prairies and in the ranch areas of Saskatchewan, more horses than there were cattle, and they were eating up grazing land required for cattle. They had American offers of five dollars a head, but they couldn't pay cowboys to round up wild horses for that price.

Mr. Sturdy, at that time Minister of Social Welfare, had just come back from the war, and headed a committee on which Dr. L.B. Thomson of the P.F.R.A. was a member; one or two of the ranchers, some of the co-operative people, and a bank manager as an advisor were also on the committee and canvassed the whole situation. Sturdy went to Ottawa, and came back with the promise of two big horsemeat contracts — one from the Belgian government, and the other from the United Nations Relief and Rehabilitation Administration. On the basis of these two contracts we managed to get an old building from the city council in Swift Current. The committee went to the bank and got a loan guaranteed by the provincial government, and they started slaughtering these horses, They paid back millions of dollars to these ranchers for these horses, and employed a couple of hundred people for several years. We supplied horsemeat to the Belgian people and the Belgian Congo, and people in Europe who were hardpressed for meat. We turned a liability into an asset. Afterward, we sold the plant to Quaker Oats as a pet food factory.

When the man heard the story, he agreed that it was the sensible thing to do, "a stroke of genius." But I couldn't get the story across to the several thousand people who read the article in *Barron's Weekly*.

The same thing happened with the oil people in the fall of 1948 in Toronto. They asked about what they read in the Liberal press, the Conservative press, and the Saskatchewan press, that we would socialize everything, all the oil wells and the refineries, after they had invested in Saskatchewan. I explained our philosophy. I said, "I believe in public ownership, but I'm telling you very frankly that if you want to put in a power system or distribute natural gas, we will say no. We've marked these industries under public ownership. But I'm prepared to give it to you in writing, that if you develop natural resources, apart from having to pay your royalty and recognizing the crown reserves, nobody will interfere with you, and you'll be allowed to operate your business just as you do anywhere else. When we put our signature to this, it is not like some of the agreements you make in Venezuela, Uruguay, and in the Middle East, where the government changes overnight as a result of a military coup d'etat and you suddenly have to make new agreements and pay twice or three times as much as you anticipated."

I gave these people a signed letter, which was printed in the oil magazines throughout Canada and the United States, that broke the resistance. But I don't think the public will ever fully appreciate just how much our political opponents deliberately held back the development of this province. I believe that the opposition was prepared to see Saskatchewan stagnate. They would rather have seen it a desolate waste, than to see it prosper under a C.C.F. government.

> We have an investment in oil alone of about 2 billion dollars.

That's right. These companies aren't afraid. Why would they be? They've got the protection of the courts. They know that. What's more, they know that the people of Saskatchewan on the whole are honourable people, and they wouldn't keep a government that broke its pledged word in office very long.

> One clause of the Regina Manifesto of 1933[13] was used extensively. Even I have been asked by oil men what it meant. There was nothing in the Regina Manifesto, was there, that didn't square with your party's philosophy when you went into office?

Not a bit. The Regina Manifesto simply pointed out that there were certain principal means of production and distribution and exchange that ought to be publicly owned. We believe that. It also made it very clear that there were areas for co-operative and private ownership. The phrase that has been repeated extensively is the closing sentence, which says that we will not rest content until capitalism has been eradicated. You have to remember the circumstances under which that manifesto was passed. There were a million people unemployed in Canada, farmers were getting twenty-three cents a bushel for their wheat, our whole economy had fallen flat on its face. Capitalism wasn't being

associated necessarily with private ownership, but with corporation ownership, and the terrible abuses that monopolies had
exercised in controlling the economy, which brought about one
of the greatest collapses in all our history.

> Wasn't it assumed that capitalism was obsolete?

That's right. Capitalism as we knew it in 1933 is gone. People don't
realize that the 1933 brand of capitalism no longer exists. The
depression was caused in part because the banks, who had the
sole control of issuing currency and credit, started to recall their
credit. In a period of eighteen months they called in $2.6 billion
dollars of bank credits. They couldn't do this today. The Bank of
Canada has complete control of issuing currency and credit;
banks have been turned into bookkeeping offices.

The same was true of the wheat trade. The Winnipeg Grain
Exchange determined wheat prices, and when there was a surplus, there was no price, and when there was a price there was no
supply. But today the Wheat Marketing Board sets the price of
wheat. The capitalism we were against, and whose abuses we
pointed out, has already been eradicated to a large degree.

> Was it a great error to equate capitalism with free enter-
> prise?

Yes, in the popular mind. Ever since the war the term capitalism
has been changed to free enterprise, and my contention is that
this free enterprise is neither free nor enterprising. Even President Eisenhower's chief economic advisor, Dr. Slichter, said that
the gigantic monopolies now set sixty percent of the prices on this
continent, and the prices they set have no relation to supply and
demand. But to condemn monopolistic capitalism does not mean
to condemn private ownership. As a democrat and a co-operator,
what I most regret in the last fifty years is the disappearance of
private ownership. The little merchant who ran his own store, the
man who ran his own business, and the artisan who did his own
work are disappearing. A man used to run his own filling station,
but now he runs one for B.A. or Imperial Oil or Husky, or some
other oil company. Private ownership as we understood it at the
turn of the century is largely being wiped out.

> But it's still being alleged in this year of 1958 that one of the main reasons industry won't come into Saskatchewan is because of the existence of the Regina Manifesto. Some clarification of that manifesto has been made, has it not?

Yes, the Winnipeg Declaration of 1956 puts the Regina Manifesto in its historical perspective. The Regina Manifesto addressed only the terrible abuses of the time and the complete lack of government control. The Winnipeg Declaration is not only concerned with the capitalism that to some extent has been obliterated, but this monopoly situation and the tremendous loss of both political and economic democracy that has resulted from it. I think it's more timely, and it recognizes the situation of the second half of the twentieth century.

But we're still being told that Saskatchewan would get more industry if we had a better political climate in the province. I have two answers to that claim. First, in a province that has consistently had 600 million dollars of public and private investment annually, a lower unemployment ratio than either Alberta or Manitoba, and a higher per capita investment than the national average, it doesn't look like the political climate has kept anybody out. In the last decade we've had more industrial development than in any ten-year period in our history.

Second, what do people mean by the political climate keeping people out? They're never specific as to what they would change about the political climate. If they feel that the Farm Security Act is keeping people out, they should say so. Do they think the labour legislation is keeping people away? Do they mean that they would be prepared to abolish our labour legislation? Or do they mean that the government should get out of power and telephones, insurance and gas distribution, and turn these over to private monopolies? This they never say. We need to make the public aware that if we want business to come to this province, and we have to sell our birthright, then we are adopting a policy of economic slavery.

> Isn't there another factor? There is quite a degree of practical and physical co-operation between industry and the government.

That's right. I think we've made the kind of move that the British Labour party is now advocating. We have an industrial development fund to help develop private and co-operative industry.

A moment ago I mentioned the crown reserves. We have put some of our crown reserves up for public auction, and received very good sums of money: two and a quarter million dollars in some cases for one parcel of land. But some of our land we've made available on a net royalty basis to allow the small investor, who can't lay out the million or two million dollars, to have it in return for seventy or eighty percent of the net return after expenses. This has enabled many small companies to get into the oil business without a very heavy outlay. They need just enough money to pay for their drilling costs and so on. If they find no oil, they've lost; we've lost nothing. But if they find oil, we make a very heavy percentage.

We have also taken some of the most promising oil reserves and turned them over to co-operatives on a net royalty lease basis. We are paid either in oil or in cash. We've always taken the cash, and they put the oil into their refinery. This is perfectly in keeping with C.C.F. policy. In the old days we used to talk about production for use and not for profit. Well, here it is. Here are farmers and now many urban people who belong to the co-ops — the oil comes out of the ground and belongs jointly to the co-operatives and the people of Saskatchewan through their government. That oil goes by pipeline or by truck to the refinery, where it is processed and distributed to the filling stations. When it comes out of the ground and goes into the farmer's truck or the citizen's car, nobody's making any profit. The money either comes to the government under our net royalty lease, or it is paid back to the consumer in patronage dividends.

When I think of all the sneering we listened to in the 1930s and the 1940s, this is a fantastic argument and a concrete example of production for use and not for profit.

Private enterprise is still flourishing.

Yes, but the co-operatives and small independent producers have prevented the oil resources of Saskatchewan from being held by half a dozen big companies who can form a cartel. They represent

an effective balance wheel. This is important in a mixed economy: the public and private segments of the economy must, in
my opinion, represent at least twenty to twenty-five percent of
the total economy if they're to be an effective balance wheel
against big monopolies. Big monopolies can only throttle the
economy when they have ninety or a hundred percent of the
control. Monopolies must be compelled by competition to keep
their prices down and not to exploit the public.

> When you advocated a planned economy, you began by
> getting the best advice and setting up an economic plan-
> ning board.

That was one of the first things we did when we came into office.
The planning board has been of tremendous value, not only industrial development, but in planning our government programmes by giving them some sense of priority and perspective.

One of the outstanding men we hired was George Cadbury
of the Cadbury Chocolate people in England, who is now working for the Technical Assistance Committee of the United Nations.[14] Mr. Cadbury was very efficient and gathered around him
very able people; his job since he left has fallen on the shoulders
of Mr. Tommy Shoyama,[15] a very competent economist. The
actual promotion of industrial development has been delegated
to the Industrial Development Office, headed by Mr. D.H.F.
Black, and they have been very effective in attracting industry to
Saskatchewan.

> In conclusion, do you think that this population problem,
> if one exists, can be solved, and by what means?

It won't be solved quickly because the process of farm mechanization has proceeded very rapidly. We need to at least provide
enough jobs to permit employment for those who come off the
farms, and then work toward attracting people from other parts of
Canada and from other countries of the world, so that our population can grow. But our main job now is to stabilize our existing
population.

> You don't visualize then any of these western provinces

> becoming what you might call highly industrialized, such
> as we find in Toronto or Montreal? Will our base, rather,
> always be agriculture?

Our base will certainly be agriculture for a long time. Industrialization will develop as secondary and tertiary industries come along, but for the time being our two bases are going to be agriculture and primary industries. But as time goes on, in twenty or twenty-five years, a great many secondary and tertiary industries will build around these primary industries and western Canada could become a fairly important industrial centre. Markets will limit us — we're a long way from markets. It will help when the eastern provinces of Canada and the eastern parts of the United States become more highly industrialized, and more dependent on us for raw materials. For a long time, we're going to be suppliers of raw materials.

> When we speak of raw materials, some are not renewable and could still leave us with an agricultural base. In a matter of two decades or less, do you see Saskatchewan moving from a precarious one-crop economy to a much more diversified, lasting economy? We have had a crop failure recently, in 1954. What happened then?

Our economy stood up very well because that happened to be a particularly good year for mineral production, oil production, and manufacturing. We scarcely felt the adverse effects of the crop failure. Our budget that year, which we thought we would have to cut as a result of the crop failure, was actually increased.

10

The third
C.C.F. term in office

◻ Politically, what happened to you in the year of the 1952 election?

This was a very crucial election for us because we had a setback in the number of seats in 1948, and also in the federal election of 1949, when the number of seats we held were cut from eighteen to five. The year 1952 would tell whether we were a flash in the pan and on our way out, or whether we were here to stay.

It wasn't a hard fought election. I think by this time the organized attempt to portray the government as Communists or subversives and the old cries of "Tucker or Tyranny" were ineffective. We won that election quite easily, and increased our representation in the House from thirty-one members to forty-two.

Douglas with Princess Elizabeth during a royal visit to Saskatchewan, 1951.

There were just one or two notable events following the 1952 election. In October 1952 we had a visit from Prince Philip and Princess Elizabeth, shortly before the death of King George VI. What impressed you about your meeting with the royal couple?

They were originally scheduled to come early in October, right in the midst of an Indian summer when they would have seen the prairies at their very best, the leaves changing colour, the golden stubble, and the blue skies. However, the visit had to be postponed a whole week, and they landed here in a blizzard. It's not often that we get blizzards in October, but I'm sure their impression of Saskatchewan must have been pretty grim. In spite of the inclement weather, we had arranged for them to be seen as much as possible, and I think they got a very hearty welcome.

Like most young couples, they were very much interested in their children. We gave them some gifts to take back to Prince Charles and Princess Anne. Princess Elizabeth was deeply touched by the fact that we were thinking of their children. They had a very fine reception. At the luncheon and at the dinner in the evening, I was quite pleased to be sitting next to Princess Elizabeth, and found her very charming and intelligent. She had been briefed before with penetrating, intelligent questions about the province. Prince Philip was also quite interested. Like most English people they were interested in horses, and we took them out to the R.C.M.P. barracks and showed them the musical ride, which unfortunately had to be done inside, but even then they got a very great thrill out of it.

My other impression was the Princess's obvious fondness for her father. She spoke very feelingly about him; at this time he was quite ill. She was in daily communication by telephone with Great Britain. A few weeks later, he died.

> Wasn't there also quite a scramble to get the moccasins flown in from the far north?

They arrived that morning, just in time to be presented as gifts for the royal children. The moccasins were of white caribou with Indian beadwork. We also presented them with four paintings of Saskatchewan by Robert Hurley, summer, spring, fall, and winter scenes. They were very glad to have these paintings, a very fine tribute to Mr. Hurley, who is a very fine Saskatchewan painter. As a result, a great many Canadians in London and in eastern Canada have started to buy Mr. Hurley's paintings, which has helped Saskatchewan art somewhat.

◿ In the February 1953 session, there was a Liberal opposition of eleven members. Something rather dramatic happened at this session. Here's an excerpt from a broadcast I made:

Somewhat abruptly, nearly four weeks of inquiry by a Saskatchewan legislative committee ended on Saturday. It was an inquiry into allegations by Joseph Rawluk that a cabinet minister and the government insurance manager received kickbacks on insurance commissions. This inquiry, an ordinary legislative committee sitting as a semi-judicial body, heard twenty-eight witnesses, who testified for more than one hundred hours. In Regina, public interest in the inquiry was high. Hundreds of people jammed the legislative chamber for four weeks, many of them lining up for two hours before the doors opened mornings and evenings.

Later the committee brought in a majority report which exonerated everybody involved. Mr. Tucker's minority report said in effect that the people involved had not proved themselves innocent. Do you recall how it started?

We were sitting in cabinet that morning, running over some final business for the Legislature. Since the crown corporations committee was just in the process of being organized for the year, it wasn't felt necessary that all the ministers be there, so just Mr. Fines went down to be present at the organization meeting and most of the cabinet ministers were at the cabinet meeting.

Mr. Fines returned to the cabinet meeting at about noon and told us that Mr. Tucker had read an affidavit signed by J.R. Rawluk making very serious charges, and Mr. Tucker had demanded an immediate investigation. He moved that the crown corporations committee of the Saskatchewan Legislature should investigate the whole matter, and Mr. Fines, in a burst of enthusiasm, seconded the motion. Had either of them stopped to read the rules, they would have known that neither the crown corporations committee nor any other committee has authority to start an investigation. A legislative committee, like the House of Commons committee, operates under the terms of reference given to it by the Legislature, and all this committee really had power to do was to report the matter back to the House and ask for instructions, at which time the government and the majority of members would have decided how they wanted to conduct this investigation. If the matter had been referred to the House, I would have favoured some other type of investigation, either a judicial investigation or a Royal Commission. I know that an investigation by a committee made up of politicians from two different parties is not likely to reach any conclusive results. There would be a majority report and a minority report, and the government members would remain convinced on one score, and the opposition would be convinced of something different. Whereas a committee of judges or a Royal Commission could investigate the matter under the proper rules of court procedure, and could have come to some fairly definite conclusions.

But as Mr. Tucker had moved the motion, and Mr. Fines seconded it, we could not change the situation. To do so then would have been taken as an attempt by the government to white-wash the whole affair and refer it to some other group. Under the rules of the House we had no authority to go ahead, and so I introduced a motion that gave the committee the authority to do what it had already begun to do. I moved that the crown corporations committee should have the authority to carry on an investigation into the allegations and charges made in this particular affidavit. I expressed my preference for an investigation by a judicial committee or a Royal Commission, but Mr. Tucker said he didn't want any behind-the-barn investigation, and that this was going to be investigated by the members immediately without any stalling. Because we were going to have a federal election in June, a few months away, he probably had in mind that this was a chance to have a Roman holiday.

Frankly, when I heard about the case it sounded a bit far-fetched, but I've always taken the position that when you have ten thousand employees in government service, you always have the possibility that someone is going to be dishonest, or is going to accept bribes or some monetary return for giving favours. Consequently we must always be ready to investigate such charges. I've always made it clear to every cabinet minister that when they make mistakes in matters of judgement, I will stand by them, recognizing that any human being can make a mistake. But if they were guilty of any dishonesty in mishandling funds, accepting bribes, or accepting expensive presents, as far as I was concerned, even if they were my best friend or my own brother, I would accept their resignation.

In the meantime the committee had chosen a counsel, Mr. E.C. Leslie, Q.C.,[1] a very prominent barrister in Regina. When he called me he said, "I've been asked by a committee of your Legislature to act as counsel, and before I take such a job I want to know what I'm supposed to do." I said, "As far as I'm concerned, there's only one thing you're supposed to do, and that is to elicit the truth." He said, "Are you sure you want the truth?" I said, "I want it no matter who's involved. The people of Saskatchewan have a right to know the truth and if any of these people are involved then I shall ask for their resignation. If I'm involved in any way, then the people will get my resignation, too. The only job you have is to ferret out the facts and place them before the committee." I think the great majority of the committee felt exactly the same way.

> I suppose from your viewpoint as premier you must always feel much more deeply concerned when allegations are made against one of your cabinet, although the gentleman accused in this case was a close friend.

He was a very close friend indeed, one of my closest friends, and a man for whom I had a very high regard and so it came as a great shock to me. Nevertheless, I've had enough experience over the years to know that you never know anyone, and that people can make mistakes. Had the allegations against Mr. Fines been proven, I would have taken the same position with regard to him as I would have taken with regard to Mr. Allore, who was a government employee.

> But it would have reflected on the government.

Oh, yes, and it was very serious.

> There were tremendous crowds, and such public interest that people were sitting on the floor of the Legislature.

There wasn't enough room for everyone. What really stands out in your mind about it? It was somewhat of a nightmare to those in the press gallery. We didn't know if it was real or unreal.

It was a nightmare to us, too, as you can well imagine. The Legislature was supposed to be dealing with the budget and the estimates of the departments, but this and all the other business of government were completely forgotten. Everything revolved around the Legislative Committee and the crown corporations. We started out by meeting as usual in the legislative committee rooms, but in a very short time this was completely inadequate, and so we moved into the Legislative Chamber. The Legislature was restricted to meeting in the afternoon, and the investigating committee met morning and evening. Everybody turned up to watch the fireworks in the committee, which stole the show.

One of the newspapermen asked me about the session a few days before and I said, "It'll be a quiet session. We have just finished the provincial election and it will probably be a very dull session." It was anything but dull. It was the most exciting session I ever attended, and a very difficult one, because naturally we still had to keep legislation moving, but at the same time we spent hours and hours of mornings and evenings in this committee. Then we'd work half the night going over the evidence submitted, preparing the questions for the next day, and arranging for witnesses. It was very hectic.

As I recall it there were also some lighter touches. For instance, in the middle of the recital of important evidence the chairman would get up and say, "Is Billy Jones in the audience? Your mother wants you to call her at LA 26405." There were also some Hollywood dramatics. Mr. Rawluk's wife was brought in to answer a few questions, and then at a judicious moment, she collapsed and was taken out in a semi-fainting condition. There were a lot of Damon Runyan characters, Billy George, gamblers, and other people from the underworld here. But it wasn't all fun. There was a lot of bitterness, but it was such a fantastic story: the idea that a Provincial Treasurer would

> meet some unknown person on a street, whom we could only identify by a purple coat, and take from him an envelope containing what was said to be between one and two hundred dollars. It was such a bizarre touch.

Yes. It sounded like a cloak-and-dagger mystery. Rawluk was in so deep that nothing could be worse. He'd gone broke and his books were taken by the committee. Mr. Leslie demonstrated that he had been forging cheques and had on two occasions misappropriated funds. He also admitted to perjury on a number of occasions. The poor fellow to some extent was a victim of political viciousness, who ought to have been dealt with kindly by some good psychiatrist rather than being dragged into this investigation.

> He said that he had not wanted Mr. Tucker to bring up the affidavit.

I had heard rumours, even during the election campaign in 1952, that there was a fellow called Rawluk who was talking about some affidavit he had. I paid no attention except to say to the person who mentioned it to me, "If this man has any affidavit about any misconduct on the part of any person in the government, tell him to come and see me and there'll be a full investigation." Of course Rawluk didn't come, and when he got on the stand, he said that he had never wanted an investigation. I don't know why he gave this affidavit to Mr. Tucker, but I don't think he really wanted the matter publicized. His bankruptcy and the possibility of going to jail had worked on his mind. He had a lot of grievances, real or imagined, and drafted this affidavit.

> I was discussing the matter with a man who knows politics probably better than anybody in this province, and he said, "After all, it's good fun, and good for elections, but you should never go ahead with a complete scrutiny unless you're a hundred-percent certain that you've got the evidence." It was rather amazing that Mr. Tucker did this: he was an experienced politician and a lawyer. It always struck me as peculiar.

His judgement wasn't good, because you remember that Rawluk

admitted on the stand that Mr. Tucker had come to see him about five days before the Legislature opened. He had seen this affidavit, and asked to take a copy of it away with him, and apparently on the basis of this affidavit and the charges contained in it proceeded to raise the matter at the very first meeting of the crown corporations committee. I'm certain now, that if he had taken the time to ascertain the facts from anyone regarding Rawluk's credibility and his standing in the business community, he would never have raised the matter without a very full investigation. It's amazing that a man who sat as a Member of Parliament, who had been parliamentary secretary in the House of Commons to the Minister of Veterans' Affairs, and who had experience as a lawyer, wouldn't have thought twice before exposing himself to this scandal on the basis of an affidavit from an obviously emotionally upset individual.

> You carried a great weight of the defence yourself. The committee finally brought in a majority report exonerating everybody involved.

We prepared a report on the basis of the evidence elicited by Mr. Leslie. The understanding when he took the job was that there would be no attempt to whitewash anybody. The facts stated that Rawluk was completely discreditable, that no evidence of any sort whatsoever had been produced to support a single one of his assertions regarding wrongdoing or kickbacks. We debated this in the committee behind closed doors for some days, and finally the majority of the committee agreed with this report. This report had to be presented in the Legislature, and then there was an awful fiasco when of one of the opposition members, Mr. Horsman, M.L.A. for Wilkie, moved an amendment, which was about forty-eight pages long. It was terrific, it had thousands of words, and purported to be a reply to the committee's report. While he was reading the first page, the whole thing fell out of his hands and onto the floor. He hastily gathered the pages together again, and I'm not even certain they were reassembled in chronological order, because it was a most fantastic reply.

The only case they could make was that the parties charged had not completely proven their innocence. We pointed out that a party was innocent until proven guilty. Then they asked for what I had wanted in the first place, a judicial investigation. At this point it was completely contrary to justice. You cannot try a man under one court and then ask another court to try him — play the game all over again, with a different umpire and a different playing field.

> In the final speech you went after Mr. Tucker, saying that he was discredited as a politician by these tactics. Mr. Tucker had his head down on his desk and didn't raise his head until you were finished with him. In my experience of reporting it was one of the most devastating criticisms I'd ever heard, and I think Mr. Tucker felt it very keenly. Did this long trial, with all its bizarre aspects, have any effect on the C.C.F. party?

I thought that it might, and that was why I went into a good deal of detail on the evidence in my speech. The opposition whips had told us that afternoon that the debate would go on for at least another day, and so I made no arrangements to get the lieutenant-governor to prorogue the House, because both Mr. Tucker and I had long speeches, and several other people were going to speak.

When I finished summarizing the whole case and sat down, nobody got up. At half-past nine in the evening, the debate collapsed. That probably was the end of Mr. Tucker's influence. Most people had been quite shocked at the charges and were quite prepared, if the evidence was forthcoming, to demand that stringent disciplinary measures be taken with those who were guilty. None of us knew just what the effect would be. While you can prove that something is wrong, whether you can wash off the dirt is another story. But in June we went into the federal election with five M.P.s and came out with fourteen.

> This brings us to Mr. Tucker's swan song. He had come here with the idea that he wouldn't leave until he was Premier of Saskatchewan.

The Liberal party representation dropped by half from twenty-two to eleven in the 1952 election, which proved that all these innuendoes hadn't worked. After the resounding defeat, as far as

C.M. Fines, T.C. Douglas, and C.C. Williams at a presentation of a brief by the Trades and Labour Congress, 1951.

Saskatchewan was concerned, in the 1953 federal election following the Rawluk inquiry, it became apparent that the public generally didn't go for irresponsible character assassination. There isn't any doubt that two or three people had been marked for attack by character assassination, and Mr. Fines was one of them. In summing up the case, this was one of the points I tried to make. It was virtually apparent that because Mr. Fines was one of the best administrators we had, and because it had been largely due to his financial adroitness that we had been able to finance many of our programmes, he was a man they wanted to destroy. I think the public became aware of this and reacted accordingly.

I am quite convinced that legislative committees were never intended as a means of carrying on investigations regarding charges of dishonesty. They should examine accounts and find out whether money had been properly spent, but when it comes to a matter of investigating the private affairs of an individual, the matter ought to be turned over to the courts or to a judicial committee or to a Royal Commission. This is a British tradition. The Americans, however, specialize in committees of investigation — the McCarthy committee is the most noted one — which can stray from the point and can ruin people's reputations without any responsibility. This is the danger of allowing people whose business is legislating to set up a quasi-judicial court. The courts have the machinery and the objectivity and they have no political bias and no axe to grind.

> You and Eleanor Roosevelt were to be presented with citations by the League of Industrial Democracy on 11 April 1953. You were unable to go because of the Rawluk case, is that right?

I had anticipated that the Legislature would be finished by 2 or 3 April, as was usually the case. But with the Rawluk investigation underway, I felt it would have been most inappropriate for me to have been absent, and so Mr. Coldwell, the national leader of the C.C.F., went on my behalf and accepted the citation.

> The Rawluk case was very significant because it was probably the end of a political era as far as Saskatchewan was concerned. It was Mr. Tucker's end as a leader. After that, the party was disgruntled with his leadership. What happened to him then?

He then decided to resign, and to run as a federal candidate in Rosthern constituency in the election of June 1953. Mr. Boucher, the incumbent M.P., very conveniently withdrew in Mr. Tucker's favour, and Mr. Tucker once more became M.P. and Mr. Boucher was later elevated to the Senate.

> For one year after that we had Mr. Asmundur Lopston[2] as the House leader, one of the two veteran members [the other was Mr. Herman Danielson] whom you once christened the "dead-end kids."

During the 1954 session, Mr. Lopston was the leader of the opposition, and in 1955 Mr. Alexander Hamilton McDonald came in as leader of the opposition.

◻ You went to England again for the Coronation in 1953. What do you recall about it?

There is no nation with the capacity for pageantry of the British. They have made a study of it down through the centuries, and can put on a spectacle that makes Hollywood look like a bunch of amateurs.

The Duke of Norfolk, who was in charge of the arrangements, was a Catholic organizing an Anglican service to crown a Queen. He did a magnificent job, and he told some of us that the crown was put on the Queen's head thirty-one seconds ahead of schedule, and that the Queen's carriage entered Buckingham Palace seventeen seconds behind schedule. That's how closely it was timed. Everything was done to the most minute detail. There was one special directive on liquid intake prior to the ceremony, and for three days before, people were to reduce their intake gradually until the morning of the Coronation, when they were to have no liquid intake at all so that they would not be embarrassed by having to leave the ceremony at a most inappropriate moment.

Speaking of liquid intake, I remember an incident in the Abbey. Apparently in the previous Coronation of King George VI, there had been no washrooms or lavatories in the Abbey, and thousands of people who were there from early in the morning weren't able to get out of the Abbey because of the crowds until late in the afternoon. There was a good deal of physical discomfort encountered by those in attendance. There had been so much protest about it that when the 1953 Coronation came along, temporary comfort stations were established in the Abbey.

My wife and I got there about seven o'clock in the morning. The ceremony didn't take place until eleven o'clock, and wasn't over until probably one o'clock, and we didn't get out of the

Abbey until about 5:30 P.M. You just couldn't get out in the streets from about eight o'clock in the morning. Traffic in the streets was just impossible, and so you had to be in the Abbey by eight o'clock unless you were part of the procession. Even at 5:30 you proceeded at a snail's pace. I'm sure it took us an hour and a half to go from Westminster Abbey to the Park Lane Hotel.

This was a long time to be in. Fortunately my wife, with considerable foresight, had hidden some sandwiches and some chocolate bars in the cuff of her fur jacket. Premier and Mrs. Smallwood from Newfoundland were sitting next to us. Smallwood had filled his top hat with chocolate bars, and so between our sandwiches and chocolate bars and Joe Smallwood's confectionery, we managed to hold out until the luncheon, at about 1:30 or two o'clock.

After we had been sitting for about three hours, Mr. Smallwood decided he wanted to find a washroom, and I told him where I had seen one on my way in. He said, "You come along and show me." So I went along with him. On one door, a sign said "Gentlemen" and the other door, "Peers," the latter referring to Members of the House of Lords. At the "Gentlemen" door there was a line-up of about sixty men. Joe Smallwood took one look at this line, and then saw the other door with nobody there. I caught him by the arm and said, "You can't go in there, that's for Peers." He said, "That describes me exactly," and in he went.

It was a very brilliant and a very moving ceremony. We were sitting right behind the British cabinet ministers, and the prime ministers from the various parts of the Commonwealth. To my mind it was one of the great highlights of my life to see that ceremony.

There were innumerable social functions: garden parties, receptions, and dinners. The lieutenant-governor of Saskatchewan, the Honourable W. J. Patterson, and Mrs. Patterson were there, and I know they enjoyed going to these functions very much, as we did.

You had to be specially dressed, did you not?

Oh, yes. At seven o'clock in the morning you had to be in full evening dress, and the women had to be in their evening gowns. It was all very formal.

In the intervening time between 1953 and the next election in 1956, there were two exciting years with very little reference to politics. Did you see the Saskatchewan Golden Jubilee as a very successful and worthwhile event?

Yes, I think it was a very historic occasion. We started in 1952 by passing an act of legislation setting up a Golden Jubilee Committee. We wanted to get started early, so that there'd be plenty of time to plan and get the maximum amount of participation by every possible community. We wanted the committee to have complete freedom. It wasn't a government committee just of civil servants, but included people from all walks of life. The committee had an independent budget and was encouraged to get various groups, irrespective of their political or religious affiliations, all working together in celebrating this Jubilee.

We were fortunate to have Mr. Justice Culliton, who had been a former member of the Legislature, and who now is on the Appeal Court of Saskatchewan, as our chairman. Much of the success of the Golden Jubilee is due to his hard work and his personality. He had a great ability to get along with different kinds of people, he was strict about the budget, and at the same time he had lots of imagination.

We were also fortunate to have Mr. Fred McGuinness, a very skilled public relations man. I was on the train coming from Toronto, and I ran into Pat O'Dwyer, who worked at one time for *The Leader-Post* and was then working for the *Winnipeg Free Press*. I said I was looking for a man who was a combination of Barnum and Tchaikovsky. I wanted somebody who could put on a first-class show, but I didn't want just entertainment. When the Jubilee celebration was over, I wanted the people of Saskatche-

Douglas participating in the dog derby at the Hudson Bay Saskatchewan Golden Jubilee celebrations, 1955.

wan to have a better understanding of their own history, particularly their own local history. Everything had to be directed toward our background, the part the pioneers played, and what still had to be done to make Saskatchewan a great province. I didn't want a circus, but at the same time I didn't want it so long-hair that nobody but intellectuals would take any interest in it. Pat O'Dwyer suggested Fred McGuinness, who was also on the train. Fred was quite intrigued with the idea, and came in the fall of '52 and stayed until about 1956, when he later went to manage one of the Southam papers.

Fred McGuinness had all the qualifications of a showman. He also had a deep understanding of what we wanted to do, and he was ably assisted by the secretary of the Golden Jubilee Committee, Mr. John Archer, the legislative librarian. They made a good team along with Dr. Lewis Thomas, the provincial archivist, who helped to supply the factual data, and see that they kept the presentations historically accurate.

All through the year there were Golden Jubilee activities, the MacDonald Brier contest, the North American skating championships, and the Dominion Drama Festival. We must have had fifty national conventions that year. It was an unusual year for us, and there was hardly a week or a month when there wasn't some national event taking place in the province, all beamed toward the idea of drawing public attention to Saskatchewan's Golden Jubilee.

The celebration officially began with the visit of Governor-General Massey, who opened the Natural History Museum dedicated to the pioneers of the province. We thought this was the most useful way we could honour the pioneers so that the young people would understand something of the natural history of Saskatchewan. Over five hundred communities wrote local histories and established little local pioneer museums. They collected things that others didn't know existed: old flintlocks from the Battle of Waterloo, old candlesticks, old spinning jennies, old-fashioned looms, an old pump that pumped water from hot air from burning wood (something any politician should be interested in), old farm implements from the early days, and things that had been brought out from Ontario and from Europe. The Golden Jubilee Committee helped these communities, sometimes financially, and also by giving them material, but the great part of the work was done by the people themselves. The children were very involved. They wrote histories of their own communities and did their own research.

> Dr. Thomas said that this wonderful research would never have been done by any other means. There were hundreds and hundreds of schoolchildren going out and interviewing old-timers.

I read at least a couple of hundred of these school histories, which are now in the archives. Some of them are remarkably well done, and contain a lot of historical data that would have been lost forever had it not been collected at that particular time. And at all these ceremonies, the guests of honour were the pioneers, the people who had been here in the early days. It wasn't just the larger places like Regina, Saskatoon, Prince Albert, North Battleford, and Weyburn that produced very fine ceremonies. Communities of three or four hundred people put on celebrations. Just north of Regina and Lumsden on No. 11 highway, they had taken the entire community hall and filled it with relics of the pioneer era that had been picked up in that community. Some of these were museum pieces.

A history of the province was written by Jim Wright,[3] and Dr. Carlyle King did a collection of Saskatchewan literature and poetry in a little book called *Saskatchewan Harvest*.[4] Some Saskatchewan songs were written, and collections of Saskatchewan paintings were made, with prizes awarded to the best submissions.

We wound up the whole affair on Labour Day, 1955, with a closing ceremony. Prime Minister Louis St. Laurent was here along with several of the former Saskatchewan premiers: Mr. Dunning; Mr. Martin, the Chief Justice; Mr. J.G. Gardiner; a son of Dr. Anderson; a daughter of Mr. Scott; and Mr. W.J. Patterson, the lieutenant-governor, were all in attendance. We had a parade and a state dinner in the evening at which the prime minister and the former premiers and I all gave speeches. The proceedings were broadcast over a provincial network.

It was an outstanding occasion. Not just because of the entertainment, but it helped give Saskatchewan people an appreciation and understanding of the pioneers and provided an opportunity for thanking the pioneers for what they had done. Also, it gave us a chance to look ahead, and to see that if the future was to be successful, we would have to maintain the same kind of vision and imagination and courage of the pioneers.[5]

> Saskatchewan was looked upon as a kind of Siberia in art, music, drama, libraries, and particularly, archives. However, there has been quite a surprising development considering the province is only fifty years old.

I've always maintained that the people on the prairies, by virtue of the fact that we haven't got many of the advantages of living in a city like New York or London, are hungry for what are commonly

described as things of the mind and the spirit: good music, literature, drama, paintings, and folksongs. This is why the Saskatchewan Arts Board was established. I think it has done a remarkable
job making it possible for people to see good paintings and hear
good music. They have brought artists here and they have encouraged writing. They've interested people in folk singing and
handicrafts.

The Archives Board and the Arts Board have worked very
closely together. People like Mrs. James and Mary Ellen Burgess
have done a good deal in stimulating interest in drama throughout the country. The Department of Education has taken paintings and recordings of music around to the schools. I can remember when record players and movie projectors were oddities in
schools. There's hardly a school now of any size that hasn't got
both, and a radio. We have a small studio in the Legislative Building from which music, French, drama, and a whole series of
courses are broadcast to the children in rural areas.

> Probably one of the greatest achievements was, histori-
> cally speaking, in archives. Saskatchewan is probably the
> only western province that has developed its archives to
> this extent.

Yet it is unfortunate that we have so few records. Men like Nicholas Flood Davin,[6] and a great many of the other early figures did
not take any time to keep a record when the province was
developing so rapidly.

> This record in itself is an example of the first of its kind. If
> we had a record of Motherwell[7] and people of that de-
> scription, we would be much richer.

Yes, and also if we had Walter Scott's[8] own story of the formation
of the province.

> The Jubilee and various other measures established by
> the government have made Saskatchewan a more interest-
> ing place in which to live. People know that it is not just a
> bald prairie where only wheat grows.

I can remember in the thirties, when the dust and the grasshoppers and the drought had us all down, children's choirs and adult choirs took on a great significance. I remember hearing a British adjudicator say that he had never listened to children singing so sweetly. For the children, singing was almost their only escape from the grimness and harassment of their everyday lives. It's undoubtedly true, in my opinion, that as the economic pressure lessens and people have a little more leisure, the arts will become increasingly important.

In the pioneer days when just the sheer task of staying alive took almost every waking hour, when keeping warm and fed was a mammoth undertaking, there wasn't much time for cultural activities. There was the odd square dance, husking bee, or barn raising, but there wasn't much time for drama and music, thinking, and reading good literature. This is a tremendous challenge, because I think one of the great problems of our time is that, with technological advancement, we're going to need less human labour and we're going to have more leisure time as a result. What are we going to do with it? We're either going to vegetate in front of the T.V. watching Wyatt Earp, or we're going to develop an interest in music, drama, sport, recreation, or hobbies. Unless these are along constructive lines that enable people to feel that they have some personal significance, life will be fairly empty.

In 1952 a Royal Commission on Agriculture and Rural Life was appointed, and in 1955 it reported. Can you tell us of the benefits of this commission? How did it originate?

I'd had the germ of the idea for many years. As an amateur sociologist, I could see not only an economic revolution, but a sociological revolution taking place in the province. I've watched it over the last thirty or thirty-five years. I can remember when I was a young minister in Manitoba going to the various churches, some of them in little schoolhouses, some in little villages, and we would have young people's meetings or little societies. We used to have debates, and one of the favourite subjects for debate every year was "Be it resolved that the horse is more important than the automobile," and every year the horse won the debate, and yet every year there were more automobiles in front of the school and less horses. In other words, while all the sentiment was with the horse, time was with the automobile.

No matter how much you may revere the past or love the past, you can't live there. Bit by bit, society has changed on the prairies. In 1924, a quarter-section farm was a big farm, and a well-off farmer was the fellow with a half section. Everybody worked with horses. A few people had a Ford car, but they were few and far between. I drove horses a good part of the time, both in the winter and in the summer. But this has changed. Farms have got bigger, the number of people are fewer, and consequently people have to go longer distances to shop, for their amusements, and for social intercourse. There's been a steady change in the whole pattern of rural living. Better roads, better means of communication by telephone, radio, and T.V. have come to the rural areas. The little towns and communities are dying out, and the bigger centres have grown very rapidly. This is important when deciding where schools should be located and where hospitals should be built.

While we knew that this social and economic revolution was taking place, and that there was a shifting pattern of life in the rural areas, nobody had ever tried to plot it. With this in mind I began to think of a Royal Commission on Agriculture and Rural Life. There were a great many economic questions that had to be settled. Is farm machinery becoming so expensive that it is no longer possible for a small farmer to be completely equipped because this would cost him twenty-five or thirty thousand dollars? Is the co-operative use of farm machinery feasible? Is there any way that people can buy farm machinery together and share it? What are the needs for rural credit? What about our municipal and school organizations? Are these nine township municipalities, which were set up in the days when people travelled by horse and buggy and when five miles was an hour and a half journey, adequate units for today, or should we look at larger units? Should we look at the possibility of counties? All these questions came to the fore, and this is why we set up the Royal Commission under Professor Baker of the University of Saskatchewan.[9]

Twenty-five years from now people will go back and read the reports and recognize that the blueprint they set is sociologically and economically sound. Dr. Black, who is head of the Department of Agricultural Economics at Harvard University, came here about a year before this commission had finished their report, largely because he knew Mr. Meyer Brownstone, our chief economist. After he had spent two or three days looking over the work of the Royal Commission Dr. Black said, "I tried twenty-five years ago to get the New England states to undertake a study like this. I'm confident that if they had undertaken that study when I had suggested it twenty-five or thirty years ago, they would have saved millions of dollars and they wouldn't be in the hodgepodge that they're in today. As soon as your report is ready I'm going to put it before the five New England states again, and say 'This is what's been done out in the prairies by Canadians and it's not too late even now to make this kind of a study'." He said that this was the first attempt, to his knowledge, on this continent, to undertake a study of this nature.

> This was an entirely different type of Royal Commission. Normally there are judges and expert witnesses, but here they have tried to involve all the people, or at least as many as they could, in this vast province.

In the ordinary sense it really wasn't a Royal Commission. It really was a continuing sociological and economic study of the whole framework of local government, a social study of population trends, utilization of labour, and modern technological facilities. They held public forums in which the people expressed their views and set forth their problems. They used a sociologist's technique applied to a Royal Commission investigation format.

> Revolution was in progress, but people weren't aware of how it was affecting anyone but themselves. The commission suggested means whereby the hardships caused by the revolution could be eliminated. The federal government have taken chapters or parts of these volumes, and every so often you hear them quote the report.

It shows that a lot of top federal officials have studied the report. When you are in a period of transition, sometimes the tempo is accelerated more than at other times, and a good many problems are thrown up. The tendency is always to fight these problems in the wrong way. What's the reaction of the small farmer amidst a transition from the small quarter-section farm to the big mechanized farm? We have hundreds of representations from various small farm groups saying that we should forbid people to have farms over a certain size, or that people farming more than a section of land should pay double taxation. We hear cries that we ought to encourage people to raise horses so that they will have their own fuel, and not have to buy gasoline, and that we should put up windmills instead of having electrification.

They're confused, and take the wrong way of trying to find the answer, resulting in a good deal of discord and bad feeling. The Royal Commission helped in this way even more than in finding solutions. They helped people to see their own problems, to see the trend that was going on. The commission said that two things must be done. One was to see that people aren't hurt in the process of adjustment, and secondly, that we must direct this adjustment toward desirable social objectives. This was the great value in getting people to participate in the whole survey.

> This went on for about five years.

It's still going on. There's a continuing committee, on which the municipalities (urban and rural), the trustees, the health regions, and the teachers' association are all involved in carrying on the investigation started by the Royal Commission.

> A premier anywhere, I imagine, can be quite a lonely man at times. He sometimes faces a decision but he can't discuss it with his cabinet colleagues. We've had leaders all through history who had a confidant, someone they could turn to, a man who has no axe to grind and is not interested in politics. Have you ever had any friend of that kind, whom you could turn to away from the official lights, and ask, "What's your advice?"

No, I don't think I've ever had anyone outside the government to

whom I could go. The closest friend outside the government
would be Mr. M.A. MacPherson, who was formerly attorney-
general and provincial treasurer, and who was a runner-up for the
Conservative leadership at the second-last national convention. I
would never discuss with Mr. MacPherson something that involved the confidences of the government or the party, but he's
certainly one of the people on whose judgement I would rely,
knowing as he does the problems of government. I think my main
confidant would be Mr. Coldwell, and, until his death, Dr. Hugh
McLean, whose advice I valued greatly. He was a great humanitarian and a great idealist, and he and I exchanged letters right up
until he died.

[Dr. Hugh MacLean was born in Glasgow and immigrated
with his family to Ontario in 1887. He worked as a labourer and
later as a teacher to earn money for a college education. After
graduating from the University of Toronto as an M.D. in 1906, he
first practiced in Lang, Saskatchewan, from 1906 to 1913, then
moved to Regina, where he became a noted surgeon. During
World War I, he served as a medical officer. He was a leader of his
profession on both the provincial and national levels, and became
very active in the affairs of the Y.M.C.A. in Regina. In 1921 he ran
as a Progressive candidate for election to the House of Commons,
and again in 1935 for the C.C.F., but was unsuccessful on both
occasions. In the early 1930s he was vice-president of the provincial party. Due to illness, he moved to Los Angeles in 1938,
where he resumed active practice during the war years, continued his constructive support of the Y.M.C.A., and made fre-
quent visits to Regina. On 13 July 1944, he gave a comprehensive
and eloquent address to the C.C.F. annual convention in support
of socialized medical and hospital services. MacLean helped in
the foundation of the medical school at the University of Saskatchewan, and established a fund to support needy students. In
1947 he helped prepare a report on the advanced system of
medical services in New Zealand. Known for his philanthropy
and Christian convictions, he died on New Year's Day, 1958.]

Dr. Harry Laidler[10] of the League for Industrial Democracy
is another man I often confided in, and whose views I prized. But
I think most of them would be people within our own group,

including yourself, Chris. I think your political judgement is of the best. Among my cabinet colleagues, I would go to Mr. Fines for financial matters and Mr. Lloyd[11] for questions of basic policy. Mr. Lloyd has one of the best minds I have ever met, and I've met a lot of able men, but his judgement, when you get down to basic fundamentals, is not easily equalled.

[Woodrow Stanley Lloyd (1913–72) was born in Saskatchewan, the son of a farmer. He was educated at Moose Jaw Normal School and the University of Saskatchewan, where he earned his B.A. in 1940. He taught in various schools from 1932 on, and ultimately became principal of the large high school in Biggar. He was an active member of the Saskatchewan Teachers Federation, of which he became president in 1940, the Federation of Home and School Clubs, and the Senate of the University of Saskatchewan. He became involved in politics as early as 1934, when he campaigned for the Farmer-Labour party. He ran as a C.C.F. candidate in 1938, but was first elected to the Assembly in 1944, and re-elected in five succeeding general elections. He was Minister of Education from 1944 to 1960, and Provincial Treasurer from 1960 to 1961, when he succeeded Douglas as premier. As Minister of Education, he introduced many fundamental reforms in educational administration, including the establishment of larger school units. As premier he was responsible for implementing the C.C.F. party's demand for a universal prepaid medical insurance plan, which the Assembly enacted in 1961. This was opposed by most of the medical profession, the Liberal party, and "save our doctors" committees. The famous Medicare dispute ended in a compromise, and Medicare became an established feature of Saskatchewan society and was later copied by all the other provinces, with federal government endorsation. The C.C.F. was defeated in 1964 and Lloyd became leader of the opposition until 1970. In 1971 he retired from politics to accept the position of resident representative of the U.N. Development in South Korea, where he died shortly thereafter. Lloyd was a shy, rather quiet man, but a profound thinker, and it is not surprising that Douglas held his younger colleague in such high regard.]

What about Mr. Bentley?[12] He's a self-educated man

Hon. J.H. Brockel-
bank signing
certificate for
15,000th mineral
claim, 1953.

with lots of experience in weighing the rural element.
Would you turn to somebody like him?

Yes, if I wanted to know the practical answer. But if I wanted
someone with a very original mind, a deep rooted philosophy, and
an understanding of the purpose of a proposal, I'd talk it over with
a man like Woodrow Lloyd. You've got to divide people into two
categories: the people who are interested in how, and the people
who are interested in why.

When a problem comes up in cabinet, a premier is in a
very tough situation. There must come a time when only
his judgement must prevail. How do you look on that?

We have a very complicated set-up for arriving at decisions in the
C.C.F. For example, something that caused a good deal of dispute was the question of how we would develop our oil resources.

Douglas at opening
of Regina Co-op
Refinery, 1951.

Because we then had developed considerable quantities of oil in this province, Mr. Brockelbank, the minister concerned, asked what our policy would be. Usually, we put our trained people to work on it through the Economic Advisory and Planning Board. We have a working committee of economists and technical people—geologists, petroleum engineers, or whoever is required—and they go over the physical aspects. By the time they bring their conclusions to cabinet, I've had two or three sessions with the Planning Board, of which I am chairman. At this stage, I usually have a fairly clear idea of what I think the policy should be, and I make my recommendations to cabinet.

Sometimes cabinet ministers see something unresolved, and toss it back in my lap. It doesn't happen often. By discussion and removing features that are not acceptable, we work out something that is agreed upon by everyone. Then the report goes to the caucus and to the legislative advisory committee. The Provincial Council of the C.C.F. appoint a legislative advisory committee of three people to sit in with caucus, and as soon as the legislative advisory committee and the caucus are all in agreement with it, then it goes to the provincial council. If it is a very far-reaching decision, which is going to involve the whole movement, it will finally go to the convention in the form of a resolution presented by the executive to all the constituencies. It can be discussed in the constituencies, and then all the delegates come to the convention knowing that this resolution is going to be accepted or not.

> There have been cases where the premier is put on the spot.

Take this matter of oil development. There was a very strong feeling in the C.C.F. organization that the government should set up a crown corporation, drill for oil ourselves, and not permit this vast reservoir of oil to get into the hands of big oil companies. Here was a chance for Saskatchewan to refine and market its own oil. This was one of the places I personally stepped in and said that would be impractical for a number of reasons. In the first place, the people of Saskatchewan would never stand for the government gambling with the taxpayers' money. You could spend, as some companies have, twenty or thirty million dollars and never find a drop of oil. The shareholders of a company may be disappointed, but they can't do much about it. It's different to build a gas pipeline or a power-generating station with the taxpayers' money, knowing the venture would be self-liquidating. But there's no such guarantee when you drill for oil.

Also, even if you are eventually very successful and uncover a big oil field and go into the refining business, are you going to go into the distribution business? There are a hundred and one problems connected with distribution. There's the whole question of pipelines, which are under federal jurisdiction because they cross provincial boundaries.

We had some bitter battles at the conventions with those who wanted socialism for the sake of socialism. I take the position that socialism works only in areas where the situation demands socialization.

> If there was any immediate crisis, the final decision would depend on the premier. If you have a decision that can't wait until the C.C.F. hold its convention, you have to take a stand.

That happened two weeks ago, when I made an announcement regarding the increase in freight rates. I had to make a decision, first of all, that we would appeal this to the federal cabinet, but I only had forty-eight hours in which to make the appeal. I couldn't wait for anybody. Second, I had to go to Ottawa and appear before the cabinet and make the appeal at a time when it could have been easily misunderstood. I think some places it was misunderstood that we were opposing the increased wage rate for the railway employees.

◻ The 1956 election was characterized by a rise of the Social Credit party.

The upsetting factor in the 1956 election was that we would have won easily if the Social Credit party had not suddenly entered the political picture. They had elected two members back in 1934, both of whom were later defeated; in 1938 they elected Mr. Herman from Melville; but in 1944, 1948, and 1952, there weren't any Social Credit members at all. The Social Credit party had disappeared in Saskatchewan. The same was true in the federal House. In 1935 two M.P.s from Saskatchewan were Social Credit, and later defeated. At no other time did we have Social Credit M.P.s from Saskatchewan.

But just prior to 1956, Social Credit had captured the province of British Columbia. Premier Bennett had his eyes on Ottawa. The Social Credit controlled British Columbia and Alberta, but to get into the federal field they decided to use Saskatchewan.

Their slogan was, "On to Ottawa—we've got two, let's make it three," which was combined with a very strong campaign. They spent a great deal of money on radio and T.V., and had mass rallies. Mr. Manning's "Back to the Bible" hour was the surprise element in the campaign.

The Liberal party under Mr. McDonald put on a lack-lustre campaign, and the Conservatives did almost nothing. The result was that many Conservatives voted Social Credit. The Social Credit, which had got about five percent of the vote in days gone by, went away with over twenty percent of the vote in this campaign. Quite a lot of fairly progressive people who had voted C.C.F. in the past thought that Social Credit looked like something new and that it was going somewhere, on its way to Ottawa. It had captured two provinces on monetary reform, a very simple concept to understand. As a matter of fact you didn't even have to understand it, because their main thrust was the slogans and ballyhoo and enthusiasm.

Looking back on it now, it's surprising they didn't do better, because they put on a good campaign. No doubt Mr. Bennett thought that they were going to sweep the country. Mr. Manning was hardly in the campaign, but Mr. Bennett was sure, with all his publicity people and the amount of money they poured into the province, that Saskatchewan couldn't resist the pressure.

> They did, though. What is the prognosis? What about the Social Credit?

I don't think they will make any gains at all in Saskatchewan. They will find it very difficult to hold the seats in the Legislature they have now. Social Credit has no fundamental philosophy, apart from a monetary policy, which is open to as many interpretations as there are leaders. On all the other issues such as fiscal policy, taxation policy, trade and tariffs, freight rates, international affairs, and methods of running a government, they have no common basis. They lack roots. They're like the Russian thistle, which blows around but never takes root anywhere for very long.

> Many of those votes could possibly go Conservative.

Some will, but many will come back to us. In my own constituency, the Social Credit candidate got about 2,700 votes, and many of those were ours. Many of these votes were in Scandinavian communities with a social democratic background from the old country; some votes belonged to co-operatives and nonconformist religious groups, the Pentecostals and the Evangelicals, who were tremendously taken with the religious fervour of the Social Credit movement. When there's no Social Credit candidate in the running, most of those people will come back to the C.C.F.

[In the election of 1956, the Social Credit party nominated 53 candidates, the same number as the C.C.F. They received 21.5 percent of the vote, and elected 3 members; the C.C.F. gained 45.2 percent of the vote and 36 members. The Liberals secured 30.3 percent, and elected 14 members.]

> The Social Credit party has said they're through. They haven't had a convention, and they haven't had anything to show that the party is actually here, although they have an election in Alberta this coming year.

Yes, they have an election in Alberta in 1959 and the following year in British Columbia in all likelihood. But the Social Credit people have never been active in the municipalities or trustees' associations. People of this calibre do not belong to the Social Credit movement.

11

Reflections on
life and politics

We'll go into a typical day in your life. What time do you get up in the morning?

I get up at about 7:30. I've had the same breakfast for at least the last ten or fifteen years: orange juice and porridge, toast with marmalade or honey, and coffee. I don't think my breakfast has varied, except for the years when I was in the army, when I had bacon and eggs. But at home, or if I'm away, that's my standard breakfast. I listen to the eight o'clock news and the weather reports.

Quite frequently you walk. How far do you walk to work?

About a mile. I seldom use the car unless I'm having some trouble with my leg. I find if you take the car every place you're going, you get no exercise at all, and I take this advantage of getting a little exercise and fresh air.

I've seen you walking in somewhat severe weather, too.

Yes, unless my leg is acting up. I usually get to work somewhere between 8:30 and 9:00, and read the morning paper while the girls are opening the mail. Then I start to answer the mail. This is probably the bugbear of any man in public life, the mail. I've tried to follow a policy that is becoming increasingly difficult — I try to answer every letter myself. I know it's customary, and certainly if I were serving a larger constituency, I would have my secretaries follow the usual course of culling, and writing to say the premier wishes to thank you for your letter. Instead, I answer the letters, but that does not mean that I dictate every one. Someone will write in about an old age pension, and the girls will know what to say, but it's still a letter from me, saying that we received the letter, which is being forwarded to the proper authorities, and that they'll be hearing from them in due course. I sign the letter, and I also request a copy of the reply to this person, so that I can keep it on file and know that it has been followed up rather than having landed in somebody's basket.

I get between a hundred and three hundred letters in a day. Part of it is routine, but many of these letters take a good deal of time, particularly when three or four subjects are included in one letter, which involves sending copies to different ministers and different crown corporations. But I feel there's a good deal of value in answering the mail personally. It keeps you in touch with people, lets you know what people's complaints are and whether or not your government service is working efficiently. So far I've been able to keep up with it.

The mail goes on all day in every spare moment. Then by ten o'clock I chair a cabinet meeting or a staff meeting. We hold cabinet meetings regularly. Before the session is about to start we meet daily, and during the session we always meet every day. Then there are numerous appointments with people and delegations, inter-departmental committee meetings, cabinet committee meetings, and Treasury Board meetings. The Treasury Board is made up of several ministers, and the presiding officer is the Provincial Treasurer. They meet for hundreds of hours in a year, going over estimates, preparing the budget, dealing with various applications from different ministers for additions to their staff and for extra expenses.

Delegations from different organizations take a lot of time. This has grown almost alarmingly. We used to meet probably twenty different organizations prior to the opening of the Legislature. Now it's grown to about sixty or seventy, and some of them, like the Saskatchewan Federation of Labour, the Farmers' Union, the Trustees' Association, the Association of Rural Municipalities, and the Association of Urban Municipalities, take at least half a day. We've even had requests from some of them to make it a whole day. We try to confine these meetings somewhere between 15 October and 15 or 20 December so that we have them all out of the way by January, when we're working on the legislation.

> Invariably you have your lunch in the legislative cafeteria in the Legislative Building.

That's right. I have a standing order for a glass of tomato juice, one poached egg on toast, a dish of prunes, a bottle of buttermilk, and a cup of tea. That's standard.

> What intrigues a lot of visitors from the stuffier parts of Canada is that you line up with all the rest, and nobody thinks of giving you any precedence in the line. This great informality has struck a lot of people. You sit with a group of civil servants. It's probably one of the most uninhibited civil services I've ever known, because you and some of your friends will get into arguments in the cafeteria, and you don't get any preferred treatment from anybody.

When we came into office, the room at the back of the dining-room was reserved for cabinet ministers, and waiters took their order and brought them lunch. We abolished that practice because it took too long and because we didn't see any reason why cabinet ministers should be isolated from the rest. It's amazing how many useful discussions we've had over lunch, and how often we've listened to people argue about political and economic questions. It's great for a public man to be able to go where people talk frankly and argue and hear various points of view. The biggest difficulty about public life, especially for those who stand on ceremony, is that they hear only what people think they want to hear, and so they are told exactly what people think they would like to be told. Also, you're wrestling with many problems on your own, and it's good to get someone else to tackle the problem without any inhibitions, without feeling that they have to pull their punches. You can take a particular idea and try to knock it into a cocked hat. If it won't stand up among a group of top-flight civil servants, then it won't stand up when the public takes it to pieces.

> You have some first-class people among your top administrators.

Oh, yes. We have been extremely fortunate, but it has been by design that these kind of people are around us. We searched to find top-flight people, irrespective of their age or their political views. If they were competent people in their field, we brought them in. We've gone far afield in our search: Dr. Mott is from Washington, Len Rosenfeld is from New York, and we've also brought people from Great Britain and from other parts of Canada. We've never been able to give them the kind of remuneration that industry or private practice would give them, but we've tried to compensate for this in two ways. One is providing satisfaction of doing a job. We give them a great deal of freedom in putting forth their ideas and arguing for their different programmes. We've taken the attitude that they are advisors, and that they should be advising us what the programme is, having in mind our overall philosophy. Second, we have allowed them to go away for refresher courses and post-graduate work; we pay two-thirds of their salary while they're on leave, and also foot the bill for their transportation and tuition. They are then obliged to return for at least two years after they have completed their course. Two deputy provincial treasurers have gone away to take their Ph.D. at Harvard; we have a number of social workers, psychiatrists, medical staff, health officers, sanitary officers, public health nurses, psychiatric nurses, engineers, petroleum engineers, and geologists who have all gone away at different times for refresher courses. This gives them a feeling that they're keeping abreast with their own profession. To a man who is really dedicated, this is more important than earning five thousand dollars more a year, at least three thousand of which is taken away in income tax. We have a remarkable civil service. The fact that so many of them have had offers from the federal government is one way of knowing that they are outstanding. We're recognized as having the best personnel of any provincial government in Canada, and in some cases better than their federal counterparts. Both our deputy provincial treasurers[1] and Mr. Shoyama of the Economic Advisory and Planning Board could walk out of here today and make ten thousand dollars a year more than they're earning now.

> When you get into arguments in the cafeteria, you often get back late for your appointments, causing your secretary a great deal of stress and worry.

My secretaries have an invariable greeting when I come in late for an appointment. They say, "You've met Chris Higginbotham again." You have a bad reputation for keeping me late for my appointments.

> What are your afternoons devoted to?

I always try to have half an hour or more on the afternoon mail, and appointments take up a good bit of the afternoon. The most difficult job of a public man is apportioning your time. Many people think you shut them out or brush them off, but the fact is that there just aren't enough hours in a day to see everyone you'd like to see. You can't possibly meet and talk with them all. The days are gone when you can have a friend in and both put your feet up and say, "What's cooking?" Sometimes people don't understand this, and many supporters and friends come in and want to visit, but they don't understand that chatting is the one thing you don't have time for. You haven't time to see people in order to keep your organization functioning properly. You should confer with your ministers individually as well as collectively at cabinet meetings; you should be available to discuss their problems and give them the odd bit of prodding where you feel they're falling down. You should be meeting inter-departmental committees, officials, your own staff, and periodically you should be meeting people outside the government, to find out how programmes are working.

Many a time I would gladly have given somebody a hundred dollars just to go away. You can be free with your money, but you can't be free with your time when it isn't yours anymore. You're not the master of your own time.

> Today it is difficult for a man to sit down leisurely and write his memoirs.

Few people realize how much writing you have to do. I have requests for twenty or thirty articles a year from newspapers and periodicals, and some of these I don't write. For a mineral or mining magazine, I get one of the geologists to put the article together, and then I dress it up a little with an introduction and a conclusion and try to include some government policy, but the basic work has been done by someone else. But there are a great many that you have to write yourself, especially those consisting entirely of a statement of government policy. I get requests for fifty or sixty short non-political broadcasts a year, opening comments for fire prevention week, safety week, the Y.M.C.A. drive, the cancer drive, or the crippled children's drive. At least two or three times a week I have to do a short three- to ten-minute broadcast. These have to be done by me so that they sound like me. The amount of writing is terrific, and can't be done during the day at all. This means coming back at night and doing it over the week-end.

> What time do you try to get home in the evening when your work is through?

I try to be home by six o'clock and I usually am. I've found that Mr. Coldwell was right about the business of eating. It doesn't matter if you don't eat much, but you must eat regularly. The old habit I used to have of going for ten hours without eating, and then having a big meal, is bad for you. I had some trouble with an ulcer many years ago, although I've had none recently. This got me on a regular regime, and so I am usually always home by six. I'm back at least three nights a week, and when we get close to the session or during the session I'm back every night. The exception is the summer, when I go back to the office only occasionally.

> When you have an evening when you've got nothing to do, which I suppose is very rare, what do you do?

I try to do something that is not related to work. I play records or watch T.V. or listen to the radio, but mainly try to catch up on my reading. I try to save Sunday afternoons for reading all the periodicals that I haven't been able to read during the week. I get an air mail edition of the *Times*, *The Socialist Commentary*, put out by the Labour party, the *Forum*, the *New Statesman* and *Nation*, *Harper's*, and *The Atlantic Monthly*. Just simply trying to keep abreast in your own thinking and current trend thinking on a variety of problems takes an enormous amount of time.

> Do you ever get time to do what might be called creative meditation, or is it almost impossible these days for public men to sit down somewhere alone and think for an hour?

I take time. I have a little time for thinking when I'm walking to work. Sometimes before going to bed, my wife and I will go for a walk, and I attempt to do a little thinking then. I try to have Saturday afternoons to myself to read in general fields, sociology or history or philosophy. Sometimes, if I have some particular problem that is coming up on Monday or Tuesday, and there's some field I can read to get background on what's being done elsewhere, I do that, or I may just sit down and think about it and make notes on possible approaches to this particular problem on the week-end, leaving my regular reading aside.

> It's a curse of the times.

My wife and I have often wondered if we do the right thing: we don't do too much entertaining, and have very little social life, and probably ought to have more. But you can't do everything. My feeling has been that other cabinet ministers can go to the

Buying Red Cross
seals from crippled
child at Red Cross
Hospital in Regina,
1950.

cocktail parties and other functions for me, and let me spend time working on the whole philosophy of the movement. I suppose Miss McKinnon could give you some figures, but I suppose I speak at fifty banquets or luncheons a year. The number of meals I have at home are pretty limited. In some months of the year, particularly October, November, April, May, and June, I'll be lucky to get three meals a week at home, except for breakfast. You get to treasure and conserve the little time you have to yourself.

> Have you got the faculty attributed to President Truman, who could say at a certain period in the evening, "That's that, I'm going to bed and that's the end of it"?

Oh, yes, you have to. The first year we were in office I found myself tossing all night, because I worked every evening. I found myself getting up in the morning completely worn out. I decided

With Governor-General and Mrs. Vanier in 1960.

this had to stop. So when I finished a day's work I'd go to sleep. I used to keep a book beside the bed and I'd read a chapter or so, and then drop off to sleep and just forget about work. If you don't, you're useless. I'm sure that in terms of the nervous energy used up, five years in public life equals ten years of normal wear and tear. You just have to add up the number of speeches you make in a year. On my annual speech to the Wheat Pool, for instance, I spend a good part of two weeks gathering data.

You don't drink at all?

No, I've never taken any alcoholic beverages. I did get a shot of brandy twice when I gave blood, and once in the hospital when I was recovering from my leg operation and got up too soon and fainted.

> There is quite a temptation when men have a heavy load
> to take a glass of wine or whisky before going to bed.

I never have found it necessary. I should probably explain that I've never quite understood the people who do. Most of the men with whom I was educated were fanatical prohibitionists or temperance people. My background probably has something to do with it. My father always had a bottle of beer in the ice box, and when he came home from the foundry after sweating before a steel furnace he was a tired man. He used to lose two pounds in perspiration a day, and so when he came home he'd have a bath and a bottle of beer before supper. There was always whisky in the house. When my father's friends would come on New Year's Eve, the Hogmanay as we called it, they'd have a wee drink. When I was about eighteen my father said, "If you want a drink you have it here. I don't want you drinking any place else." But I never did.

I was in boxing training at that time. I didn't start, and I've always been glad I didn't, for a couple of reasons. A lot of people start and can't stop, and so drinking becomes a problem for them. Also, I think most of the indiscretions people commit, particularly in public life where you can talk too much, are owing to a few too many drinks. Liquor legislation is one of the matters to the fore. I've always taken the position that mankind would have been better off if we had never discovered how to make alcoholic beverages. It has become one of the great problems of our time. It has caused a lot of heartache and sorrow, and crime in some cases. I don't think there's any doubt that liquor has been an escape mechanism. And I don't think we've provided such a happy society that we can condemn people for looking for an escape mechanism. Somebody once said that the pub was the easiest way out of the limehouse. The pub was the only escape for people whose lives were a dreary monotony, for whom life was just one day's hard work after another, with poverty always breathing down their necks, never having enough money for security, enjoyment, holidays, or recreation. I often think that some bigots should spend more time thinking about why people drink, rather than trying to keep them from drinking.

While I would much rather see people be temperate or even abstainers, I don't think that you can solve the problems of drinking in this age or any other age by legislative and prohibitory methods. The only kind of worthwhile discipline is the discipline that comes from within. You don't make a good man or a good woman by prohibiting or refusing them. On this continent we have inherited the mores and the social attitudes of the Puritans, who tried to make people good by legislation. Determining how long skirts should be, how many square feet of cloth had to be in a bathing suit, whether certain words in a play were obscene, or whether or not people could drink or smoke or swear didn't work. Even if it had worked, I wouldn't give a five-cent piece for any person who was good because he had been prevented from being bad. There's no credit in that. It's like giving a man credit for not being a woman-chaser because he's on a desert island where there are no women. This hardly makes for moral fibre. If you can resist it, you certainly won't be any better because a law says it's wrong.

I think we should all look at this problem of alcohol. In the old days of Bobbie Burns, when people gathered in the pubs to have a real night of it, and Tam O'Shanter could stagger home at the end of the evening because his good wife Maggie was able to get him home, it didn't matter. But now when the fellow comes out of the pub and gets behind the wheel of an eight-cylinder car, it's not quite as simple. We're in a mechanized age, and we've got to face this problem of liquor. But I'm convinced you're not going to solve anything by more restrictive legislation. Liquor for those who want it should be legal in certain situations and places. We need to develop within people the kind of discipline that makes them say they've had enough and want no more. I don't know why we need to confine this to liquor when I see all the people who are overweight. They need to establish the same kind of discipline with reference to their eating habits. I always remember a man I used to visit when I was about six years of age. He was a great teetotaller who might take the odd glass of beer, but was never drunk. When he came home, his wife would make the house untenable for him after he had a glass of beer with the boys. I often spent the whole week-end there when my father and mother were away somewhere. Finally in my childish innocence I said, "Auntie Bella, why is it wrong for Uncle Peter to have a bottle of beer, and you drank twenty-three cups of tea today?" She kept a teapot full of the blackest tea you can imagine, and would pour herself tea about every fifteen minutes. I think self-discipline is necessary in every field.

☐ A lot of people are intrigued about your speeches. I've seen you make speeches completely without notes. Even when you have notes full of figures, you never look at them. Some of your biographers say that you have a photographic memory; some said that you were able to memorize columns and columns of the *Winnipeg Free Press* and recite them afterwards. What are these trade secrets, if you don't mind divulging them?

There are no trade secrets. I've been fortunate in having a very good memory. It's not as good as it was. As a student I was able to read a column or an editorial in the *Free Press* three times, and then I could recite it. I can actually see the words and simply read them. I've done it from force of habit, but I never thought that it was any gift.

When I was writing my master's degree in 1933, and I had gone away each summer to Chicago and to Manitoba to do class work, I remember one book I had great difficulty in finding, and I only got it the night before the exam. There were about fifty-odd books on this particular course and this one text was about eight hundred or one thousand pages long. I skimmed through it, and in the centre there was an anthropological chart, which I looked at for a little while and then put away. There was no guarantee that this book would be in the exam, but at least I had looked through it. It turned out that there was a question on this book, which I left until the end. I just shut my eyes and leaned back for a few moments, and took a ruler and pencil and reproduced the chart I had only looked at for two or three minutes. This made a fair impression on people.

You never trained this talent.

No, I've always had it. So did my mother and my father.

I have read a speech probably two or three times in my life where there had to be a script for the record, for example, when I opened the Provincial-Municipal Conference, where every word matters. It wasn't an oratorical event, but important for the government in terms of municipal reorganization and reallocation of finances and responsibilities between the provincial and municipal governments. But for most speeches, I make an outline of my introduction, the points I want to make, and then the conclusion. It is important to know how you are going to drive home your final point. Your last two or three sentences shouldn't be left to chance. Otherwise you keep talking and talking, hoping to find the right conclusion. When I was preaching at a little church, one man said to me, "That was a good sermon, but you passed a lot of good stopping places." You should know where you're going, and when you get there, quit and sit down. Once I get the outline, it's comparatively simple. I look at the outline for a while and then I don't need it.

> I notice that when you do prepare notes there may be only two words, but you can get complete sense out of the note, which is almost impossible for most people. Would you advise a man just going into public life to write everything out first, read it carefully, and then throw it way? Not everybody has the gift that you have. What would you recommend?

During the 1945 Federal-Provincial Conference in Ottawa, the conference at which Mackenzie King announced that an atomic bomb had been dropped on Japan, Mr. King put on a dinner just for the premiers and the governor-general, who at that time was Lord Athlone. It was a very delightful evening. After we had finished dinner, everybody milled around chatting, and those who wanted to had a drink. Mr. King sat on the chesterfield holding court. He motioned for me to come over and sit beside him, and we chatted about a variety of things. That evening he made a very witty little speech to the premiers, completely off the cuff, and I told him, "I'm sure that ninety-nine percent of the people of Canada have no idea you have the capacity for suave and urbane witticisms as you demonstrated tonight." I've never forgotten what he said: "You know, Douglas, I made the great mistake when I started in public life of writing all my speeches. I have a terrible horror of being misquoted or saying something on impulse that could be held against me." You and I know that he wrote his speeches with a back door in every sentence, so that he could back out of anything. Every sentence was qualified by another sentence, which gave him a perfect escape. But he said, "Most of my speeches have been formal; once started on a speech I have to go through to the end, even though I may recognize that the audience is not responsive, and that I'm not following a line which is interesting. This has really spoiled a lot of my public speaking. Don't ever get yourself tied down to it. It's such a crutch now that I really couldn't do in front of a large crowd what I did tonight in front of a small informal gathering." That was a good lesson, I thought.

I would say that every person has to follow what comes most naturally. I think it's a mistake to write out a speech and throw it away. Once you've written out a speech you get sentences with which you're very pleased, and so you want to keep them, and you keep trying to remember the words, and then if you lose part of the words the sentence becomes meaningless. You are far better off to remember the ideas, and trust in your capacity to handle the English language to clothe the ideas with words as you go along. I would suggest that any young person should make an outline. It doesn't matter if they take the outline with them or not; preferably I'd take it on some inconspicuous small cards that they can hold in their hands. Eyes are the most important part of a person when he's making a speech. The best way to hold people's attention is to look at them.

> When you're speaking, do you look at the audience or do you look at the back of the room?

Don't look at the audience, keep your eyes to the back of the room, because there's a natural thermostat in your make-up that makes you throw your voice to where your eyes are looking. Let your eyes run over people; people will not wander and talk if you're looking right at them. If your eyes keep meeting theirs, they will look back at you and listen. They certainly won't look at you if you're looking at a piece of paper or looking at the ceiling or looking at your shoes. Your eyes can play over the audience from person to person and keep their attention. These small cards are large enough that you can read them, but not so large so they're conspicuous and detract from what you're saying. In making an outline, the most important parts of the speech are the introduction and the conclusion. You must know exactly how you want to start. You shouldn't have to go round and round in circles trying to find a starting place. Your outline is the skeleton and you put flesh on the bones as you go along.

From my own personal observation, you seem to be in your best health and spirits when you are in a fight.

About two weeks ago I was very tired and a bit low. We got word that the C.P.R. had been granted a seventeen-percent freight rate increase by the Transport Commission, in spite of appeals to the cabinet; and I went down with some of the other provinces to meet the federal cabinet. From ten in the morning to a quarter past twelve at night, I had the battle of my life with C.P.R. lawyers and officials, and I suddenly felt ten years younger. I've been going on the momentum of that fight with the C.P.R. ever since. I don't know whether it increases the adrenalin in my system, but a fight always makes me feel better.

Have you had what you would call any grievous disappointments, any regrets, or have you made any decisions that you wish you hadn't made? Can you recall anything either personally or politically that you would do otherwise now?

I've had disappointments, of course. The loss of my father is probably the greatest personal loss that I've ever sustained. We've had political disappointments of not making the progress in the federal field that we had hoped to make. When you look back at it now, it's understandable that we haven't made as much progress as we expected. In twenty-five years, you can't suddenly displace one of the major political parties overnight. But it has been disappointing that we haven't moved faster; and you're always tortured with the idea that it's not because your philosophy and programme are wrong, but that somewhere along the way we haven't developed the techniques for conveying and communicating our story to the public, and that the fault lies with those of us who are charged with this responsibility. Looking at the political field in Saskatchewan, I wouldn't say that there is anything we have done that I greatly regret. There are some things that, if we had to do over again, we wouldn't do. We did too much in the first four years, and we unsettled a lot of people by trying to bring about a social revolution in almost every aspect of human life, instead of tackling two or three fields, and bringing people to this gradually. But this was not just an error of judgement at the moment, it was an error of judgement long before we got in office, when we built up political programmes passed at the annual conventions, which committed us to do these things. And so we had to do them, even though we recognized that we were probably going faster than the public was ready to go with us.

If we knew then as much as we know now, we wouldn't have tackled some of the experiments with crown corporations.

> You replied to a member who said you'd lowered yourself by turning from a Baptist minister to a Socialist premier. You said: "It's true that I, some eighteen years ago, dedicated myself to teaching the Kingdom of God. I'm still engaged in that work standing here, and I believe I can do it here better than anywhere else." Do you think that you have achieved more? Have you any regrets in taking the course you did?

No, I have no regrets. It's always difficult to say what would have happened if I hadn't gone into politics. I had prospects of some fairly large churches in the United States and in Canada, or I would have probably gone to Chicago University to teach social ethics, and what kind of a contribution I could have made there, I don't know. Irrespective of whether my contribution in the political field and in the field of social and economic development in Saskatchewan will prove to have been valuable or not, there were scores of other men who were quite willing to take on the big churches, or to be professors of social ethics, New Testament interpretations, or Christian sociology. But there weren't any, at that particular time, who were prepared to enter the dust and the din of the political arena. I felt somebody had to do it. The greatest lack we have in any people's movement is a lack of trained leadership. We've all kinds of farmers, workers, people who want to build a better society, but where do they get leadership? Very few have had the advantage of a university education. Not too many are able to meet the debate on fairly even terms with corporation lawyers and big business representatives. The economic ruling class has always been smart enough to buy the best brains in the community and use them to defend their special privileges.

I feel that if people like Woodsworth and Coldwell and others and myself hadn't been prepared to enter the fray and provide leadership, much of the legislation on the statute books of Canada today would not be there. This is a consolation. At times you wonder whether you can keep moving people along fast enough to show any appreciable gains. So many countries have made progress and then slipped back. You see the reactionary forces becoming very strong in the United States, Great Britain, and in Canada, and you wonder sometimes if maybe it isn't worthwhile. Bucking the snowdrifts, and working sixteen or eighteen hours a day, you wonder if you wouldn't be better off in a university somewhere, lecturing two or three hours a day and reading books and doing pleasant things for the rest.

But in the long pull, I have never regretted it. It has disadvantages. You haven't got economic security. You live from election to election. You don't know what will happen if you're defeated, you've no financial means, and you've burned your bridges behind you as far as going back and picking up another career. You're never sure whether the things you're doing are going to prove to be advantageous. On balance I'm more than satisfied that this was what I have done.

Broadcasting "Opinions Unlimited" on CKCK-T.V. in 1960. The subject of debate was the government-sponsored prepaid medical care programme. *Left to right:* Dr. E.W. Barootes, Alex Jupp, T.C. Douglas.

I'm satisfied when I go through the restoration centre and see youngsters with polio being cured, or when I go to the hospital and am told by an old man, "I broke my back six months ago, and I'll be here on the flat of my back for another two months. If it hadn't been for this hospital plan, I don't know what I'd have done. It's hard enough for my family to manage without me working, but if I had to pay hospital bills, the outlook would be hopeless." I don't think there's any chance that the type of health insurance programme we've launched can ever be taken away from the people. I still think I'll live long enough to see a complete health insurance programme in Canada from the Atlantic to the Pacific. But even if we don't do it, I'm sure that the standard of public morality we've helped build will force government in Canada to approve complete health insurance.

[The premier's remarks were prophetic. By 1969 a nation-

wide system of medical and hospital insurance had been insti-
tuted, following the proven success of the Saskatchewan plans.
The chief landmarks in the evolution of the system were the
passage in 1961 of the Medical Care Insurance Act, which
supplemented the compulsory Hospital Insurance Act of 1946.
On the national scene in 1961, the Diefenbaker ministry appointed the Hall Royal Commission on Health Services, which
reported in 1964 in favour of a comprehensive universal medical
plan. In July of that year, Prime Minister Pearson announced at a
federal provincial conference that his government would give
financial aid to any province that had a satisfactory medicare
system, and in 1966, Parliament passed the Medical Care Insurance Act. Prolonged negotiations with the various provinces
followed, but by the end of 1969 most of them were participating
in the programme, and fifty percent of the costs were met by the
federal treasury.]

You also preach about twelve or fourteen times a year.

I take services in the Baptist church, but also in the United
churches, Jewish synagogues, Lutheran churches, and nearly
every year I've gone to speak at the Salvation Army retreat.

You're still a young man, politically speaking. Do you intend to stay in politics?

There are only two ways to get out of politics, unless you quit,
which I wouldn't do. But the only two ways to get out of politics
are to be defeated or to die. Someone once said that the one is so
humiliating, and the other is so final. I would stay in politics as
long as the electorate felt that I could be some use. I certainly
wouldn't hang on if it appeared that there was no useful purpose
to be served. I would go and do something else. I don't think of
politics as a way of making a living; it's a poor way to make a living.
If the time came when it was apparent that the things we stood
for weren't generally accepted, and there was little prospect of
convincing people to move along much more progressive lines,
then I would certainly want to quit politics.

Most men look toward some kind of retirement. What is

your Shangri-La? Is it a cottage by the sea with a book and
your memory, a monkish life of meditation, or the pulpit
and the academic life? Do you ever think of that?

Oh, yes. Everybody thinks of what he is going to do on retirement. This is one of my nightmares, because I haven't any
hobbies, and I'm too old to start developing them. I can't imagine
myself spending my retiring years down in a basement making tie
racks and flower boxes, leather tooling, or making paper flowers
for the Ladies' Aid. This wouldn't appeal to me at all.

I could be reasonably happy with just my books and some
long-playing records, but I think this would eventually get boring.
I couldn't see myself living in an ivory tower unless I were
physically incapacitated. I would hope that if I were out of active
politics I could teach. I've always hoped that some day we will
have a people's college, at which we would train men and women
for co-operative organizations, for labour unions, and for political
life. Such a college would specialize in fundamental training in
political science, economics, sociology, social philosophy, organization, and business methods. That's a training I didn't have.
We've made a start with the co-operative institute, and the
Labour people are now looking at the possibility of Labour col-
leges. I would be very happy at a place like that. But I can't
imagine myself spending my declining years, unless I was physically or mentally incapacitated, reading books and watching the
passing scene. I would be out organizing something, even if it
were only a society of broken-down and retired politicians.

[After a decade of service as national leader of the N.D.P.,
Douglas resigned, but continued as a private member, acting as
energy critic for the party. He did not participate in the 1979
election. Following his retirement, he has been constantly on the
move across the country addressing meetings of all types, in great
demand as a speaker and lecturer. At his home in Ottawa he has
an office at the Douglas-Coldwell Foundation—an organization
that encourages research in Socialist principles and the history of
socialism in Canada.]

◿ Have you any particular dislikes? Are there things that anger you? What are the things about which you feel most keenly?

My chief minor irritation is that unfortunately I daren't show anger. I can get awfully annoyed, and I show it sometimes when boring people come to me with their private little axes to grind, the kind of people who say: "I know the government doesn't hand out special favours, and I know that you've got a public works act that says the lowest bidder should get the job, but my case is different, and I want you to cut corners a little." I'm afraid I haven't too much patience in those situations. I'm afraid I make enemies with my sharp tongue. My wife says it is a sarcastic tongue that gets the better of my judgement.

On the larger issues, social or economic injustice arouses me particularly. I ought to be thankful that I'm not in a Baptist church in the southern States right now, with the whole integration and desegregation controversy. My place would be with Martin Luther King, and with the Negroes there who are fighting for the ordinary fundamental right to be treated as human beings. Any type of discrimination against people because of race, colour, or creed makes me very angry. The same is true of any violation of civil liberties. I have always felt very strongly about the question of war, especially after my visit overseas in '46. I have always had a tremendous admiration for soldiers; it was part of my family tradition — my father and his father, and most of the family have fought in wars — and soldiers, wherever you find them, have got a marvellous esprit de corps, a wonderful sense of fellowship, and great unselfishness. When you think of the men who risked the loss of life and limb for the mere pittance that society pays them, you must have great admiration for soldiers. But I have a terrific hatred of war and what it does to people.

I think I can honestly say that I have never really thoroughly disliked any person in public life. There are a few people I've despised. But that is different. These are people whose conduct I've really despised, and they're not necessarily political opponents. I'm thinking of men like a C.C.F. M.P. who tried to get everything he could inside the party, and when he couldn't get it, he went over to another political party, proceeded to malign his former colleagues, and criticized all the things that only a few years before he himself had been advocating.

But I've never hated my political opponents. People have talked about the Right Honourable J.G. Gardiner. He's not a lovable figure. He's a tough, hard-bitten politician, the last of the old-ward healers, who believes in building a political machine based on intimidation, and in some cases graft and corruption. But when people have criticized Gardiner, I've always said, "Have you ever thought of the other side?" You've got to think of his good points. First, he has tremendous courage. He was one of the few men in the House of Commons on the government side who would tackle R.B. Bennett when Bennett was leader of the opposition. I never saw him run away from a fight of any sort. He has high personal moral principles. I don't think anybody's ever suspected or even hinted that he ever took a five-cent piece. He might bribe other people with campaign funds, and bribe some-body to work for him, but I don't think he's ever taken a dollar he didn't earn. One of his best attributes is that he's not a snob. Jimmy Gardiner, when he was a Minister of the Crown and one of the few members of Her Majesty's Privy Council, met with the ordinary people and lunched with the private members and was democratic, friendly, and approachable. You might not particu-larly like him, but if you wanted to, you could always see him. The same with Mackenzie King, who could exasperate you with his shilly-shallying, trying to be on both sides of every question, and yet he had some great qualities. He had a great feeling for humanity. He was ruthless where politics was concerned, he'd cut another politician's throat, even in his own party, to advance his own end, and yet the overall welfare of Canada was always in the back of his mind. I can honestly say that I have never hated or disliked any of my political opponents.

> In 1958, you are Premier of Saskatchewan and the leader
> of the Saskatchewan C.C.F. party. Have you any national
> aspirations in the political field at this date?

No, I honestly haven't. If I'd stayed in the House of Commons, I might have had aspirations federally, and if it became absolutely clear that the C.C.F. was in danger of collapsing across Canada if someone didn't take hold of it, then I might do it. But I would do it reluctantly. And this is not because I have any innate modesty, or that I want to be a shrinking violet — nobody can accuse me of that. But I have felt, first of all, that Saskatchewan has had an unfortunate history. Geography has been against us. Climate has been against us. We've had periodic drought, and we were late in getting industrial development. We're far from markets, which affects the cost of everything we bring in and everything we ship out; and we've been the step-child of Confederation. I feel that the province deserves everything I and others can give it for the next twenty years to put Saskatchewan on par with the other provinces, where it has a chance to grow and attain a well-balanced and diversified economy. For this reason I think there's a full-time, permanent job for me here. I can probably be of much more use to the people of this province than I could be running up and down the length and breadth of Canada trying to rally people around the C.C.F. as a national movement.

The picture might change. If we had a right-wing government that I felt was oppressing people, and we were facing social injustice and desperate economic conditions comparable to the depression in the thirties, then I would have to reassess my opinion.

> What you think about the future of the Conservative party in Canada, which is now in power? Do you think we're reaching the age of material plenty? What do you think the world will be like one hundred years from now?

The Progressive Conservative government has just been elected by the biggest majority ever given to any government in the history of Canada.[2] As far as the political future in this country is concerned, I have always held that eventually we will return to a two-party system. But it has to be a system with some meaning and significance, that is, a party of the right and a party of the left, relatively speaking.

For fifty years we alternately had the Liberal and Conservative parties. One believed in a slightly higher tariff than the other. One might be a little more friendly to public ownership, but the degree was so small that it really didn't matter much; so the vested interests of the country, who always want governments to protect their special privileges, could with complete equanimity support one, and then when they saw public opinion turning against it, swing their support to the other. It is a game of the ins and outs, what George Bernard Shaw called the case of tweedle-dee and tweedle-dum.

In every country in the world, and I think Canada must follow the same pattern, we will eventually develop a party of the right and of the left. There will be ideological differences, in which one party will stand for the maintenance of the status quo, the preservation of the rights and privileges of certain economic groups, and another party will represent the disinherited, people who live by the sweat of their brow or the effort of their hands, people who work for wages and salaries, small business people, and all the people who haven't got the privilege of living off unearned income. The latter is bound to grow stronger and eventually become the government of Canada.

What makes the situation so difficult to analyse is that the Progressive Conservative party got elected because people felt that it was left of the Liberal party. They felt that the progressive part was more important than the conservative part. I'm coming to the conclusion, after only eighteen months of this government in office, that they were progressive before the election and conservative after, and that they're going to move right. If they move to the right, where does this leave the Liberal party? The Liberal party could move left of centre, and if it could be revived, it might become the logical alternative. But if it does, there isn't any place for the C.C.F., except possibly as a small protest group constantly throwing forth ideas and popularizing certain concepts that the Liberal party will gradually assimilate. This is what happened to the Socialist party in the United States. The Socialist party of the United States has been little more than a protest and a popularizing movement; the Democrats have picked up their ideas, and obtained the benefits.

The other alternative is that the Liberal party will not move left of centre, that it is tied down too much by the people who control its finances. Consider the recent appointment of Brigadier Matthews as national chairman, who is head of the Excelsior Life Insurance Company, a brigadier in the army, and well known as a strong right-winger and a sound money man. If he represents the thinking of the Liberal party, and if one may judge by his personal associates the kind of people he will go to for campaign funds, I don't think the fact that Mr. Pearson himself may be left of centre means that the party has any chance of being left of centre. It may pay lip service to being left of centre, and if it's successful in selling the people a bill of goods, as Diefenbaker did with the Progressive Conservatives, the Liberal party may stage a comeback. If they do, this postpones for a considerable time the likelihood of a C.C.F. government coming to power in Canada.

This is why there's talk of a new party, which is predicated on the idea that the Liberals will not be able to form an effective left of centre party that will unite all the progressively minded people who want to see a fairer distribution of wealth between those who live off capital and those who live by their own efforts. If there should be such a party to take the place of the Liberal party or absorb the left wing of the Liberal party, then it has to be broad based. The talk of the new party first came up in the Canadian Labour Congress, who passed a resolution at their convention saying that the executive should invite farm organizations, co-operative organizations, the C.C.F., and liberally minded people to sit down together and discuss the possibility of a new political party in Canada.[3] These discussions have only gone on for a matter of months, on more or less a hit-and-miss basis. Whether anything will come out of it or not, I don't know. Of this I am sure, that the idea of such a party is sound, but I'm equally sure that unless it represents a genuine feeling in the grass roots that the time is ripe for such a party, it will not succeed, even though the people at the top in various organizations get together and form a new party. It must be at the constituency basis that people start working together. This is going to be the interesting struggle in the next five or ten years.

> Do you think that parties and governments are behind the people or are they ahead? Are they lagging behind technological advances? Bernard Shaw and various other people have commented on this, saying that govern-

ments or political parties are always so many years
behind the people. What do you think?

It's one of those generalizations for which George Bernard Shaw
was famous. Shaw was notorious for making statements that contained a half-truth stated in such a way that it irritated the people
who believed the other half of the truth. Sure, there will always be
people who are ahead of government. But the tragedy is that
there are great masses of people who are far behind government.
When you see thirty, forty, fifty, and, in the case of municipal
elections, seventy percent of the people not exercising their right
to vote, you begin to realize how little people are generally concerned. There are some people who are ahead of the government
in their basic thinking. I'll give you an illustration. When I talked
to members of the Ontario government a few months ago, they
told me they were setting up a health insurance plan, and they
were only going to make it compulsory for employees who worked
for an employer who had more than fifteen people on staff; the
rest didn't have to participate in the plan unless they wanted.
They thought that sixty percent of the people will be covered by
this plan. The doctors told me, however, that they won't get sixty
percent because all the self-employed people will stay out, people
on a staff of less than fifteen will stay out, and that they only expected fifty percent. To everybody's surprise, ninety-five percent
of the people in Ontario are now registered under the hospital
plan, and the same percentage is registered in Manitoba. This
proves that the hunger for social security has been far deeper
than governments have so far recognized. People want to know
that if they have sickness or misfortune, they will be secure, not
from some hypothetical pot of gold at the end of the rainbow, but
out of their own contributions. They don't need to be told they
can't get something for nothing. They've been getting nothing for
something for years. They'll be satisfied if they even get something
for something.

The first thing that the privileged class does is to spend
money to see that they maintain the status quo, so that they will
not only own the community but also will run it, and they will run
it through their agent, a particular political party. Whether people have come along far enough in their political development to

recognize that there can be no hope for average citizens until they elect a government they control and finance, this is the big question.

> I want you to think in general terms. Huxley says that man hasn't made any great progress in morals and ethics since the beginning of history. How do you see the world today? Is man improving; is he making any progress or not?

This is the sheerest kind of nonsense that only intellectuals like Huxley can possibly utter. It's not long ago that people were owned like cattle. Less than a hundred years ago in the United States, less than a hundred and fifty years ago in Britain, human beings were bought and sold, and had no rights or privileges. The Tolpuddle martyrs [1834] were seeking to project a new ethic of working by earning their living by the sweat of their brow. They did not have the right to associate themselves together for their mutual betterment. This was not only against the law at that time, but against the social mores. It was immoral as well as illegal, and so they were shipped off to Australia. But by the time the few that were left came back from Australia, public indignation had grown, and people said it may be illegal but it's not immoral; if there's anything immoral, it's the law that says that this is wrong, and consequently the law is amended to give to these people their rights of association. This is a great step forward.

All our co-operative movements, our trade union movements, the rights of groups like retail merchants or filling station operators, or anybody else to associate themselves together for their mutual benefit and advancement are accepted and written into our laws today. It's hard to realize that only a comparatively short time ago it was illegal and immoral to associate. People were supposed to do what their betters told them. The aristocracy decided what you would work at, how much schooling you'd get, what church you would go to; you were little better than a serf. You had only one function, and that was to work for your betters in whatever way they thought fit. You couldn't sell this ethic today in any part of the civilized world. This is the progress we've made, and while one gets discouraged at the struggle over segre-

gation in the United States, the fact does remain that we are indignant about it. Who would have been indignant about the right
of Negro children to go to school with white children a hundred
years ago? It was part of the social mores not only that Negro children should not be going to school with white children, but that
they shouldn't be going to school at all.

It is rather fantastic to say that man has not made any progress. Take the realm of international affairs: the mere fact that
you have millions of people questioning the atomic bomb pact
and questioning the morality of war is progress. Who was questioning the morality of war in the days of the Hundred Years War,
and in the days when Caesar's legions were marching over Europe and Asia?

> You sometimes hear that this is the age in which man will
> conquer poverty. What else is there to conquer after you
> conquer poverty?

I'm afraid I'm not an intellectual; I'm a pragmatist. I always think
that if you've got an immediate problem you oughtn't to spend
too much of your energy—you've got to spend some but you
oughtn't spend too much of your energy—worrying about the
problems ahead. Sometimes intellectuals tend to weaken the
drive of good social and economic reform movements by constantly saying, "If you solve this problem, then what are you going
to do?"

We must first solve the problem of supplying all the basic
needs of all the people on the earth in terms of food, clothing, and
shelter. In this province, we must look at the fact that per capita
food production in the world today is less than it was in 1939.
We're producing more food, but we're not increasing our production of food as rapidly as the population of the world is increasing.

> Does it disturb you when we see millions of dollars being
> spent on sputniks and space travel when we know that if
> we're going to feed our growing population that we
> should be spending those millions on food research right
> now?

Yes, and it disturbs me even more when I hear governments

talking about destroying surpluses of food, curtailing production, and threatening farmers that if they don't reduce their production, they're going to have to drop their support prices at the very time when we're producing less food per person than we were twenty years ago. And remember that in that twenty years, our technology has made it possible for us to produce more food with new kinds of fertilizer and chemicals and new varieties of seed. We should be producing much more.

While it's true that modern science and technology have potentially solved the problem of poverty, the social sciences must now be brought forward to provide the ways and means by which this abundance we're capable of producing is made available to the people who need it. This is a staggering job. This is the task of the economist, the business executive, the sociologist, and all those in the field of social science. One of the tragedies of our time is that we are so concerned about producing more physical scientists, so that we can compete with one another in putting satellites into orbit; we're so afraid that some other country will make a bigger inter-continental missile than we produce. But if we were prepared to spend the same amount of money in the field of social science, determining how we could make this potential abundance available to people, it is my contention that this would remove one of the fundamental drives to war, namely hunger. Nations have invaded other nations through all the centuries because of the desire for food and for raw materials. This pressure is going to get greater with antibiotics and better medical science. The population is growing more rapidly than it has ever grown in world history, and countries are going to look around for resources with which to care for this growing population. While the first half of the twentieth century has belonged to the physical scientist, the second half better belong to the social scientist or we face the possibility of destroying what has become to be known as our civilization; somewhere in some distant part of the earth's surface some unknown tribe will have the task of beginning all over again to build another new civilization, because ours will have passed away just as the civilizations of Rome and Greece and Egypt and Babylonia and Syria passed away in their time.

Do you think we will ever conquer poverty?

When we solve the problem of food distribution, and when every person has all the food, clothing, and shelter they need, this will become not only socially moral but law, the law of the world. A new ethic will then spread for the improvement of mankind. While physical wants are taken care of, we haven't even begun to explore the intellectual appetite of man, the whole field of psychology and psychiatry, and how to live with other people. Man has always needed some type of goal. He's always needed a devil with which to do battle. Whether that devil was injustice, the wilderness that had to be conquered, or the frozen north that had to be penetrated, man has always needed something to fight against. His devil doesn't have to be other people, and it doesn't have to be conquest and war, it can be a struggle to eradicate ignorance, superstition, and disease, mental maladjustment, psychoneuroticism, and in time he will move out into space, and try to find out about other planets. There will always be plenty of realms to conquer. How to live together and how to curb the population growth will be another great problem. By the year 2000 we're going to have six or seven billion people on earth. If this is doubled in the next two or three hundred years there won't be standing room. We're going to have to face the problem of birth control, or migrate to another planet.

> As you see it now, just shortly before Christmas in 1958, it's still your thought that the first priority of the world is to feed the hungry, clothe the naked, and lift up the fallen.

Yes.

12

Editor's conclusion

The last three years of Douglas's premiership were as innovative and exciting as his first three years. There were notable developments in the economy of the province, in legislative and administrative activity, in party politics, and party leadership. During this period, administrative activity continued along familiar lines — family farm improvement, and extension of electrification of rural areas, welfare benefits, highway construction (particularly in the north), and guarantees or loans to private industry. The most remarkable event in 1959 was the beginning of construction of the South Saskatchewan River dam — one of the world's largest earth-filled dams, whose 140 mile-long reservoir would provide for electric power generation, urban water supply, recreation, and irrigation (if farmers desired). A largely attended ceremony on 27 May 1959 inaugurated the project, the costs of which were to be met by a sixty-percent contribution by the province and forty percent by the federal government.

One of the most exciting administrative activities was the resolution by the beginning of 1959 of the vexing and potentially explosive confrontation between the Hutterites of southwestern Saskatchewan and surrounding communities in the area, which was resolved by patient negotiation beginning a year earlier.[1] Instead of resorting to restrictive legislation as had been done in Alberta, the Saskatchewan government sought to resolve the problem by securing a voluntary agreement by the Hutterites to locate new colonies in areas where they would not disrupt community life. A Provincial Committee on Hutterite Settlement had been set up under the chairmanship of the Honourable J.H. Sturdy, with a sociologist-field worker, who after protracted and complicated negotiations, was able to arrange a written agreement with an important group of Hutterite leaders in August 1958.

During this time the national economy exhibited an uneven series of advances and declines, which coincided with the Conservative party's period of power under John Diefenbaker. Increasingly, inflation, unemployment, rising interest rates, and economic deterioration in certain regions of the country were consciously felt, and hence became the currency of political discussion. The C.C.F. view was concisely articulated by Provincial Treasurer C.M. Fines in his 1960 budget speech:

> The fundamental problem is that the so-called free play of the market-place has proved itself unable to allocate resources and income in a manner which will meet the tests of economic efficiency or social justice. I repeat again, in my view, these are objectives that can only be achieved by recognizing that governments increasingly have an urgent and legitimate role in directing the economic affairs and advancing the social well-being of the nation.[2]

The Saskatchewan economy, on the other hand, displayed remarkable resilience in 1959, 1960, and 1961. In 1959 the gross value of manufacturing jumped by seven percent, and mineral production increased to record-breaking levels. Forestry, fishing,

At the opening ceremonies of the South Saskatchewan River Project, 1967. *Left to right:* T.C. Douglas, W.R. Thatcher, J.G. Diefenbaker, L.B. Pearson.

and trapping were stable. The construction industry worked at capacity. The only dark feature was the drought and early snow-fall, which reduced the grain harvest and farm income, without any off-setting aid from the federal government. The chief economic difficulty was that the cost-price squeeze was increasingly affecting the farmers' situation. A severe drought in 1961 resulted in the poorest grain crop since 1937 and there was a marked decline in farm income. Under these circumstances the increased volume and value of livestock production became important. Equally significant was the sharp rise in petroleum production and the continued rise in electric power production, manufacturing, and construction activity. The government could derive some satisfaction from policies that assisted the development of an increasingly diversified economy.

There were no changes in the personnel of the fifteen-member cabinet in 1959. A by-election in Kinistino in June gave the C.C.F. candidate a substantial majority in a three-way fight, and was a good omen for the general election, due in 1960.

Following the resignation of A.H. McDonald early in 1959, the Liberals selected a former C.C.F. Member of Parliament, the dynamic W. Ross Thatcher, as party leader. He immediately launched a vigorous campaign against the government. The leadership convention had adopted a platform that the Saskatoon *Star Phoenix* described as follows:

> It is somewhat ironic that the Liberal delegates in their policy decisions matched the C.C.F. point for point in many instances and even went beyond C.C.F. policy in a number of respects, and then chose a former C.C.F. M.P. to campaign on this new platform.[3]

The convention endorsed a prepaid medical care scheme along with other welfare programmes. Thatcher promised that if the people favoured the medical scheme in a plebiscite, he would introduce it on a "fee-for-service" basis.

In the autumn of 1959 Douglas spent a month on an overseas visit, where he contacted firms doing business in Saskatchewan, and also studied the national health programmes in Britain and Israel. He undoubtedly had in mind making universal medical care insurance the chief issue in the 1960 election. A dissenting opinion had been expressed privately by the widely respected C.C.F. pioneer, O.W. Valleau, former Minister of Social Welfare, who argued that the slogan for the next election should be, "Make Saskatchewan people the best educated on the continent."[4]

In December the government received a 370-page report of the Stanford Research Institute, *Study of Resources and Industrial Opportunities for the Province of Saskatchewan*, which had been commissioned by the Economic Advisory and Planning Board. The report stressed the wide variety of the province's natural resources, and analysed the production that had been so far achieved and the potential for the future in the development of industries associated with these resources. It commended the government's efforts to diversify the economy through the Industrial Development Office, the Industrial Development Fund (involving loans to private industry), and the Saskatchewan Research Council. In general, the Douglas administration could gain considerable satisfaction from the findings of this prestigious politically independent research organization.

Early in 1960 the government suffered a grievous loss when Clarence Fines announced after the spring session that he was retiring from politics after sixteen years' service as Provincial Treasurer. Fines was one of the influential pioneers of the C.C.F. During his career as a Regina school teacher he had been in civic politics and was also one of the founders of the Independent Labour party, and had presided at the Calgary conference of 1932 that had created the C.C.F. Later he served as provincial president of the party in Saskatchewan (1942–44). Not an extrovert like a number of his cabinet colleagues, he was something of an enigma to many members of the party. One writer has described him as follows:

> Fines had a cool image, a pale oval face, dark hair brushed smooth to his head, dark eyes that were hard to the interrogator, with a tendency to amusement, dapper in appearance.... He wore a neat bow tie in early photographs, but his most flamboyant bit of haberdashery was the salmon pink brocade tie he sported on budget day.[5]

There could be no doubt about his loyalty to C.C.F. principles as enunciated by Douglas. Another writer refers to him as "a dedicated socialist with the acumen of a tycoon."[6] His budget speeches were models of clear and cogent economic and fiscal policy analysis, and successive Liberal party leaders found his budgets very difficult to attack with any degree of success.

Fines's management of the provincial treasury, more than anything else, made it possible for the government to implement programmes involving the expenditure of money. During his years in office, every budget was balanced, and by 1961 the provincial debt had been reduced to the point where only $1.2 million were required for interest charges in a budget of $148,605,000. Fines's 1960 budget was the highlight of the session, increasing by

$15 million over the previous fiscal year. The budget had two goals, which were the same as in previous years:

> First, the budget has as one objective the development of industry and resources in the Province, and frequently substantial public expenditures are necessary to open the way for such development. Second, the budget proposes continuing improvements in education, health, and welfare services.
>
> I believe that this budget, like all my earlier budgets, leads to a greater fulfilment of these two goals. It does so on the basis of the expanded revenues resulting from development, yet at a rate and level within the bounds of prudent and reasonable financial management.[7]

Fines included an item in the budget to cover the expenses of an advisory Planning Committee on Medical Care. The duty of the commission was to investigate medical care schemes in other countries and recommend a plan for Saskatchewan. On 16 December 1959, Douglas announced that the government would introduce a plan that would be universal and acceptable "both to those providing and those receiving the services."[8] The scheme would be administered by the Department of Public Health or an agency responsible to the government.

The general election was held on 30 June 1960 and the campaign was hard fought. The government campaigned on its record and pledged "to make all medical services provided by physicians available to every resident for a premium which he can afford to pay."[9] Thatcher conducted a very vigorous campaign, addressing more than 250 meetings following his election as leader. He focussed on the need for a plebiscite on the medical care issue. His main assault, however, was on the C.C.F.'s association with the move to form a new party. "The socialists are selling out agricultural Saskatchewan for the interests of a few labour bosses in Eastern Canada," he declared. "Farmers will be the junior partners in this merger because most of the money for the new party will come from labour."[10] That Thatcher had touched a sensitive nerve was reflected in the speech the premier made in the Legislative Assembly on 9 March, in which he defended the action of the national C.C.F. in assisting the formation of a new national party. In view of the decline in the numbers of the farming population,

> What chance are the farmers of this country going to have in the Parliament of Canada, where the laws of the nation are made, unless they find economic allies? Those who vote for the C.C.F. will know that the members elected are the same; our platform will be the same, and the name of our party will be the same — the Saskatchewan C.C.F. The fact that our provincial convention may or may not decide to affiliate with an enlarged national federation ... will in no way alter our status or our policies in this province.[11]

The issue Thatcher raised, though it prompted this cogent response, was to be a durable one, as we shall see later. Professor Otto Lang, campaigning for the Liberals, declared that high tariffs "will be the inevitable result of the proposed union of the C.C.F. with the C.L.C. ... Eastern labour depends on the tariff wall as a protection for their ever-increasing wages which we in the west pay for when we buy Canadian products."[12]

The Progressive Conservatives also campaigned actively, nominating candidates in every constituency, as compared with the nine they had presented in 1956. Their new leader, Martin Pederson, relied on organizational and moral assistance from the federal party. The Conservative platform was a mixture of social welfare and free enterprise ideology, and pictured a state where "people would have the freedom to conduct their own business if they desired without government interference."[13] One Conservative candidate went even further, declaring that "The only purpose of government in a Christian society is the protection of life, liberty, and property."[14]

The Social Credit party elected Martin Kelln as leader early in the year, and nominated a full slate of candidates. Their campaign stressed the achievements of the Social Credit governments in Alberta and British Columbia, and featured the direct support of Premier Manning.

The opposition parties were joined in their assault on the government by the medical profession, and the College of Physicians and Surgeons waged an all-out, well-financed and organized campaign on the issue of Medicare under the slogan, "Political Medicine is Bad Medicine." The press also joined in a sustained attack. The doctors' case was not strengthened when a British-born Regina doctor stated: "What will happen if British doctors pull out of the province en masse? They will have to fill up the profession with the garbage of Europe."[15]

The result of the election was the return of 38 members for the C.C.F. and 17 for the Liberals, with the other parties unable to obtain a single seat. The government received 40.8 percent of the votes and the Liberals increased their share to 32.7 percent. The Conservatives received 14 percent , approximately 2 percent more than that secured by the Social Credit party.

Clarence Fines's retirement produced some changes in the Douglas administration in August. Woodrow Lloyd became Provincial Treasurer and Allan Blakeney succeeding him as the Minister of Education. New ministers were George Willis (Highways), W.G. Davies (Public Works), A.M. Nicholson (Social Welfare), and Olaf Turnbull (Co-operatives). Since Medicare had become the major issue in the election campaign, for Douglas the C.C.F. victory was "a mandate for the party's medical care plan. A government's mandate gains from the number of members it has elected, not from its share of the vote."[16] Thatcher, on the other hand, and the doctors, considered the minority vote a rejection of the plan. Thatcher is quoted as stating that "he would fight to the end an attempt by the government to force its medical plan upon the people...who are by no means in even half way agreement with Mr. Douglas...."[17] In his budget brought down on 26 February, Fines had included an item for a planning committee on medical care.[18] A month earlier the medical profession had been asked to name representatives to the committee. Three months of negotiations followed concerning the terms of reference, which were never completely accepted by the doctors.

On 25 April the Advisory Planning Committee was appointed under the chairmanship of W.P. Thompson, president emeritus of the University of Saskatchewan. Again, protracted and acrimonious bargaining continued with the College of Physicians and Surgeons. After eight months of extensive investigations, the committee issued an interim report recommending a system of universal coverage, financed by direct taxation and general revenues, and run by a non-political commission. Doctors would be paid on a fee-for-service, rather than by salary as in a state medicine system.[19] The doctors responded by officially stating they would neither join nor co-operate.

A second session of the 1961 Legislature opened on 11 October and adjourned on 17 November. On 13 October the medical care insurance bill was introduced by the Minister of Public Health, J. Walter Erb. Since Douglas did not resign as premier until 7 November, it was possible for him to participate in the debate. A report of the second reading of the bill follows:

> It is the government's "hope and intention" to eventually have a large part of the administration handled on a regional basis.
>
> [Douglas] maintained there is much to be said for regional administration because "the closer you can keep an administration to the people, the better."
>
> But, he said, the plan must be centrally financed because not every region in the province has the tax base to finance a plan of its own, and gaps in service would be left in areas that need it most.
>
> By spreading the cost over the whole province, he said, taxes can be levied on ability to pay while regions would have only land or per capita tax to use. In addition, a province-wide plan would allow residents to move freely from one area to another without affecting their coverage.
>
> The premier said he agreed with the Opposition Leader that this is "an important piece of legislation,"and added, "If Canada is to have a model plan for a national scheme, this one will be a good one to follow...."
>
> Dealing with the proposal to set up a commission to establish and administer the government plan, Premier Douglas admitted that it has disadvantages.
>
> Opposition members have protested strongly that the

medical care plan was being taken out of the hands of the Legislature. He agreed that it would be better to have the plan run as a part of the health department, but he said the commission was recommended because it was requested by the doctors, and because it would assure no political interference.[20]

The second reading of the bill was given unanimous consent on 26 October with the opposition reserving its criticism for committee debate.[21] After second reading, Douglas withdrew from the Assembly after thirteen days of legislative activity in view of his candidacy for national leadership of the new party.[22]

The intra-provincial events of 1959–61 took place during a period of intense discussion of a merger of the national organization of the C.C.F. with the Canadian Labour Congress, which in 1958 had proposed the creation of a new party embracing farmers, trade unionists, and liberally minded elements of the middle class. The new party movement had progressed to a point that it became an issue in the 1960 election campaign that Douglas was forced to confront, producing the declaration in the spring session of the Assembly that has already been noted, and which concluded with the statement, "No broadening of the base of the national organization will alter the status and program of the C.C.F. organization in Saskatchewan."[23]

The provincial convention of the C.C.F., held in late July 1960, almost unanimously endorsed the move to affiliate with the new party, and Douglas and Argue gave their support. At the same time, existing and potential opposition was defused with the following statement:

> Be It Resolved ... that the Saskatchewan C.C.F. will continue to operate under its present constitution and will have, as heretofore, the fullest autonomy in determining its provincial policy and program.... Resolved that the C.C.F party retain its present name and identity in Saskatchewan.[24]

The 1960 national convention was held in Regina in August. It endorsed the principle of a new party "to strengthen democratic forces in Canada and further the principles and objectives for which the C.C.F. was founded."[25] Tension centred on the position of Hazen Argue, parliamentary leader of the C.C.F. A prolonged ovation during his speech to the convention, and the dramatic revolt of eight M.P.s against the national council's proposal that the choice of a national leader be postponed until the founding convention in 1961, led Argue to accept election to the latter office.[26]

During the lengthy discussion of the new party proposal, no attention seems to have been paid to the statement of C.L.C. President Claude Jodoin at the April 1960 national convention, that the organization would not become "an appendage of any political party." He said, "We shall retain our rights as trade unionists regardless of what party happens to be in power. Should the New Party gain power we must remain independent of it, free to praise when it is deserving of praise, and, yes, free to criticize and castigate it should it forget its obligations to the Canadian people." This was a forecast of the ultimate failure of the N.D.P. to attract the loyalty of trade unionists who, whatever its top brass might say, usually voted for the two old parties. The philosophy of Samuel Gompers, the American Labour leader who believed in non-intervention of trade unions in politics, was still a force to be reckoned with.

The 1961 N.D.P. platform, unlike the Winnipeg platform of 1957, contained no reference to socialism. It was a long document, with something for every interest group in the country. It stressed economic planning, "cooperative federalism," and a comprehensive national health plan. It was a victory for the eastern wing of the C.C.F., who wanted a new image: "secular, accelerating, affluent, urban, American. Only a party tuned to this key could hope to get the vote of pragmatic, beer-drinking, car-proud, sportsminded, T.V.-watching, thousand-strong, 'ordinary' voters."[27]

Seemingly traumatized by the result of the federal election of 1958, the C.C.F. establishment in Ottawa responded enthusiastically to the C.L.C. initiative. In Saskatchewan, voters who still favoured the C.C.F. provincially had succumbed to the magnetism of John Diefenbaker, who had won the Progressive Conservative leadership by overcoming the influence of the Toronto and

Montreal tycoons, the traditional ogres of the western farmer. Stanley Knowles, who had become C.L.C. vice-president following his defeat in the Diefenbaker sweep, and National President David Lewis, who in his long association with the party had fought ceaselessly to transform the movement into a Canadian version of the British Labour party, were the leading architects of the new party. The party was never a "grass roots" organization, as claimed by Knowles in his book, *The New Party*, published in 1961, but, as Professor Walter Young was to write later, "was grown artificially, from the top down, in the way the Liberal and Conservative parties came into being."[28]

As the most successful and dynamic C.C.F. politician, it was inevitable that T.C. Douglas would be pressed to run for the national new party leadership. Coldwell and Lewis were particularly insistent, but Douglas was reluctant to leave the province. "Thinking with my heart, I'd rather be here," he told the Saskatchewan caucus in February 1961.[29] Early in July he encountered Clarence Fines in Toronto. Douglas's biographer, Doris Shackleton, reports Fines's recollections:

I knew he was still undecided. I told him I disagreed very much with the C.C.F. going into the new party, and of him going in as leader. The job wasn't finished by any means in Saskatchewan. And I felt Tommy shouldn't take on anything new, because of his health. I wanted to see him live to enjoy some leisure, just as I had felt in my own case that it was foolish to stay on. But he made the decision the other way, and Saskatchewan lost its C.C.F. government.[30]

The 5 July issue of *The Commonwealth* carried a report of a press conference in the executive council chamber. Douglas's remarks included the following comments:

During the past year it has become increasingly apparent that the most pressing problems facing the people of this province must be solved at the federal level of government. I refer particularly to the cost-price squeeze on the farms and to unemployment in the towns and cities. These problems have been further aggravated by the fact that the Canadian economy has lost its momentum to the point where our real wealth production on a per capita basis has actually declined....

It seems to me that the issues at stake today are so vital to the people of Saskatchewan whose cause I have championed for over a quarter of a century that I must do everything I can to ensure the successful launching of the New Party. I have therefore decided to allow my name to stand for the national leadership of the New Party at its Founding Convention in Ottawa.

This decision has not been taken lightly. My natural inclination would be to stay in the provincial field and continue the work my colleagues and I have been doing for the past seventeen years....

I have now been relieved of my provincial obligations by the governing council of the C.C.F., by the almost unanimous decisions of constituency conventions and by my own people in Weyburn. I am free and willing to serve as leader of the New Party if the majority of the Founding Convention delegates so decide, but I will definitely not campaign for the office nor seek it in any other way.[31]

Three weeks later at the founding convention of the New Democratic Party, Douglas defeated C.C.F. national leader Hazen Argue with 1,391 votes to 380 for the leadership of the N.D.P. It was the end of an era, the most creative and exciting seventeen years in twentieth-century Canadian political history. Perhaps the most notable summation of Douglas's career was contained in an editorial in the Liberal-oriented Regina *Leader-Post*, his most constant critic over the years. On the occasion of his retirement under the heading, "The indefatigable Mr. Douglas," the editor wrote:

Despite sincere differences over some of his government's policies, the people of Saskatchewan generally have respected Mr. Douglas while from his followers he has received their utmost admiration and adoration. He has stood forth during his 17 years which have seen premiers come and go in other provinces as one of the most dynamic to hold this office in the nation. He has been an indefatigable worker, a zealous crusader, and an inspired and inspiring leader. These personal attributes in the main have been responsible for his record of more than 17 years in office. His was a personal achievement which it is difficult to match elsewhere in Canada. Certainly, it has no parallel in Saskatchewan's political history.

To the tributes being paid to Mr. Douglas on his relinquishment of the premiership, *The Leader-Post* desires to add its acknowledgement of the friendly and co-operative attitude of the premier during the 17 years. There were sharp differences over some government policies, and there was occasional barbed criticism of the newspaper by Mr. Douglas, but personal relations between him and the editors and writers of the paper at all times remained on a warm, friendly basis. While Mr. Douglas often has not agreed with views expressed by this newspaper, he never has questioned the paper's right to voice them.

It is a saddening thought to many ... that colorful "Tommy" Douglas as of this day ceases to be the premier of Saskatchewan.[32]

Notes

Foreword

1. All quotations from Burns's poems are taken from *The Complete Poetical Works of Robert Burns,* Cambridge edition (Boston: Houghton Mifflin Co., 1897).
2. *Off the Record: The C.C.F. in Saskatchewan* (Toronto: McClelland & Stewart, 1968).

1 Scottish immigrant

1. For a biography of T.C. Douglas covering the years from his birth in Scotland to 1974, *see* Doris F. Shackleton, *Tommy Douglas* (Toronto: McClelland & Stewart, 1975).
2. T.C. Douglas's trip overseas is chronicled in Chapter 7, pp. 204–16.
3. An account of the early history of the Carron Ironworks will be found in H.

Hamilton, *The Industrial Revolution in Scotland* (London: Oxford University Press, 1963), pp. 155–61.

4. For a history of Winnipeg, *see* A.F.J. Artibise, *Winnipeg: A Social History of Urban Growth, 1874–1914* (Montreal: McGill-Queen's, 1975).

5. Grace MacInnis, *J.S. Woodsworth, A Man to Remember* (Toronto: Macmillan, 1953).

6. From "Is There For Honest Poverty" by Robert Burns.

7. For accounts of the Winnipeg General Strike of 1919, *see* D.C. Masters, *The Winnipeg General Strike* (Toronto: University of Toronto Press, 1971); D.J. Bercuson, *Confrontation at Winnipeg: Labor, Industrial Relations, and the General Strike* (Montreal: McGill-Queen's, 1974); and K. McNaught and D.J. Bercuson, *The Winnipeg General Strike: 1919* (Toronto: Longman, 1974).

8. For an account of the riot in Estevan, *see* S.D. Hanson, "Estevan 1931," in I.M. Abella, ed., *On Strike: Six Key Labour Struggles in Canada, 1919–1941* (Toronto: James Lorimer, 1974), pp. 33–77.

    For accounts of the Regina riot, *see* E.G. Drake, *Regina: The Queen City* (Toronto: McClelland & Stewart, 1955), pp. 197–202; V. Hoar, ed., *Recollections of the On to Ottawa Trek by Ronald Liversedge, With Documents Related to the Vancouver Strike and the On to Ottawa Trek* (Toronto: McClelland & Stewart, 1973), pp. 105–19, 221–324; B. Broadfoot, *Ten Lost Years 1929–1939: Memories of Canadians who survived the Depression* (Toronto: Doubleday, 1973), pp. 363–68; and G.M. Stone, "The Regina Riot, 1935" (M.A. thesis, University of Saskatchewan, 1967).

9. John Martin Harvey (1863–1944) was a distinguished English actor, producer, and theatre manager. He was knighted in 1921.

2 Baptist minister

1. Charles Haddon Spurgeon (1834–92), English Baptist minister, was one of the most popular and influential preachers of his day, with congregations numbering six to ten thousand. He published over fifty volumes of sermons and a number of his books were widely translated. He also founded a theological college and an orphanage.

2. Walter Rauschenbusch, author of *Christianity and the Social Crisis* (New York: Macmillan, 1908), an American theologian, was the chief early proponent of the social gospel and a pioneer Christian Socialist in the United States.

3. Harry Emerson Fosdick was the leading Baptist preacher in New York City, who gained a wide influence through his sermons, lectures, and writings, including *Christianity and Progress* (New York: Association Press and Fleming H. Revell, 1922). He was a supporter of the Modernist movement in American theology as contrasted to fundamentalism.

4. Martin Niemöller, a theologian, preacher, and founder of the German Confessional church, publicly opposed Hitler's racial policies in 1933, and preached throughout Germany. Arrested by the Gestapo in 1938 and interned in concentration camps until 1945, he became a pacifist in 1954, and in 1961 was elected as one of the presidents of the World Council of Churches.

5. Fred Henderson's *Case for Socialism* was originally published in England in the early 1920s, and was used extensively by the Labour party. It was re-printed there and in the United States and also in Canada, where it was produced by the national Co-operative Commonwealth Federation (C.C.F.).

6. J.T.M. Anderson (1878–1946) was Conservative Premier of Saskatchewan from 1929 to 1934.

7. For a succinct account of the formation of the Farmer-Labour party (later the C.C.F.), *see* D.E. McHenry, *The Third Force in Canada: The Cooperative Commonwealth Federation 1932–1948* (Berkeley: University of California Press, 1950), pp. 13–14, 23–26, 209–10. *See also* W.D. Young, *The Anatomy of a Party: The National C.C.F., 1932–61* (Toronto: University of Toronto Press, 1969), pp. 43–44, 303–4.

8. *See* Frank Scott, "The C.C.F. Convention," *Canadian Forum*, vol. XIII, No. 156 (September 1933), pp. 447–49. *See also* pp. 443–44 and W.D. Young, op. cit., pp. 43–50, 304–13.

3   C.C.F. politician

1. *See* S.M. Lipset, *Agrarian Socialism: The Cooperative Commonwealth Federation in Saskatchewan: A Study in Political Sociology* (Berkeley: University of California Press, 1950; 3d ed., 1968), p. 109.

2. For a sympathetic but somewhat uncritical biography of Williams, *see* F. Steininger, "George H. Williams, Agrarian Socialist" (M.A. thesis, University of Regina, 1977).

3. Douglas's memory is remarkably accurate. The official figures were: Liberal, 2,281, Conservative, 1,544; Farmer-Labour, 1,343.

4. These were the famous "quintuplets" of C.C.F. legend in Saskatchewan.

5. T.C. Davis was the Liberal M.L.A. for Prince Albert from 1925 to 1939, Minister of Municipal Affairs and Provincial Secretary from 1926 to 1927, and Attorney-General from 1927 to 1929 and 1934 to 1939.

6. E.J. Young was the Liberal M.P. for Weyburn from 1925 to 1935.

7. Apparently the backers of the dummy "Social Credit" candidate also held a convention at which he was nominated, but without the Saskatchewan party's sanction. *See* news report in *The Weyburn Review*, 3 October 1935.

8. A.A. Heaps (1885–1954) was arrested in 1919 during the Winnipeg General

Strike, and subsequently released. One of the founders of the C.C.F., he was elected to the House of Commons in 1925 and defeated in 1940.

9. Charles Grant MacNeill was C.C.F. M.P. for Vancouver North from 1935 to 1940.

10. *See* W.R. Graham, *Arthur Meighen*, vol. III, *No Surrender* (Toronto: Clarke, Irwin, 1965), p. 141.

11. W.A. Riddell's version of the episode is set forth at length in *World Security by Conference* (Toronto: Ryerson Press, 1947), pp. 85–145, in which he notes the support he received from Sir Robert Falconer and N.W. Rowell. Riddell had the support of his deputy and successor in Geneva, L.B. Pearson. *See* L.B. Pearson, *Mike: The Memoirs of the Right Honourable Lester B. Pearson* (Toronto: University of Toronto Press, 1972), pp. 87–96. *See also* R. Bothwell and J. English, "Dirty Work at the Crossroads: New Perspective on the Riddell Incident" in Canadian Historical Association, *Canadian Historical Papers*, 1972, pp. 263–86; J.A. Munro, "The Riddell Affair Reconsidered," *External Affairs*, vol. 21, (1969), pp. 266–375; J.G. Eayrs, *In Defence of Canada*, vol. 2, *Appeasement and Rearmament* (Toronto: University of Toronto Press, 1964); and J.E. Hislop, "A New Perspective on the Riddell Incident: A Comparative Analysis of the Attitudes and Policies of Richard B. Bennett and William Lyon Mackenzie King" (Honours Essay, University of Alberta, 1979).

12. R.H. Tawney (1880–1967) was a brilliant English economist and historian whose book cited by Mr. Douglas, originally published in 1926, has been many times reprinted, and is regarded as a classic.

13. Norman McLeod Rogers (1894–1940), professor of history and political science at Acadia and Queen's universities, was elected to the House of Commons in 1935. He served as Minister of Labour from 1935 to 1939 and as Minister of National Defence from 1939 to 1940.

14. *See* Hugh Thomas, *The Spanish Civil War* (London: Eyre & Spottiswood, 1961; enlarged edn., New York: Harper & Row, 1977).

15. *See* ibid., p. 294 for confirmation of Douglas's statement.

16. Arthur Greenwood (1880–1954), one of the most popular leaders of the British Labour party, though not an effective administrator, was born in Leeds and graduated from the university there. He taught economics at Huddersfield Technical College and the University of Leeds. He was elected as a Labour member to Parliament in 1922 and served as Minister of Health from 1924 to 1931. He was re-elected in 1932 and became deputy leader of the Labour party in 1935. He was a member of the Churchill coalition cabinet from 1940 to 1942 and a member of the Attlee ministry from 1945 to 1947.

17. *See* note 4 to chapter 2.

18. *See* J.F. Wagner, "The Deutscher Bund in Saskatchewan," *Saskatchewan History*, vol. XXXI, no. 2 (1978) pp. 41–50.

19. O. Douglas was a pen-name for Anna Buchan.

20. James Maxton (1885–1946), a teacher, was chairman of the Independent Labour party from 1926 to 1931 and from 1934 to 1939. He was a Member of Parliament from 1922 to 1946.

21. *See* House of Commons Debates, 1938, pp. 583–92, 1475–84, 1497, and 2725.

22. The Right Honourable James G. Gardiner (1883–1962) was first elected to the Saskatchewan Legislature in 1914, and in subsequent elections till 1935. He was premier of Saskatchewan from 1926 to 1929 and from 1934 to 1935, Member of Parliament from 1936 to 1958, Minister of Agriculture from 1935 to 1948, and Minister of National War Services from 1940 to 1941.

23. Charles Avery Dunning (1885–1958) was born in England and migrated to Canada in 1903. He became a farmer and was active in farm organizations, and was elected to the provincial Legislature in 1916 as a Liberal. He became premier of Saskatchewan from 1922 to 1926, and resigned to enter the federal cabinet in 1926. He served as Minister of Finance from 1929 to 1930 and from 1935 to 1939 and retired from politics in 1940.

24. George Alexander Drew was a veteran of the First World War who became leader of the Ontario Conservative party in 1938. He was elected to the provincial assembly in 1939 and was premier of Ontario from 1943 to 1948. He became leader of the Progressive Conservative party of Canada in 1948 and served as leader of the opposition from 1949 to 1956. He resigned in 1957.

25. King reacted to Drew's charges by promptly appointing Supreme Court Justice Henry H. Davis as Royal Commissioner to investigate the matter on 7 September 1938. His report was given to the government on 29 December of the same year. He found no corruption or misconduct by government members or civil servants. *See* H.B. Neatby, *William Lyon Mackenzie King,* vol. III, *1932–1939* (Toronto: University of Toronto Press, 1976), pp. 279–80.

26. *See* House of Commons Debates for the fourth session of the 18th Parliament (1939), pp. 538, 588–97, 842–92. The House of Commons adopted a motion on 13 February 1939 to refer the Davis Commission report to the Public Accounts Committee.

27. Charles Grant MacNeill had served with the Canadian Motor Machine Gun Brigade in World War I. He was a business man in Vancouver, and a C.C.F. Member of Parliament from 1935 to 1940.

28. Gerald Gratten McGeer (1888–1947) was a lawyer, an M.L.A. from 1916 to 1920, and mayor of Vancouver from 1935 to 1936. A monetary reformer, he was elected as a Liberal M.P. and served from 1935 to 1945, when he was appointed senator.

4 War years in Parliament

1. House of Commons Debates, 1939 (Special War Session, 18th Parliament), p. 24.

2. Ibid., pp. 41–47.

3. For an account of the career of H.H. Stevens and the origin of the Reconstruction party, *see* J.R.H. Wilbur, "H.H. Stevens and the Reconstruction
Party," *Canadian Historical Review*, vol. XLV, no. 1 (1964), pp. 1–28.

   Henry Herbert Stevens was born in England and moved to Canada in
1887. He was a member of the House of Commons from 1911 to 1940 and a
member of the Meighen ministries in 1921 and 1926. He was Minister of
Trade and Commerce in the Bennett administration from 1930 to 1934. He
became a highly controversial figure in the Conservative party because of his
advocacy of state intervention to solve the problems of the depression, which
he attributed to the influence of big business monopolies, and particularly
the mass buying practices of the chain stores, traditional supporters of the
party. Stevens enjoyed widespread popular support among small business-
men, farmers, and workers.

   Unable to convert the Conservative hierarchy and the prime minister to
his views, Stevens formed the Reconstruction party to contest the 1935
election. He was elected, but all his other candidates were defeated,
although the votes they received probably cost the Conservatives the
election. Stevens rejoined the Conservative party in 1938.

4. The biographers of Woodsworth include O. Zeigler, *Woodsworth, Social
Pioneer, An Authorized Sketch* (Toronto: Ontario Publishing Company,
1934); G. MacInnis, *J.S. Woodsworth, A Man to Remember* (Toronto:
Macmillan, 1953); and K. McNaught, *A Prophet in Politics: A Biography of
J.S. Woodsworth* (Toronto: University of Toronto Press, 1959).

5. *See* W.R. Graham, *Arthur Meighen*, vol. III, *No Surrender* (Toronto: Clarke,
Irwin, 1965), pp. 107–31.

   Joseph William Noseworthy (1888–1956) was a Toronto high school
teacher who had been an unsuccessful C.C.F. candidate in the 1940 general
election. When Arthur Meighen became leader of the Conservative party in
1941, the Member of Parliament for York South (a traditional Conservative
constituency) resigned, permitting Meighen to gain a seat in the Commons.

   The by-election, which the Liberals did not contest, was a hard-fought,
bitter campaign. It was obvious that many Liberals voted for Noseworthy,
who won by a large majority on 9 February 1942. He was defeated in 1945, but
re-elected in 1949 and 1953. Meighen remained leader until 1942, when he
called a national convention to select his successor — John Bracken, Premier
of Manitoba.

6. *See* C.P. Stacey, *Official History of the Canadian Army in the Second World
War*, vol. 1 (Ottawa: Dept. of National Defence, Queen's Printer, 1955), chap.
XIV, particularly pp. 446, 490.

7. *See* House of Commons Debates, 1942, pp. 489–95. *The Globe and Mail*, 13
February 1942 and 28 July 1942, contains reports on Douglas's speeches on
the Hong Kong affair.

8. C.P. Stacey, op. cit., pp. 325–408. *See also* Terence Robertson, *The Shame and the Glory: Dieppe* (Toronto: McClelland & Stewart, 1962). The best account of the raid — its origins, events, and aftermath — is J. Mellor's *Forgotten Heroes — The Canadians at Dieppe* (Agincourt: Methuen, 1975).

9. Douglas's first impressions would be affected by the confusing and inadequate press reports issued at the time (*see* Stacey, op. cit., pp. 393–96). Douglas's account of the Dieppe raid coincides almost exactly with the oral testimony of the survivors expressed in the two-hour documentary programme, "Dieppe, 1942," on C.B.C television on 11 and 12 November 1979.

10. *See* C.P. Stacey, op. cit., pp. 374–75.

5 Provincial leader

1. F. Steininger, "George H. Williams, Agrarian Socialist" (M.A. thesis, University of Regina, 1977), claims that quarrels between Coldwell and Williams continued unabated.

2. A notable exception was Professor Carlyle King of the English Department of the University of Saskatchewan, who was a pacifist. King, a popular teacher, was a graduate of the universities of Toronto and London (England). He was provincial president of the Saskatchewan C.C.F. from 1945 to 1960.

3. *See* Doris F. Shackleton, *Tommy Douglas* (Toronto: McClelland & Stewart, 1975) p. 120.

4. For an intensive study of the campaign, *see* R.M. Sherdahl, "The Saskatchewan General Election of 1944" (M.A. Thesis, University of Saskatchewan, 1966).

5. Escott Meredith Reid was born in Ontario in 1905 and was educated at Trinity College, Toronto, specializing in political science. He won the Rhodes scholarship for Ontario in 1927, and distinguished himself at Oxford. He was national secretary of the Canadian Institute of International Affairs from 1932 to 1938. He taught political science at Dalhousie University, and in 1939 began a long and very distinguished career in the Canadian diplomatic service, including ambassadorships in India and Germany. His article on the Saskatchewan Liberal machine is regarded as a classic and has been reprinted in H.G. Thorburn's *Party Politics in Canada*, 3d ed. (Scarborough: Prentice-Hall, 1972).

6. *See* E. Chambers, "The Referendum and the Plebiscite," in N. Ward and D. Spafford, eds., *Politics in Saskatchewan* (Toronto: Longman, 1968), pp. 59–77.

7. Timothy Buck (1891–1973) was born in England and became a machinist. He migrated to Canada in 1910, and settled in Toronto. He had been a member of the Socialist Independent Labour party in his homeland, and in Canada

he was first introduced to Marxian socialism. During the First World War he became a convert to communism and helped found the Communist party of Canada in 1921. He was party leader from 1929 to 1962, and was a tireless spokesman and a prolific author of books and pamphlets. He ended his stormy political career as national chairman of the party. *See* O. Ryan, *Tim Buck, A Conscience for Canada* (Toronto: Progress Books, 1975).

8. Walter Tucker, later Judge Tucker, was born in Manitoba but received his law degree from the University of Saskatchewan and began the practice of law at Rosthern in 1925. He served with the Canadian army in the two World Wars. He was a Member of Parliament for Rosthern from 1935 to 1948 and leader of the Saskatchewan Liberal party from August 1946 to July 1953. Elected to the Legislature in 1948, he was Leader of the Opposition from 1949 to 1953, and re-elected to the House of Commons in the latter year. He was appointed to the Court of Queen's Bench of Saskatchewan in 1963.

9. William John Patterson (1886–1976) was born and educated in Grenfell, and served overseas in World War I. He became an insurance and financial agent, and was elected to the Legislature as a Liberal. He held various portfolios in the Gardiner ministries from 1926 to 1929 and from 1934 to 1935. He succeeded Gardiner as premier in 1935, and was leader of the opposition from 1944 to 1949. In 1951, he was appointed lieutenant-governor of Saskatchewan. He retired in 1958.

6   First months of office

1. This was a major broadcast made on 12 July 1944 describing the policies and plans of the government. It was printed in the *Saskatchewan Commonwealth*, 26 July 1944, p. 8.

2. *See* pp. 77–78 above. Williams held the agricultural portfolio in the Douglas ministry from 10 July 1944 until 26 February 1945. He died in a military hospital in Vancouver on 12 September 1945.

3. This is why there are no Patterson ministry files in the Archives of Saskatchewan.

4. *Saskatchewan Commonwealth*, 26 July 1944, p. 8 (C.B.C. broadcast).

5. There were sixty-eight resignations from the Farm Loan Board, the Liquor Board, the Provincial Tax Commission, the Bureau of Publication, and the Tourist Bureau. C.M. Fines to T.C. Douglas, 6 February 1945, T.C. Douglas Papers, Archives of Saskatchewan, file 10-2.

6. S.M. Lipset, op. cit., chap. XII, states that the C.C.F. originally proposed "the complete elimination of private enterprise," (281) and that after the party gained power in Saskatchewan, it abandoned socialist principles (as defined above) in response to bureaucratic conservatism, financial difficulties, conflict with trade unionists, and farmer satisfaction with the new *status quo*.

He completely ignores the fact that Douglas and the Saskatchewan C.C.F. defined their socialism in terms of creating a mixed economy combining public, private, and co-operative enterprise.

7. Edward Milton Culliton was born in North Dakota and later moved to Saskatchewan and became a Canadian citizen. He took his law degree at the University of Saskatchewan and practiced in Gravelbourg. He was a Liberal M.L.A. from 1935 to 1944 and from 1948 to 1951, and Provincial Secretary in the Patterson ministry from 1938 to 1941. He served with the Canadian army from 1941 to 1946. Appointed to the Saskatchewan Court of Appeal in 1951, he was chairman of the Saskatchewan Golden Jubilee Committee from 1953 to 1955. Later he was Chancellor of the University of Saskatchewan from 1963 to 1969. His latest post is Chief Justice of the Court of Appeal.

8. William Melville Martin (1876–1970) was born in Ontario, educated at Osgoode Hall, and began practicing law in Saskatchewan in 1904. He was elected as a Liberal to the House of Commons in 1908 and re-elected in 1911. He resigned in 1916 to become Premier of Saskatchewan, a position he held till 1922 when he was appointed to the Court of Appeal as Chief Justice of Saskatchewan from 1941 to 1961.

9. Hutchison's biography of King, sub-titled *A Candid Portrait of Mackenzie King: his works, his times, and his nation*, was published in 1952, two years after King's death. It caused a considerable stir, since it was the first candid analysis of a man who had dominated national politics for a quarter of a century.

10. King's description of the conscription crisis of 1944 that follows does not correspond in several respects to the much more detailed and fully documented account in C.P. Stacey's *Arms, Men and Governments: The War Policies of Canada 1939–1945* (Ottawa: Ministry of National Defence, Queen's Printer, 1970), pp. 441–74. Readers should consult this carefully before arriving at conclusions on the policies and actions of King as he described them to Douglas. J.L. Granatstein, in *Canada's War: The Politics of the Mackenzie King Government 1939–1945* (Toronto: Oxford University Press, 1975), pp. 350–57, 363–73, gives an account that corresponds more closely to Douglas's report of King's conversation.

7 Saskatchewan government reforms

1. In 1937 the Alberta Legislature passed the Accurate News and Information Bill, the Bank Taxation Bill, and the bill amending the Credit of Alberta Regulation Act. Lieutenant-Governor J.C. Bowen refused to assent to them and reserved them for consideration of the federal government, which subsequently disallowed them. *See* L.H. Thomas, *William Aberhart and Social Credit in Alberta* (Toronto: Copp Clark, 1977), p. 114.

2. For a comprehensive analytical account of the development of the public power system in the province, *see* C.O. White, *Power for a Province: A History of Saskatchewan Power* (Regina: Canadian Plains Research Center, 1966).

3. The maximum speed of the *Aquitania* was 23 knots: *see* C.R.V. Gibbs, *Passenger Liners of the Western Ocean,* 2d ed., London: Staples Press, 1957), p. 78.

4. This was not "a green book," but was officially designated the *White Paper on Employment and Income,* tabled in Parliament by the Minister of Reconstruction, in April 1945. It was written by Dr. W.A. Mackintosh, then Director General of Economic Research in the Department of Reconstruction and Supply and subsequently Principal of Queen's University. *See Canadian Economic Policy Since the War* (Ottawa: Carleton University, 1965).

5. In 1946 the National Health Service Act was passed in Britain under the sponsorship of Aneurin Bevan; it came into effect in 1948.

6. *See* pp. 273–75 below.

7. Saskatchewan Health Services Survey Commission, *Report of the Commissioner* (Regina: Government of Saskatchewan, 1947).

8. Dr. John R. Mott won the Nobel Peace Prize in 1946.

9. Dr. Mott to the editor, 8 August 1980.

10. The salary of the cabinet members was cut by $1000 by the Douglas government. Members of the cabinet received $5,000 (the premier $6,500). The sessional indemnity, payable to all Members of the Legislature, amounting to $2,000, remained unchanged. The latter sum was to meet travel expenses and living accommodation while the Assembly was in session.

11. Rupert Ramsay, Professor of Extension at the University of Saskatchewan, was chosen Conservative leader on 16 February 1944, and resigned 28 November 1948. He did not secure a seat in the Legislature in the elections of 1944 and 1948. He also lost the by-election in Morse in 1946.

8   The 1948 election

1. Then the largest hotel in the city, owned by the C.P.R. and situated in the central business area of Regina.

2. Alexander Hamilton McDonald, M.L.A. for Moosomin, was leader of the Liberal party from November 1954 to July 1959. He was succeeded as leader by Ross Thatcher in October 1959.

3. *See* pp. 259–62.

4. Joseph Lee Phelps farmed at Wilkie, Saskatchewan. He was active in the Saskatchewan Trustees' Association and the Wilkie Board of Trade. Elected as a

C.C.F. Member of the Legislature for Saltcoats in 1938, he was re-elected in 1944 and appointed Minister of Natural Resources and Industrial Development. He was narrowly defeated in 1948, and subsequently active in the Saskatchewan Farmers' Union and as Chairman of the Board of the Western Development Museum.

5. Oakland W. Valleau (1892–1976), an Ontario-born farmer, was elected as a C.C.F. Member of the Legislature for Melfort in 1938 and re-elected in 1944. He held the portfolios of Provincial Secretary and Minister of Social Welfare from 1944 to 1948, and was the minister responsible for the Saskatchewan Government Insurance Office. Defeated in the election of 1948, he was subsequently Chairman of the Workmen's Compensation Board.

6. The trial did not take place until 27 October 1949 because the original writ was issued in the wrong district. According to a report in the Regina *Leader-Post*, Judge Taylor had "long experience" and had tried some of the most noted slander actions in the history of the province.

7. Everett Clayton Leslie (1893–1978) of the firm of MacPherson, Leslie, and Tyerman was one of the most distinguished barristers in the province, and president of the Canadian Bar Association. A graduate of the University of Saskatchewan, he was later awarded honorary degrees from Saskatchewan and Queen's universities. He was counsel for the premier in the proceedings in the Saskatchewan Appeal Court and the Supreme Court of Canada. MacPherson (former Attorney-General from 1929 to 1934, and Provincial Treasurer from 1931 to 1934) also participated in the trial as a member of Douglas's counsel.

8. See Tucker *v*. Douglas, Saskatchewan Court of Appeal, 3 May 1950. *Dominion Law Reports 1950*, vol. 2, pp. 827–41, noting particularly the judgement on p. 841, allowing the appeal with costs and directing that a new trial be held.

9. See Supreme Court of Canada, 1952 *Canada Law Reports*, vol. 1, pp. 275–91. The decision was rendered 17 December 1951.

9   At home and abroad

1. Sir Howard D'Egville (1879–1965) was a Cambridge-educated barrister and the author of several books dealing with the parliamentary institutions of the British empire and imperial relations. He travelled widely. First Secretary of the Commonwealth Parliamentary Association, he founded and edited the *Journal of the Parliaments of the Commonwealth*, 1920–60 . He organized many conferences and meetings of parliamentarians in various parts of the Commonwealth and the United States from 1910 to 1959.

2. Herbert Morrison (1888–1965) was born in modest circumstances in Kingston upon Hull, England. He started work as an errand boy, later becoming a shop

assistant, and finally a newspaper circulation manager. He became actively involved in London city government from 1920 to 1940. A prominent figure in the Labour party on the civic and national levels, he was Labour Member of Parliament from 1923 to 1924 and from 1929 to 1959. He held various portfolios in Churchill's war cabinet and the Attlee ministry, as well as serving as Deputy Prime Minister from 1945 to 1951 and Leader of the Opposition from 1951 to 1955. He wrote several books on government and received honorary degrees from four universities in Britain and one in the United States. He was appointed a life peer in 1959.

3. *See* p. 269.

4. *See* note 16 to chapter 3.

5. Sir Walter Nash (1882–1968), a distinguished New Zealand statesman, served in the Labour government from 1935 to 1949, and was the chief initiator of the world-famous welfare and socialist policies. First elected as a Labour Member of the New Zealand Parliament in 1929, he was First New Zealand Minister to Washington, from 1942 to 1944, and deputized for Prime Minister Fraser at the conference of Commonwealth prime ministers in 1946. He served as Leader of the Opposition from 1950 to 1957 and Prime Minister of New Zealand from 1957 to 1960.

6. Hugh Todd Gaitskell (1906–63) was educated at Oxford, specializing in philosophy, politics, and economics. He was Head of the Department of Political Economy, University of London. A Labour Member of Parliament from 1945 to his death, he served as Minister of Fuel and Power from 1947 to 1950, Chancellor of the Exchequer from 1950 to 1951, and Leader of the Labour party from 1955 to 1963.

7. J.H.C. Griffiths (1890–1975), was educated at the Central Labour College, London. Active in Welsh miners' affairs and organizations, he became a Labour Member of Parliament from 1936 to 1970, Minister of National Insurance from 1945 to 1950, and Secretary of State for the colonies from 1950 to 1951. His last post was Secretary of State for Wales from 1964 to 1966.

8. Jennie Lee, M.A., L.L.B., daughter of a Fifeshire miner, was educated at the University of Edinburgh. A writer and lecturer, she was elected Labour Member of Parliament and served from 1929 to 1931 and from 1945 to 1970. She married Aneurin Bevan in 1934.

9. Mrs. B.A. Castle was the most oustanding female Member of Parliament of her day. Educated at Oxford, she became parliamentary private secretary to Sir Stafford Cripps in 1945, Labour Member of Parliament from 1945 to 1975, and Chairman of the Labour party from 1958 to 1959. Her positions included: Minister of Overseas Development, 1964–65, Minister of Transport, 1965–68, Secretary of State for Employment and Productivity, 1968–70, and Secretary of State for Social Services, 1974.

10. David Lewis was born in Poland. Educated at McGill in Montreal, he was a Rhodes scholar and the first Canadian to be elected president of the Oxford

Union. Called to the bar in 1936, he practiced law in Toronto. He was national secretary of the C.C.F. from 1936 to 1950, national chairman of the party from 1954 to 1958, and national president from 1958 to 1961. Active in the Woodsworth Memorial Foundation, the Canadian Council of Christians and Jews, the Human Rights Commission, and the Jewish Labour Committees, he was first elected to the House of Commons in 1962 after several unsuccessful attempts. National leader of the New Democractic Party (N.D.P.) from 1971 to 1975, he was defeated in the 1974 general election.

11. Graham Spry was born in Ontario and served in the First World War. He graduated in 1922 from the University of Manitoba, was a Rhodes scholar at Oxford, and took classes in Grenoble and at the Sorbonne. He worked for the *Manitoba Free Press* and the International Labour Organization, under the auspices of the League of Nations, and was national secretary of the Canadian Clubs from 1926 to 1932. Co-author of *Social Planning for Canada* (1935), he was chairman of the Ontario C.C.F. from 1934 to 1936. He became an executive of the California Standard Oil Co., London, 1937, and later personal assistant to Sir Stafford Cripps from 1942 to 1945, when he accompanied Cripps on his historic mission to India in 1945. He conducted an economic survey of Turkey for the 20th Century Fund from 1946 to 1947, and he was Agent-General for Saskatchewan in the United Kingdom and Europe from 1947 to 1967.

12. Vernon Hunter headed a drilling crew that spudded Leduc No. 1 well at Leduc in November 1946. *See* E.J. Hanson, *Dynamic Decade* (Toronto: McClelland & Stewart, 1958), p. 66. Whether Hunter was the "Red" referred to here is not apparent.

13. *See* M. Horn, "Frank Underhill's Early Drafts of the Regina Manifesto 1933," *Canadian Historical Review*, vol. LIV, no. 4 (1973), pp. 393–418.

14. George W. Cadbury was born in 1907, and educated at Cambridge University, specializing in economics, and at the School of Finance and Commerce, University of Pennsylvania. He was president of Toynbee Hall, 1929–35 and 1941–43; managing director of British Canners Ltd., 1929–35; managing director of Alfred Bird and Sons Ltd., 1935–45; deputy director of Material Production of the Ministry of Aircraft Production, 1941–45; chairman of the Economic Advisory and Planning Board and Chief Industrial Executive of the Province of Saskatchewan, 1945–51; employed by the United Nations in various capacities to 1960; president of the Ontario N.D.P., 1961–66; and latterly chairman of the International Planned Parenthood Federation.

15. Tom Shoyama was a former national president of the Japanese Canadian Citizen's Association in the early 1930s and graduated from the University of British Columbia in 1938. He worked in a logging camp during World War II, and later edited *The New Canadian*. Shortly after the end of the war he was appointed economic advisor to the Douglas ministry. Following the defeat of

the C.C.F. in 1964 he was appointed as a senior economist in the federal government, became Deputy Minister of Energy, Mines, and Resources in 1974, and in 1975 became Deputy Minister of Finance, holding this post until 1979.

10   The third C.C.F. term in office

1. *See* p. 388, note 7.
2. Asmundur A. Lopston (1885–1972) was born in Iceland and came to Canada in 1887. He became a highway contractor and a large-scale farmer and was elected mayor of Bredenbury, Saskatchewan. He was elected as a Liberal Member of the Legislative Assembly for Saltcoats and served from 1929 to 1938 and from 1948 to 1960.
3. J.F.C. Wright, *Saskatchewan: The History of a Province* (Toronto: McClelland & Stewart, 1955). Wright was an experienced newspaperman who had previously written two books, one of which is *Slava Bohu, The Story of the Doukhobors* (New York: Farrar and Rinehart, 1940).
4. Carlyle King, ed., *Saskatchewan Harvest: A Golden Jubilee Selection of Song and Story* (Toronto: McClelland & Stewart, 1955).
5. For a full account of the events of that year *see Report of the Saskatchewan Golden Jubilee Committee* (Regina: Government of Saskatchewan, 1956).
6. Nicholas Flood Davin (1843–1901), a brilliant Irish lawyer who migrated to Canada in 1872, was educated at Queen's College, Cork, and was called to the bar in the Middle Temple, London. He worked for the Toronto *Globe* and *The Mail* following a notable journalistic career in England. He was secretary to two federal Royal Commissions. He moved to Regina, N.W.T., in 1883 and founded the *Leader*. Elected as a Conservative to the House of Commons for the constituency of Assiniboia West from 1887 to 1900, Davin was much in demand as a speaker and was the author of *The Irishman in Canada* (London: Sampson Low, 1877; reprint ed., Irish University Press, 1969) and other works, including a book of poetry. *See* C.B. Koester, *Mr. Davin, M.P.: A Biography of Nicholas Flood Davin* (Saskatoon: Western Producer Prairie Books, 1980).
7. William Richard Motherwell (1860–1943) was born in Ontario and educated at Guelph Agricultural College. He moved to Abernathy, Assiniboia, in 1881 and was active in farmers' organizations before 1905. Elected as a Liberal member to the Saskatchewan Assembly in 1905, he was Minister of Agriculture from 1905 to 1918. He was elected to the House of Commons in 1921 and Minister of Agriculture in the King administration from 1921 to 1930.
8. Walter Scott (1867–1938), the first premier of Saskatchewan, was born in Ontario. He received a public school education and became a printer and journalist, and moved to Regina in about 1892. He owned and edited the Moose Jaw *Times* from 1894 on, and purchased the Regina *Leader* of which

he was editor from 1895 to 1900. Succeeding Davin, he was the Liberal member for Assiniboia West from 1900 to 1905. Invited by the lieutenant-governor of Saskatchewan to form the first ministry in 1905, he held the portfolios of Public Works from 1905 to 1912, and Education from 1912 to 1916. He gave up politics due to illness in 1917.

9. The establishment of the Royal Commission on Agriculture and Rural Life was approved by the Legislative Assembly on 17 March 1952. The Commission was appointed by Order-in-Council on 31 October 1952, and brought in its report on 18 March 1955 after extensive hearings throughout the province.

10. Harry Wellington Laidler (1884–1970) was an American author and economist and a graduate of Columbia University and Brooklyn Law School. He was an active Socialist and executive director of the League for Industrial Democracy from 1921 to 1957. He lectured widely and was director of the National Bureau of Economic Research from 1920 to 1970. A member of the social welfare department of the Federal Council of Churches, 1951–53, he was active in several other related national organizations and in Socialist politics in New York State. He also authored three important books and many brochures.

11. *See* C.B. Koester, ed., *The Measure of the Man: Selected Speeches of Woodrow Stanley Lloyd,* (Saskatoon: Western Producer Prairie Books, 1976); and D. Lloyd, *Woodrow: A Biography of W.S. Lloyd* (Regina: Woodrow Lloyd Memorial Fund, 1979).

12. Thomas John Bentley was born and educated in Nova Scotia, and later moved to Saskatchewan to farm near Swift Current. He became active in the wheat pool organization and was a C.C.F. Member of Parliament from 1945 to 1949. Elected to the Saskatchewan Legislature in a by-election in 1949, he was re-elected in 1952 and 1956. During this time he served as Minister of Public Health, 1949–56, and Minister of Social Welfare, 1956–60. He retired from politics in 1960.

11 · Reflections on life and politics

1. These were T.H. McLeod and A.W. Johnson. T.H. McLeod was born in Weyburn, Saskatchewan, and had degrees from the University of Manitoba and Pennsylvania State University. He was Economic Advisor to the Saskatchewan Cabinet from 1944 to 1950; Deputy Provincial Treasurer from 1950 to 1952; Dean of Commerce and Business Administration, University of Saskatchewan from 1952–1964; and Dean of Arts and Acting President, University of Regina from 1964–1971. He moved to Ottawa in 1971 and joined the staff of C.I.D.A., and was later advisor or administrator of various federal government agencies, including the Anti-Inflation Board.

A.W. Johnson was born in Insinger, Saskatchewan, and received degrees from the University of Saskatchewan and University of Toronto, and served with the Canadian Army in 1942. He was Deputy Provincial Treasurer and Secretary of the Treasury Board, Government of Saskatchewan from 1952 to 1964; Deputy Minister of Welfare, Secretary of the Treasury Board, Assistant Deputy Minister of Finance, Government of Canada; and President of the C.B.C. since 1975.

2. The result of the 1958 federal election was a severe blow to the C.C.F. The Progressive Conservatives under John Diefenbaker won sixteen of the seventeen seats in Saskatchewan, and C.C.F. representation declined from ten to one.

3. S. Knowles, *The New Party* (Toronto: McClelland & Stewart, 1961), p. 132.

12   Editor's conclusion

1. "The Hutterite Program — Final Report," by Vern Serl, Premier's Papers, file 57, Archives of Saskatchewan (hereafter A.S.).

2. Budget Speech 1960, Friday, 26 February 1960 (Regina: Saskatchewan Government, 1960), p. 3.

3. Saskatoon *Star-Phoenix*, 26 September 1959. *See also* D.E. Smith, *Prairie Liberalism: The Liberal Party in Saskatchewan* (Toronto: University of Toronto Press, 1975), pp. 277–79.

4. Valleau to Douglas, 15 September 1959, Premier's Papers, A.S.

5. Shackleton, op. cit., p. 146.

6. D. Lloyd, op. cit., p. 62.

7. *See* p. 365, note 2.

8. E.A. Tollefson, *Bitter Medicine* (Saskatoon: Western Producer Prairie Books, 1964), p. 45.

9. *C.C.F. Program for 1960* (Campaign Leaflet), A.S.

10. *The Leader-Post* (Regina), 4 June 1960.

11. *The Commonwealth* (Regina), 16 March 1960.

12. *The Leader-Post*, 4 June 1960.

13. Ibid.

14. *The Leader-Post*, 14 May 1960.

15. *Canadian Annual Review*, 1960, p. 25.

16. *The Leader-Post*, 9 June 1960.

17. Ibid.

18. *See* p. 369.

19. *Canadian Annual Review*, 1961, p. 63. For a detailed account of the

protracted negotiations, *see* Tollefson, op. cit., chaps. 2, 3, and 4, pp. 27–87.

20. *The Leader-Post,* 26 October 1961.
21. Ibid.
22. Ibid., 28 October 1961.
23. *The Commonwealth,* 16 March 1960.
24. Ibid., 22 July 1960.
25. Knowles, op. cit., p. 132.
26. *The Commonwealth,* 17 August 1960.
27. Shackleton, op. cit., p. 248.
28. *See* D. Morton, *NDP: Dream of Power* (Toronto: Hakkert, 1974), p. 28; Shackleton, op. cit., p. 248; and W.D. Young, *The Anatomy of a Party: The National C.C.F., 1932–61* (Toronto: University of Toronto Press,1969), p. 133.
29. Shackleton, op. cit., p. 253.
30. Ibid., p. 255.
31. *The Commonwealth,* 5 July 1961.
32. *The Leader-Post,* 7 November 1961.

Index